Jews, God, and Videotape

D1173223

Jews, God, and Videotape

Religion and Media in America

Jeffrey Shandler

NEW YORK UNIVERSITY PRESS

New York and London

NEW YORK UNIVERSITY PRESS
New York and London
www.nyupress.org

Library of Congress Cataloging-in-Publication Data
Shandler, Jeffrey.
Jews, God, and videotape : religion and media in America / Jeffrey
Shandler.
p. cm.
Includes bibliographical references and index.
ISBN-13: 978-0-8147-4067-5   (cl : alk. paper)
ISBN-10: 0-8147-4067-7   (cl : alk. paper)
ISBN-13: 978-0-8147-4068-2   (pb : alk. paper)
ISBN-10: 0-8147-4068-5   (pb : alk. paper)
1. Mass media—Religious aspects—Judaism.   2. Communication—
Religious aspects—Judaism.   3. Technology—Religious
aspects—Judaism.   4. Judaism—United States.   5. Judaism—
20th century.   6. Judaism—21st century.   7. Jews—United
States—Communication.   I. Title.
BM729.M37S53—2009
296.3'7—dc2   2008045773

New York University Press books are printed on acid-free paper, and
their binding materials are chosen for strength and durability. We
strive to use environmentally responsible suppliers and materials to
the greatest extent possible in publishing our books.

Manufactured in the United States of America

C 10 9 8 7 6 5 4 3 2 1
P 10 9 8 7 6 5 4 3 2 1

Contents

DL

Acknowledgments

This book brings together research and analysis undertaken over much of my scholarly career. I am therefore indebted to a host of individuals and institutions for their contributions to this undertaking.

The intellectual approach that I offer in *Jews, God, and Videotape* is inspired by meeting with the members of the Working Group on Jews, Media, and Religion at the Center for Religion and Media, New York University. It has been a special privilege and thorough pleasure to serve as co-convener of this group since its inception in 2003. I am profoundly indebted to the dozens of scholars and artists who have been involved in the working group over the years for the intellectual stimulation and generous camaraderie that has been its hallmark. I owe special thanks to Faye Ginsburg, Angela Zito, and Barbara Abrash for making the working group possible and, most of all, to Barbara Kirshenblatt-Gimblett, who, as its other co-convener, has been a source of endless enthusiasm, inspiration, and wisdom.

I have also benefited from presenting parts of this project at a number of scholarly gatherings, including the Conference on Religious Pluralism in America, Center for the Study of American Religion, Princeton University; the series on Arts of the Sacred, University of Illinois Urbana-Champaign; the Conference on Spirituality, Performance, and the Jewish Stage, University of Maryland, College Park; the American Studies Symposium, Rutgers University; the Workshop on Visual Cultures and Religion in the United States and Israel, Haifa University; the Conference on Imagining the American Jewish Community, Jewish Theological Seminary; the Conference on the Lubavitcher Rebbe—Life, Teachings, and Impact, New York University; the Jews and Performance Seminar, Jewish Theological Seminary; and the Jewish Music Forum, New York.

Much of this manuscript was completed during a sabbatical from the School of Arts and Sciences at Rutgers University, and I am most grateful for this generous opportunity to concentrate on research and writing for an extended period of time. I am also very thankful to all the faculty and staff of the Department of Jewish Studies at Rutgers for their collegiality and support of my work.

Two chapters in this volume revisit work done in collaboration with other scholars: part of chapter 2 originally appeared in an essay, coauthored with Elihu Katz, in *Tradition Renewed: A History of the Jewish Theological Seminary of America,* ed. Jack Wertheimer (New York: Jewish Theological Seminary of America, 1997); and part of chapter 5 originally appeared in an essay, coauthored with Aviva Weintraub, in *Material Religion* 3, no. 3 (2007). I gratefully acknowledge the publishers for granting permission to use this material. In addition, both Elihu Katz and Aviva Weintraub have kindly consented to allow me to draw on these collaborative essays for this project.

At NYU Press, Eric Zinner's support for this project, even before it was completed, has been invaluable, as has the assistance of Despina Papazoglou Gimbel and Ciara McLaughlin. For their many contributions to the realization of this book, I also thank Roger Bennett, Alan Berliner, Lauren Shweder Biel, Charlotte Bonelli, Matti Bunzl, Sally Charnow, Lynn Schofield Clark, John DeNatale, Drew Friedman, Rela Geffen, Henry Goldschmidt, Samuel Heilman, Andrew Ingall, Miriam Isaacs, Ellen Kastel, Maya Balakirsky Katz, Arthur Kiron, Mark Kligman, Rebecca Kobrin, Marcia Littell, James Loeffler, Julie Miller, Fred Myers, Edna Nahshon, Chana Pollack, Edward Portnoy, Peter Pullman, Gary Rendsburg, Michele Rosenthal, the Schear family, Lawrence Schiffman, Naomi Seidman, Rona Sheramy, Melissa Shiff, Elkanah Shmotkin, Nancy Sinkoff, Michael Sittenfeld, Lorin Sklamberg, Mark Slobin, Karen Small, Alisa Solomon, Jeremy Stolow, Samuel Weiss, Jack Wertheimer, Azzan Yadin, and Yael Zerubavel.

My ultimate thanks go to Stuart Schear, who has been a guiding light throughout this project. It would never have been begun, much less completed, without his generous gifts of insight, patience, and devotion.

Author's Note

Romanization of Hebrew and Yiddish terms, other than those that have standard spellings in English (e.g., bar mitzvah), follow the rules of the *Encyclopaedia Judaica* and the YIVO Institute, respectively. In citations, original spellings, formatting (capitalization, italicization), and other conventions (e.g., "G-d") are maintained. In some instances, therefore, readers will encounter a multitude of romanizations for the same term (e.g., Hanukkah). All translations from Hebrew and Yiddish are mine, except where indicated. Quotations from the Bible, other than those included in citations, are given in the Jewish Publication Society of America translation.

Introduction

Let me begin with a joke someone sent me by email in 2001:

> Gottlieb called his Rabbi and said, "I know tonight is Kol Ni-
> dre [the service that marks the beginning of Yom Kippur], but
> tonight the Yankees start the playoffs. Rabbi, I'm a life-long Yan-
> kee fan. I've got to watch the Yankee game on TV."
>
> The Rabbi responds, "Gottlieb, that's what VCRs are for."
> Gottlieb is surprised. "You mean I can tape Kol Nidre?"[1]

This joke assumes that the medium of videotape is in tension with religious life, an assumption often made about other new media of the past
century in relation to religion. At the same time, though, the joke voices
a desire to resolve this tension, rethinking the possibilities of religious
practice (why not watch a "replay" of Kol Nidre on one's home VCR?)
and challenging the protocols of religious authority (though one might
well imagine the rabbi's response, Gottlieb's innovative suggestion is left
unaddressed). As an artifact of turn-of-the-millennium American Jewish
culture, the joke testifies to the community's ongoing attention to interrelating Americanness (baseball) and Jewishness (Kol Nidre), in which
desires understood as competing might be resolved through mediation, in
more than one sense of the term. Moreover, the joke evinces the dynamics of American Jews' engagements with new media—from the telephone
to broadcast television to videotape to email—which variously unite this
community with and distinguish it from other Americans and other Jews.
This is a fast-paced dynamic; in the summer of 2007, the *New York Times*
reported that the Jewish Television Network, a "nonprofit television production and distribution company," was planning to offer streaming video
on the Internet of religious services during Rosh Hashanah and Yom Kippur, suggesting yet another resolution to Gottlieb's dilemma, one unavail-
able when this joke was sent to me.[2]

Slight though it is, this joke exemplifies the topic of *Jews, God, and Videotape*—American Jews' encounters with new media during the past century and the implications of these encounters for religious life—and demonstrates its rich potential for scholarly inquiry. Over the course of the twentieth century, a succession of new media became fixtures of daily life for millions of Americans, as well as for many others living in technologically advanced societies, starting with the arrival of sound recordings and silent movies during the first decade of the century and continuing to the advent of the Internet, digital media, and their various devices (email, web browsers, DVD players, digital cameras) in the 1990s. These innovations have appeared so frequently and regularly that not a single generation has passed without engaging at least one new communications technology and often dealing with more than one concurrently. Such encounters are hardly new; in a volume on the phenomenon of new media, Lisa Gitelman and Geoffrey Pingree start with the advent of zograscopes (viewing devices that impart a sense of depth to a flat image) in mid-eighteenth-century England, and of course it is possible to look back further in time, especially to the beginnings of print culture in the fifteenth century. Gitelman and Pingree call attention in their study to the social significance of a medium's "newness":

> There is a moment, before the material means and the conceptual modes of new media have become fixed, when such media are not yet accepted as natural, when their own meanings are in flux. At such a moment, we might say that new media briefly acknowledge and question the mythic character and the ritualized conventions of existing media, while they are themselves defined within a perceptual and semiotic economy that they then help to transform.[3]

Although the moment of a medium's newness constitutes a distinctive and strategic opportunity for reflecting on the meanings invested in various modes of communication, established as well as new, these encounters are not all of a kind. In the United States, even as encounters with new media have provided many Americans with a shared experience—occasionally transcending the nation's vast geographic dispersal and divisions of class, religion, gender, race, or politics—responses to the opportunities and challenges that these media present have varied greatly. In fact, these encounters have proved to be highly contingent, shaped not only by the particular new technology in question but also by the particular community engaging this new medium.

This contingency is readily evident in American religious communities' encounters with new media, given the self-consciousness that religions generally bring to the form and means as well as content of communications. Consider, for example, the advent of telephone service in Lancaster County, Pennsylvania, at the turn of the twentieth century, which sparked a debate among Amish and Old Order Mennonites over the use of this new technology, embraced by some as rendering "a divine service" while denounced by others as "the devil's wires."[4] According to communications scholar Diane Umble, telephone usage provoked larger concerns in these religious communities, complicating their interactions with the society beyond their closely guarded social and cultural confines and even challenging their understanding of faith in God. Examples of popular or folk religious practices involving new media are especially revealing, as they can contest widely held assumptions about the compatibility of technology with religiosity, especially at its most traditional, and with folkways, generally thought of as artisanal. Thus, anthropologist Jo Ann Koltyk has noted, "researchers of Hmong culture in America have focused on traditional folk narratives such as folktales, songs, needle work 'story cloth,' and personal narratives," while neglecting the immigrant community's use of self-made videos to transmit memories of Old World customs and rituals. Folklorist Linda Dégh has studied how a Pentecostal community in Indiana, which largely eschews mainstream media (including Hollywood films and most television programming), uses audio recordings of testimonies made during group worship and regards this documentation not as inimical to but rather as enhancing the dissemination and understanding of ecstatic religious narratives. And another folklorist, Daniel Wojcik, has observed how Roman Catholic pilgrims to an apparition site in Queens, New York, used Polaroid photographs to "document miraculous phenomena, produce signs of the supernatural, and create sacred images," thereby extending the spiritual impact of a pilgrimage site and, moreover, redeeming technology and the "fallen" modern society that has embraced it.[5]

As these examples demonstrate, responding to new media does not simply enable innovations in religious engagement. The response itself constitutes a significant cultural proving ground, even when a new medium is rejected, prompting members of a religious community to consider larger issues that are central to its understanding of religious propriety, literacy, and authority, of its place in history or in the sociopolitical present, or even of its relation to the numinous. Studying American Jews offers a wealth of opportunities to consider the interrelation of new media and religious life, for these encounters have engendered responses that have proved defining for American Jewish culture. Engaging new media has at times situated Jews as an exceptional or paradigmatic religious community in America in unprecedented ways and has distinguished Judaism in the United States from the way it is practiced elsewhere. American Jews' responses to new media have variously challenged the role of clergy or transformed the nature of ritual; facilitated innovations in religious practice and scholarship, as well as efforts to maintain traditional observance and teachings; created venues for outreach, both to enhance relationships with non-Jewish neighbors and to promote greater religiosity among Jews; prompted religious legal debates regarding the proper use of certain media; even redefined the notion of what might constitute a Jewish religious community or spiritual experience.

The extent and variety of these examples demonstrates that, far from being inimical to spirituality, new communications media can instigate innovations in religious practice, including when their use is characterized as extending or maintaining traditions, rather than diverging from precedent. Engaging these new media also stimulates members of religious communities to examine the larger relationship of religious practice and thought to media practices, both established and novel, even when use of a new technology is disallowed. Given the array of new media technologies, the internal diversity of American Jews, and the dynamics of their lives over the past century, it is hardly surprising that the results of these encounters are far from consistent. Some American Jews reject outright new media practices avidly adopted by others, and Jews' attitudes toward a particular medium can change over time, responding to technological or social developments or to the dynamics of religious thought and conduct. There is value in this diversity of responses in itself, for it demonstrates that new technologies do not limit or predetermine the possibilities for their place in religious life. At that same time, the ongoing imperative of considering new media and their implications for religious life has become a common experience for Jews, as it has for other American religious communities, and this demand has itself become an important new means of advancing and affirming notions of religious life. Thus, American Jews' encounters with new media have become a means of continually redefining their notions of religious literacy, propriety, authority, communality, and spirituality.

By focusing on media practices, *Jews, God, and Videotape* enriches the historiography of this community during the period when the United States emerged as a major center of Jewish life and when Jews attained unprecedented prominence in American public culture. For people familiar with the history of twentieth-century American Jewry narrated in terms of immigration patterns, communal institutions, political activities, or other frequently studied elements of its experience, examining American Jews' encounters with new media offers new insights into this history. Intergenerational dynamics, for example, typically discussed in terms of work, education, or religious observance, can also be studied in relation to new media. Thus, a 1924 feature in the English section of America's most widely read Yiddish newspaper, the *Jewish Daily Forward* (itself an intergenerational mediation), on whether Jewish families should buy a phonograph or a radio, observed that inclinations were split between immigrants (who preferred the phonograph, which enabled them to "listen to their heart's content to Jewish tunes") and their children (whose "faculties are young and pulsating" and therefore inclined toward the radio, enabling them to "get in touch with any broadcasting station and open the floodgates of noise and merriment").[6] Or consider a study of American Jewish youth that was undertaken at the turn of the millennium by Reboot, a nonprofit organization that strives to help younger American Jews "'reboot' the traditions we've inherited and make them vital and resonant in our own lives"[7]—thereby analogizing Jewish consciousness with computer technology. Reboot identified its study's subject in terms of another new medium—dubbing American Jewish youth members of the "iPod generation"—and characterized the new technology as epitomizing this cohort's cultural moment, wherein "the desire and ability of the individual to mix and match . . . translates into the power to choose the way he or she defines personal identity in America."[8] These examples concern all manner of engagements with new media, secular as well as religious. By focusing on those encounters related to Jewish religious life, this book expands the scholarly discussion of Jews and media in America, which has mostly dealt with Hollywood film, stand-up comedy, and other secular entertainment genres and has primarily addressed issues of Jewish image and identity.[9]

To the relatively new field of media and religion, *Jews, God, and Videotape* offers the first book-length study of American Judaism within this rubric. Beyond examining a religious community infrequently discussed in this field, this book also essays a distinctly expansive approach to religion, media, and their interrelation. In this study, American Jews—including various major religious denominations (Orthodox, Reform, Conservative, Reconstructionist), hasidim, unaffiliated, and secularist, among others—are a subject of interest in their own right and in relation to the nation's Christian majority. Several chapters examine interfaith efforts, both official, such as ecumenical broadcasting on national networks in the mid-twentieth century, and popular, as in the various media practices responding to the "December dilemma" (that is, the challenges posed by the seasonal coincidence of Christmas and Hanukkah). Besides studying various forms of Jewish agency in relation to new media (as producers, writers, advertisers, performers, critics, consumers), this book also considers Jews as objects of Christians' moral and theological reflection, notably in media works of Holocaust remembrance. Some chapters focus on phenomena that are distinct to Jewish experience (for example, hasidism or the cantorate), and others engage media practices for which there are parallel phenomena in other religious communities, especially the photodocumentation of life-cycle rituals.

Moreover, this book approaches the nexus of media and religion differently by dint of the uneasy fit between the category of "religion" and Jewishness, which can also be conceived as a comprehensive way of life, as an ethnic (or national or racial) identity, or as a consciousness or sensibility. (Considering this array of paradigms in 1949, anthropologist Melville Herskovits asserted that perhaps "no word . . . means more things to more people than does the word 'Jew.'")[10] As Michael Satlow observes in his recent analysis of the challenging task of defining Jewishness as a religion, "to the extent that Jews have understood themselves as practitioners of 'Judaism' [that is, of a religion], they have primarily adopted a model of a religious tradition that emerged from the Enlightenment's adaptation of a Christian notion."[11] Similarly, Lynn Schofield Clark argues that research into media and religion is epistemologically informed by the protocols of what she terms "Protestantization"—that is, "values emergent with the Reformation," including "the rise of intellectual inquiry as an endeavor separated from religious aims and the cultural norm of religious tolerance and relativism." These values, she writes, are a product of Protestantism as "first and foremost a movement that signaled a new independence from the institutions of religion."[12] *Jews, God, and Videotape* interrogates the rubrics of "religion" and "media" through close examination of Jews' uses of new media in which the notion of religiosity is itself under scrutiny, as is its relation to mediation. Given the challenges that the word *religion* poses, it is not surprising that use of the term (as well as the terms *belief, faith,* and *spirituality*) varies considerably in this book's examples. More-over, these examples often engage the subject of religion and media less as "putatively distinct realms," in which a medium serves as an instrument of religion, but rather, as sociologist Jeremy Stolow has suggested, as a more complexly integrated phenomenon, "religion *as* media":

> "Religion" can only be manifested though some process of mediation. . . . It is only through . . . media that it is at all possible to proclaim one's faith, mark one's affiliation, receive spiritual gifts, or participate in any of the countless local idioms for making the sacred present to mind and body. . . . By the same token, every medium necessarily participates in the realm of the transcendent, if nothing else than by its inability to be fully subject to the instrumental intentions of its users.[13]

Therefore, one task of this study is to consider how, in engaging new me-dia and the special self-consciousness of mediation that doing so entails, Jews are also engaged in mediating the idea of religion itself. They do so both in relation to Christians, by challenging a generalized notion of re-ligiosity that looks beyond denominationalism and creed, and in relation to Jews themselves, by problematizing the Christian paradigm of religion while, at the same time, working within it.

What can be identified, however imperfectly, as traditional rabbinic Ju-daism has its own distinct paradigms, and these also inform this book's approach. The Talmudist Joseph Soloveitchik has argued that the religios-ity of rabbinic Judaism, what he terms the worldview of "halakhic man," is "as far removed from the [Christian notion of] *homo religiosus* as east is from west," in large part because the hands of halakhic man are "soiled by the gritty realia of practical Halakhah [rabbinic law]." The centrality of rabbinic Judaism's many commandments, elaborated through custom and learned, to a considerable extent, through mimesis, privileges behav-ior over thought and the practices of daily life over theological doctrines, mystical strivings, or eschatological projections. Soloveitchik character-izes this phenomenon not as limiting but as expanding opportunities: "Halakhic man prefers the real world to a transcendent existence because here, in this world, man is given the opportunity to create, act, accomplish, while there, in the world to come, he is powerless to change anything at all. . . . The universal *homo religiosus* proclaims: The lower yearns for the higher. But halakhic man, with his unique mode of understanding, declares: The higher longs and pines for the lower."[14] This principle is frequently extended to explaining more generally how "the good Jewish life is achieved." In his popular "anthropology of the Jews," Melvin Konner writes that this is accomplished "not by philosophy, . . . but by deeds large and small," and he references the oft-cited biblical prooftext for this sensibility, "We will do and we will understand" (Exodus 24:7).[15] The privileging of deed over thought that is central to rabbinic Judaism also informs the Jewishness of many Jews who do not observe rabbinic law, including those who variously characterize themselves as nonreligious, secular, cultural, "non-Jewish," "imaginary," or "post-halakhic" Jews.[16] In delineating the distinctive character of the "non-Jewish Jew," Isaac Deutscher explains that most of his exemplars have a "great philosophical idea in common—the idea that knowledge to be real must be active. . . . It was Spinoza who said that 'to be is to do and to know is to do.' It was only one step from this to Marx's saying that 'hitherto the philosophers have interpreted the world; henceforth the task is to change it.'"[17]

Indeed, although the history of Jewish modernism is usually recounted in terms of Jewish philosophy that, starting with Spinoza, challenges traditional rabbinic thought, this history could be traced just as effectively (if not perhaps more so) according to modernists' quests for new Jewish practices, which mediate between those who perform them as Jews and the ideas that conceptualize these behaviors as defining Jewishness. New media have often figured in these practices. For example, attendees of Jewish film festivals, of which there are now several dozen held annually in North America, sometimes describe the experience as the equivalent of going to synagogue.[18] Although these new practices are occasionally conceptualized as replacements for religious observance, others are characterized as enhancing religiosity—such as Jewish *Star Trek* fans' elaboration of speculative *halakhah* as it would pertain to life in outer space as portrayed in the science-fiction series.[19] Conversely, these new practices can be deemed religion's subversion, as in the case of a 1996 poll of students in a Manhattan Jewish day school, who, when asked to identify their favorite Jewish heroes, named performers Jerry Seinfeld, Adam Sandler, and Howard Stern ahead of God (who came in fourth).[20] Uniting all these undertakings is a desire to forge new ways of behaving as Jews, always conceived—if often tacitly and sometimes defiantly—in relation to established practices understood as religious.

In keeping with this sensibility that assigns behavior a defining, meaningful primacy in Jewish religious life, *Jews, God, and Videotape* approaches the nexus of religion and media among American Jews by centering attention on the social practices of new media as they engage religiosity, broadly defined. Beyond discussing the form or content of media works, theories of mediation, or communication in the abstract, this approach entails examining how certain media technologies figure in Jewish life comprehensively, including the contexts in which media works are created, distributed, consumed, scrutinized, and collected; the epiphenomena of media works (for example, publicity materials promoting a new film); the protocols of media use, both official and actual; the discussion of media in public forums, usually facilitated by other media (such as reviews of television programs published in newspapers or posted on weblogs).

The notion that the social practices of media can be key to understanding Jewish religious life is not without precedent. Long known as the "People of the Book," Jews are often defined in relation to a fundamental media work and its attendant social practices, including institutionalized study and ritual public reading, as well as an elaborate set of practices around the creation, adornment, storage, celebration, and interment of the Book in its most traditional (and sacred) form, the Torah scroll. For post-halakhic Jews, the notion that texts, broadly conceived, and textual practices are definitional persists in the form of Jewish book fairs and book clubs, as well as other text-based phenomena, such as guided tours organized around the films (both based on novels) *Exodus* (1961) and *Schindler's List* (1993).

Organizing this study around the spectrum of social practices involving new media necessitates a consideration of the term *media* in its full variety and complexity. As Raymond Williams observes, this word encompasses a convergence of meanings, including "the conscious technical sense," distinguishing various communications technologies (print, audio, visual, digital, and so on), as well as "the specialized capitalist sense," in which a particular institution or service (such as a newspaper publisher, radio station, recording label, or video production company) serves as "a medium for something else." (Sometimes the term also refers to media works themselves.) In addition, Williams notes "the old general sense of an intervening or intermediate agency or substance," most often expressed as a verb, to *mediate*, meaning to make a connection or negotiate between distinct entities or notions.[21] Just as this book attends to diverse uses of the word *religion*, it considers various uses of the term *media*, as well as how these uses resonate and intersect with one another.

To do so, *Jews, God, and Videotape* takes an expansive approach to new media, examining both new communications technologies of the past century as well as older media that are new to Jews during this period (for example, the Yiddish daily newspaper and the Jewish holiday greeting card). New mediating practices are also examined as they engage more established cultural institutions, such as museum displays and tourist productions. The approach to time and place in this book is similarly expansive. Though this study is centered in twentieth-century America, it looks back before 1900 and forward into the present century, as well as beyond the borders of the United States, when doing so is important to the analysis of particular phenomena.

At the same time, *Jews, God, and Videotape* takes a selective approach to its subject, analyzing a set of case studies in depth, rather that seeking to offer an all-inclusive overview, delineate a master narrative, or posit a comprehensive theory. Each case study—variously organized around a particular issue, medium, community, time period, or occasion—has been selected as being especially revealing of a different aspect of the religion/media nexus in twentieth-century American Jewish life. The approach to each case study responds to the phenomenon at hand, each engendering its own research questions, analytic methods, scope, and organization of writing.

The first chapter examines the impact of sound recordings, broadcasting, film, and other media on the role of cantors in Jewish community life throughout the twentieth century. As these new media aestheticized cantors' devotional musicianship, they have transformed the cantor from a spiritual messenger into a celebrity performer, who has become the center of communal attention as opposed to a conduit to the divine. These media have also situated cantors as protagonists in a variety of narratives in which cantors figure as exemplars of American Jewry, negotiating the demands of communitarian tradition and the lure of modern culture, centered on individual consciousness and creativity.

Chapter 2 analyzes the involvement of Conservative Judaism in ecumenical broadcasting during the middle decades of the twentieth century. Considered pioneering efforts in public-service radio and television, these broadcasts were especially innovative in their use of drama as a vehicle of Jewish religious culture. In addition to playing a strategic role in redefining the image of Judaism in American public culture during the years following World War II, these broadcasts became the center of new definitional rituals of listening for a widely dispersed audience of American Jews. The rise and fall of these broadcasts sheds light on the dynamics of religious pluralism in twentieth-century America.

The place of new media—including feature and documentary films, television broadcasts, tourist productions, and museum installations—in the civil religion of Holocaust remembrance in the United States is the subject of chapter 3. During the latter half of the twentieth century, Americans came to embrace the Holocaust as a mainstay of its civil religion, thanks largely to works of media. These media also prove strategic in adapting the protocols of established religious practices—inspirational dramas, rituals, moral instruction, pilgrimages, and monuments—to realize projects of Holocaust remembrance and moral edification for this large and diverse nation, in which few citizens have any direct connection to this profoundly disturbing historical event.

Chapter 4 examines how films and videos documenting life-cycle celebrations have transformed the nature of many American Jews' experience of ritual. Within the expansion of personal photodocumentation over the course of the past century, film and video making have had a remarkable impact on planning, enacting, and recollecting rituals associated with birth, coming of age, marriage, and death. In addition to serving frequently as the organizing principle of staging and remembering rituals, these films and videos have at times become an integral component of the ritual experience itself, which some participants deem incomplete until they have witnessed the ritual's photodocumentation.

Chapter 5 considers the implementation of various media, including advertising, television drama, and greeting cards, to address the challenges that Christmas poses to American Jews. Known since the mid-twentieth century as the "December dilemma," the coincidence of Christmas and Hanukkah not only has transformed how American Jews observe Hanukkah but also has engendered an array of Jewish responses to the near-ubiquitous public celebration of Christmas. These responses address changes within the American Jewish community—most significantly, shifting responses to intermarriage—and in the United States generally, notably the dynamics of identity politics as it relates to religion. The December dilemma has inspired a remarkable array of new Jewish media practices that center on productivity, thereby partaking in—and, at the same time, often subverting—the consumer rites of Christmas in America.

The final chapter explores how Lubavitcher hasidim, based in Brooklyn, New York, have used broadcasting, video, and the Internet, among other media, to advance their distinctive mission during the past half-century. Unique among ultra-Orthodox Jews, these hasidim deploy media extensively in their outreach campaigns, which strive to encourage other Jews to become more observant of traditional religious precepts. Media also play a provocative role in the group's messianism, which has become more complicated since the death, over a decade ago, of the last Lubavitcher rebbe, who left his followers without a successor to his leadership. Consequently, the extensive inventory of media documentation of his public appearances has come to serve many of his followers as a "virtual rebbe," providing them with a source of devotional inspiration and solidarity as an international religious community.

Although each of these chapters can be read as an independent study, there are revealing resonances among them. For example, though the Holocaust is dealt with specifically in chapter 3, it is also discussed, in one manner or another, in all the other chapters. Moreover, several key analytic issues recur: how the notion of Jews as an audience, defined by their engagement with new media, engenders new understandings of this community; the importance of celebrity as a new cultural force in religious life; how new consumer practices inform discussions of religiosity; the emergence of new modes of storytelling in conjunction with new media; how new media challenge traditional notions of religious authority and literacy; the impact of new media on the relationship of theology to religious behavior; and the advent of new modes of self-scrutiny through innovations in self-reflexive media practices.

From among these resonances, the value of studying the interrelation of religious life and new media emerges: far from being incompatible or destructive, new media can enable a wealth of possibilities for enhancing religiosity. Nor are these media simply means that serve some distinct end for religious communities; rather, these media are imbricated in that end. And the ongoing demand to consider the implications of a cascade of new media demonstrates the centrality of mediation in religious life, not only by virtue of the extent and variety of media practices but also as a catalyst for stimulating religious thought and practice.

1

Cantors on Trial

Shmulik had a sackful of stories about cantors, one better than the
next. He had learned these stories from their original sources. . . .
But the cantors of old are not to be found nowadays. Where,
for example, can you find today a cantor like Arke Fiedele, the
Vitebsker? The whole world flocked to hear his voice. . . . Or, for
instance, someone like the Vilner Balabeysl, as he was called?
Where can you find his equal today?
                              —Sholem Aleichem, *Yosele Solovey* (1886)[1]

Cantors have long inspired talk, quite apart from the attention
paid to their musicianship. In particular, they serve as key figures in discussions interrelating spirituality and art in Jewish life. The position of
hazzan (the modern Hebrew word for cantor) has a long dynamic, with
its origins in the Talmudic era, as synagogue worship was inaugurated
two millennia ago. As synagogue rites developed during the Geonic period (the sixth to eleventh centuries C.E.), the role of the *hazzan* was con-
solidated as the official *sheli'ah zibbur* (community messenger), charged
with leading communal worship during services. During the Middle Ages
the *hazzan* emerged as a professional mainstay of synagogue life.[2] Rabbis
have long discussed the qualifications for this role, which have entailed
not only familiarity with liturgy and musical talent but also matters of
character—the cantor's marital status, physical appearance, demeanor,
and personal history have all been subject to scrutiny.[3] In the person of
the cantor religiosity, artistry, and public comportment converged, often
uneasily. Historian Israel Abrahams, writing about social morality among
medieval Jews, noted, "There was one class only against which suspicion
pointed its finger—the *Chazan* . . . , an official who was more musician
than minister, and who shared some of the frailties apparently associated

with the artistic disposition." Abrahams felt obliged to caution that "the comparative frequency with which the chazan was suspected of unchastity must not lead us to the supposition that the whole order was tainted with the same vice."[4]

In the modern era, cantors became the subject of an extended public discourse in which Jews negotiate their ideals of devotion to God in relation to the realities of daily life and the demands of the Jewish public sphere. Thus, the 1756 constitution of the Jewish community of Sugenheim, Franconia—in which the only paid communal official was the cantor (whose duties included religious instruction and kosher slaughtering, among other tasks, in addition to leading worship services)—required that a candidate for the post "be able to account for his origins and for his conduct in the past by means of the proper documents."[5] As subjects of ongoing scrutiny and discussion, cantors became the protagonists of narratives.

Over time, these narratives grew more elaborate and engaged new concerns. By the late nineteenth century, cantors had become central characters in larger contests between the demands of Jews' traditional communal worship, on one hand, and desires for modern, personal artistic expression, often engaging the aesthetics and mores of the non-Jewish world, on the other hand. These narratives appeared in cultural forms new to Jewish culture, including Yiddish novels, such as Sholem Aleichem's *Yosele Solovey* (*Yosele the Nightingale*), and plays, such as Mark Arnshteyn's 1902 *Der vilner balebesl* (*The Young Gentleman of Vilna*). Both works retell the story of the ill-fated cantor Yoel-Dovid Strashunsky (1815–1860), whose vocal talent attracted Christian admirers who lured him from the synagogue to the secular world, resulting in his professional and moral ruin.

In twentieth-century America, stories about cantors reflect larger concerns of the American Jewish audience, for whom they serve, in ethnomusicologist Mark Slobin's words, as "representatives of the group's strivings."[6] As in Europe, these narratives have appeared in new cultural forms and a cascade of new media. These include print media (novels, memoirs, periodicals, sheet music, advertisements, cartoons) as well as new technologies that record performances (sound recordings, from wax cylinders to digital files, as well as film, broadcasting, video). Cantors simultaneously explored new forums for live performances, including recitals, fundraising events, and vaudeville. This unprecedented array of opportunities for performance helped transform the cantor's public profile from communal messenger to star—that is, from a mediating figure, strategic to traditional Jewish worship, to a subject of mediation him- (and sometimes her-) self.

דער נרוויסער קונדס
מעטעממארפאזע נומער 4

אין דער היים איז ער געווען א בעל־תפלה און האט געהייסען זעליקאוויץ — אין אמעריקא איז ער א איטאליעגישער טענאר און הייסט — ס ע נ י א ר
ז ע ל ק א נ י נ י.

"In the Old World, he was a cantor named Zelikovitsh; in America he is an Italian tenor named Signor Zelkonini." This Yiddish cartoon (read from right to left) by Saul Raskin, one of a series portraying the disparities between Jewish life in Eastern Europe and in the United States as tales of "metamorphoses," appeared in the American humor magazine *Der groyser kundes* (*The Big Prankster*) in 1909.

In becoming a star, a cantor engendered what film scholar Richard Dyer has termed a *star text*—that is, an accumulation of performances and discussions of them, together with discussions of the performer, both while performing and while not, which are circulated and remediated in public relations materials and press accounts, as well as gossip. Dyer characterizes stardom as a social and ideological phenomenon with intimations of the miraculous. A synthesis of fictional representations and actual people, stars effect a "magical reconciliation" of these seemingly contradictory states.[7] The star texts of American cantors also engage a series of contradictions of their own, concerning religiosity and art, Americanness and Jewishness, Old World and New World sensibilities, communal concerns and individual desires. By examining narratives about cantors created in twentieth-century America and how these stories have been mediated, this chapter considers what these practices of storytelling and mediation reveal about American Jewish religious life in ways that often extend far beyond the cantor's art.

"Chazunes in America"

Among the array of technologies that presented cantors to the public, early sound recordings—wax cylinders and 78 rpm discs—are especially important, being the first new media that could reproduce, albeit in a limited fashion, a cantor's vocal performance. The first published recordings of *hazzanut* (cantorial music)—or, as the great majority of American Jews at the time would have pronounced the word in Yiddish, *khazones*—date from the turn of the twentieth century. By the early 1940s, there were over one thousand recordings made by several dozen cantors in the United States, with considerable inventories produced in Europe at the same time.[8] Cantorial music was but one of several genres of music identified as "Jewish" (or, sometimes, "Hebrew") available on commercial recordings in the early twentieth century, along with Yiddish theater songs, instrumental dance music (what is now called *klezmer*), and spoken performances, including comic routines and dramatic monologues. Jews who had recently arrived from Eastern Europe were the primary audience for these recordings, which were one of an array of "cheap amusements"—some of which (most notably, the nickelodeon) involved new media—primarily targeting America's burgeoning, largely working-class, immigrant population. In the American Yiddish press, advertisements for phonographs vied in number with those for pianos, the epitome of domestic refinement for many immigrants, during the 1910s and '20s.[9]

These newspapers also ran advertisements for recordings, vaunting a wide variety of performances—"serious and comic songs, folksongs and Zionist songs, . . . as well as the best comedy and dramatic duet sketches"—all of which promised to "delight the Jewish soul." According to advertisers, the purchase of Jewish recordings not only offered the consumer "world famous singers in your home" but also constituted an act of communal loyalty: "Not a single Jew should fail to buy the following wonderful records," exhorted a 1917 promotion for Columbia Gramophone Company. In addition, recordings were marketed as transcending the geographic and cultural upheaval of immigration, offering immigrants an emotional palliative for their homesickness. A 1918 advertisement for Columbia asserted that its recordings "will remind you of the sacred, divine hymns of praise, sweet national melodies, and joyous, genuinely Jewish dance music that you used to hear in your native land. Your troubles will disappear, you will forget your cares, and every corner of your home will become lively and happy." Though often included with secular music in the roster of these advertisements, recordings of *khazones* were sometimes promoted separately, especially around the High Holy Days. A 1920 advertisement for Pathé Records intimated that listening at home to holiday liturgy was on par with hearing it chanted in the synagogue: "Every prayer that is sung in synagogue on the holy days of Rosh Hashanah and Yom Kippur can be found on our list, and our Jewish patrons will have the greatest pleasure on hearing the following records by the greatest and most famous cantors in New York."[10] In these advertisements, live performances were doubly mediated; advertising copy transformed the experience of listening to recordings into an encounter charged with affect, political significance, or spiritual value.

Of course, a sound recording does not simply replicate live cantorial performances; it, too, transforms them. As historians of recording regularly note, recording technology in the acoustic era was kinder to some sounds than to others, and the capacity of the recording medium, whether wax cylinder or 78 rpm disc, limited the performance to a maximum length of three to four minutes.[11] Early recordings of *khazones* thus isolate from the full length of Jewish worship services, which can extend for hours in actual performance, discrete musical "numbers." These include selections from Sabbath and weekday services, High Holiday worship (most famously, the Yom Kippur-eve prayer Kol Nidre), as well as the liturgy for other holidays. In addition, cantors recorded prayers associated with mourning (El Male Rahamim, Kaddish) and home worship, especially for the Sabbath (Kiddush, Havdalah).

Most significantly, sound recordings are what R. Murray Schafer calls *schizophonic* phenomena, separating sound from its original source.[12] In the case of *khazones*, recordings remove cantorial singing from the synagogue and the specific occasion of worship. Even when these recordings feature choral accompaniment, they foreground the cantor rather than replicate the interrelation of cantor and congregation that takes place during worship. Besides the performance's removal from sacred place and time, it is separated from its original sacred intent—addressing God within the rubric of communal worship—thereby situating cantorial music in some other listening context. Cantors, record producers, marketers, and audiences have all demonstrated their awareness of this transformation. For example, many recordings of *khazones* feature instrumental accompaniment that would not be heard when this music is performed in those synagogues where playing instruments is forbidden on the Sabbath and holidays. The shift away from worship is also signaled on many (though not all) recordings, in which cantors substitute the words *Adoshem* and *Elokeinu* for names of God traditionally uttered only when actually praying. Thus, within the protocols of *khazones* itself, performers marked their recordings as something other than worship.

Audiences were likewise aware both of the distinction between *khazones* in the synagogue and on recordings and of their close interrelation. The context of listening could provoke discomfort, especially when it took place not in enclosed private venues, such as the home, but in open public spaces. At the beginning of the twentieth century, cantor Pinhas Minkowsky denounced the Victrola as a "disgraceful screaming instrument" and expressed outrage that in Odessa, cantorial recordings could be heard through the windows of prostitutes' rooms in the city's red-light district.[13] Decades later, author Judd Teller noted a comic irony in the behavior of crowds that gathered in front of phonograph stores on New York's Lower East Side, which played amplified music outside their doors. Devoted fans of *khazones* "waited patiently for the moment when a cantorial record was put on. Then they exploded into a minor riot of heated polemics, drowning out the voice pouring through the horn [as] each coterie of fans acclaimed the records of its favorite cantor."[14]

Some cantors who made recordings defended their efforts as having a moral benefit for the Jewish community. Gershon Sirota, one of the first to record *khazones*, refuted Minkowsky's condemnation of this practice with anecdotes of Jewish soldiers, fighting in the Russo-Japanese War, who found solace listening to Sirota's recordings on the battlefield and of a Russian aristocrat who received some of the cantor's records as a gift from a Jewish tenor of the St. Petersburg Royal Opera. According to the singer, "This high ranking lady, who was never a friend of the Jewish people, changed her biased viewpoint thanks solely to the direct influence of [Sirota's] voice. . . . As a consequence of her having listened to the laments in Sirota's prayers, . . . she felt instinctively that his people suffered innocently."[15] The value for Jews attributed to these recordings is distinct from the sacred purpose of the original performances that they document; instead, through an affective appeal to their listeners, these recordings variously boosted morale and a sense of ethnic solidarity for Jews on the battlefield and, for the non-Jewish listener, prompted sympathy for Jews as victims of oppression.

As early recordings dislocated *khazones* from the synagogue, they transformed the cantorial repertoire into a selective inventory of modular performances that had to compete in the marketplace for consumers' attention both alongside other kinds of music and among different cantors' recordings. Produced like other works of popular culture, cantorial recordings straddled a tension between the expected and the novel. Cantors responded to these demands by offering multiple versions of the most popular selections from their repertoire (sometimes rerecorded by the same cantor), performing what are, in effect, "covers" of familiar repertoire distinguished by musical variants and arrangements. This pursuit of variety and innovation engendered the occasional novelty recording, such as performances by cantorial duos and quartets.

As Slobin has noted, cantors' musical sensibility is eclectic by nature.[16] Just as they listened to and learned from a variety of musical idioms, some cantors demonstrated their command of music beyond *khazones* on recordings, as they had already been doing in live recitals. Given their stature as public figures in the Jewish community, it is not surprising that most of the nonliturgical music that cantors recorded on 78s was some other kind of Jewish music, including songs in modern Hebrew, in particular Zionist songs (and especially the anthem "Hatikvah"), and in Yiddish. The most frequently recorded Yiddish numbers were secular works with religious subjects: "Eyli, Eyli" ("My God, My God"), an emotional avowal of faith and plea to heaven to protect Jews from persecution, written by Jacob Sandler for a Yiddish play in 1896; and "Afn pripetshik" ("On the Hearth"), Mark Warshavsky's early-twentieth-century song describing the traditional teaching of the Jewish alphabet to young children, which is celebrated as an exemplar of Jews' endurance in the face of hardship.[17] Some cantors' recorded repertoire included opera arias, art songs, and even Judaized versions of Tin Pan Alley numbers (Cantor David Putterman recorded "Zindelle Meins" and "Kadishil Mains," Yiddish versions of the Al Jolson tearjerkers "Sonny Boy" and "Little Pal").[18] Besides demonstrating individual artists' range, these recordings expanded the notion of cantorial performance generally, demonstrating a modern Jewish musicianship across languages, genres, and subjects and displaying musical virtuosity in the idioms of mainstream elite and popular culture. Offered in the same modular format as cantors' recordings of *khazones*, their renditions of non-Jewish and secular Jewish music appeared as works of equivalent stature, at least as commodities.

Of particular interest in cantors' recorded Yiddish repertoire are a number of self-reflexive songs about cantors, which were especially popular during the interwar years. Most famous of these is "A khazndl af shabes" ("A Cantor on the Sabbath"), a folksong first published by M. Kipnis in 1918 and recorded by several cantors.[19] The song describes a cantor's Sabbath prayers as appreciated by three Jews in his town—a tailor, a carpenter, and a coachman—each of whom savors the cantor's skill in terms of his own trade (for example, the tailor likens the cantor's singing to a needle's stitching and an iron's pressing). "A khazndl af shabes" both celebrates *khazones* (the song allows for ample embellishment in performance) and mocks it, albeit good-naturedly, likening cantorial talents to the work of laborers. Just as a cantor singing this song both impersonates and distances himself from the provincial cantor who is the subject of the song, "A khazndl af shabes" separates *khazones* from its spiritual purpose and offers it up as an artisanal skill.

Other self-reflexive songs that cantors recorded include their own compositions, such as Pierre Pinchik's performance of "Der Chazen Un Gabbe (The Cantor And The Sexton)" and Joseph Shapiro's of "A Chazon Oif Probe (Cantor For A Trial)." Other vocalists also recorded Yiddish songs about cantors in the 1920s, including Michal Michaelsko's rendition of Sholem Secunda's "A Probe Oif Chazonim (Cantor's Test)" and Joseph Winogradoff's "A Chaz'n's Debut In A Klein Shtedtele" ("A Cantor's Debut in a Small Town"). And cantors were the subject of recordings by Yiddish theater star and impresario Maurice Schwartz, who performed his own composition "A Chazen A Shiker (A Drunken Cantor)"; vaudevillians Sam Silverbush and Sadie Wachtel, who recorded "A Chazan Auf Der Elter" ("A Cantor in Old Age"); and "character singer" Myra Sokolskaya, who made a recording of "Der Chasendl (The Cantor)."[20]

Even as some cantors demonstrated musical eclecticism in their recordings, they recorded discrete parts of their repertoire under different names. Cantor Abraham Jassen recorded *khazones* under that name and issued secular Hebrew songs as A. Jassen; similarly, Cantor Shlomo Beinhorn recorded both *khazones* and Italian songs under the name Mr. S. Beinhorn, while as Cantor Shlomo Beinhorn, he issued only cantorial selections. Most remarkable is the case of Meyer Kanewsky, who recorded *khazones* under the name Rev. Meyer Kanewsky; under the name M. Mironenko, he issued Ukrainian songs; as M. Guttman (or Gutmann),

Poster advertising a Yiddish radio program starring Sheindele the Chazente (female cantor), heard on New York station WEVD in the 1930s. (Jewish Museum, New York)

he recorded Yiddish songs; as M. Kanewski, he recorded Yiddish, Russian, and Ukrainian songs; as M. Kanewsky or Meyer Kanewsky, he issued some *khazones* as well as songs in Ukrainian, Russian, Yiddish, and Hebrew; and, as M. Kanewsky-Katz, he recorded in Russian.[21]

Conversely, a number of vocalists who were not cantors performed *khazones* as part of their recorded repertoire, including tenors Morris Goldstein, Kalman Juvelier, Simon Paskal, and William Robyn; a boy soprano (Kamele Weitz, recording several selections for Victor in 1928); and several women: Rose Herringer, Dorothy Jardon, Delphine March, Estella Schreiner, Regina Prager, and Lady Cantor Sophie Kurtzer, who recorded three discs for Pathé in 1924–1925.[22] The phenomenon of "lady cantors," or *khaznte*, as they were called in Yiddish, epitomizes the transformation of *khazones* through new media. Forbidden by rabbinic law from serving as cantors—or, among more stringently observant Jews, from singing before men generally—women could not perform this music in synagogues in the official capacity as leaders of worship (until the Reform and Conservative movements began ordaining women cantors in the 1970s and 1980s, respectively; most Orthodox Jews still prohibit women from singing in the synagogue). But secular venues, including sound recordings and radio, provided women with opportunities to sing the cantorial repertoire. Indeed, the media used in these performances marked them as outside the bounds of devotional singing, while, conversely, the presence of *khazntes* marks these media as facilitating something other than worship.

Further complicating the distinction between music for sacred worship and other kinds of engagement, as well as between the musicianship of cantors and other singers, are recordings by both men and women of selections of *khazones* as they were performed in Yiddish theater works: Joseph Feldman and Morris Goldstein recorded "Kaddish, fun 'Yeshiva Bocher' ['The Yeshiva Student']"; Jennie Goldstein recorded "Rachem, fun 'Der Golem'" and "Ovinu Malkeynu, fun 'Dem Chazen's Tochter' ['The Cantor's Daughter']"; and David Kessler recorded "Mismore Ledovid, from 'Gott, Mensch & Taifill' ['God, Man, and the Devil']."[23] Goldstein's rendition of Ovinu Malkeynu as performed in the play *Dem Chazen's Tochter* demonstrates how, even within the confines of a recording lasting a few minutes, *khazones* can be situated in a complexly layered performance. The recording begins with Goldstein, as the eponymous cantor's daughter, delivering a spoken introduction in Yiddish, over orchestral accompaniment, recalling her father's chanting of the penitential prayer Ovinu Malkeynu on Yom Kippur: "Dressed in his white robe, he stands before the holy ceremony of Kol Nidre and beseeches God on behalf of all sinners, all the unfortunate." She performs a verse from the prayer, as the orchestra continues to play, then sings in Yiddish, describing the prayer's emotional plea to God for forgiveness ("Dear God, see my tears, and remove the stain from my brow") and concludes with an elaborate cantorial flourish. The original prayer for communal forgiveness is framed in an affective personal narrative, translated into vernacular language, and—mediated by a female singer with orchestral accompaniment—transformed into an object of nostalgia. The first 78s made of *khazones* thus played with and at times contravened the persona of the cantor and the parameters, protocols, and contexts of his repertoire, even as these recordings drew on this music's aesthetics, authority, and sanctified affective value.

Transcriptions of cantorial selections were first published in sheet music at the turn of the twentieth century as well, thereby reinforcing some of the transformations wrought by sound recordings. Sheet music similarly separated *khazones* from its original performance context, atomized the cantorial repertoire into discrete musical "numbers," and set it to instrumental accompaniment (usually piano) or rendered vocal melodies for instrumental performance (for example, on the violin or mandolin). Moreover, sheet music further democratized *khazones*, making not just hearing but also performing this repertoire available to anyone able to read music. The Hebrew texts were typically romanized (which facilitated reading the words in the same left-to-right direction as musical notation), removing the obstacle of Hebrew literacy. At the same time, the professional authority and acclaim of celebrity cantors were affirmed on sheet music, which occasionally credited a well-known cantor as the source of the arrangement and reported that he had performed it "with great success." Portraits of cantors, sometimes framed in drawings of synagogue facades, frequently grace the covers of sheet music of *khazones*, and these covers occasionally cross-promoted recordings by the featured cantor.[24]

Sheet music of *khazones* both vaunted cantorial authority and sometimes situated cantors in competition with one another, as in the case of multiple editions of "A khazndl af shabes," variously arranged for "the Famous Cantor Rev. Joseph Hoffman," "Cantor Hershman," and "the Famous Cantor Rev. Rabinowitz."[25] In the case of "Eyli, Eyli," cantors vied in the public marketplace with other vocalists; besides sheet music of arrangements by the renowned cantor Josef (Yossele) Rosenblatt, there were versions arranged for actress Sophia Karp, opera singer Rosa Raisa, and popular chanteuse Belle Baker, who credited her rendition as having helped make the song "the world's most famous Hebrew melody."[26] In an unusual extension of cantorial authority to support another commodification of Jewish observance, the publication of one of Rosenblatt's versions of "Eyli, Eyli" was underwritten by the Loose-Wiles Biscuit Company, Bakers of Sunshine Biscuits, and the back page of this sheet music featured the cantor's endorsement of the company's kosher products. "When I am traveling, they literally save my life," Rosenblatt explained, in Yiddish. "In all the Jewish homes that I visit throughout this country they serve Sunshine Kosher Cookies."[27]

Sound recordings were also commodities in an open, competitive market. But whereas sheet music was often issued by Jewish publishing houses, almost all early recordings of *khazones* and other Jewish music in America were produced by major labels as one of a series of inventories of ethnic or national musics: Italian, Russian, German, Irish, and so on. In this taxonomy, recordings of *khazones* were indexed as music for a traditional constituency conceived in new terms as an audience, a niche market. At the same time, because these recordings were sold by major labels, music traditionally associated with a particular community became potentially accessible to anyone with a phonograph. The modular nature of sound recordings enabled listeners to establish their own inventories of listening, crossing linguistic, ethnic, and generic boundaries, and to create their own listening practices. As recordings and sheet music separated *khazones* from its context of origin, they commodified and aestheticized it, thereby challenging the value of the music as well as the sacred calling of its traditional performers.

The advent of sound recordings coincided with the peak of mass immigration of East European Jews to the United States, during which other cultural forces contributed to the transformation of *khazones*. As Slobin notes, the start of this wave of immigration was marked by the "cantorial craze" of the 1880s and '90s, when newly arrived American Jews elevated cantors into local and, occasionally, national celebrities.[28] Historian Jonathan Sarna argues that, for these immigrants, the celebrity cantor represented "the ultimate synthesis of the Old World and New . . . : observant yet rich, traditional yet modern. . . . He personified the great heritage of a European world-gone-by, yet succeeded equally well in Columbus's land of the future. In short, a cantorial performance simultaneously served both as an exercise in nostalgia and as living proof that in America the talented could succeed handsomely." Significantly, Sarna notes, this was "a synthesis most immigrants sought to achieve but few succeeded" in realizing.[29]

The disparity between this synthetic ideal and the complex, often unresolved realities of immigrant life is reflected in the consequences of mediating *khazones* on recordings. Significantly, both immigration and sound recordings separated cantors and their music from a context regarded as sacred and indigenous. Separating *khazones* from its traditional milieu disrupted an established understanding of the signifying power of this music and, at the same time, opened it up to new symbolic possibilities. This development also informed early-twentieth-century cantorial narratives in America, which project the particular challenges that immigrant cantors confronted onto larger trials that immigrant Jews in America faced as individuals, as families, and as an entire people. These narratives center on conflicts that are defining for immigrants, articulated through cantors in terms of competing modes of expressive culture.

The cantor's status as the embodiment of American Jews' relocated past grew more complex with the end of mass immigration from Europe in the early 1920s. What American Jews regarded as "native" (that is, Old World) music practice was increasingly understood as having been transformed by multiple phenomena of modern life: immigration, commodification, mediation, and professionalization. By the mid-1920s some complained that *khazones* had become overly standardized, its sound reduced to what one critic termed a "phonographic character."[30] At the same time, members of the profession showed growing interest in artistic standards as defined by Western art music: "While in former days the natural qualities of the chazan's voice have been sufficient for his cantorial tasks, the cantor of today needs more voice culture and more understanding of the general vocal art in order to keep up honorably his position as a leading factor in the musical life of his community," wrote Bernard Kwartin, a voice teacher at the New York College of Music (and brother of renowned cantor Zavel Kwartin) in "The Cantor and the Vocal Art," an essay in the 1937 anniversary journal of the Jewish Ministers Cantors' Association of America. There follows an overview of principles derived from Kwartin's "Prinzipien fuer Stimmbildung und Gesang," including an anatomical diagram of the vocal apparatus and a musical passage from the tenor aria "Il mio tesoro" from Mozart's *Don Giovanni*. "It can not be urgently enough suggested to every cantor to pay the utmost attention to the proper training of his voice and of the culture of his singing," Kwartin concludes. "It would help materially to create higher standards in the cantorial profession and accordingly to raise the prestige of the cantor as *the* leader of the musical activities of the community."[31]

Further complicating the public profile of cantors in interwar America is the most famous cantorial narrative of the period—indeed, of the twentieth century: the 1927 Warner Bros. film *The Jazz Singer*, based on the 1922 story ("Day of Atonement") and 1925 play (*The Jazz Singer*) by Samson Raphaelson. These works were in turn inspired by the life of entertainer Al Jolson (né Asa Yoelson), who starred in the film as Jack Robin (né Jakie Rabinowitz). The film centers on an elaborate symbolic struggle—between Old World and New World, parent and child, tradition and modernity, religious devotion and secular entertainment, communal obligations and individual desires—enacted in the person of this Jewish musician, an immigrant cantor's son, who is asked to make the (improbable) choice between his Broadway debut as a jazz singer and replacing his dying father on the eve of Yom Kippur in a Lower East Side synagogue. In *The Jazz Singer*, Slobin notes, music making is not merely a vehicle but is the self-reflexive subject of the work: "The entertainer, the actual transmitter of the musical style that characterizes the group . . . , reflects the concerns that make the entertainment important to its audience."[32]

Critics and scholars have long regarded *The Jazz Singer* as a complex exercise in American Jewish self-portraiture, reenacting not only Al Jolson's personal history but also American Jews' communal struggles with the challenges of assimilation and the prickly dilemmas of race in American cultural politics.[33] Moreover, film critic J. Hoberman argues, the film's producers "were uneasily aware that the story of *The Jazz Singer* was not only that of Jolson or many of their employees, but also of themselves." The film offers both an oblique retelling of the Warners' journey from immigrant Jewish origins to success as American entertainers and an ambivalent homage to their father.[34] The souvenir program from the premiere of *The Jazz Singer* explains that the film's "faithful portrayal of Jewish home-life is largely due to the unobtrusive assistance of Mr. Benjamin Warner, father of the producers and ardent admirer of *The Jazz Singer*."[35]

Moreover, Hoberman notes, *The Jazz Singer* has endured as an "American Jewish myth," projecting forward to future generations via a series of remakes, adaptations, and parodies that run throughout the twentieth century.[36] But *The Jazz Singer* and its various versions relate only one such cantorial narrative. Other twentieth-century stories present cantors who did not choose the path taken by Jolson (or Robin). Indeed, these cantorial stories can be read as counternarratives to *The Jazz Singer*, even when having occasion to intersect with it.

The Dream of My People

The career of Yossele Rosenblatt constitutes one of the most elaborate of these counternarratives. Born in Belaia Tserkov, Russia, in 1882, Rosenblatt came to America in 1912, having already achieved acclaim as a cantor in Munkács, Pressburg, and Hamburg (where he made his first sound recordings). Rosenblatt was soon the most celebrated cantor in the United States, renowned among not only Jews but also the general public. Rosenblatt made dozens of recordings, published sheet music of his vocal arrangements, and appeared in concerts, vaudeville, and films. His face was widely reproduced in advertisements, news reports, and cartoons in the Yiddish, Anglo-Jewish, and mainstream American press. The cantor's celebrity status persisted beyond his death in 1933. In 1947, for example, the *Jewish Daily Forward* ran an advertisement for Yuban coffee featuring a portrait and capsule biography of Rosenblatt; the ad's copy begins, "When Yossele Rosenblatt used to pray, Jews would happily pay the price. When it comes to enjoying the good things in life, people will always gladly pay the price for the best. This explains why so many housewives are ready to pay a few more cents for the rich quality and flavor of Yuban coffee."[37] His reputation continues to be invoked in the twenty-first century, for example, in "Shirei Yosef: The Songs of Yossele," a concert tribute "dedicated to the memory of Yossele Rosenblatt"—hailed as "a Legend"—on the occasion of the seventieth anniversary of his death. The concert, held in New York City on December 2003 at Lincoln Center's Alice Tully Hall, featured performances by six contemporary cantors.[38]

Through an extensive array of live, notated, and recorded performances, Rosenblatt established his renditions of the traditional repertoire as a (if not *the*) standard against which other cantors would be measured. Like his published sheet music, his recordings of *khazones*, mostly for Victor and Columbia, frequently identify Rosenblatt as the arranger. His recordings also included Jewish art music (such as an aria from Moyshe Horowitz's opera *Yzias Mezrajum* [*Exodus from Egypt*]), Zionist anthems (I. B. Arnstein's "Soldiers of Zion"), Yiddish songs ("Pastuchel" ["Little Shepherd"]), and Tin Pan Alley Judaica ("My Yiddishe Momme"), as well as vocal recital standards in English ("The Last Rose of Summer") and Russian ("Song of the Volga Boatman"). Several of Rosenblatt's recordings were issued to mark special occasions, such as a version of the memorial prayer El Male Rahamim for victims of the *Titanic,* released in 1913; Massenet's "Elegy" in 1917 for victims of World War I; and "Onward, Jewish Legion" in 1919, honoring Jewish soldiers who fought in the British army during World War I.[39] Rosenblatt's recordings sold well and steadily during his lifetime; in the early 1920s he earned "at least $8,000" in royalties annually.[40] Posthumous reissues of his recordings have continued to appear on long-playing records, cassette tapes, CDs, and as MP3 files, providing ongoing opportunities for future generations to hear his *khazones*.

Like other celebrities, Rosenblatt cultivated public attention to his life outside the synagogue and other performance venues. Among the most significant episodes in his star text was a performance he chose *not* to give: In 1918, Cleofonte Campanini, general director of the Chicago Opera, invited Rosenblatt to sing the lead role of Eléazar, a beleaguered Jewish goldsmith, in Jacques Fromenthal Halévy's *La Juive* for one thousand dollars per performance. Rosenblatt's eventual refusal—despite assurances that he would not have to perform on the Sabbath or cut his beard—received national attention. The *New York Times* even reprinted the full text of Campanini's letter to the president of New York Congregation Ohab

Zedek, which then employed Rosenblatt as its cantor, in which the impresario stated that Rosenblatt had agreed to sing in *La Juive* only if the congregation would permit it.[41] While the story proved more of a passing curiosity in the mainstream American press, in Jewish newspapers it occasioned a more extensive discussion, addressing larger issues of Jewish artistry and its place in the modern world.[42]

Rosenblatt took a proactive role in this public discussion, especially in the Jewish press. Responding to a reporter from the *Yidishes Tageblatt*, who questioned the cantor's decision, Rosenblatt invoked the story of Yoel-Dovid Strashunsky: "When he was the cantor in Vilna's Great Synagogue, he had his voice, his honor, his greatness. There was nothing that he lacked. But then he left to sing for *them*—sang for a countess—and what happened? He sang 'Kol Nidre' for her . . . without covering his head! And what was the result? He lost his voice, went mad, and died a stranger, without his voice, without honor, without a Jewish community." As for the offer to sing at the Chicago Opera, Rosenblatt admitted, "For a moment I was taken aback by the proposal. For a moment the proposal enticed me. But a voice inside me said: 'Yossele, don't go! It's a dangerous path!'"[43] Thus, Rosenblatt used the Jewish press as a forum for articulating his own narrative as a counterexample to Strashunsky's, while exploiting the same elements of temptation and tension straddling Jewish tradition and modern Western culture. The Jewish press, in turn, offered its own commentary on Rosenblatt's career, notably in cartoons, which occasionally poked fun at the cantor's much publicized performance of piety outside the synagogue. For example, Rosenblatt's struggle with the temptation to perform in the opera was limned provocatively in a cartoon by Lola (Leon Israel), which ran in the Yiddish satirical weekly *Der groyser kundes* (*The Big Prankster*) in May 1918. The cantor is shown, dressed in top hat and tails and gripping a prayer book, fleeing a scantily clad woman, labeled "Grand Opera," who beckons with outstretched arms: "Come, Yossele, a thousand dollars a night!" to which the cantor replies by praying: "Shma Yisroel [Hear, O Israel]!!!"[44]

Despite rejecting opera, Rosenblatt gave recitals in concert halls and even performed in vaudeville in the 1920s, in order to wipe out debts from bad investments he had made in a Yiddish newspaper and a ritual bath, projects intended to enhance Orthodox Jewish life in New York. In Rosenblatt's 1954 biography, written by his son Samuel, the cantor's concert and vaudeville appearances are characterized not as compromising his commitment to *khazones* but rather as an extension of his values as a pious Jew and a Jewish artist.[45] Indeed, the cantor's son championed his father's touring the vaudeville circuit as an opportunity to perform religious ideals quite apart from his musicianship:

> His very conduct on the variety stage and the demands he made from the managers to satisfy his religious scruples were an ideal medium for teaching the non-Jewish masses of America something of the tenets of the Jewish faith while acquainting them with Jewish music. The announcements on the billboards that Josef Rosenblatt would not be heard on Friday evening or Saturday matinee, because he was observing his Sabbath, constituted a real *Kiddush Hashem*, a glorification of the Jewish religion.[46]

Samuel Rosenblatt claimed that press coverage of his father's vaudeville performances offered more opportunities to explain to the American public such Jewish religious practices as not uttering divine names in profane settings, keeping kosher, and not traveling on the Sabbath. The press also provided the cantor with a public forum in which he could bracket his onstage performances of "The Last Rose of Summer" and "Eyli, Eyli" (which he pronounced "Keyli, Keyli," to avoid pronouncing a sacred name of God on stage) within a public enactment of Jewish piety, reverence, and modesty. But other observers of Rosenblatt's vaudeville appearances seem to have witnessed another performance entirely, plotted on a different narrative trajectory. Teller wrote of the cantor's variety appearances, "The regular customers were mystified by the diminutive Yossele alone in the spotlight, and his large personal following had no desire to see their Yossele in his degradation, a Samson shorn of his locks parading before the Philistines in their temple. Nor could Yossele bear this very long. His heart gave out."[47]

Rosenblatt's variety performances may well have inspired his first participation in a film: a cameo appearance as himself in *The Jazz Singer*. At a strategic moment in the film, Jack Robin attends a recital by Rosenblatt while on tour in Chicago. As described in the film's novelization, Jack thinks to himself as the cantor sings:

> How fitting it seemed that he should be sitting here now. He had never told his associates in the theater of his home or his parents. He had never talked of the years of training given him by his father that he might be a Cantor. He had felt that he was a part of the theater—that the old years had been completely lost to him. He had even felt a little queer about

coming into the concert. . . . And yet now, as he sat there, he could feel all the old impulses rising; all the old sentiments stirring. This belonged to him.[48]

This encounter with Rosenblatt foreshadows later scenes in the film, in which Jack's devotion to the theater reveals both its tension with and its indebtedness to *khazones.*

In the screenplay for *The Jazz Singer* drafted by Alfred A. Cohn in the spring of 1927, Rosenblatt is described as performing "Eyli, Eyli" at the recital that Jack Robin attends. (In the film itself, Rosenblatt sings "Yohrzeit," a Yiddish song by Rhea Silberta about reciting the Kaddish on the anniversary of a relative's death.) Jack sits and watches Rosenblatt, transfixed. "It is a fairly close shot of the singer alone as Jack would see him from a seat well in front of the house. The figure slowly dissolves into the figure of Jack's aged father, Cantor Rabinowitz," singing in the synagogue, and then dissolves back to Rosenblatt performing on stage.[49] (This transformation prefigures the more famous dissolve, later in the film, when Jack looks in his dressing-room mirror and sees first a reflection of himself in blackface and then a vision of his father singing in the synagogue.)

The screenplay both elaborated and ironized the symbolic value of Rosenblatt's performance as bridging the stage and the pulpit in the next scene (which does not figure in the final film), set in Cantor Rabinowitz's home. The cantor's choirboys gather around the piano, waiting for their lesson with him. One boy plays and sings "Yes Sir, She's My Baby" (a Tin Pan Alley song made popular by Jolson). As soon as the cantor enters, the boy, "with hardly a change in tempo, starts playing and singing 'Eli, Eli,' with a very sanctimonious expression on his face," and the other boys join in. The cantor looks perplexed. "He is sure that the music he heard from outside was not 'Eli, Eli.' Yet, he is getting old and perhaps his ears are failing."[50]

Rosenblatt's biography describes his participation in the film differently than what appears to have been the case, claiming that the cantor did not agree to appear in the film but only agreed to record several "non-liturgical Jewish melodies" for its soundtrack. (He is only heard performing "Yohrzeit" in the film, and he is seen singing it on a stage.) Moreover, the biography claims that Warner Bros. originally approached Rosenblatt to cast him as Cantor Rabinowitz (eventually played by Warner Oland). The studio reportedly offered to pay Rosenblatt "$100,000 and appealed to him: 'Think of what it would mean for raising the prestige of the Jew and his faith if a man like you were to be held up as its representative to the non-Jewish public.'" Rosenblatt is said to have rejected the offer and a request to record sacred music for the soundtrack, including Kol Nidre, which figures as a musical and dramatic motif in *The Jazz Singer*: "Under no circumstances would I permit that to pass my mouth anywhere except in a house of God."[51] (He did, of course, record Kol Nidre for both Victor and Columbia.) In this story of rejecting the studio's proposals, Rosenblatt once more affirmed his commitment to his calling by discussing a role he chose not to perform—while, at the same time, identifying himself as that role's ideal performer.

Complicating the biography's claims of what Rosenblatt did or did not do in relation to *The Jazz Singer* is an article in *Moving Picture World*, which announced that the cantor had agreed to appear in the film in late May 1927. Hailed as "the greatest Cantor in America, if not the world," Rosenblatt is reported to have been participating in the film "as a singer, not as an actor. . . . Rosenblatt will appear as a singer and teacher of Cantors. He will take no part in the dramatic action of the production. He has already made two songs in New York on the Vitaphone" for use in *The Jazz Singer*.[52] A recording of Rosenblatt singing both "Yahrzeit" and Kol Nidre, identified as being from the film's soundtrack, was issued in the summer of 1927.[53] (Joseph Diskay sang Cantor Rabinowitz's performance of Kol Nidre as heard in the film; Jolson, as Jack Robin, sings Kol Nidre at the film's denouement.)[54]

This confusion about Rosenblatt's participation in *The Jazz Singer* may reflect not only the dynamics of negotiations with the cantor as the film was being produced but also some discomfort with his appearance in the film—especially in light of the cantor's own narrative, in which rejecting the film parallels his earlier rejection of opera and, in a way, also addresses his appearances in variety. Rosenblatt's biography characterizes his involvement in the film as "helping reduce the importance of vaudeville as the most popular form of amusement . . . of the American masses."[55] In his own *Jazz Singer* narrative, Rosenblatt both refuses the role of the Old World cantor—who fails to find his way in America and, at the film's end, dies an honored but defeated figure—and enacts the role of the successful New World cantor, who is able to stir the conscience of the wayward Jack Robin. Moreover, Rosenblatt does so from the stage, the same locus that tempts Jack to stray from his responsibility to the Jewish community. Thus, embedded within the *Jazz Singer* narrative is a counternarrative, in which the autobiographical exemplar is not Jolson but Rosenblatt.

In what proved to be the final journey of his life, Rosenblatt traveled to Palestine in 1933 to appear in another film, *The Dream of My People*. Produced by the Palestine American Film Company, the hour-long film brings "present day Palestine before your eyes," together with performances by Rosenblatt, hailed in the opening credits as "The Greatest Omed [pulpit] Singer in His Last Song." *The Dream of My People* is primarily a Zionist travelogue, taking viewers on a tour of sites in Palestine that reveal "the romance of the modern Jewish Renaissance." Typical of Zionist propaganda films of the interwar period, Jewish agricultural colonies and new civic institutions (Hadassah Hospital, the Technion) are contrasted with ancient landmarks evoking the biblical era and with Arabs, who embody an Orientalized past.[56]

Rosenblatt appears in the film at selected moments to perform six solos. At the opening, the cantor stands, dressed in a top hat and morning coat, with a small group of people atop Mt. Zion, overlooking Jerusalem. As the camera pans the landscape, Rosenblatt is heard singing a selection from his cantorial repertoire with organ accompaniment. He reappears over the course of the travelogue at different sacred sites, including the "Wailing Wall" in the Old City of Jerusalem and Rachel's Tomb. At each location Rosenblatt sings a selection from his repertoire, including Ovinu Malkeynu at the Cave of Machpelah, "B'tzes Yisroel" ("When Israel Went Forth"), his own setting of Psalm 114, sung while standing in a small rowboat on the Jordan River, and finally "Aheym, aheym" ("Homeward, Homeward"), a Yiddish Zionist song, back atop Mt. Zion. The musical performances are from earlier recordings, and there is no effort made to synchronize Rosenblatt's on-camera singing with the soundtrack, emphasizing the overall incongruity of his presence in the film.

Indeed, Rosenblatt's role in *The Dream of My People* is somewhat uncanny. His formal attire is strikingly out of place, compared with the appearance of both young Zionist pioneers and elderly religious Jews. Similarly, his stentorian performances contrast with livelier, less formally rendered modern Hebrew songs and Arab tunes heard elsewhere on the soundtrack. Rosenblatt is positioned as a tourist, yet one who engages the environment selectively (he is never seen at modern, secular sites), delivering performances in formal postures that seem disengaged from the surroundings that are ostensibly inspiring his singing (at the Wailing Wall, for instance, old pious Jews who have gathered there to pray seem oblivious to his presence).

Cantor Yossele Rosen-
blatt, singing at the
"Wailing Wall" in Jeru-
salem, from the 1933 film
The Dream of My People.
(Center for Advanced
Jewish Studies)

During filming, Rosenblatt died suddenly of a heart attack while at the
Dead Sea. News of his death is incorporated into the film's penultimate sequence, making his role in *The Dream of My People* that much more complicated and strange. After Rosenblatt sings "Aheym, aheym," the narrator
intones, "Saw the land and died," as a collage of notices of Rosenblatt's
death appears on screen, followed by footage of the crowds attending his
funeral in Jerusalem. The film continues with a sequence on Tel Aviv, the
"city of youth and gaiety," and concludes with the sun setting on the city's
shore and a Zionist flag fluttering in the breeze, as a lively Hebrew chorus
is heard on the soundtrack.

The Dream of My People positions Rosenblatt at the juncture of two
contrasting narratives. In the film's tourist narrative of Palestine, the cantor seems the embodiment of the diaspora Jew, who has come to venerate
the old and admire the new, but who is ultimately unable to disencum-
ber himself from an exilic sensibility and engage with the Zionist project.
Thus, after his interment, the tour proceeds to Tel Aviv, the modern Jewish city of the future. At the same time, *The Dream of My People* offers a
narrative that centers on the sacred, more so than on the secular, and on
Rosenblatt, rather than on Palestine, in which the cantor figures as a mod-
ern-day Moses, a venerated Jewish leader who comes to see the "promised land" and then to die. Read this way, the film—another problematic
commercial venture of Rosenblatt's, which, like his sound recordings and
stage appearances, tested the protocols of traditional *khazones*—becomes
a vehicle that successfully relates the final chapter of the cantor's life as

the culmination of a sacred journey. Samuel Rosenblatt's biography of his father seems to confirm this second narrative, explaining that the cantor had long wished that "his last pulpit might be in the Land of Israel."[57]

Cantorial films became a popular genre in the decade following the advent of "talking" pictures. Between *The Jazz Singer* and *The Dream of My People*, Rosenblatt also performed in two short films for Vitaphone, *Omar Rabbi Elosar* (*Rabbi Elosar Said*) and *Hallelujah*, and he appeared as one of nine soloists in *The Voice of Israel*, a 1931 compilation by Judea Films of cantorial performances. Among the earliest Yiddish "talkies" were one-reelers featuring cantors, the novelty of the medium coinciding with the high profile of star cantors in America. Leibele Waldman, a young American-born cantor, appeared in several of these shorts and in feature-length films. Some of Waldman's one-reelers offer performances of *khazones* in stories tailored to showcase the singer's virtuosity, positioning the cantor and his artistry at the center of narratives that engage the challenges that modernity posed to contemporary Jewish life.

The 1931 short *The Feast of Passover* contrasts a seder celebrated in decorous English by wealthy American Jews in formal evening dress with the traditional piety of a parallel celebration, conducted in Yiddish and Hebrew by an Old World family in their much humbler home. An extended performance of the Kiddush (blessing over wine) by Waldman (with off-screen orchestral accompaniment) is the cantorial centerpiece of the latter ritual, which elicits engaged devotion of both young and old, as seen in reaction shots. This seder culminates with a ghostly vision of the prophet Elijah entering and blessing the family when the ritual calls for the door to be opened to welcome his symbolic arrival. Returning to the American seder, its leader (who has conjured up the Old World celebration as a childhood memory) asks his son to open the door to their home for Elijah. A policeman enters instead, having come to search the home for a bottle of (illegal) liquor. The host reassures the officer that they only have sacramental wine, permissible under the Volstead Act, and offers him a glass. The policeman quickly recites the Hebrew blessing over wine, drinks, and the film ends. Waldman, a cantor popular with American audiences on records as well as films, here enacts the traditional Jewish art of fulfilling religious obligations elaborately and artfully, which the film associates with Eastern Europe. By contrast, Jewish prosperity and universalism in America, where Passover is characterized as "a feast of freedom embracing liberty to all mankind," appears spiritually tepid and passive. In *The Feast of Passover* a beat cop's spontaneous blessing over wine (contrasted with Waldman's extended, bravura recitation) serves as both a comic surprise and an emblem of tradition's diminished tenacity among American Jews.[58]

Waldman also starred that year in the one-reeler *A khazn af probe* (*A Cantor on Trial*), a satirical look at the cantorial profession in America. In this short, a bumbling, argumentative committee auditions potential cantors to lead High Holy Day services in their synagogue. Waldman impersonates a series of cantorial types applying for the position: an Old World East European cantor in a long coat, broad hat, and full beard, who delivers a traditionally ornamented solo; a German cantor with trimmed beard and top hat, who performs in the decorous style of oratorio; and finally an Americanized cantor, preceded by his manager, who promises the committee a cantor who has "personality," "pep," and can sing "Kol Nidre with a two-step melody." A clean-shaven Waldman enters, in a fashionable light suit and fedora, and performs a syncopated version of the prayer Yismakh Moshe, ending with a refrain of "boob-boop-a-doop." Enthralled, the committee members proclaim this candidate their choice and join in his jazzy dance around the room as the film ends. Waldman's series of impersonations is framed by him singing, in top hat and tails, a Yiddish song that ridicules this annual rite of auditioning cantors: "Cantorial tryouts are an endless affair. / They gargle and screech, hoping to please. / Many prayer leaders come in, / Even jazz singers acclaim the [Rosh Hashanah prayer] El Orech Din."[59] *A khazn af probe* puts both America's cantors and the congregations who engage them on (mock) trial, finding them guilty of frivolity. Waldman's performance in the context of this playful satire is complex, displaying his virtuosity as a musician and actor while reducing *khazones* to an act of mimicry.

The Cantor's Son

By the end of the 1930s, cantors appeared in feature-length Yiddish films as characters that contribute dramatically as well as musically to more elaborate plots. In *Hayntike mames* (*Mothers of Today*), a 1939 melodrama about the struggle between traditional virtues and modern vices, Solomon, a young cantor (played by Max Rosenblatt), enacts the ideal pious American Jew by singing the Kiddush in an extended sequence. More complex are the cantors played by tenor Moishe Oysher in *Dem khazns zindl* (*The Cantor's Son*, 1937) and *Der vilner shtot-khazn* (*The Cantor of Vilna*, also known in English as *Overture to Glory*, 1940), in no small measure due to the resonance of the films' stories with Oysher's star text. As Hoberman notes, both films offer narratives that run counter to that of *The Jazz Singer*, and both resonate with Oysher's own struggles to negotiate between careers as a cantor and as a performer on stage and radio.[60]

Whereas Yossele Rosenblatt's public persona exemplified a stalwart commitment to piety—reinforced by public demonstrations of his refusing to abandon the synagogue for other venues—Oysher was known as a transgressive figure whose career provocatively straddled the stage and the pulpit and whose personal life similarly flouted and embraced piety. The descendant of generations of cantors, Oysher began his professional career in the theater, shortly after emigrating from his native Bessarabia, where he was born in 1907, to Canada at the age of fourteen. He subsequently turned to *khazones*—most famously, by accepting the post of cantor at the First Roumanian-American Congregation, one of the oldest and largest of East European Jewish congregations on the Lower East Side, in 1935.

Controversies over whether Oysher was morally acceptable as a cantor (sparked not only by his secular performances but also by a reputation for being a womanizer and lax in religious observance) repeatedly provoked public demonstrations and press coverage.[61] Even promotional material for Oysher's performances characterized his career in terms of conflict between the sacred and the profane. In a pamphlet issued by the Second Avenue Theatre for its 1935 season, a biography of the singer states that "in spite of all his glories, [Oysher's] immediate family remained indifferent to his triumphs. They felt hurt that their son should snap the traditional golden chain of Cantors in their family for the lure of the footlights."[62] Interest in Oysher's public persona extended beyond the Jewish community; his dilemma was the subject of an item in *Variety*, which reported, "Moishe Oysher is in trouble because he couldn't make up his mind whether he wants to be a Yiddish actor or a cantor. Now, he seems to be caught between the two, with no jobs at either."[63] Beyond a matter of gainful employment, Oysher had come to exist, in the public eye, in a constant state of suspension between transgression and penance.

Oysher's performances in films contributed to this public image by staging his dilemma through dramas in which cantors confront the lure of the secular stage. In *Dem khazns zindl*, Oysher both enacts and undoes the journey of the wayward son, first abandoning his shtetl and the pursuit of his father's calling as cantor to become a popular performer in New York, then renouncing the stage for the pulpit and quitting America for Europe. Audiences can savor the range of Oysher's musical talents, from sentimental theater songs to bravura displays of *khazones*, in a series of set pieces performed throughout the film. At the same time, the film mocks the American cantorial craze, poking fun at synagogue committees and artistic managers, much like Waldman's short *A khazn af probe*.

After appearing as a shtetl playboy who mends his ways in *Der zingendiker shmid* (*The Singing Blacksmith*, 1938), Oysher played the quintessential penitent cantor in *Der vilner shtot-khazn*, based on Arnshteyn's dramatization of the life of Yoel-Dovid Strashunsky. Oysher's performance in this film situates his personal narrative in relation to a historical trajectory dating back to Strashunsky's experiences in Vilna and Warsaw in the early nineteenth century. Released during the first months of World War II, Strashunsky's (and Oysher's) attraction to Western culture becomes emblematic of larger questions about the limits of Jewish-Christian relations, which had acquired a new urgency as Jews in Europe experienced unprecedented levels of persecution. Music figures in *Der vilner shtot-khazn* as a powerful cultural force with the potential for promoting amity as well as strife between Jews and Christians. When Strashunsky tells his family and congregants that he has been invited by the Polish composer Stanisław Moniuszko to sing in the opera in Warsaw, they express indignation and remind the cantor of his communal obligation and sacred calling: "Your voice is ours, you hear? Ours! . . . Who will speak for us to God?" After his enraged father-in-law tears up the sheet music that Moniuszko had given to Strashunsky, the cantor replies, "You inflict your hate on something that is full of love for all people. People kill each other, fight each other. . . . But not in this music. This speaks to the soul of all peoples. No hatred is in it. I want my voice to reach everyone. In every language they will feel my Jewish sorrow." The rabbi warns Strashunsky that if he leaves the cantorate for the opera, he will be "left between two worlds, in neither of which will you really be."[64]

In the course of his performance, Oysher enacts music's potential to transcend boundaries of cultural mistrust by singing *khazones* and opera with equal vocal skill and emotional fervor, demonstrating how Strashunsky enchanted the Polish aristocracy as readily as he inspired his Vilna congregants. In *Der vilner shtot-khazn* the notion of music as a universal language exists in a performative tension with the spoken word. Like other Yiddish films of the prewar era, the language is uttered not only by

Moishe Oysher (right), as cantor Yoel-Dovid Strashunsky, performs for Polish composer Stanisław Moniuszko, in the 1940 Yiddish film *Der vilner shtot-khazn* (*The Cantor of Vilna*).

Jewish characters but also, as the language of the film's audience, by Polish characters, even when conversing among themselves. Ultimately, Jewish particularism trumps musical universalism in the film's narrative. The tragic ending of *Der vilner shtot-khazn*—following news that his young son has died, Strashunsky abandons the opera and returns to Vilna, where, after singing Kol Nidre in the synagogue, he dies a broken man—belies its early, optimistic voicing of the possibility of accord between Jews and their neighbors.

In these films Oysher enacts tales of a prodigal cantor that resonate with his own career narrative as they strive to countervail against it. They enable—indeed, they require—him to demonstrate his talents as cantor and showman. The films' narratives tell of renouncing secular musicianship for the cantorate, but Oysher's career narrative moves back and forth, relativizing these two opposing callings with a musicianship that bridges ideological divides through aesthetic virtuosity. If anything, the secular trumps the sacred in these films, as these stories of returning to *khazones* are enacted in the medium of movie musicals.

Singing in the Dark

The devastating upheavals wrought by World War II had their impact on the cantorate no less than any other segment of the American community. As devotional representatives of Jewish communities before God, cantors faced unprecedented cultural and, for some, theological challenges. Slobin notes that American cantors responded to the war—in particular, its destruction of what had been the "European cradle" of *khazones*—by taking "giant steps toward professionalization." They established training programs and professional organizations as part of a larger expansion of American Jewry's corporate religious movements, especially Reform and Conservative Judaism. At the same time, Slobin notes, Orthodox Jews, who had been "staunch supporters of the cantorate in the immigrant era," grew "less interested in the institution" after the war.[65]

Both new cultural challenges and new media have contributed to innovations in American Jews' cantorial narratives in the postwar period. Whereas immigration figured as modern Jewry's ultimate challenge in most prewar narratives, it was replaced in postwar narratives by the aftermath of the Holocaust, though the Holocaust's presence is often oblique. In postwar cantorial narratives, America is no longer viewed as central to the problems that Jews face; on the contrary, it is often explicitly characterized as Jewry's salvation. Similarly, opera no longer appears as the pernicious seducer of cantors but comes to be portrayed as compatible with *khazones*. Notwithstanding all these changes, postwar cantorial narratives revisit personalities, plots, and works familiar from before the war, reconfiguring them in new symbolic stories.

Sometimes, new media play a defining role in how cantors present themselves to the American public during the postwar era. Consider the case of Bela Herskovits, who had been a prominent cantor in Budapest before the war. Surviving as a member of the Hungarian underground, he immigrated to the United States in 1947, where he became the cantor of the Ocean Parkway Jewish Center in Brooklyn. Herskovits was dubbed the "Cantor of the Ghetto," as an early postwar recording explained in its liner notes: "During the War Cantor Herskovits lifted the morale of his stricken brothers in bombed areas, shelters and subterfuges, bringing comfort and consolation to thousands of Ghetto dwellers."⁶⁶ Later, Herskovits acquired the sobriquet "The 'This Is Your Life' Cantor" on recordings made after his appearance in 1956 on the eponymous popular television program, on which he was one of several Holocaust survivors and rescuers of Jews from Nazi persecution whom the series honored.⁶⁷ In 1956 Herskovits also made his New York recital debut at Carnegie Hall, thanks to the efforts of comedian Eddie Cantor, who had heard Herskovits perform in Brooklyn. This recital was recorded and issued on a long-playing record titled *Two Cantors at Carnegie Hall*. The recording features introductory remarks by the comedian (who characterizes Herskovits as offering "a great human interest story" in addition to being "a very fine singer") and performances by the cantor demonstrating the range of his artistry: selections of *khazones*, Hungarian folksongs, a Russian lullaby, "Eyli, Eyli," and several opera arias, including "Rachel, quand du Seigneur," from *La Juive*.

Halévy's opera, perhaps best known in the prewar discourse of *khazones* as a work not performed by America's most illustrious cantor, has continued to figure in postwar cantorial narratives. The opera's signature aria, sung by Eléazar at the conclusion of Act IV, was a favorite of cantors, performed in recital and on records, sometimes in Yiddish translation.⁶⁸ In the postwar era, such a performance imbues the aria with new symbolic value, as evinced in a live recording of a recital in the United States by Moshe Koussevitzky, a cantor who had an accomplished career in interwar Poland and came to America after surviving the Holocaust. The recording, probably made in the 1950s, begins with him announcing in English that he will sing the aria from *La Juive*. "In Yiddish," Koussevitzky adds, after a pause, and the audience responds with laughter, followed by applause.⁶⁹ Singing this aria in Yiddish is a provocative act; it ostensibly "restores" the aria to the "original" language of its Jewish protagonist (the opera is set in fifteenth-century Constance), thereby underscoring the tension between the milieu of French grand opera and this work's historical subject of European anti-Semitism. Moreover, a Holocaust survivor's performance of what was perhaps the most famous nineteenth-century work of European theater about anti-Semitism in the language of the majority of European Jews murdered during World War II transforms Eléazar's aria of agonizing over his daughter's fate at the hands of Christian anti-Semites into a moving statement of cultural tenacity.

Oysher never recorded "Rachel, quand du Seigneur," but the Chicago Opera is reported to have engaged him to perform the role of Eléazar (and Canio in *I Pagliacci*); the singer had begun to study these parts, but a heart attack ended his pursuit of an opera career.[70] Instead of expanding his repertoire to include opera, Oysher employed the new medium of the long-playing record during the last years before his death in 1958 to create three innovative works, each centered on the celebration of a Jewish holiday: *The Moishe Oysher Seder, Kol Nidre Night with Moishe Oysher,* and *The Moishe Oysher Chanuka Party.* This series exploits the medium's capacity to record up to twenty-five minutes on each side of a disc to present a synthetic performance combining narration, orchestral accompaniment, and singing, both choral and solo. The series's producers conceived it as forging a novel approach to Jewish tradition: "These albums assume a brand new flavor as they delve into the musical background of these ancient religious rites."[71] More than a compilation of excerpts from each holiday's musical repertoire, each album is conceived in dramatic terms, not unlike a radio drama (and, in fact, they were produced with broadcast in mind).[72]

The Moishe Oysher Seder, the first of the series, follows the order of the Passover ritual but does not simulate it. Rather, it most resembles a cantata, in which Passover's liberating possibilities are celebrated in multiple languages and musical idioms—ranging from traditional melodies, such as the Ashkenazic trope for chanting the Four Questions (which are sung in English translation), to Oysher's Yiddish scat-style performance of the Aramaic song "Had Gadya" ("One Goat") at the album's conclusion—unified by the performer whose eclectic musical sensibility brands the ritual.[73] *Kol Nidre Night with Moishe Oysher* elaborates the series's approach to mediating a Jewish holiday by rendering the spiritual power of the service that inaugurates Yom Kippur in the affective idiom of music drama. Listeners are offered an account of Jewish ritual that is not only solemn and dignified but also rich in emotional suspense and compelling spectacle. Cantorial performance, the service's centerpiece, is presented in an elaborate frame of sound effects, chorus, orchestra, and narration, rendered in the decorous style of the ecumenical radio dramas of the period heard on *The Eternal Light* (see chapter 2).

The Moishe Oysher Chanuka Party is also not a recording of a worship service, as its liner notes explain: "It is rather a collection of highlights of the Moishe Oysher repertoire, used during the years for Chanuka Festivals in Synagogues and Jewish Centers."[74] Traditional blessings and hymns sung when lighting the Hanukkah menorah are joined by Oysher's original holiday composition "Drei Dreidele" ("Spin, Little Top"), as well as songs that variously recall his Bessarabian roots, memorialize the victims of Nazi persecution, and celebrate the establishment of the State of Israel.

This sequence relates Hanukkah's ancient rededication of the Temple in Jerusalem with a contemporary narrative, then embraced by growing numbers of American Jews, in which the destruction of European Jewry during the Holocaust is redeemed with the establishment of the State of Israel. Linking this wide-ranging selection is narration delivered by Oysher's eleven-year-old daughter, Shoshanna, described in the liner notes as "a student at the Westchester Day School, (Yeshiva), in Mamaroneck, New York." Like her father, "Shoshana has a flair for Dramatics, and intends to concentrate her studies on Drama, Dance, and Music."[75] Far from being configured as moral compromise or cultural confusion, as was often the case in prewar descriptions of Oysher's musicianship, his merging of Jewish devotion with entertainment here becomes a heritage maintained by the next generation.

The liner notes to all three albums feature a biography of Oysher that centers on his dual career as cantor and secular entertainer, capped by his work in film. The notes argue that the career of "Moishe of the movies" may seem to be "a far cry" from his Bessarabian origins, "but the change is merely environmental, not spiritual"; indeed, "the journey was inevitable." Although the biography admits that "Hollywood" may be "an odd field in which to sow the flower of Jewish culture," Oysher's divided interests—"his soul in the synagogue and his heart in the theatre"—are characterized as "inseparable, unbreakable fibres of his consciousness." Oysher is quoted championing film as "the most potent instrument with which to combat religious prejudice and to reveal the light, the beauty, and the truth of Jewish life." At the same time, the liner notes assert that Oysher continues to perform as a cantor and is "a worthy successor to the late Rosenblatt. . . . Like Rosenblatt, he also concertizes and acts in the movies. He has never played on Broadway because he will not break the Sabbath."[76]

In 1954, Oysher returned to film, this time an English-language feature, in which he plays another errant cantor's son. In *Singing in the Dark* (based on an original story by Oysher and director Max Nosseck), the singer plays a Holocaust survivor who has no memory of his prewar life; he cannot remember his name and so is called Leo by fellow survivors. Leo comes to America and his musical talent is discovered while working as a hotel clerk. When a friend gets Leo drunk, alcohol liberates him, and he begins singing, to the delight of the hotel's nightclub clientele. Leo is an overnight success but, haunted by his inability to remember his past, seeks psychiatric treatment. Under hypnosis, he recalls that his father was a cantor who, with the rest of Leo's relatives, died during the war. Later, when struck on the head during a fight, Leo remembers that his real name is David, and in a hallucinatory sequence he is seen alone inside a ruined synagogue in Europe. He mounts the abandoned pulpit and sings, in English translation, El Male Rahamim, mourning the murdered Jews of Europe. In the film's final scene, Oysher, as Cantor David, sings the Kiddush in a synagogue, as adoring congregants look on. A reprise of Oysher's penitent cantor films of the prewar era, *Singing in the Dark* is distinguished as a response to the Holocaust. Unlike *Dem khazns zindl*, America is the site not of the cantor's demise but of his recovery; here, he takes up his father's calling and, in doing so, restores the sacred music of a vanquished culture to a living Jewish community.

At the same time that Oysher filmed the last of what Hoberman has termed the singer's "anti–Jazz Singer" dramas, that landmark Hollywood film was itself remade by Warner Bros.[77] Both the 1952 remake of *The Jazz Singer*, starring Danny Thomas, and a second remake in 1980, starring Neil Diamond, situate the narrative of a cantor's son's struggles in different dilemmas emblematic for contemporary generations of American Jews. The 1952 remake removes immigration as the defining matrix for the conflict between the cantor and his son. Instead, the cantor's family, who live not on the Lower East Side but in Philadelphia, is rooted in American heritage. Thomas plays Jerry Golding, a college graduate and recently returned war veteran who longs to become a popular entertainer—but he is also the descendant of generations of American cantors, who have served the same congregation since the late eighteenth century, and Jerry is expected to follow in their footsteps. The modest tenement home of Cantor Rabinowitz is replaced by the Goldings' respectable, bourgeois domesticity. Rather than situating cantors at the center of a family drama that epitomized an intergenerational conflict between Old World mores and New World ambitions, as in the original film, the 1952 remake places its protagonists in a hyperbolic performance of Jews' Americanness. Coming at the height of the Cold War, this version of *The Jazz Singer* resonates with other undertakings—including plans by organized American Jewry to celebrate the 1954 tercentenary of Jews' settlement in America as a demonstration of their longstanding patriotism—intended in part to allay Americans' fears of Jewish sedition in the wake of highly publicized cases of Jewish "atom spies" and accusations of support for communism among Jews in the entertainment industry.

In the 1980 remake, *The Jazz Singer* returns to the theme of immigration as a sociocultural frame for its story of intergenerational tension. The
film's setting likewise returns to the Lower East Side, portrayed in the title
sequence with a vibrant montage of the neighborhood's many immigrant
cultures, accompanied by Diamond's song "Coming to America." Adapting the story to a contemporary setting, the 1980 film offers yet another
configuration of the cantorial family. Here, the paternal cantor (played by
Laurence Olivier) is a Holocaust survivor and a widower, thereby removing from the drama the emotional triangulation of rebellious son, stern
father, and sympathetic mother that animates the two previous versions.
This transformation not only situates Jews as recent immigrants in the
film's late-twentieth-century setting but also reframes the dilemma that
The Jazz Singer poses to its protagonist in terms that are meaningful in
the post–World War II era: Will the son of a cantor who survived the
Holocaust betray a commitment not only to the continuity of Judaism but
also to the survival of Jewry?

Finding Eléazar

Another longstanding contest in cantorial narratives—between *khazones*
and opera—is transformed in the star text of the singer who was arguably the most famous cantor in post–World War II America. In the career of tenor Richard Tucker, this conflict gives way to a different kind of
cantor's story, in which these two musical and cultural idioms generally
complement each other. Because of Tucker's renown as one of the most
accomplished American opera singers of his generation, his personal history appears in a wealth of popular media, including music reviews in
leading newspapers, liner notes to recordings on major labels, interviews
published in popular magazines (such as a 1952 feature in *Life*, which
proclaimed, "Met's Top Italian Tenor Is a Jewish Cantor")[78] and aired on
national television. Tucker's high visibility in the public sphere continues
after his death; posthumous tributes include a square near New York's
Lincoln Center named after him and a U.S. postage stamp featuring him
in a series honoring American opera singers. And Tucker's biography is
usually presented with a general audience in mind, as opposed to the narratives of other cantors, which are primarily told by and for other Jews.

Tucker (né Reuben Ticker), the American-born son of East European
Jewish immigrants, began his musical career as a cantor before turning

to opera. From the early 1940s until his death in 1975, he achieved international renown for his performances in lead tenor roles in the most popular operas of Mozart, Verdi, Bizet, and Italian verismo composers. While devoting the lion's share of his career to opera during these years, Tucker continued to perform and record *khazones* and other Jewish music. His recordings include the liturgy of the Friday evening Sabbath service and Kol Nidre service, Yiddish theater songs by Abraham Goldfadn, "Hatikvah" and other modern Hebrew songs, and an album memorializing victims of the Holocaust.[79] Moreover, Tucker was forthrightly visible as a Jewish performer in the American (and international) public sphere, raising funds for Jewish causes and readily acknowledging in interviews the role that Jewishness played in his professional as well as personal life. For example, when Edward R. Murrow interviewed Tucker on the CBS series *Person to Person* in 1952, the telecast included a visit to the dining room in the Tuckers' home in Great Neck, Long Island, where the table was set for celebrating the beginning of the Sabbath.[80] In this regard, Tucker's public persona as an opera star parallels that of another luminary of American opera in the decades following World War II, Leontyne Price. The soprano's solo recitals of arias and art songs regularly concluded with spirituals or excerpts from George Gershwin's *Porgy and Bess,* and her visibility as an African American in the world of opera was a subject of considerable public discussion and scrutiny during the early postwar decades.[81]

Price regularly acknowledged the foundational role that singing in the black church in her native Mississippi played in her musical career; similarly, Tucker frequently reflected in public on the interrelation of his minority identity, with its attendant religious musical culture, and his vocal artistry, sometimes doing so by invoking earlier performers' lives. Just as Yossele Rosenblatt contrasted the story of Strashunsky with his own career narrative, Tucker invoked Rosenblatt to tell his own story, for instance, recalling in a 1970 television interview rumors that Rosenblatt was going to shave his beard in order to sing in the opera. "I was the first cantor to make this transition," Tucker claimed, implicitly characterizing his career shift from cantor to leading tenor at the Metropolitan Opera as the fulfillment of others' ambitions as well as his own. In his descriptions of his career, Tucker sometimes stressed the common ground of the synagogue and the opera house, recalling, for example, looking out from the opera stage and seeing "Orthodox people with yarmulkes [skull caps]. I didn't know if I was in the Met or a synagogue."[82]

These stories obscured professional and cultural tensions that arose when Tucker began his operatic career. A letter sent by Rabbi Louis Ginzberg of the Jewish Theological Seminary to the Brooklyn Jewish Center, where Tucker served as cantor when he was invited to make his Metropolitan Opera debut in 1944, cautioned, "People would find it quite strange to see their Cantor one day recite the Neilah prayer [which concludes Yom Kippur worship] and the following day sing a love duet with some lady. My advice is therefore that you try your utmost to prevent your cantor from accepting the offer made to him by the Metropolitan."[83] Tucker, by contrast, recalls the invitation to sing at the Metropolitan as being, if anything, the fulfillment of Jewish devotional musicianship for both artist and audience: "Edward Johnson [a former opera singer, then the Metropolitan Opera's general manager] . . . came to the synagogue to hear me, . . . to convince me and my wife that 'If you can sing for two thousand Jews at the Brooklyn Jewish Center, I have no fear for you at the Metropolitan Opera.' See, he had a Jewish heart. . . . Very few people know, Edward Johnson sang in a temple choir in Newark."[84]

Reflecting on his career, Tucker invoked one singer more than any other: Enrico Caruso. Tucker frequently identified Caruso as his role model and was regularly compared to the Neapolitan tenor by music critics and fans. Indeed, Tucker's public persona as an American and as a Jew was complicated by regular mention of his Italianate sound and sensibility. Winthrop Sargeant's profile of the tenor for *Life* notes that Tucker "can sing Italian with a faultless accent. Though he has been in Italy only once, he sings Italian opera with a native passion and a garlic-scented abandon that gives the illusion of many generations of Neapolitan ancestors. He not only sounds like an Italian: he looks like one."[85] Tucker's biography includes accounts of how vocal coach Angelo Canarutto and conductor Tulio Serafin, as well as numerous critics, both were impressed with Tucker's "Italianate singing style" and "the purity of his Italian" diction and were bemused at how the tenor came by these skills that were so closely associated with national character. Tucker clearly enjoyed these accolades as well as the puzzlement. When Serafin, complimenting the tenor on his command of Italian, asked him where he learned the language, Tucker replied, smiling, "In Brooklyn."[86] In Tucker's narrative, his ability to assimilate an "alien" ethnic style is regarded with admiration, rather than the suspicion or ridicule that this skill would more likely have engendered during the early decades of the twentieth century. Alongside Tucker's agility in negotiating ethnic boundaries, he demonstrated an ecumenical

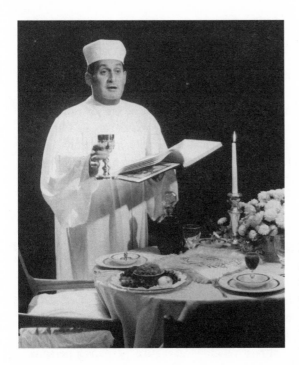

Promotional photograph of Richard Tucker for his album *Passover Seder Festival*, issued by Columbia Records in 1962. (Forward Association)

public spirit. He recorded the Lord's Prayer for Christmas albums,[87] made occasional appearances at fundraising events for Catholic charities, and enjoyed friendships with Francis Cardinal Spellman and Terence Cardinal Cooke, among other prelates. At an ecumenical memorial service for Tucker held at the Metropolitan Opera, Cooke remarked that the singer "was always ready to share that tremendous talent because he had a generosity founded on faith."[88]

At the same time, Tucker's star text repeatedly affirms Jewish pride, whether noting that a young Elvis Presley was a fan of the tenor's 1949 recording *Cantorial Jewels* or relating Tucker's refusal to make an opera recording with conductor Herbert von Karajan, because of his wartime association with Nazi Germany. (On this occasion, Tucker reportedly told record producer Dario Soria, "My Jewish people would never forgive me.")[89] In a profile of American Jewish opera singers who came to prominence in the middle decades of the twentieth century, Leonard Leff characterizes Tucker as the most demonstrative of his Jewishness among this cohort. "He would neither hide his faith nor allow himself to believe that the public would hold his faith against him. His was an almost aggressive assertion of his religion." Consequently, "what some listeners expected to hear from this *chazzan* . . . , they heard," with critics and fans arguing over whether Tucker's vocal production, technique, or histrionic sensibility was indebted to his cantorial training—a debate "that continues in internet chat rooms."[90]

Tucker's own understanding of the interrelation of his Jewishness, his cantorial training, and his opera career was complex, as revealed in interviews with him and reports by people close to him. He reportedly considered "the site of the greatest single performance of his entire career" to be a synagogue in Vienna where, in 1958, he led services one Sabbath morning before making his debut at the Staatsoper. Recollections of this episode—by Tucker's wife, Sara, and John Gualiani, the tenor's European representative, who both attended the service—characterize it as a powerful memorial to victims of Nazi persecution and a demonstration of Tucker's masterful musicianship. (Indeed, Gualiani, who "as a Gentile, . . . couldn't follow what [Tucker] was singing the way the congregation could, . . . just listened to the beauty of his voice.")[91] Tucker biographer James Drake roots the tenor's operatic career in personal convictions that conflate theology and art, arguing that Tucker owed his success as a singer to his sense of "a special mission—a calling almost religious in nature, perhaps a personalized extension of his identity as a Jew, one of the Chosen People. He believed that God had given him a wondrous gift—the gift of song, the gift of the biblical David—and had chosen him for an extraordinary life."[92] Yet Tucker seems to have understood the interrelation of his Jewishness and his operatic career differently. In an interview conducted by the American Jewish Committee in 1973, he remarked that he and his wife "used to say, 'Well, can you imagine, if I were not Jewish . . . , how much higher I would have gone?'"[93]

Jewishness and opera were conjoined most complexly in Tucker's quest to sing Eléazar in *La Juive*. The tenor long campaigned to perform the role, and although he recorded excerpts from the opera, sang it in concert in New York and London, and appeared in staged productions in Barcelona and New Orleans, he never succeeded in convincing Rudolph Bing, general manager of the Metropolitan Opera during most of Tucker's career, to stage the opera for him there. (This matter has sometimes been characterized as a conflict between Tucker's public forthrightness as a Jew versus Bing's silence on the subject of his own Jewishness; in an interview, Tucker dismissed the suggestion that Bing's resistance to producing *La Juive* had anything to do with anti-Semitism but explained that the impresario found the opera "boring.")[94] Plans to stage the opera for the tenor at the Metropolitan under the management of Schuyler Chapin were finally under way at the time of Tucker's sudden death.[95]

Discussions of Tucker's quest to perform Eléazar regularly mention that the role held special appeal for him both as one of Caruso's most admired performances and as a Jewish operatic hero. Tucker's unrealized goal of singing in *La Juive* at the opera house where his career was made is often described as a lost opportunity for both the tenor and his audiences. At the same time, Leff writes that, "paradoxically, had Tucker become even more closely associated with Eléazar, he might have reinforced the 'Jewish singer' stereotype that denied him, he believed, a greater reputation at the Metropolitan."[96] Yet when Tucker first approached Bing about staging *La Juive* for him, the singer argued that he could give a definitive performance of Eléazar not only because of his vocal capabilities but also because he was a cantor.[97] As an unrealized project, Tucker's plan to sing Eléazar at the Metropolitan remains an open-ended subject of discussion, inviting speculations about both why the project was never realized and what it might have demonstrated had it happened. Beyond musical questions about the opera or its star, this speculative exercise considers the implications for Tucker as a Jewish celebrity, in which the relation of opera and *khazones* that ran throughout his career would have somehow found its ultimate synthesis.

When the Metropolitan eventually revived *La Juive* in 2003 (having last performed it in 1936), public discussions of the work repeatedly invoked the association of Eléazar with both Caruso and Tucker.[98] The company promoted the tenor starring in the new production, Neil Shicoff, as giving a performance that both "honors the tradition of his great predecessors" and manifests a "passionate, deeply personal identification with Eléazar."[99] The insert accompanying Shicoff's video recording of *La Juive*, issued the following year, touts Eléazar as "the role that Neil Shicoff was born to sing," noting that, "like Tucker, Shicoff comes from a Jewish family and, again like Tucker, he sang as a child in a Jewish synagogue, where his father was the cantor."[100] In his own discussion of the role, Shicoff similarly honors the longstanding association of the role with *khazones* (though it should be noted that Eléazar sings no cantorial music or even traditional blessings in the opera). Of the aria "Rachel, quand du Seigneur," the tenor comments that "this piece sounds, in this modal kind of way, very cantorial, very religious, and that's a sound I know very well, as my father was a cantor."[101]

In conjunction with his performance of Eléazar, Shicoff participated in the making of a documentary film, *Finding Eléazar*, which profiles his preparation for the role, and a music video, directed by Sidney Lumet, featuring the tenor's performance of "Rachel, quand du Seigneur." This short video follows a bearded Shicoff, wearing a skullcap and vaguely old-fashioned clothing (a black frock coat and tall leather boots), from a dressing room to the interior of an old synagogue on the Lower East Side—actually, the Angel Orensanz Foundation for the Arts, an arts center housed in a former synagogue, built in 1849. In the video, the interior of the building, which bears the weathered traces of its erstwhile role as a house of worship, has been set up as a synagogue, with an ark, rows of pews, and a lectern in the center. As the aria's orchestral introduction is heard, Shicoff takes a scroll from the ark, removes its cloth mantle, and unrolls it on the lectern. He takes up a *yad* (the pointer used for reading from a Torah scroll) but, instead of chanting from the Torah, begins the aria. After singing the opening section, Shicoff puts on a prayer shawl, then looks up to see a young woman in old-fashioned dress—presumably Eléazar's daughter, Rachel—standing in the balcony (the traditional women's section) of the otherwise empty synagogue. He continues to sing, addressing the aria to her. When the aria reaches its climax, Shicoff returns to the lectern, grasps the scroll, and tears it. As the aria concludes, he collapses, face down, on the synagogue floor, and the video ends. In this staging, Eléazar becomes, in effect, a cantor, albeit a sacrilegious one—befitting, perhaps, this fusion of theater and synagogue, operatic histrionics and the fervor of religious devotion, Old World music and New World setting.[102]

Faith First

After flourishing for several generations, stories in which cantors figure as protagonists emblematic of the American Jewish community may have become obsolete, or at least vestigial. Tellingly, the last adaptations of *The Jazz Singer* made for mainstream American audiences in the twentieth century were parodies. In 1981, the comedy series *SCTV Television Network* spoofed Neil Diamond's remake of *The Jazz Singer* with a sketch about a Jewish recording executive who opposes the ambitions of his adopted African American son to become a cantor instead of a jazz singer.[103] A decade later, an episode of the animated comedy series *The Simpsons* parodied the 1927 version of the film, especially its stature as an icon of immigrant Jewish culture, rather than reconfiguring its plot to address, even in mock form, contemporary concerns. Moreover, the story's protagonist (Krusty the Clown, a children's television personality, whose troubled past occasions the *Jazz Singer* parody), is the descendant of generations of rabbis, not cantors.[104]

Cantors' life histories continue to be told at the turn of the millennium, but within different rubrics, reflecting changes in the cantorate as a profession as well as in definitional practices of American Jews. The intensely histrionic cantorial performances prized by immigrants and their children earlier in the century often fail to engage younger generations. Thus, in liner notes to *Invocations*, Frank London's 2000 recording of instrumental settings of "classic hazonos," Sarah Gershman writes, "Like many Jews, I have felt a sense of alienation from operatic, showy cantorial music. It is difficult to daven [pray] in an environment that feels more like a performance than a prayer service." (Although the recording evokes "the passionate, imploring voices of the great cantorial virtuosos" of the past, it does so in performances "scored for trumpet solo, harmoniums, glass harmonica and bass"—and no vocalists.)[105] Similarly, the cantor no longer serves as an emblematic figure for the larger community in dramas of American Jewish life; instead, cantorial narratives appear in the genre of documentary. Rather than obliquely referencing the experiences of actual cantors in fictional plots, as was done in feature films involving Jolson, Waldman, and Oysher, documentaries call on cantors to perform their life stories before the camera as themselves. Consequently, these films offer stories about professional clergy rather than epitomizing members of their community.

The 2002 documentary *Faith First: Second Career Clergy*, aired on WABC in New York City as part of local public-affairs programming devoted to religion, offers personal narratives of several Jews training to be cantors or rabbis at the Jewish Theological Seminary (JTS) who have chosen to do so after pursuing other careers, including, among the cantorial students profiled, an opera singer, an engineer, and a pastry chef. Each individual offers a narrative organized around the decision to become a cleric. Typically, these are stories of a personal quest, following frustration with earlier careers or a larger sense of dissatisfaction with the state of the subject's life. Told in the manner of conversion narratives, some of these profiles are, in fact, the personal histories of individuals whose path to studying at JTS included an earlier decision to convert to Judaism.

These stories are quite different from the cantors' narratives offered in twentieth-century American Jewish popular culture. No longer tied to larger tales of Jews' collectively confronting some disruption on a grand scale, whether mass immigration or the Holocaust, these are narratives that remain personal exercises—indeed, the individual scale of these stories is reinforced by there being a series of them, each having its own narrative integrity while resonating with the others' stories. The quest to become a cantor or rabbi is told as a journey of self-realization, linking concerns for spiritual fulfillment (interviewees speak of seeking an "inner connection," finding one's "moral compass") with bourgeois concerns for professional satisfaction, including the luxury of being willing to "trade financial stability for happiness." (As one rabbinical student explains, "If I'm not going to live forever, why do I go every day to a job I don't like?") Even when the interviewees speak of the importance of ministering to the Jewish community, the discourse is sometimes self-reflexive; one JTS student explains that, in the wake of the attacks of 11 September 2001, "helping others was just what I needed."[106] Framed as the pursuit of a personal calling within the rubric of American religious broadcasting, the decision to become a cantor is largely removed from Jewish communal concerns, whether religious or ethnic.

The 2005 documentary *A Cantor's Tale* considers the American cantorate's future by revisiting its recent past through the story of Jack Mendelson, who teaches cantorial students at the Reform movement's Hebrew Union College in New York City and serves as cantor of a Conservative congregation in the nearby city of White Plains. Mendelson grew up in Boro Park in the early post–World War II years, when the Brooklyn neighborhood boasted an extraordinary concentration of prominent cantors (among those he mentions are Mordecai Hershman and Moshe Koussevitzky), many of them Holocaust survivors. The film follows Mendelson as he revisits his childhood haunts, noting that, when he was growing up there, "*khazones* was in the air," heard not only in synagogues but also on Yiddish radio (where the occasional commercial was set to cantorial modes) and even sung by waiters in delicatessens. Mendelson, along with other cantors and aficionados of *khazones* profiled in the documentary, waxes nostalgic for the cantors of the mid-twentieth century and, moreover, for the culture in which they were celebrities. Describing his mission as working "to keep *khazones* alive," Mendelson bemoans the current generation of cantorial students who have no "style" and need to be taught the idiomatic ornaments of traditional *khazones*; Mendelson calls these, in

Yiddish, *kheyndelekh*—that is, grace notes—which he translates, tellingly, as "ethnicities." Over the course of the documentary Mendelson narrates his personal history (from high-school dropout to president of Conservative Judaism's Cantors Assembly of America) not as an exemplary tale but as testimony to the cultural continuity inherent in his musicianship, which he maintains in the face of extensive rupture and innovation. With an outsize vocal and physical presence and boundless energy, Mendelson demonstrates his pedagogical skills with cantorial students and young children, and he exhorts Jews whom he encounters in Brooklyn shops and on Tel Aviv beaches to sing *khazones* with him—all part of a ceaseless performance of self that strives to reanimate a "lost" Jewish sacred musical culture among both performers and listeners.[107]

As a consequence of these many mediations of cantors, their music, and their personal histories, community messengers become celebrities, their sacred performances become entertainments, their private lives become popular narratives, their coreligionists become fans, and their performance venues become sites not of affirming Jewish devotional tradition but of interrogating it. In this complex of cultural transformations, new media, like the cantors whose music and stories they present, are not merely vehicles of transmission. Rather, they figure as proving grounds, catalysts, and forums for the fashioning of narratives in which cantors' careers epitomize the Jewish encounter with modernity.

The attention to cantors' lives is itself not new in Jewish culture, but presenting a cantor's life story as an exemplary or cautionary tale for Jews as a whole is a modernist innovation, for this approach situates the "project of the self," a paradigm of modern, secular Western culture, as being central to Jewish life.[108] In these stories, the cantor performs not only devotional music but also the quest for a career, and God is no longer the ultimate recipient of cantorial performances; rather, the cantor's fellow Jews are. Endowing cantors with celebrity is another novelty of the modern age, elevating them from figures of occasional suspicion and even ridicule in traditional Jewish culture (according to a Yiddish proverb, *khazonim zaynen naronim*—cantors are fools) to a stature in which cantors embody the contradictory sense of intimate familiarity and awe that distinguishes the relationship of audiences with stars.

Positioning cantors as leading protagonists in Jewish dramas of personal—and, implicitly, communal—striving brings *khazones* into new contexts that challenge established, facile notions of the interrelation of sacred and secular. Attributes of twentieth-century new media figure strategically in this transformation of cantors and their music, none more so than the earliest of these technologies. Evan Eisenberg suggests that sound recordings can facilitate a new kind of ritual behavior by enabling the repetition of a performance. Indeed, given recordings' ability to repeat endlessly and completely, they appear to be the fulfillment of ritual's aspiration toward "exact repetition." At the same time, Eisenberg argues, "most . . . phonographic ritual is secular," and recordings can facilitate new kinds of listening rituals inimical to the religious rites that they ostensibly reproduce.[109] In the case of *khazones*, recordings of sacred music intended for performance on the Sabbath or holidays can be listened to on those occasions, but doing so violates traditional prohibitions against playing recordings as a form of work. Thus, sound recordings produced in recent decades for Orthodox Jews typically bear labels warning consumers not to play the recordings on the Sabbath or holidays.[110] A recording thus has the potential not only to document and disseminate sacred music but also to undermine the original intent of its performance.

Early listeners were apparently either horrified or delighted to discover how this new medium enabled *khazones* to be heard in all manner of contexts outside the synagogue and perceived the consequence as either defiling the spiritual intent of this music or, conversely, freeing it to acquire new signifying powers. The salient transformation wrought by sound recordings and then other new media took place not in the music or the musicians but in their listeners, who came to be defined as an audience rather than a congregation. Audiences are constituted not according to religious protocols but by individual desires in relation to market forces and consumer practices. Therefore, even when an audience and a congregation comprise the same individuals, the nature of their engagement with a performance of sacred music is different. This development complicates the signifying potential of cantorial performance. As artistry is foregrounded, spirituality may be marginalized or ironized, and music's meaning may be defined by individual interests in relation to public discourses rather than by religious authorities.

All this would seem to suggest that new media at best attenuate (and at worst undo) conventional notions of religiosity, especially the sanctity of devotional performance. But it is also possible to see these mediations of cantorial music as proving grounds for exploring new possibilities for engaging with sanctity. Cantors from Josef Rosenblatt to Jack Mendelson have ventured into unconventional modes of performing their music and personal histories in efforts to enhance Jewish religious life, taking an expansive approach to the notion of being a communal messenger. Cantors who have straddled conventional boundaries between sacred and secular performance, such as Moishe Oysher and Richard Tucker, repeatedly insist on their performances as extending, rather than compromising, the significance of the sacred music that they claim as their artistic inspiration.

Essential to all these efforts is the imbricating of mediating musical performances with mediating life stories. These efforts enable a larger concern for transmitting not only a musical repertoire but also a sense of its place in a Jewish way of life understood as authentic, traditional, communitarian, and comprehensive, a way of life that has been roiled by geographic dislocation, by modern social, economic, and technological phenomena, and ultimately by genocide. Through these new media practices, American cantors and their audiences have engaged in an array of efforts to reconfigure this imagined past in terms of an expressive culture that is readily accessible, thanks to various recording technologies, even as it invokes a bygone way of life.

Ultimately, mediating cantors and their music has effected new conceptions of art in relation to religiosity. The cantor has become a signifier of the quest for an understanding of spirituality. Because *khazones* is perceived as something displaced (by immigration, the Holocaust, and, for some, new media), listeners' engagement with it becomes a process, an interrogation, a struggle. An organic, inevitable, immediate (and unmediated?) relationship with spirituality through this music is projected away from the here and now to a chronotope—the Old World—that only grows further away from the American present with the passing of time, and in the wake of the Holocaust this separation becomes an abyss. The processual, interrogative nature of this relationship is key—for engaging the numinous is not understood as inherent or as the ultimate goal of this quest. Because the New World problematizes spiritual engagement through *khazones*, its spirituality is not inevitable. Instead, cantors and their art are constantly put on trial in the American marketplace. In this forum it is possible for each listener to assign meaning to the cantor's life and art in response to personal aspirations. The cantor's life narrative models for the listener a project of one's own—investigating what this traditional expression of Jewish spirituality might mean in the unfolding life of the listener.

2

Turning on *The Eternal Light*

In the mid-1940s, a rabbi who allegedly never listened to the radio, a broadcasting executive who characterized the medium as a manifestation of divine power, and a Jewish playwright who was a self-confessed agnostic worked together to create a body of religious media unprecedented in form, content, and scope: hundreds of hours of radio and, later, television drama portraying Jewish life, past and present. In these programs' heyday, which lasted some two decades, they reached millions of listeners across North America and were hailed as outstanding achievements in broadcasting and in public religion. Today, they are largely forgotten in the annals of both American Judaism and religious media.

The broadcasts were created by the Jewish Theological Seminary (JTS), the intellectual center of Conservative Judaism, in conjunction with, at one time or another, all three major national networks. For the most part, these dramas were aired on the ecumenical series *Directions* (ABC television), *Frontiers of Faith* (NBC television), *Lamp Unto My Feet* (CBS television), and the program most widely associated with JTS, *The Eternal Light* (NBC radio and, later, television).

This venture took place at a strategic moment both in JTS's history and in the development of American broadcasting. During its early years, JTS's Radio and Television Department provided the Seminary with its most extensive outreach effort, as its leaders sought to combat anti-Semitism and to position Judaism in the public sphere as a significant moral resource for Americans generally. For broadcasters, this programming was part of ongoing efforts to situate religion in their offerings to a national audience, as they negotiated between notions of radio as a public service and as a commercial enterprise.

JTS's religious broadcasts came into being thanks to a singular convergence of agendas; they were as much a result of the visions of exceptional individuals as they were responsive to political, social, cultural, and aesthetic sensibilities of the early post–World War II years. These dramas celebrated a spirit of communion, looking beyond differences to promote harmony between American Jews and their Christian neighbors, between the demands of commercial broadcasting and the public good, and between the ideals of art and religion. At the same time, the inception, production, and reception of these programs reveal a complex of tensions, constituting something of a "backstage" drama of its own. Indeed, the story of the making of *The Eternal Light* and similar Jewish ventures into ecumenical broadcasting seems at times to demonstrate the inverse of the accord that these programs sought to advance. Both in their flourishing and in their decline, these broadcasts demonstrate the dynamics of what has been thought possible for religious media in the American public sphere.

"The World's Best Kept Secret"

The Eternal Light made its debut during the final months of World War II, as American Jews began to confront a threshold in their lives of unprecedented magnitude, defined by the many consequences of the war's end. To a considerable extent, this threshold moment entailed changes that these Jews faced alongside their fellow Americans: the new prominence of the United States as a world power and a postwar economic boom, as well as expanding social, educational, and professional opportunities prompted by the return of the millions of men and women who had gone to war. At the same time, Jews faced issues at the war's end that set them apart from other Americans. The vast scale of the destruction of European Jewry was revealed, confirming—if not surpassing—American Jews' worst fears. The struggle to establish the State of Israel raised high expectations for an important new center of Jewish life but also prompted great anxiousness for its viability. And American Jews found themselves suddenly the largest and most stable of the world's Jewish communities, albeit by default. This new status prompted an urgent sense of what Jonathan Sarna terms a "special responsibility"—not merely for the welfare of other Jews, which had been an abiding concern for American Jewry, but for the future of Jewish culture, including its religious life. Consequently, Sarna argues, "religion became a major vehicle for [American] Jewish identity" in what he, among others, characterizes as a postwar "revival" of Judaism, which entailed large-scale growth of Jewish religious institutions as well as new attention to "Judaism's status as an accepted American faith."[1]

During the postwar years, the Conservative movement, the youngest of the three major denominations of organized Judaism in America, experienced more rapid growth in affiliation than either Reform or Orthodoxy. Sociologist Marshall Sklare links the Conservative movement's expansion to American Jewry's large-scale internal migration from cities to suburbs, their rapid upward socioeconomic mobility, and their integration into an American cultural mainstream.[2] Conservative Judaism was also at the forefront of efforts to reshape the American public's image of Jews. This project was a central concern of Rabbi Louis Finkelstein, whose tenure as the president of JTS had begun in 1940. Under his leadership, the Seminary inaugurated several innovative institutions, all intended to increase the visibility of Judaism in the American public sphere and position Judaism as strategic to the nation's moral well-being. These undertakings, which included establishing the Radio and Television Department, were committed to promoting common ties among Jews of different convictions as well as fostering mutual understanding and respect between Jews and their Christian neighbors.

Finkelstein characterized this Judeo-Christian ecumenism as essential to the principles of American democracy. And while he understood "the preservation of religion as a vital force in America" to be a universal good, Finkelstein saw this principle as having special implications for the future of world Jewry, which became increasingly dire as the horrors of World War II unfolded. By 1944 JTS articulated its mission as building for Jews "a vital life in America, which will take the place of the devastated European Jewries. . . . The Seminary is engaged in a battle for the survival of Judaism in the Western Hemisphere."[3] For Finkelstein, American and Jewish concerns were interdependent; he insisted that "Judaism as a faith can survive only in an atmosphere of general faith."[4]

Finkelstein proposed several major projects for promoting the value of Judaism to Americans, deploying institutional models already familiar to the general public, if relatively new in Jewish life. In addition to JTS's ventures into broadcasting, these projects included expanding the Seminary's Jewish Museum from a modest display of Judaica within its library to a much more substantial institution, housed in a Fifth Avenue mansion; an unrealized plan to establish an American Jewish Hall of Fame at JTS; and the creation of two intellectual colloquia, the Institute for Religious and Social Studies and the Conference on Science, Philosophy, and Religion (both initiated at JTS in the late 1930s, when Finkelstein was provost).[5] These gatherings realized another of Finkelstein's commitments to

Louis Finkelstein, president of the Jewish Theological Seminary, on the cover of *Time*, 15 October 1951. The Seminary was best known in the American public sphere at this time through its weekly radio broadcasts of *The Eternal Light*, which may explain the depiction of a *ner tamid* (eternal light) in this portrait.

building bridges—in this case, mediating between religious leaders and scholars in the humanities and social sciences. Here, too, he set out to articulate commonalities across conventional boundaries, centered on a commitment to ethics understood as universal, for which Judaism served as an exemplum.

Although the emergence of JTS's Radio and Television Department is closely identified with Finkelstein's tenure as president, the Seminary made its first forays into broadcasting earlier. During the 1930s, JTS produced occasional radio broadcasts in conjunction with either local stations or one of the national networks. By 1939, it had engaged the services of Milton Krents to assist in arranging these broadcasts. Krents was an attorney for the American Jewish Committee, which had pioneered efforts to use broadcast media to promote issues of concern to the American Jewish community, including combating prejudice and political extremism. Krents continued to serve as producer of JTS's radio and television programming through the early 1980s.

The idea for a regular radio program presented by the Seminary in conjunction with a national network began to take shape during the late 1930s and early '40s. Finkelstein was interested in making effective use of radio "to explain Judaism to the American public and to give Jews a better appreciation of their own heritage." These broadcasts, he believed, would reveal Judaism, which he characterized as "the world's best kept secret," to both unaffiliated Jews and many non-Jews.[6] Remarkably, the medium itself did not seem to hold particular interest for Finkelstein. In an interview, veteran JTS staff member Marjorie Wyler recalled, "I don't think that he ever turned on the radio. I doubt very much whether he had one in the house."[7] The realization of JTS's radio series began with a meeting between Finkelstein and NBC president David Sarnoff, who was interested in presenting a Jewish program on his network. Sarnoff agreed to underwrite a series produced in association with JTS, stipulating that, as "Judaism was entitled to time as *one* of the major faiths in the United States," the Seminary's programming would have to represent Judaism as a whole and not just the Conservative movement.[8] To this end, JTS involved advisers from the Orthodox and Reform Jewish movements.

In August 1944, after a close vote by its board of directors, JTS agreed to create a weekly series of broadcasts in conjunction with NBC and hired Krents to oversee the production. The decision was made only after extensive debate, in part because some board members were "reluctant to commit scarce dollars to an avowedly experimental project"[9] or were concerned that regular broadcasts on national radio would make Jews too "conspicuous" in the American public sphere.[10] Originally to be called "Synagogue of the Air," the series was eventually named *The Eternal Light*.[11]

From its inception, *The Eternal Light* pursued an ambitious and complex agenda. A press release issued by the Seminary when the series premiered in the fall of 1944 explained that *The Eternal Light* "is designed to show Judaism as a moral force in important moments of history."[12] Elsewhere, JTS described *The Eternal Light* as "dramatizing the ideals of Judaism" and "attacking apathy and ignorance."[13] In other early publicity materials, the Seminary articulated the series's five "basic precepts":

(1) *To extol all who sanctify God's name.* The call of religion demands that every man shall sanctify God's name in acts of daily living. Particularly in these days of doubt and frustration, every man who walks in humility with his God brings glory to His name and peace to fellowmen.

(2) *To emphasize the sanctity of human personality.* Man is created in the image of God. The potentialities for good inherent in man must be developed and fostered. The gift of being a human being is the greatest of all gifts bequeathed by God to His creatures. In this sense, man must learn to be human to his fellow beings.

(3) *To declare the democratic impulse as fundamental to the good [of] society.* Democracy is the political system best suited to the creation of social and spiritual values. The contributions of all religious traditions which have influenced democratic living and thinking should find places in the overall scheme of the program.

(4) *To explain Palestine as the religious aspiration of the Jewish people.* The meaning of Palestine as the center of Judaism is to be dramatized. The listening audience should be acquainted with the centrality of Palestine in Jewish tradition and history, and the saga of modern Palestine as a great creative and religious force.

(5) *To introduce and explain Jewish ritual, ceremonial and folklore.* While these ceremonials are particularistic in form, and therefore related only to Jewish people, nonetheless, they reflect the universal spiritual strivings of all free men.[14]

Through radio, JTS sought to address subjects beyond ethics or theology, including Jews as a national and an ethnic community. Moreover, JTS imbricated these various Jewish topics with ecumenical, patriotic, and humanistic concerns. If there was an overarching goal among this complex of objectives, it was a commitment to demonstrating that Jewish particularism—whether realized in ancient ritual and lore or contemporary Zionist activism—is incidental to Judaism's fundamental universalism and its compatibility with American values and principles. And just as the lore and rites of Judaism could easily be rendered accessible to both non-Jews and estranged coreligionists, Jews could be presented to the general American public as loyal, moral, and well-integrated fellow citizens.

JTS was neither the first nor the only Jewish religious movement to produce religious broadcasts during the middle decades of the twentieth century. According to Krents, NBC approached JTS about creating a radio series in 1943, when the newly formed ABC network acquired *Message of Israel*, a Jewish religion series produced in conjunction with the Reform movement, which had been heard on NBC, leaving that network without a Jewish program.[15] Nonsectarian American Jewish organizations undertook similar ventures at this time. The American Jewish Committee initiated an array of related activities in 1937, including producing or providing information for both local and national programming; coproducing programming with other Jewish organizations, such as the American Jewish Joint Distribution Committee; and monitoring the presentation of Jews and issues concerning them on other radio programs. Like JTS, the American Jewish Committee's objectives included national concerns, such as the promotion of democracy and intergroup tolerance, as well as issues specific to the Jewish community.[16]

These efforts to use radio as a means of public education, notes historian Stuart Svonkin, "reflected the assumption that anti-Semitism was rooted in ignorance of Jews and Judaism." In the postwar years, the American Jewish Committee, as well as B'nai B'rith and the American Jewish Congress, transformed its approach to combating anti-Semitism by joining "the vanguard of the emerging intergroup relations movement." The leaders of these organizations "redefined Jewish interests in universal terms and committed themselves to the creation of a more pluralistic and egalitarian society," adopting a "unitary concept of prejudice," which understood "all forms of bigotry as inseparable parts of the same phenomenon." These organizations "invoked Jewish ethical and religious values" to make the case for adopting "a broad intergroup relations program"— though, as Svonkin notes, Jewish history "clearly demonstrates that there are few discernible connections" linking "ancient Jewish ethical concepts" and "modern ideals of social justice."[17]

Like JTS in the early postwar years, these nonsectarian Jewish institutions advocated "the acceptance of Judaism as one of the foundations of an American civil religion, . . . as the senior partner in America's 'Judeo-Christian' culture." Moreover, they considered the role of social science to be essential in planning effective educational programs for combating bigotry, and these programs were realized through an array of media: print advertising, pamphlets, films, radio, and television. These efforts included approaches similar to the rubric of JTS's broadcasts, such as educational programs with three speakers, one each to represent the views of Protestantism, Catholicism, and Judaism, as well as radio dramas, including *Lest We Forget*, a series that "celebrated the contributions made by members of various racial, ethnic, and religious groups to American history and culture."[18] And these undertakings involved some of the same personnel as JTS's broadcasts, including Krents, who served as director of the American Jewish Committee's Radio and Television Division.

"Religion at Its Highest and Best"

NBC's interests in producing *The Eternal Light* compounded and at times complicated JTS's agenda. The network's invitation to JTS was part of an ongoing effort by national broadcasting networks to situate religion in their schedules in a way that would satisfy federal regulations, avoid controversy, and enhance the networks' image as serving the public interest. In American radio's early days, religious organizations were a significant presence, as owners of individual stations and producers of programming. By 1925, over one-tenth of all stations were licensed to religious groups.[19] The advent of national networks (NBC in 1926, CBS in 1927, the Mutual Broadcasting System in 1934) engendered different policies regarding religious broadcasting: NBC donated time only to what it deemed mainstream religious organizations, deferring to them to provide programming content; CBS offered time to major Protestant denominations to provide speakers, who were heard on programs controlled by the network; Mutual sold airtime to individual churches and denominations to produce their own religious programs.[20]

NBC's policy proved to have the greatest influence on how the networks approached religious broadcasting during the middle decades of the twentieth century. In a 1928 statement of principles, the network explained that it would "serve only the central or national agencies of great religious faiths, as for example, the Roman Catholics, the Protestants, and the Jews, as distinguished from individual churches of small group movements." Moreover, NBC characterized a proper religious broadcast as "non-sectarian and nondenominational in appeal, . . . presenting the broad claims of religion, which not only aid in building up the personal and social life of the individual but also aid in popularizing religion." Such broadcasts should "interpret religion at its highest and best so that as an educational factor [they] will bring the individual listener to realize his responsibility to the organized church and to society." Though it characterized the value of religion in universalist and humanistic terms, NBC stated that "religious messages should only be broadcast by the recognized outstanding leaders of the several faiths as determined by the best counsel and advice available."[21]

This agenda conformed to Sarnoff's general vision of radio's singular moral imperative. During the 1930s, he argued that "those who have something of value to contribute to the public have greater opportunity to utilize the instrumentality of radio than they possess in practically any other field."[22] With the rise of fascism in Europe, Sarnoff characterized broadcasting as having an urgent moral responsibility, being strategically suited to advancing tolerance and democracy: "To promote the prosperity of our heterogeneous world and to lighten its burdens, a comprehensive system of intercommunications by which people may discover their common bonds is indispensable. . . . The broadcasters of the nation are impelled by the very nature of this service to ensure that the channels of radio shall be open to all matters of public interest, regardless of race, creed, color, or political party."[23] During World War II and its immediate aftermath, Sarnoff argued that the United States, in its new capacity as a world power, must take the lead in establishing international mass-communications efforts as part of the "continuing struggle of democracy against totalitarianism."[24] Promoting plans for the Voice of America and for an international broadcasting initiative by the newly established United Nations, Sarnoff employed familiar idioms of American patriotic rhetoric to position radio as epitomizing national values: "Our American concept of radio is that it is of the people and for the people. Its essence is freedom—liberty of thought and of speech."[25]

Yet while NBC championed freedom of speech for all, the network's approach to religious broadcasting engendered "a 'two-tiered' system," separating "mainstream groups"—Jews counted as one such group—from others, most notably evangelical Christians.[26] Consequently, those religious broadcasters unable to air programming on NBC, then the leading network, sought other possibilities, including broadcasting on CBS, which was on less-sure financial footing and was willing, at first, to sell air time to individual churches and religious leaders. One such individual was a Catholic priest, Charles E. Coughlin, who in 1926 began local broadcasting in Detroit. Within a few years, after his sermons began to air nationally on CBS, Coughlin became one of America's most celebrated and, thanks to his increasingly politically charged broadcasts, most controversial public figures. In 1931, CBS decided to discontinue Coughlin's broadcasts and instituted its own series, *Church of the Air*, "with speakers on a rotating basis from various religious groups, on a free-time basis."[27] Coughlin remained a popular presence on radio throughout the 1930s, broadcasting on his own nationwide syndicate. By the end of the decade, his rhetoric grew explicitly anti-Semitic, and he implicated broadcasters in these attacks, claiming that "Nazi actions elicited publicity because of 'Jewish influence in radio, journalism, and finance.'"[28]

The case of Coughlin proved a cautionary tale for both the networks and the federal agency overseeing them. Regulations issued by the Federal Communications Commission (FCC) in 1934 and self-governing rules established by the National Association of Broadcasters (NAB) in 1939 defined the rubric under which networks aired religious broadcasting, consolidating the position of religion in the public sphere for decades. The NAB code stated explicitly that radio "may not be used to convey attacks upon another's race or religion. Rather it should be the purpose of the religious broadcast to promote the spiritual harmony and understanding of mankind and to administer broadly to the varied religious needs of the community."[29]

These principles rested on the foundation of the FCC's 1934 Communications Act, which situated religious programs as part of what it termed *public service* broadcasting. The agency mandated that networks demonstrate their commitment to the public interest by presenting a regular number of hours of special programs each week. Intended to edify rather than entertain, these programs were to demonstrate that the airways are a public trust licensed to broadcasters by the federal government. Ecumenical religious programs were thus conceived (and usually aired) alongside public-affairs and cultural broadcasts, such as educational documentaries and symphony concerts. Sponsorship and scheduling also distinguished these broadcasts from the networks' other offerings. Public-service programs were typically aired in "sustaining time"—that is, at the broadcasters' expense, without the benefit of a sponsor's underwriting.[30] Networks usually aired "sustaining" programs on Sunday mornings and afternoons, as this part of their weekly schedules had proved the least profitable. Among people working in the broadcasting industry, this time period came to be known as the "Sunday ghetto."

Thus, when NBC first broadcast *The Eternal Light* in the fall of 1944 on New York station WEAF on Sunday mornings from 12:00 to 12:30 p.m., the series joined other religious broadcasts aired nationwide, such as *Church of the Air*, heard in New York on WABC from 1:00 to 1:30 p.m., and *The Catholic Hour*, aired on WEAF from 6:00 to 6:30 p.m. Other Jewish broadcasting heard in New York City on Sundays include *Message of Israel* (WJZ, 10:00–10:30 a.m.) and the *Jewish Science Program* (WMCA, 9:45–10:00 a.m.).[31] In the fall of 1946, *The Eternal Light* was rescheduled to air nationally on NBC between 12:30 and 1:00 p.m., with some local stations airing the broadcasts later in the day.[32] On television, programming produced by JTS rotated in the same time slot with Protestant and Catholic broadcasts, reinforcing the parallel status of these religious series within the rubric of public-service broadcasting.

"Tolerance Trios"

The rotating format of these programs followed a precedent set by live and broadcast panel discussions, including "Protestant-Catholic-Jewish 'tolerance trios' that toured the United States beginning in the 1930s under the auspices of the National Conference of Christians and Jews."[33] Other early postwar undertakings also realized this tripartite model of American ecumenism. For example, in 1956, architect Max Abramovitz designed a trio of Protestant, Catholic, and Jewish chapels for the Brandeis University campus, each building being of equal size and placed around a reflecting pool so that "none can ever cast a shadow on another."[34] Similarly, the Chapel of the Four Chaplains on Temple University's campus—an "interfaith memorial and sanctuary for brotherhood" dedicated in 1951 in memory of four clerics who died on the SS *Dorchester* during World War II—featured "three altars representing the three major faiths, Jewish, Catholic, and Protestant, [which] rest on a turntable [that] changes by releasing a push button to the desired chapel."[35] Whether public lecture, television broadcast, or work of sacred architecture, each of these undertakings made special efforts to position its three components as discrete and equal.

This trinitarian model of American religious pluralism received its most elaborate articulation in Will Herberg's 1955 study *Protestant—Catholic—Jew: An Essay in American Religious Sociology*. Herberg identified religiosity as essential to American society and argued that the two were "so closely interrelated as to make it virtually impossible to understand either without reference to the other." Whereas immigrants' progeny would likely change their nationality, language, and ethnic traditions, they would not change their religion, he maintained, because "from the beginning the structure of American society presupposed diversity and substantial equality of religious associations."[36] Herberg conceptualized America as a "triple melting pot," uniting citizens of diverse ethnic heritages in a national commitment to religiosity that includes respect for freedom of worship (that is, as a Protestant, Catholic, or Jew).

This argument had special implications for American Jews at the end of World War II. Although they continued to figure as a minority in this rubric, their symbolic status as one third of the "triple melting pot" far exceeded national demographic proportions (Jews were then approximately 3 percent of the American population) in relation to the Christian majority. Moreover, Jews exemplified an acceptable difference in Christian America—indeed, their acceptance constituted a model of loyalty to the American principle of religious toleration, making Jews' welcome presence in America an essential demonstration of national values.

The "triple melting pot" paradigm, as well as its realization in ecumenical broadcasting and other public cultural ventures, canonized major corporate religious movements as the American mainstream and thereby marginalized various Christian groups, from Mormons to Eastern Orthodox churches, not affiliated with coalitions of mainline denominations, such as the National Council of Churches of Christ (NCC, established in 1950).[37] Moreover, the complete absence in this model of Islam and American Indian and Asian religions locates them beyond the nation's spiritual pale—to say nothing of excluding atheists or people who claim no religious identity. Centered on immigration from Europe as the formative American experience, Herberg's rubric also fails to account for African Americans, American Indians, and others whose ancestry does not fit his model of voluntary emigration to North America. And although Jews figure prominently as a religious community in this paradigm, it poses other challenges for them, by excluding secular Jews (such as members of the Workmen's Circle or the Jewish People's Fraternal Order) and religious Jews outside the major organized movements, from Jewish Scientists to hasidim.

Even as ecumenical broadcasting embraced Herberg's rubric, which suggested that its three components are of equal stature, the networks' model for these broadcasts most closely resembled the sensibility of mainline Protestantism. This conceptualization of religion emphasized a harmonious spirituality and reasoned consensus, unlike other American visions of religiosity that privileged the particularist, the ecstatic, or the nonrational. During the mid-twentieth century, mainline Protestants produced broadcasts for public-service programming in pursuit of their own agenda. Following World War II, as religion scholar Michele Rosenthal notes, the Protestant hegemony in the United States began to wane. Recognizing that "consent to the Protestant agenda would increasingly have to be manufactured," NCC leaders championed broadcasting by mainline Protestant denominations as strategic to preserving their vision of the United States as what they termed a "Nation Under God." These Protestant leaders understood American democracy as rooted in religious values and, therefore, especially vulnerable to attack by foreign communists and domestic secularists. The NCC regarded mainline Protestantism as being, in effect, "America's semiestablished religion" and thus produced broadcasts reflecting "the language, common sense, and folk religion common to mainline Protestantism, while eliminating . . . specifically Protestant or denominational references" that would prompt disparagement by Catholics and Jews.[38]

Yet whereas liberal Protestant leaders regarded the cooperation of Catholic and Jewish religious leadership in ecumenical broadcasts as maintaining Protestantism's "cultural prominence," Rosenthal argues, Catholics and Jews were more likely motivated "by the desire to explain and legitimate their traditions to the larger American public. . . . Catholic and Jewish leaders were thankful for being recognized as two alternatives to the historical and culturally dominant faith." Moreover, "if messages [in Protestant broadcasts] were to be nonsectarian and nondenominational, and to promote religion in general," then Jews and Catholics "were not to be targets of specific evangelical campaigns."[39] At the same time, for Jewish organizations venturing into religious broadcasting, the prevalence of this Protestant model of ecumenism also shaped their notions of how Jews might present themselves as a religious community on the national airways. Ecumenical broadcasting, like Herberg's "triple melting pot," assigned Jews a position of strategic prominence in American public culture but did so within a Christian-centered (and especially Protestant) rubric that constrained Jews even as it afforded them a privileged position.

"A Common Ground for Artists and Theologians"

Further complicating JTS's venture into ecumenical broadcasting was its choice of format for *The Eternal Light*. In the course of its planning, Krents proposed that the radio program could best fulfill its mission by presenting original dramas, as opposed to worship services, concerts of sacred music, or sermons, which had been the staples of most American religious broadcasting. Radio drama emerged as a "high" art form in the late 1930s; until then, dramatic broadcasts had largely been limited to soap operas and suspense serials. Landmark scripts by Archibald MacLeish (for example, *The Fall of the City*, aired on CBS's *Columbia Workshop* in 1937), Orson Welles (*War of the Worlds*, on CBS's *Mercury Theater on the Air* in 1938), and Norman Corwin (*They Fly through the Air*, on CBS's *Words without Music* in 1939) demonstrated that radio drama could effectively present topics of serious social concern to general audiences (all three of the aforementioned dramas were conceived as anti-Fascist allegories).[40]

At Krents's suggestion, the Seminary engaged playwright Morton Wishengrad to prepare a number of scripts for *The Eternal Light*. Wishengrad, who had been educational director of the International Ladies Garment Workers Union (ILGWU), had already written radio dramas for public-service programming, including the NBC series *Labor for Victory* and *University of the Air*. Wishengrad became JTS's main playwright, writing some 150 scripts for its radio and television broadcasts from the mid-1940s until shortly before his death in 1964. An anthology of twenty-six of Wishengrad's scripts for the first seasons of *The Eternal Light* was published in 1947;[41] there and elsewhere, he discussed these dramas' distinctive aesthetic sensibility.

In Wyler's account of the origins of *The Eternal Light*, she relates the story of JTS's hiring of Wishengrad as something of a conversion experience for the writer, who had become estranged from Judaism:

> [Krents] introduced Dr. Finkelstein to Morton Wishengrad, a talented young playwright—and an avowed agnostic. After a luncheon which lasted several hours, Wishengrad found it hard to maintain his skepticism. There was a real challenge in . . . translating traditional Jewish values into the vocabulary of radio drama. The dramatist left the Seminary with an armful of books, and, by midsummer, he was ready to begin a task which would engage him for the rest of his life.[42]

Wishengrad's own writing suggests a more complicated personal relationship with *The Eternal Light,* the Seminary, and Judaism. Indeed, if this partnership entailed a leap of faith, it was rather JTS's decision to turn to drama as the rubric for its religious broadcasts. The dramatic mode—unlike the narrative and lyric modes of the Bible, the dialogic mode of Talmudic writing and scholarship, or the liturgical mode of communal worship—is largely alien to traditional Jewish religious culture. The modern Jewish stage and Jews' involvement in Western theater have generally been secular enterprises. Though some scholars see the influence of

Publicity photograph of a rehearsal for a broadcast of *The Eternal Light*, 1940s. Left to right: actor John Garfield, playwright Morton Wishengrad, orchestra conductor Milton Katims, and producer Milton Krents. (Joseph and Miriam Ratner Center for the Study of Conservative Judaism, Jewish Theological Seminary of America)

ancient Greek drama on parts of the Bible (notably the Song of Songs and the Book of Job), they regard the absence of an ancient Hebrew dramatic literature as indicating an incompatibility between drama and Jewish ritual practice, law, or philosophy. The conflict applies not only to content but also to the distinctive performance context of drama, which—with the very circumscribed exception of Ashkenazic Purim plays—is absent from traditional Jewish cultural practice.[43]

By contrast, the mission of the playwrights, rabbis, and others involved in JTS's radio and television series postulated that drama and Judaism are culturally compatible and envisioned their respective practitioners as capable of an aesthetically and spiritually valid collaboration. (This vision of Jewish religious drama was not completely unprecedented; dramas on Jewish history and religious pageants had been written for amateur performance by American Jewish schools, synagogues, and community groups since the 1910s.)[44] In a foreword to the anthology of Wishengrad's *Eternal*

Light dramas, Finkelstein wrote of the need for "the team of scholar-artist . . . to interpret Judaism. . . . The Eternal Light suggests how an artist and a group of [religious] scholars can co-operate to translate ancient, abstract ideas into effective modern dramatics."[45] Broadcasters made similar claims; Pamela Ilott, vice president for religious and cultural affairs broadcasts at CBS News, wrote of the series *Lamp Unto My Feet*, "The creation of works of art represents man's striving to express his highest aspirations, to reflect his own world and, at the same time, to influence the condition of man. Religious television presentations . . . provide a common ground for artists and theologians to work toward these ends."[46]

"What's Religious about This?"

At Finkelstein's suggestion, *The Eternal Light* debuted with a series of thirteen plays about synagogues throughout Jewish history.[47] The first drama, aired on 8 October 1944, was Wishengrad's *A Rhode Island Refuge*, inspired by the Touro synagogue, founded in Newport in 1763. Using a device he would return to frequently in *Eternal Light* scripts, the playwright designated a character within the drama to serve as narrator, selecting a figure with an oblique or unconventional perspective. *A Rhode Island Refuge* begins with Mordecai, a fictitious resident of colonial Newport, speaking from his grave in the town's Old Jewish Cemetery:

> They sleep so still beside me. Once so long ago they fled from Spain and Portugal, fled before the Inquisition and they wandered over the earth again. And here in Rhode Island they found refuge. And now they sleep . . . a final refuge . . . the last exodus. The headstones mellow in the rain . . . Lopez, Alvarez, Levy, Seixas, Touro. But over my grave there is no tablet. Only a nameless stone the color of earth.[48]

A drama of Jewish life in colonial Newport ensues, centered on the Jews' participation in the revolt against England. Characters in *A Rhode Island Refuge* repeatedly invoke the compatibility of Jewishness and Americanness. "The American colonies are your congregation," the narrator's father tells his fellow Jews during a debate about the revolution. "This is our place." Later, he exhorts his son, as Mordecai is about to join the 8th Massachusetts Regiment, to "be a good soldier . . . for Israel and for America." The drama concludes with Mordecai's return to Newport after the war.

There, Moses Seixas (an actual member of the Jewish community in colonial Rhode Island) reads to him from George Washington's famous letter to the Hebrew Congregation of Newport, in which Washington asserts
that the United States gives "to bigotry no sanction, to persecution no assistance," and thereby offers Jews a welcoming haven.[49]

The opening of *A Rhode Island Refuge* both recalls Henry Wadsworth
Longfellow's 1858 poem "The Jewish Cemetery at Newport" and transforms its portrait of this famous graveyard. Rather than viewing it as
an alien presence, from the distance of a non-Jewish perspective ("How
strange it seems! These Hebrews in their graves," writes Longfellow, "How
came they here?"),[50] Wishengrad presents the cemetery from within as a
welcome, enduring resting place. Similarly, his script removes Washington's letter from the larger context of his correspondence with Newport's
Jews and other colonial religious communities (this letter is, in fact, a response to one sent to Washington by the congregation, and its most famous passage is his iteration of language formulated by the Jews of Newport themselves). And Wishengrad avoids probing what historian Hasia
Diner characterizes as "the ambiguity expressed in Washington's letter,"
which welcomes Jews in the United States as long as they "demean themselves as good citizens."[51]

Wishengrad wrote the preponderance of the scripts for *The Eternal
Light* in its first seasons, but others also wrote for the series, including
television and theater playwrights Erik Barnouw, Ernest Kinoy, Arnold
Perl, and Shimon Wincelberg, often working under Wishengrad's editorial guidance. The range of subject matter for *The Eternal Light* dramas
expanded as well. A second series of broadcasts presented the life stories
of "builders of Judaism," including profiles of communal and religious
leaders Louis Brandeis and Isaac Mayer Wise, as well as authors Emma
Lazarus and Sholem Aleichem. Biographies of noteworthy figures, Jewish and non-Jewish, were among the most enduring genres of *The Eternal
Light* dramas. In addition to dramatizing the lives of important historical figures of Jewish letters and thought (including Rabbi Akiba, Solomon Ibn Gabirol, Moses Mendelssohn, the Vilna Gaon), *The Eternal Light*
profiled the diverse contributions of Jews to society at large, with dramas
about, among others, Dr. Bela Schick, who helped fight diphtheria; Edward Rosewater, telegraphist for President Lincoln; and Ludwig Zamenhof, inventor of Esperanto.[52]

As the inaugural broadcast of *The Eternal Light* exemplifies, JTS was
committed to using the series to demonstrate the compatibility of Jewish

and American values. This agenda inspired dramas devoted to American holidays (especially Thanksgiving), the American Revolution, and the Civil War, as well as portraits of an array of important figures in American life, including Mary McLeod Bethune and George Washington Carver. The Seminary also produced special broadcasts in 1954 marking the tercentenary of Jewish settlement in America.[53] Broadcasters played a leading role in planning this commemoration, which extended beyond radio and television programming. Both Sarnoff and CBS president William S. Paley served on the program policy committee for the tercentenary, and Sarnoff is credited with proposing the celebration's theme, "Man's Opportunities and Responsibilities Under Freedom."[54]

Many *Eternal Light* broadcasts dramatized the Jewish past, but the series also addressed contemporary issues of general concern—for example, episodes honoring the life of Mahatma Gandhi or documenting an effort to bring Japanese women, scarred as a result of atomic bomb blasts, to the United States for reconstructive plastic surgery.[55] Occasionally scripts articulated links between biblical teachings and present concerns. In October 1946, for example, as the United Nations General Assembly convened for the first time, *The Eternal Light* presented *Isaiah and the Nations*, in which "the Prophet Isaiah appears at the opening session of the General Assembly to bring the voice of the holy writ to the delegates."[56] However, the series seldom dramatized the Bible itself. According to Moshe Davis, a JTS dean who served as the series's first program editor, the creators of *The Eternal Light* asserted that the Bible was not suited to this idiom, because it is "such an epic, its passages so sacred that it cannot be transferred suitably to the medium of radio."[57]

During the first seasons of *The Eternal Light,* the series devoted a considerable number of episodes to the experiences of Europe's Jews during and after World War II. In addition to programs about the struggle to survive Nazi persecution—including one of the first American media adaptations of Anne Frank's wartime diary—were dramas about displaced persons and refugees building new lives in the postwar era.[58] In fact, more scripts in Wishengrad's 1947 *Eternal Light* anthology deal with the war and its aftermath than with any other subject. Beyond demonstrating a special concern among the series's creators with the fate of European Jewry, these broadcasts evince the powerful role that the Holocaust played in motivating ecumenical projects and, moreover, in shaping postwar notions of ecumenism itself. As historian Geoffrey Wigoder has argued, "the realization that the traditional Christian teaching of contempt [for Jews] had created the atmosphere in which a Holocaust was possible" prompted Christians to formulate a new concept of Jewry and of Judaism.[59]

Other episodes of *The Eternal Light* explored various approaches to linking moral edification with dramatic entertainment, presenting adaptations of Jewish literature, including works by S. Y. Agnon, Isaac Babel, David Bergelson, Y. L. Peretz, Henry Roth, Isaac Bashevis Singer, and Sholem Aleichem. During the series's first seasons, it also aired several adaptations of works of world literature dealing with Jewish characters (Stephen Vincent Benet's *Joseph and the Indians*, Gotthold Ephraim Lessing's *Nathan the Wise*, Jean Baptiste Racine's *Athalie*). Moral instruction was offered even in the occasional humorous episode, whether an adaptation of Yiddish folktales about the wise men of Chelm or an original script, such as Marc Siegel's *How Manny Got into the Seventh Grade*, the story of a ten-year-old schoolboy's search for a sign from God that he would be promoted to the next grade.[60]

JTS leaders recognized that the wide-ranging inventory of subjects for its broadcasts extended well beyond religious matters, as they are conventionally understood, and considered this range emblematic of the Seminary's larger vision of Judaism as central to other facets of Jewish experience, whether it be modern Jewish nationalist movements or Jews' involvement in modern Western culture and scholarship. Davis termed *The Eternal Light* a "*klal-yisrael* program"—that is, a program that takes a comprehensive approach to Jewish life—and he recalled in an interview that this approach sometimes provoked debate over the proper scope of Jewish religious broadcasting:

> The question came up from time to time, why are you doing it under the guise of religious programming? . . . The other [religious] groups began to complain. . . . One day the man in change of Public Affairs at NBC came to see Dr. Finkelstein . . . about the Solomon Schechter program, [which dramatized Schechter's discovery of a trove of abandoned manuscripts stored in the Cairo Genizah.] He . . . says, "What's religious about this? . . . Why is this a religious program for NBC to put on?" . . . Dr. Finkelstein said to him, "You know, what I'd like to tell you is that for us study is prayer." And the man said, "Well, I never knew, I never understood it that way."[61]

Wishengrad's correspondence reveals how he, too, struggled with the challenges of crafting protocols for dramatizing Jewish religion. In 1949, he wrote to Davis concerning a script about a famous Jewish physician, submitted to JTS by another playwright, whose approach Wishengrad found problematic:

> [This] script is a great distance from what I hope is an Eternal Light standard. [The author] apparently thought he was answering my objections that his first draft lacked any justification for being scheduled on a program sponsored by the Jewish Theological Seminary by tacking on a half-dozen Biblical quotations. That doesn't make this script religious, only stuffy and incredible. What would make it religious would be the parable of integration that it offers, i.e., the physician who treats the human being versus the specialist who treats a narrow, subdivided ailment.[62]

At times, the challenges of integrating religion with drama stymied Wishengrad himself. In 1960, he returned an advance he had received to write a stage play based on the life of Rabbi Levi Yitzhak of Berditchev, a topic that, he explained, "has obsessed me for more than fifteen years." (Wishengrad had written a radio play for *The Eternal Light* on this subject: "The Song of Berditchev," aired 17 September 1950.) Explaining his decision, he wrote,

> I am throwing in the towel. Levi Yitzhak, who never in his saintly life ever raised his voice or swung a fist, has knocked me flatter than Ingemar Johanssen. I am undone by exactly those same qualities of sweetness and saintliness. And I have absorbed a costly lesson: that ours is the theater of Aberration, the Dramatic Century of the Louse. Were the Berditchever a hypocrite, an adulterer, a latent homosexual, a misogynist, who concealed his hatred of mankind under a mask of love, . . . he would arouse the sympathy of his audience. But he was indeed a saint, and nothing repels more swiftly than simple, unparadoxical goodness.[63]

Even Wishengrad's most successful scripts for JTS evince the challenges he faced in negotiating dramatic, religious, and other concerns. One of his first efforts, aired a year before *The Eternal Light* had begun, was *The Battle of the Warsaw Ghetto*. Produced in conjunction with the American Jewish Committee, this half-hour play recounts the story of Jewish resistance against Nazi persecution in a form that the author characterized as "half-drama, half-documentary" (because of the script's recitation of statistics on the ghetto's population and on their deaths by disease, starvation, and deportation to death camps). First aired on NBC in October 1943, only a few months after the uprising had taken place, the drama prompted extensive response from enthusiastic listeners.[64] During the remaining war years, the network presented the play another two times, and it was broadcast internationally on Armed Forces Radio.[65] NBC reaired *The Battle of the Warsaw Ghetto* repeatedly, as late as 1985.

A landmark of early Holocaust remembrance in America—it is certainly among the very first such efforts addressed to a national audience—*The Battle of the Warsaw Ghetto* also reveals how Wishengrad first approached writing religious drama. In this script he makes pointed use of Jewish ritual music (the funeral chant El Male Rahamim, which opens and closes the drama) and prayer (the Kaddish, traditionally recited by mourners), as well as biblical language and imagery. At the drama's opening, an unnamed voice likens the dead of the Warsaw Ghetto to "the scapegoats of the centuries" and recalls the Bible's description of Aaron's ritual offering of a goat (Leviticus 16:10): "And he released the goat, and its name was Azazel—scapegoat; and it fled into the wilderness. But for them in the Ghetto of Warsaw there was no release . . . there was only the abyss." The Ghetto's Jews, now all "[a]sleep in their common graves, . . . have made an offering by fire and an atonement unto the Lord and they have earned their sleep." Here, Wishengrad employs sacred scripture and ritual both to articulate the enormity of the annihilation of Warsaw's Jews and to interrogate the notion of these murders as being somehow sanctified.[66]

The Battle of the Warsaw Ghetto offers neither a simple message of religious redemption nor one that champions armed resistance, as have many subsequent representations of this event. Rather, the script acknowledges the struggle to maintain human dignity and mourns its defeat. Wishengrad valorizes the efforts of the Warsaw Ghetto's Jews to continue pursuing humanistic, more so than religious, endeavors—running a school, planting a garden, making a sculpture, or playing in an orchestra. He mourns not merely the Jews' physical destruction but their abandonment by the Allies ("We asked England, Russia, and the United States for weapons. And there was silence. You did not answer.") and their moral degradation by Nazi Germany, which is exemplified by a man stripping and abandoning his wife's corpse, so that her death would go unregistered and he and their son could continue to use her ration card. "This is your inheritance," the man tells the boy, and an unidentified voice intones the Kaddish.[67]

Over the ensuing years, Wishengrad evolved a complex relationship with the Seminary, its broadcasting projects, and Judaism. Rather than simply finding in the mission of writing plays for JTS a new personal path, artistically or spiritually, his own convictions became yet another factor that further complicated the nexus of agendas behind *The Eternal Light*.

If religion was not a leading force in Wishengrad's life, other beliefs were. Since his years as an undergraduate at Brooklyn College, he had been active in politics, and he soon identified as a liberal anti-Communist. His political interests eventually merged with his aspirations to write and inaugurated his career as a radio playwright. Following several years at the ILGWU, Wishengrad worked for the Shortwave Bureau of the American Federation of Labor and Congress of Industrial Organizations (AFL-CIO), which broadcast during the war to organized labor in Europe. This position, as well as his political convictions, led to Wishengrad's debut as a radio playwright, as he recalled in an account of his early political activism:

> NBC was the reluctant sponsor of a series known as Labor for Victory. When it became the turn of the CIO Textile Workers Union to broadcast . . . , the liberal vice president of the union refused to hire the writer suggested by [the] publicity chief of the CIO. [The vice president believed] that the radio scripts for the CIO largely reflected the C[ommunist] P[arty] line of the period. [He] asked me to write a script because, as he said, "I refuse to hire a communist." This marked my entrance into radio.[68]

Cold War politics continued to inform Wishengrad's career as a dramatist. In 1948 he wrote *Communism—U.S. Brand*, a controversial anti-Communist script for ABC radio, which received a Peabody Award and made Wishengrad a divisive figure in progressive political circles. Wishengrad's political concerns also informed his discussions with JTS staff regarding *The Eternal Light*. In a letter to Davis about a proposed script on John Ordroneaux, Wishengrad argued against it, explaining that he had learned that this hero of the War of 1812 was not a Jew and that the left-wing author Howard Fast had identified Ordroneaux as a Jew in his work, despite having been told otherwise:

> That's a CP tactic. But for heaven's sake it isn't a Seminary tactic. If you do such a script you become allied to a communist interpretation of American Jewish History. And you will open the Seminary to attack from an entire political spectrum that will begin on the anti-CP liberal left and go to

the Catholic right. The Catholic Church is gunning for Fast, as you know. I think their victory against his books is disgraceful. But it seems to me that if you're going to pick a fight with the Church on the issue of academic freedom, the fight should be on an issue where truth is on our side.[69]

In personal correspondence, Wishengrad voiced some ambivalence about his work for JTS. Writing to a literary agent in 1953, he described the plays that he wrote for the Seminary as "luftmensch [here: "insubstantial"] operations which have paid my rent" and characterized his employers there as "the assorted rabbis from whose phylacteries I dangle."[70] In 1961, Wishengrad responded to a letter from a former JTS student, thanking him for telling the playwright some years earlier "that there was a vast Jewish desert in America where kids were daily betrayed by pedantic, tone-deaf, unloving, doctrinaire teachers and rabbis, and that some of [Wishengrad's] scripts had given them an emotion which spoke of another kind of Jewishness." And yet, when reporting in the same letter on his health (Wishengrad was recovering from a stroke), he wrote, "I limp only when exhausted, but unlike the standard hero of Eternal Light drama I have not been ennobled by what happened to me."[71]

"I Pray That Millions Hear Your Program"

Within the limitations of the relatively unpopular "Sunday ghetto," *The Eternal Light* acquired a considerable following. In its inaugural season, the series was aired by thirty-three of NBC's affiliate stations and was carried in Canada over the CBC. By the mid-1950s, over one hundred radio stations across the United States presented *The Eternal Light*. The earliest information on its audience share comes from Hooper ratings for the autumn of 1946; these figures suggest that *The Eternal Light* then reached more than five million listeners in the United States alone, comparable to the audience for other religious, cultural, and public-affairs programs of the time.[72] Early publicity materials for *The Eternal Light* frequently mentioned an audience of six million.[73]

During the early postwar years, various efforts were made to bring *The Eternal Light* to audiences beyond North America. *Jüdische Rundschau*, a periodical for Jewish displaced persons in Germany, printed transcripts of the series; episodes were performed in German and Yiddish for live audiences in displaced-persons' camps; and German-language radio stations

Cover of a promotional brochure for *The Eternal Light*, printed by the Jewish Theological Seminary, ca. 1950. (Joseph and Miriam Ratner Center for the Study of Conservative Judaism, Jewish Theological Seminary of America)

in Munich, Frankfurt, Bremen, and Cologne aired the *Eiwige Licht Programme*. The Palestine (later Israel) Broadcasting Service presented selected installments of *The Eternal Light* in Hebrew into the 1950s. For many years, *The Eternal Light* was heard on Voice of America and Armed Forces Radio Service.[74]

The Seminary also developed other means for extending the reach of *The Eternal Light* during its first seasons. Listeners could write to JTS for offprints of individual scripts or could receive them by subscription. By 1948, JTS reported nine hundred regular subscribers to these offprints.[75] To encourage Jewish educators to make use of the broadcasts or scripts, the Radio and Television Department prepared teacher's guides to facilitate classroom discussion of individual broadcasts.[76] In 1947, the Seminary made recordings of ten *Eternal Light* episodes available for purchase.[77]

These efforts were doubtless fueled by the generally positive attention accorded to *The Eternal Light* in its first years. This acclaim extended well beyond Jewish support. Among the program's earliest admirers was

Eleanor Roosevelt, who mentioned it in her nationally syndicated column two days after the series's debut.[78] The program was almost as widely recognized as an important contribution to the development of radio drama as it was for its innovative approach to religious broadcasting. *Variety* praised both the agenda of *The Eternal Light* and its production values:

> NBC rates a nod for this Sunday noontime public service show. Any attempt in these crucial times to further goodwill and tolerance, break down homefront prejudices and foster greater understanding of minority groups should of necessity be encouraged. . . . [NBC] has projected itself as a definite force for good. . . . The dramatizations are of a pattern that reflects painstaking effort to realize a fuller understanding of the problems and invest them with top entertainment values: the acting [is] . . . out of the top drawer, and the direction and all around production [is] a distinct credit.[79]

A 1948 manual on producing religious radio programming cited *The Eternal Light* as a pioneer of broadcast drama and praised it for being "not only one of the best religious programs on the air, but also one of the leading dramatic shows in all radio."[80] Reviewing the series for the *New York Times* in 1950, Val Adams wrote that *The Eternal Light* "bubbles with more real sense of good theatre than some of radio's star studded productions" and praised the series for its "fundamental new approach . . . to religious broadcasting," which "suggests spiritual uplift and moral integrity with never a trace of sanctimony."[81] In its first ten years on the air, *The Eternal Light* received awards from the National Conference of Christians and Jews, the Radio-TV Critics Circle of New York, and *Variety* magazine, among others.[82] In later years, the series twice received the George Foster Peabody Broadcasting Award.[83]

Given the Seminary's strong commitment to outreach, audience response to *The Eternal Light* was of special interest to its creators. Five years after inaugurating the series, the Seminary reported receiving an average of five hundred letters per week from listeners.[84] JTS collected and studied listeners' letters and cited selected comments in publicity materials. These selections do not, of course, offer a comprehensive view of audience reception, but they do evince which listener responses fulfilled the Seminary's expectations. At the same time, these selections from audience mail reveal a slippage between the Seminary's vision of its audience in relation to the larger goals for public-service broadcasting to a national audience.

While committed to an ecumenical focus on the commonalities among different faiths and their followers, JTS also conceptualized its audience as divided between Jews and non-Jews and envisioned distinct goals in addressing each group. For non-Jews, the series strove to demystify Jewish history, beliefs, and practices and thereby combat anti-Semitic prejudice. For Jews, JTS's broadcasts offered a point of entry for the unaffiliated, isolated, or culturally illiterate, encouraging them toward further engagement with Judaism.

This double agenda is evident, if obliquely, in a promotional brochure that JTS issued during the first seasons that *The Eternal Light* was on the air. The brochure consists almost entirely of excerpts from the Seminary's collection of audience letters, which "speak for themselves." Most of the thirty listeners sampled identify themselves as either Jews or Christians; their comments are printed anonymously, though their towns of origin are given. Typical of the Christians' testimonials is this one, from a listener in Kinderhook, New York:

> Like too many others not of the Jewish faith, I am ignorant of much that the great and small alike of that faith have contributed to our world through the ages, and hope that through programs similar to the one presented today, there may be more enlightenment for us who want to know that we may be better educated in our individual efforts for better understanding among all people in this terrible struggle today.

Other letters similarly relate the mission of *The Eternal Light* to contemporary concerns, as does one from a Catholic in New York City, who writes, "I am troubled . . . by the unchristian apathy, ignorance and intolerance [regarding Jews] of so many, many of my Christian brethren. I pray that millions hear your program, that millions may gain a new insight of the Jew as a person: a working, loving, living . . . and dying individual, rather than a race apart."[85]

These testimonials were clearly selected to model the Seminary's vision of audience relationships to *The Eternal Light* among a growing national listenership, as exemplified by the comments of one listener from Chicago: "With each succeeding broadcast of the 'Eternal Light' I become more and more convinced that this is the 'light' that will dispel the dark ugly shadows of anti-semitism and misunderstanding which plague the Jew." Several correspondents, both Christians and Jews, report using the broadcasts or offprints of scripts in religious schools or other community educational settings. And the series itself is held up as a paradigm for other religious communities to emulate, as a letter from Charlotte, North Carolina, states: "I want to write to the Federal Council of the Churches of Christ in America, suggesting that their next radio enterprise be presented with some of the dramatic listener-appeal which *The Eternal Light* brings to an audience, which I am sure will grow."[86]

Responses selected from Jewish listeners speak of the broadcasts' value for those Jews whose relationship with their Jewishness is attenuated, as in the case of another letter from Chicago: "I would like to tell you how much we look forward to these broadcasts. . . . We are an average Jewish family with no religious connections; all we remember is what memories we have of our fathers and mothers. After listening to these programs, we have resolved to be better Jews if we can possibly help it." Other letters from Jews praise *The Eternal Light* for fostering Jewish pride: "The program was the best I ever heard," writes one listener from Venice, California. "What courage it gives to young Jews!—boys who are afraid to be Jewish, afraid to mention the word, Jew."[87]

Letters from Jewish listeners further suggest that *The Eternal Light* inspired new forms of engagement with their Jewishness that center on the radio series itself. One correspondent from New York City was prompted by the program to make a donation to JTS, having experienced the broadcast as simulating an intergenerational communion with one's ancestors: "May I take the liberty of enclosing a small contribution to the work of the Seminary in the name of my father, Jacob. I could feel a part of him speaking through most of the characters portrayed in today's presentation." And a letter from a listener in Denver describes *The Eternal Light* as the focus of one family's weekly ritual:

> I would like to give you a picture of a Sunday morning in our home. It is really exciting. The whole family gets up early enough to listen to the fascinating pageant you present each week. We are all dressed up, the table is set in the dining room, and we are in a festive mood. We are all participants and would like to keep on listening and learning from our rich and sad, but hopeful and promising past.[88]

Similar self-styled rituals, linking family gatherings and food with listening to the radio program, were enacted in other American Jewish homes during the early post–World War II years. Consider, for example, the account that Philip Roth offers in one of his quasi-autobiographical novels:

> Fifty-two Sundays a year, for most of my lifetime, my father went out to the corner for the smoked fish and the warm rolls, my brother and I set the table and squeezed the juice. . . . Then, after my parents had read the Newark Sunday papers and listened on the radio to "The Eternal Light"— great moments from Jewish history in weekly half-hour dramatizations— we two boys were rounded up and the four of us set off in the car to visit relatives.[89]

Davis described *The Eternal Light* in its heyday as having become "a kind of sacred hour for Jews all over America."[90] His qualification points to the novel, inchoate nature of the series's apparent sanctity. This uncertainty was due, in no small part, to the distinctive way that radio engages the public sphere. Though heard for the most part in individual homes, the broadcasts situated listeners in a virtual public space, in which they could imagine themselves part of a vast, nationwide audience. For Jewish listeners, this context had particular implications. The Seminary's oft-mentioned statistic of six million listeners for *The Eternal Light* configured listening to the broadcasts as a symbolic act for the American Jewish community, invoking both the estimated Jewish population of early postwar North America and the number of Jewish victims of the Holocaust. Listening to *The Eternal Light* could thereby be construed as a definitional and a memorial rite.

"Gracious Opportunity"

Even as the Seminary's official agenda placed equal emphasis on Jewish and non-Jewish audiences—and notwithstanding its distinctive investment in addressing Jewish listeners' particular needs—JTS actually considered its primary audience to be non-Jews, according to Wyler. In addition to their expressions of admiration and concern for Jews, Christian listeners held strategic symbolic value for the Jews who created and listened to *The Eternal Light*. Knowing that there was a non-Jewish listenership for the series allowed Jews to perceive themselves as subjects of the respectful attention of their Christian neighbors. This much larger non-Jewish audience validated Jews' worth above and beyond any internal sense of their significance. The desire for this kind of attention is manifest in a concern for respectability, construed in mainstream American middle-class terms, which is fundamental to the aesthetic of *The Eternal Light* and which similarly informed other new cultural, social, and political concerns for postwar American Jewry.

Ecumenical broadcasting modeled a new kind of contact between American Jews and Christians. Radio and television served both the geographic decentralization of American Jews and their entry into the American cultural mainstream, by offering them direct and simultaneous access to centers of culture (Jewish as well as general), regardless of where these Jews resided. Through these domestic media, American Jews were also symbolically inviting themselves into the homes of their non-Jewish neighbors for a Sunday social call. This virtual engagement coincided with actual new encounters that Jews were having with other Americans in the postwar era, due to rapid and large-scale embourgeoisement, epitomized by Jews' participation in a mass movement to the suburbs. For many Jews, suburban migration constituted, in Arthur Hertzberg's words, a symbolic "move into America."[91]

In a study of Jewish life in postwar suburbia, Albert Gordon likewise tied this move to significant changes in "the character of Jewish community life in America. . . . The new Jewish suburbanites believe . . . that since we are all Americans, it is not good for Jews—or any other ethnic or religious group—to live together, forming their own community. They *fear* segregation, in contrast to their parents, who in many cases sought it."[92] So powerful was the integrationist impact of postwar suburban migration on American Jewish culture, according to sociologist Nathan Glazer, that this "great movement" offers a "more persuasive" explanation for the transformation of American Jewry in the postwar period "than either Hitler or Zionism. . . . Aside from the economic and social shift, though certainly allied to it, was the rise of new values in American life, values that may be included under the general heading of . . . middle-class respectability."[93]

In the context of postwar American middle-class life, respectability demanded a demonstration of conformity to bourgeois sensibilities, in which the visual and performing arts figured as an important ennobling and civilizing force. This privileging of the arts informed JTS's desire to realize the compatibility of religion and art through its broadcast dramas and its expansion of the Jewish Museum. These undertakings were part of a larger interest in aestheticizing Judaism that flourished in early postwar America, manifest in new synagogue design and innovative approaches to Jewish education in which the arts were regarded as essential to facilitating what historian Deborah Dash Moore terms "spiritual recreation." This interest in middle-class respectability also informed American Jewish home decor and cuisine, through which Jews strove to demonstrate that "civility and aesthetics" could be compatible with traditional practice.[94] Central to these acts of aestheticizing Judaism—whether at the synagogue, in the kitchen, on the airwaves, or elsewhere—is a concern for demonstrating Jewish respectability. In his 1959 dissertation on American Jewish broadcasting, Zev Zahavy argued that aesthetic concerns for respectability are essential to realizing the "gracious opportunity" that broadcasting provided for "expanding the moral, ethical and divine principles of Jewish life." The "proper utilization" of Jewish religious broadcasting, Zahavy maintained, "may create tastes and motives for better Jewish living."[95]

JTS realized its aspirations for respectability in broadcasts that maintained an elevated, dignified tone, whether striving for a somber, histrionic, or amusing affect. The aesthetics of *The Eternal Light* are epitomized by its signature opening: For many years, each radio broadcast began with a stentorian performance by a male vocalist of the Hebrew song "Shomer Yisrael" ("Guardian of Israel") with orchestral accompaniment. There followed a reverberating male voice intoning the following biblical passage (Exodus 27:20): "And the Lord spake unto Moses, saying, 'Command the children of Israel that they bring unto thee pure olive oil beaten for the light, to cause lamps to burn continually in the tabernacle of the congregation, and it shall be a statute forever in your generations.'" This opening sequence linked traditional Jewish language and scripture with the highbrow aesthetics of classical music and the lofty English of the King James translation of the Bible.

This aesthetic continued throughout the broadcasts, epitomized by the voices of such performers as Alexander Scourby and Roger De Koven, who were regularly heard as narrators or protagonists on the radio series. The carefully inflected speech of these trained radio announcers bore no trace of "ethnic" accent or colloquial rhythm. They performed the equivalent of the ideal sound that JTS had sought for its rabbinical students, who had been required to study elocution during the Seminary's early years.[96] Thus, the aesthetic of the Radio and Television Department conformed to JTS's longstanding agenda of "Americanizing" the "East European" character of the majority of American Jews.[97]

Enacting middle-class respectability, especially in relation to religiosity, also had political value for American Jewry during the first years of the Cold War, when Jews were frequent, if often oblique, targets of American anti-Communist activists' scrutiny of the broadcasting industry, which was targeted as a potential instrument of "un-American" propaganda.[98] Ecumenical programs allowed both American Jewry and the broadcasting industry to situate themselves at the center of American values, distancing themselves from "godless" communism, voicing their patriotism, and promoting democratic freedoms of expression and of worship. Thus, on the tenth anniversary of *The Eternal Light*, Sarnoff characterized broadcasting as embodying a democratic ethos of divine origin: "Radio waves, which are a manifestation of an 'Infinite Reason,' . . . do not discriminate against race, religion or creed. Freedom is their essence—and they enter the homes of Protestants, Catholics and Jews alike."[99]

"Like a Good Deed in a Naughty World"

Although the networks and JTS touted the airwaves as a locus of spiritual democracy, American public-service broadcasting actually provided Jews with a marginal and highly circumscribed, albeit respectable, venue in which to present themselves to the American public. Aired only in the "Sunday ghetto," ecumenical programs confined Jews to the equivalent of a segregated neighborhood, ostensibly separate but equal, within the virtual "cultural forum" or public "gathering place" of American broadcasting.[100] By designating Sundays as the appropriate time for Jews to be presented regularly as Jews, demonstrably and with dignity, on the national airwaves, broadcasters implicitly limited other possibilities for Jewish representation.

The decorous presentation of Jews on ecumenical radio and television did, in fact, provide a marked contrast to most other Jewish characters and performers who populated these media during the middle decades of the twentieth century. Like so many other ethnic, regional, national, and racial types featured in American popular culture of the time, characters identified as Jewish were largely comic figures. Nevertheless, it is instructive to compare *Eternal Light* broadcasts with the only other regular, forthright presentation of Jews on the airwaves during the 1940s and '50s: the radio and, later, television series *The Goldbergs*. Although it might appear to exemplify a public image of Jews that *The Eternal Light* strove to counter, *The Goldbergs* engaged similar concerns about Jewish representation and also employed the regular broadcast of drama on domestic media to present Jews as comfortably at home in America.

The Goldbergs was a popular radio series, having been aired in various formats and on different networks for fifteen years when *The Eternal Light* debuted in 1944. At the time, *The Goldbergs* was a daytime drama heard on CBS, and it continued to be heard on radio until 1950. In 1949, *The Goldbergs* had become one of the first situation comedies on television, where it was seen on different networks until 1956. Thus, for a quarter century, broadcasts of *The Goldbergs* defined American Jewish family life for a national audience.

In all its various incarnations (which also included a vaudeville act, a Broadway play, a comic strip, and a feature film), *The Goldbergs* offered a portrait of American Jewish domestic life through the quotidian adventures of the multigenerational Goldberg family.[101] At the family's center was its matriarch, Molly Goldberg, portrayed by Gertrude Berg, who was also the creator, producer, and writer of all permutations of *The Goldbergs*. The Goldbergs' Jewishness was signified by their name and their Yiddish-inflected English dialect, following the convention of representing various ethnic types on American radio.[102] Against this portrayal of Jews, *The Eternal Light* offered a counterportrait, focusing on the grand sweep of Jewish history and eschewing dialect and other markers that might be construed as stigmatizing Jews as comically undignified, alien, or sinister.

Nevertheless, through *The Goldbergs*, Gertrude Berg pursued an agenda that was, in some respects, akin to JTS's aspirations for its ecumenical broadcasts. While working within the rubric of commercial entertainment programming, Berg, too, regarded radio as a force for doing public good on behalf of her fellow Jews. Literary scholar Donald Weber argues that *The Goldbergs* constituted "a gigantic effort to soften the jagged edges of [the] historical alienation [of Jews] through the supremely maternal figure of Molly Goldberg and her special accommodating vision—the dream of a loving family, of interdenominational brotherhood, of the political ideas associated with the American founders." (Indeed, a portrait of George Washington was displayed prominently in the living room of the Goldbergs' Bronx apartment in the television series.) *The Goldbergs*, Weber suggests, offered its audience something akin to religious inspiration—"a utopian dream vision providing a redemptive light illuminating how 'life should be'"—and Molly "inspired faith—and faithful listeners—during an interval of economic doubt and historical uncertainty."[103]

Like the creators of *The Eternal Light*, Berg was also concerned with performing an accommodating and respectable Jewish self-portrait before an American audience as she made herself a virtual guest in their homes. In her memoirs, Berg attributed her success as an entertainer to her family's background in the hotel business, which taught her to be considerate toward guests and to avoid offending them.[104] Elsewhere, she explained that, in her approach to dramatizing American Jewish family life on the airwaves, "I don't bring up anything that will bother people. That's very important. Unions, politics, fund-raising, Zionism, socialism, inter-group relations, I don't stress them," and she argued that such issues were of secondary importance in portraying a family's daily life. And as for her characters' identity as Jews, she stated, "The Goldbergs are not defensive about their Jewishness, or especially aware of it."[105] Occasionally, radio episodes of *The Goldbergs* did include portrayals of Jewish holidays (Yom Kippur and Passover) and life-cycle events (a wedding and a bar mitzvah), acknowledged Yiddish culture (a 1933 broadcast included a performance from Abraham Goldfadn's operetta *Shulamis*), and even addressed the issue of anti-Semitism in America.[106]

Berg's fan mail reveals that audience members ascribed values to her broadcasts similar to those that listeners who wrote to JTS found in *The Eternal Light*. A listener from Oklahoma City wrote, "The fact that [the Goldbergs] are Jews does not at all detract from our enjoyment, but rather adds to it. We like the democratic and friendly feeling they have for Jew [and] Gentile. . . . We like their patriotism, their constructive, charitable acts, their sympathy for friends." And another wrote from Maine, "Truly, The Goldbergs 'shine like a good deed in a naughty world.' 'May they live long and prosper.'"[107]

Berg characterized her broadcasts as a corrective to images of Jews in popular culture that she found "revolting."[108] Like JTS, she saw her program as employing radio and television to redress wrongs that had been directed at Jews in these media. Although both these efforts considered performing the respectability of Jews as paramount, their approaches differed: Berg did so in the role of the good neighbor, who, along with the rest of her fictional family, made regular visits to American homes with stories centered on the drama of daily life, in which Jewishness was normalized as an occasional presence. JTS, by contrast, realized respectability through an image of Jewry as a venerable moral exemplar, manifest in an anthology of historical episodes and figures that focused on the accomplished and the inspiring.

"Disincorporation"

Despite the acclaim that *The Eternal Light* garnered and the pride that its creators voiced in its accomplishments during the late 1940s and '50s, JTS produced fewer ecumenical dramas in the ensuing decades. During the early 1960s, the series continued to present both new radio plays and re-broadcasts of scripts from earlier seasons. By the mid-1970s *The Eternal Light* devoted more episodes to interviews with authors, religious leaders, performers, and other public figures; still, the series offered the occasional new play and continued to reair selected dramas. This practice continued into the mid-1980s, when *The Eternal Light* ceased regular broadcasting. The decline of JTS's production of ecumenical broadcasting reveals the extent to which its success depended on a complex of contingencies. When this constellation of interests and possibilities came undone, the creators of these broadcasts could no longer sustain their distinctive mission and approach.

One factor leading to the decline of *The Eternal Light* appears at first to be an expansion of its agenda—namely, JTS's ventures into television. While maintaining its radio series on NBC, the Seminary entered into arrangements with all three major commercial networks to produce religious television broadcasts. The first of these aired in 1948 on the CBS ecumenical series *Lamp Unto My Feet*. In 1951, the Seminary produced episodes for *Frontiers of Faith*, NBC's first televised ecumenical series; starting in 1958, these episodes were aired under the title *The Eternal Light*. Beginning in 1961, JTS produced installments of *Directions*, ABC's ecumenical television series. All these broadcasts were aired in rotation with Protestant and Catholic television programming during the same time slot.

The formats of JTS's television programs varied. *Directions* was originally conceptualized as a "living magazine" with multiple segments, but it soon switched to presenting a variety of programming, including dramas, documentaries, interviews, and panel discussions. On NBC's television series, JTS continued to present dramas, some adapted from scripts originally heard on the radio version of *The Eternal Light*.[109] In the 1960s, JTS aired fewer television dramas on *The Eternal Light* and began producing original documentaries. Topics ranged from Jewish themes in Rembrandt's art and the Jewish contribution to the Renaissance to profiles of rabbinic scholar Solomon Schechter and Holocaust survivor Elie Wiesel. During this decade, *The Eternal Light* also began to televise interviews with prominent public figures, including ambassador Sol M. Linowitz, author James Michener, violinist Itzhak Perlman, Jewish Museum director Karl Katz, and theologian Abraham Joshua Heschel.[110]

These changes responded, in part, to budgetary constraints (notably, the much greater cost of producing television versus radio) and also reflected the general disappearance of radio drama from American broadcasting, as well as the decline in popularity of televising original dramas. Once considered the epitome of the medium's potential as a "high" art form, television's drama anthology series all but completely disappeared by the end of the 1950s, as production shifted from New York to Los Angeles and from live studio broadcasts to dramatic series filmed on location.[111] Moreover, these changes reflected a signal shift in American broadcasting policy. Beginning in 1960, a series of FCC rulings eliminated the requirement that national networks underwrite public-service programs as part of their licensing. The networks subsequently cut back the time and money allotted to ecumenical broadcasting, especially as selling airtime on Sunday mornings to individual churches proved increasingly profitable, thanks to the rise of televangelism. Media scholars Stewart Hoover and Douglas Wagner argue that "the relative advantage of . . . access to 'sustaining time' rather quickly turned to disadvantage" for mainstream religious organizations, when "economic and technological change made it possible for a range of evangelical and para-church institutions to achieve national distribution outside the network system."[112] Consequently, increasing numbers of network affiliates and independent stations dropped the ecumenical series from their schedules. Mainstream religious groups were eventually obliged either to purchase air time for theses broadcasts or to watch the size of their audience dwindle.[113] Thus, whereas over one hundred television stations carried *The Eternal Light* in the early 1970s, a Hanukkah special presented on the series in 1982 was aired by only twenty-two stations.[114]

Rather than increase the budgets for religious programming, mainstream religious groups proved more likely to shift their approach to broadcasting. Mainline Protestant groups, notes Rosenthal, "rejected television as an appropriate site for the production of liberal Protestant culture and instead focused upon cultural critique," for example, by establishing media watchdog groups.[115] Nor did JTS aggressively pursue new broadcasting ventures during the 1970s and '80s. Instead, the rising costs of media production, as well as institutional shifts in agenda away from general public outreach, led to a reduction of resources committed to the Radio and Television Department.

JTS's decision reflected a larger trend among American Jewish organizations regarding their involvement in intergroup relations. Svonkin notes that, beginning in the 1960s, "without abandoning their commitment to liberal activism, leaders and staff members [of these organizations] . . . increasingly distinguished Jewish interests from broader 'American-centered' concerns. This reassertion of ethnoreligious particularism reflected a significant change in the way that Jewish intergroup relations professionals conceived of anti-Semitism," regarding it less as a "model prejudice" that could be effectively addressed through "propaganda, education, and legal action" than as "a unique form of prejudice that was more pervasive and resilient than they had previously imagined." This growing attention to Jewish particularism also reflected the rise of American Jewish organizations' concern for "the problem of assimilation," which they viewed as an "erosion of a distinctively Jewish culture in the United States" that was the consequence of Jews' "socioeconomic, cultural and political achievement" in America.[116]

This shift in concern from anti-Semitism to assimilation resonates with changing strategies for American Jews' self-presentation, which religious broadcasts, especially those on television, problematized. Public-service broadcasting had enabled Jews to "adopt the attitude of the public subject," which literary scholar Michael Warner characterizes as entailing a "disincorporation" of the self, addressing "an abstract audience" that is the public. Such an approach to engaging the public space, pioneered in the print culture of eighteenth-century Western Europe, facilitated "a utopian universality that would allow people to transcend the given realities of their bodies and their status." The public sphere realized by this rhetorical strategy has, Warner argues, "a logic of abstraction that provides a privilege for unmarked identities: the white, the male, the middle class, the normal."[117]

With regard to the public sphere created by mid-twentieth-century American broadcasting, one could add to this list of "unmarked" categories the Protestant—or, at the very least, the Christian. (Hoover and Wagner note that "the fact that certain religious voices—specifically mainline Protestant and Roman Catholic—could be so facilely integrated into [national network broadcasting] is a measure of the prominence of institutional religion and of the relative consensual harmony that existed" at the time.)[118] "Publicness," Warner asserts, "is always able to encode itself through the themes of universality, openness, meritocracy, and access, all of which . . . guarantee . . . at every step that difference will be enunciated as . . . an ineluctable limit imposed by the particularities of the body, . . . [which] cannot translate or neutralize itself . . . without ceasing to exist."[119]

Wishengrad said of radio drama that, like dreaming, it "is always best when your eyes are closed."[120] This text-based medium, when enacted by unseen performers whose voices were ethnically "unmarked" (that is, they sounded like WASPs), facilitated the disincorporation of both subject and audience very effectively—so much so that, when American Jews' concerns about the loss of Jewish particularism came to the fore in the 1960s, this medium no longer seemed to serve as an effective vehicle for Jewish self-presentation. On television, conversely, the limitations of the "rhetorical strategy of personal abstraction" on which ecumenism relied became readily evident, as the medium compromised the power of invisibility enabled by radio. (As Warner notes, "Where printed public discourse . . . relied on a rhetoric of abstract embodiment, visual media . . . display bodies.")[121]

The dynamic dilemma of Jewish self-presentation on the airwaves occasionally complicated JTS's self-reflexive discussions of its efforts. For example, in listing actors who had performed on the radio version of *The Eternal Light*, a twenty-fifth-anniversary press release mentioned "Juano Hernandez, an extremely gifted Negro actor who found on the Eternal Light the opportunity to play a wider range of roles than he was able to secure in commercial radio. The program has never used the shield of 'type casting' to bar performers of any race or creed."[122] Here, in an effort to champion the values inherent in its radio dramas, JTS took the public "behind the scenes" to reveal that, even in the production of these broadcasts, it enacted an ethics of combating prejudice. To demonstrate this, however, the Seminary had to expose its efforts to render difference invisible, revealing a different drama—one of struggling with racial typing and discrimination—at work.

As *The Eternal Light* dramas disappeared from the airwaves, so did most other ecumenical programming. According to media scholar Hal Erickson, this attrition was not only a consequence of changes in the networks' protocols regarding public-service broadcasting, the rise of televangelism, or budgetary concerns but also because these series were increasingly addressing controversial topical issues, especially the war in Vietnam.[123] Instead of facilitating a national consensus, these programs became forums for divisive debates. After the heyday of the ecumenical series, Judaism was engaged only occasionally on network religious broadcasts, such as the short-lived children's series *Marshall Efron's Illustrated, Simplified and Painless Sunday School*, which aired on CBS in the early 1970s. And a very different kind of religious programming targeted Jewish viewers, with the advent in the 1970s of various proselytizing broadcasts produced by the Evangelistic Jewish movement (popularly known as Jews for Jesus).

At the same time, new forms of Jewish self-portraiture emerged on prime-time American broadcasting, as a consequence of changes in television programming and general notions about Jewish presence in American public culture.[124] In the 1970s, dramatic and comedy series increasingly took up the subject of Jewish religiosity, following the precedent of *The Goldbergs*, offering occasional episodes about a Jewish holiday or life-cycle celebration or addressing the problem of anti-Semitism. Topics in Jewish history, from the Bible to the Holocaust, once only dramatized on ecumenical broadcasts, became the subject of prime-time television mini-series (*Moses, the Lawgiver*, CBS, 1975; *Holocaust: The Story of the Family Weiss*, NBC, 1978). Broadcast documentaries, especially on public television, explored subjects ranging from Jewish popular culture to the broad sweep of Jewish history (*Heritage: Civilization and the Jews*, PBS, 1984). And Jews as a political force, both in Israel and in the diaspora, are now regularly discussed on local and national newscasts.

Newer technologies have also had their impact on Americans Jews' use of the media for self-portraiture. Just as the advent of radio and television facilitated JTS's efforts to address the American public in the mid-twentieth century, video, satellite broadcasting, and the Internet have played strategic roles in the more recent, very different approach to outreach by Lubavitcher hasidim (discussed in chapter 6). Home videotape and DVD players have extended the opportunities for disseminating and collecting media of Jewish interest, exemplified by the Jewish Heritage Video Collection, assembled in 1990s by the Jewish Media Fund "to explore Jewish heritage through the unique resources of film and television," thereby addressing "vital issues of Jewish history, identity, and culture."[125] Among this library of some two hundred media works are several telecasts originally produced by JTS for ecumenical programming. But most of the Seminary's hundreds of radio and television broadcasts are no longer accessible for repeat listening or viewing, even in media archives.

Striving to articulate a public image of Judaism as a source of enduring, universal values, the creators of *The Eternal Light* encountered an unstable complex of challenges: the shifting interests of commercial broadcasting, the dynamics of new media, the problematics of conjoining art and theology, the less-than-perfect fit of Jewishness with the rubric of religion, the changing social and political landscape of postwar America. As JTS fashioned its approach to ecumenical programming, it engendered more than the innovations in religious broadcasting and radio drama for which it was lauded. The broadcasts themselves, as well as the context of their production and reception, enabled new possibilities for Jewish religiosity by creating a new phenomenon perceived as existing somewhere between established notions of the sacred and the secular. Instead of being centered on liturgy or scripture, *The Eternal Light* placed drama at the fore— and with it, a humanistic focus on affect and interpersonal relations. Rather than convening in a synagogue or other established Jewish locus, JTS spoke from the virtual platform of broadcasting, with its own distinctive hybridization of private and public space. Through regular scheduling, *The Eternal Light* created its own kind of ritual, making the day after the Jewish Sabbath a new high point in Jews' weekly calendar. Instead of convening a congregation, JTS addressed an audience—one that not only symbolically brought together Jews and Christians (while each remained in their own homes) but also existed in the minds of each individual listener who imagined this attenuated communion among fellow Americans. On *The Eternal Light,* the authority of rabbis or other scholars often yielded to the leadership of media artists, and Judaism was transformed from a devotional practice into a complex of mediations: facilitating the promotion of Jewish ethics as universal, reeducating Americans about the worthiness of Jewish heroes and the general compatibility of Jews as a people, exhorting a dispersed and disaffected Jewry to take pride in its Jewishness, and situating Judaism as a point of entry to Jewish history and culture.

The Eternal Light proved to be a highly contingent phenomenon, a result of the confluence of dynamic social, political, cultural, economic, theological, and aesthetic factors. Its decline gave way to new possibilities (and impossibilities) for conjoining Judaism and broadcasting in the United States. Beyond its value as an artifact of a distinct moment in the histories of American religion or broadcasting, Jewish ecumenical broadcasting endures obliquely as a threshold moment in the public culture of American Judaism, in which the possibilities of finding cultural, even spiritual, value in self-portraiture as seen in the imagined gaze of others were first explored on such a grand scale.

3

The Scar without the Wound

And the Lord spoke to Moses, saying: Speak to the children of
Israel, and tell them to make a yellow star upon their garments
throughout their generations, one star over their heart and one on
their back, of equal size and proportion: and it shall be for you a
sign, that you may look upon it, and remember all the commandments of the Lord, and do them.
—from the service for Holocaust Remembrance Day, First United
Methodist Church, Santa Monica, 29 April 1984

As Holocaust remembrance became pervasive in American
public culture during the final decades of the twentieth century, continuing into the present with no signs of abating, it has frequently been conceptualized in relation to religion. Given the complexity of the Holocaust
and the means of remembering it, these conceptualizations are far from
uniform. The Holocaust has engendered its own theological discourses, in
which different Jewish and Christian denominations have been compelled
by the mass murder of Jews and other European civilian populations
during World War II to respond anew to age-old questions of theodicy.[1]
Holocaust remembrance has also been incorporated into established religious practices. Among Jews, these range from Orthodox *kinot* (elegies)
recited on Tishah b'Ab (a day of mourning the destruction of the First
and Second Temples in ancient Jerusalem) to the official liturgy of Reform Judaism.[2] Christian examples of Holocaust commemoration include
special worship services, sermons, and performances, as well as memorial
artwork installed in churches.

More extensive, and more exemplary of a distinctly American response,
are an array of practices characterized as the civil religion of Holocaust
remembrance. Among these practices are official days of Holocaust

remembrance, both national and local, marked by public ceremonies; memorial sites, such as monuments and museums; and pedagogical undertakings, including state-mandated Holocaust education programs. Not only do these practices make frequent use of all manner of media—publications, films, broadcasts, displays, works of visual and performance art— but they are also by their nature mediating practices, bringing Holocaust remembrance to a population that, with few exceptions, has no direct experience of or personal connection to these events.

The term *civil religion* has been in use since its coinage by Jean-Jacques Rousseau in the mid-eighteenth century to identify definitional beliefs and practices of civil societies as having the authority and gravitas, if not the numinous aura, of religion.[3] A term now employed by historians, political scientists, sociologists, and communications scholars to identify a wide range of social practices, civil religion is generally characterized as either paralleling or replacing religion, which serves as the paradigm for conceptualizing the fundamental nature of how civil societies establish collectives in thought and deed.[4] Holocaust memory practices exemplify but also complicate the notion of civil religion, perhaps because of the disturbing questions about religious beliefs and practices that the Holocaust raises. Both Christians and Jews are haunted by questions of theodicy (where was God?) and about the efficacy of religious practice by clergy and their followers (where was humanity?). Religious differences both during the Holocaust and afterward complicate desires for a communion among faiths in Holocaust remembrance. Civil religion more typically is understood in relation to nationalism, and this concept, too, is problematic regarding both the history of the Holocaust and its memorialization among various nations. Moreover, the commitment of civil religion to finding something edifying, inspiring, or unifying in Holocaust remembrance is tested by the nature of such an abject event, which, if anything, demonstrates the extent to which civil societies can fail to be civil.

These concerns challenge the civil religion of Holocaust remembrance in all nations, but they do so differently in each case, due not only to matters of national history and contemporary politics but also to cultural configurations. In the United States, the salience of mediations distinguishes its practices of Holocaust remembrance from others. As I have noted elsewhere,

> The Holocaust's singular place in the moral vocabulary of so many Americans is largely a product of the distinctive nature of Holocaust memory

culture in this country. In Europe, the former Soviet Union, and Israel, Holocaust remembrance has been realized as powerfully, if not more so, through the extensive presence of survivors of World War II or geographical landmarks. But in America this subject has almost always been mediated through newspapers, magazines, books, theaters, exhibition galleries, concert halls, or radio and television broadcasting.[5]

Not only do mediations help bridge the geographic, cultural, and temporal distances between Americans and the Holocaust, but they also help negotiate the challenges that Holocaust remembrance poses to American civil religion. Besides addressing the dilemma of sacralizing the remembrance of mass murder, these works engage the challenge posed by the mediated nature of Holocaust remembrance in America. Often these works respond self-reflexively to widespread concerns about the appropriateness—or even the possibility—of mediating this episode of history.[6]

Yet even as scholars and critics problematize these mediations, they are readily embraced by creators of public culture as vehicles for rendering the Holocaust morally significant for Americans. As a result, Holocaust mediations have prompted an extensive series of public conversations on the nature of mediation itself, situating the Holocaust as an exemplum of collective memory, of juxtaposing history against memory, of deriving ethical lessons from destruction, of the challenges that aesthetics poses to remembrance, and so on. Especially revealing are conversations inspired by Holocaust remembrance in new media, exemplified by television, wherein the concomitant novelty of the medium and of Holocaust remembrance provided especially protean opportunities for new memory practices. Similar innovative practices take place in other new media, such as video and the Internet, and in novel uses of established media—notably, the emergence of Holocaust film, music, pedagogy, museums, and tourism.

This chapter considers the wide array of Holocaust memory practices in America as sites where new media and religion converge within the rubric of civil religion. In particular, this chapter examines how established religious practices—performing redemptive dramas, enacting rituals, imparting moral instruction, undertaking pilgrimages, erecting monuments—inform Holocaust remembrance, simultaneously serving as sources of inspiration and posing challenges to the possibilities of memory. At the same time, this chapter explores the interrelation of Holocaust remembrance with religion as bilateral, in which efforts to commemorate recent events not only draw on longstanding religious traditions but also inform or challenge religious practices—and, at times, the very idea of religiosity.

Redemptive Dramas

Discussions of mediating the Holocaust regularly fault American feature films on the subject, especially those made by major Hollywood studios, for failing to confront "the darker realities of World War II." In the 1980s, pioneers of Holocaust film studies, such as Annette Insdorf, suggested that "perhaps the cinema of a country that has never experienced occupation cannot plumb the depths of the Holocaust experience." Ilan Avisar similarly wrote of "Hollywood's inherent incapacity when it comes to dealing with a subject of the magnitude of the Holocaust."[7] In these and similar arguments, American naiveté or the venality of its commercial film industry prevent the creation of works of Holocaust cinema sufficient in their historical accuracy, intellectual insight, moral complexity, or aesthetic gravitas. Holocaust scholars reiterate this sentiment as they scrutinize popular mediations of this epoch. Tim Cole, for example, decries the "Hollywoodization" of the Holocaust, in which films such as *Schindler's List* (1993) offer a Holocaust "with a happy ending." The trope continues into the present century: in a 2005 survey of American Holocaust films, Trudy Gold writes, "The fear is that we will only be left with Hollywood."[8]

These sentiments are part of a larger discourse on Holocaust representation that repeatedly expresses concerns over the irresolvable character of this subject's enormity; literary scholar Lawrence Langer, for example, has long warned against works that "misleadingly identify the Holocaust as a healable offense."[9] Yet such critiques of American feature films on the Holocaust tend to overlook what motivations prompt the attraction of uplifting, restorative Holocaust dramas among both their creators and their audiences. Indeed, Hollywood films frequently decried for their redemptive messages—notably *The Diary of Anne Frank* (1959) and *Schindler's List*—are among the most widely popular mediations of the Holocaust, both in the United States and abroad.

These films' uplifting messages are far from exceptional. Indeed, they iterate sentiments of some of the earliest American works of Holocaust remembrance: dramas produced by religious and civic Jewish organizations for national broadcast media in the immediate postwar years. Among these are scripts for the NBC radio series *The Eternal Light* (see chapter 2), which valorized Jewish heroism during the war (such as *The Lantern in the Inferno*, a 1945 drama about resistance fighter Hannah Senesh) and celebrated the reaffirmation of life after the war's end (*Zipporah*, a 1948 portrait of concentration camp survivors).[10] Similar dramas were televised throughout the 1950s on both Sunday ecumenical programs (including *Anne Frank: The Diary of a Young Girl*, the first American dramatization of that book) and prime-time drama anthology series (Paddy Chayefsky's *Holiday Song*, on *Philco Television Playhouse* in 1952; Rod Serling's *In the Presence of Mine Enemies*, on *Playhouse 90* in 1960).[11] One of television's most popular entertainment series in the 1950s, *This Is Your Life*, offered a half-dozen tributes to Holocaust survivors and rescuers of victims of Nazi persecution, relating their life stories as narratives of triumph over adversity through the program's unique format of reuniting honorees with figures from their past—including, in the earliest of these telecasts, aired in 1953, a reunion of one Holocaust survivor with her brother, whom she had not seen since before the start of World War II.[12]

These redemptive broadcasts echo sentiments often expressed in educational programs, sermons, memorial ceremonies, and publications that American Jewish communities began offering in the early postwar years. According to historian Hasia Diner, these efforts typically responded to the horrors of the Holocaust with valorization of Jewish resilience and messages of hope for the future.[13] Such impulses are hardly unprecedented. The pervasive desire for an uplifting response to the Holocaust conforms with foundational Jewish and Christian narratives of redemption following adversity (the Exodus, the Passion) and with American memory practices that emphasize optimism, consensus, and a "quest for reconciliation."[14]

By the late 1950s, redemptive Holocaust dramas had become mainstays of the American broadcasting calendar, especially as an integral component of Passover programming, following the precedent of earlier American Jewish commemorations.[15] With regular scheduling of programs on the topic aired at that time of year, the Holocaust joined other fixtures of American broadcasting's annual calendar of occasions for special programming, such as national holidays and the Christmas and Easter seasons. Thus, the *Jewish Daily Forward* of 19 April 1959 noted on its television and radio page that, "as happens every year," broadcasters had scheduled several special programs in honor of Passover, including an installment of the religion series *Look Up and Live* (CBS) entitled *The*

John Cassavettes (left) in *The Final Ingredient*, Reginald Rose's original television drama about Jewish spiritual resistance in a Nazi concentration camp, aired on ABC on the day before Passover, 1959. (Joseph and Miriam Ratner Center for the Study of Conservative Judaism, Jewish Theological Seminary of America)

Razing of the Warsaw Ghetto and *The Final Ingredient* (ABC), an original play by Reginald Rose, who, like Chayefsky and Serling, was among the most celebrated authors of prime-time television dramas in the 1950s.[16] Set in a concentration camp, Rose's half-hour play depicts Jewish inmates' efforts to celebrate a Passover seder, focusing on one young man's struggle with his faith. A critic who reviewed *The Final Ingredient* for *Variety* described Rose's play as "a blend of drama and ritual that had an added sock," coming on the eve of Passover.[17]

Linking these dramas with religion entails more than their frequent portrayal of Jewish religious practice (just as *The Final Ingredient* is set on Passover, *Holiday Song* takes place on the eve of Rosh Hashanah) or discussions among characters of theological questions. Nor is the association of Holocaust films and broadcasts with religion primarily a matter of the way these media are understood as either constituting something analogous to popular religion, "instruct[ing] us in the basic values and myths of our society," or offering an experience that inherently inspires devotional engagement by the audience, given the medium's potential "to be transformative."[18] Rather, the notion that Holocaust media provides something akin to a religious experience—that is, an encounter with something morally or spiritually galvanizing—lies outside the films and broadcasts themselves. This notion is instead manifest in the epiphenomena of Holocaust media, especially the exceptional circumstances of their presentation and reception, which strive to differentiate the experience of these films and broadcasts from the protocols of the entertainment genres in which they are created. Indeed, the exceptional character of the way audiences are meant to experience these dramas affirms the public's investment in the Holocaust as a singular subject of moral engagement.

In 1961, United Artists presented the feature film *Judgment at Nuremberg* as both a star-studded courtroom drama and an exceptional, morally charged experience. The film's structure merges the audience's act of watching with the task of sitting in judgment of Nazi war criminals and, ultimately, with the onus of witnessing atrocity footage, screened at a climactic point in the trial.[19] American audiences were also invited to consider their own watching of *Judgment at Nuremberg* in relation to the film's world premiere (at the Kongresshalle in Berlin on 14 December 1961) and American premiere (at a benefit for the U.S. Committee for the United Nations), each of which was conceived as a morally infused symbolic performance. United Artists explained to exhibitors that the Berlin premiere drew attention by coinciding with the city's "crisis over 'the wall' incident"; literary scholar Alan Mintz notes that the premiere also resonated with the recently concluded war-crimes trial of Adolf Eichmann in Israel.[20] United Artists also suggested that, besides arranging special student screenings, exhibitors could localize the moral force of *Judgment at Nuremberg* by staging their own "Hollywood type opening night" for the film in conjunction with "a worthy and important charity."[21]

A generation later, *Schindler's List* was screened in American theaters with special protocols, eschewing trailers or commercials during its original theatrical release. When the film premiered in Germany, the question was raised of whether it was appropriate to eat popcorn during the screening.[22] These efforts to transform a night at the movies into a moral touchstone were deftly lampooned in a 1994 episode of the television situation comedy *Seinfeld* (NBC), in which Jerry Seinfeld's friends and family are shocked to discover that he and his girlfriend were necking during a screening of *Schindler's List*—that is, behaving as if it were just another movie.[23]

In fact, audiences regularly assign their own meanings to popular works of Holocaust remembrance, negotiating among the possibilities of entertainment, civil religion, or other valences, and sometimes assigning these works the value of a definitional rite. Consider Mintz's recollection of how, as a teenager in 1961, he anticipated seeing *Judgment at Nuremberg*:

> I realized that I had been permitted to go to an over three-hour movie on a school night because this was not an entertainment but an event, an event that was significant in the life of the small but intense Jewish community of which we were a part. . . . *Judgment at Nuremberg* was the first time in general American mass culture in which the terrible things that had been done to the Jews of Europe were being publicly acknowledged. Although it was not talked about very openly, the murder of European Jewry was a tragedy we [in our Jewish community] were all aware of. . . . But as Jews, we regarded this knowledge as a private sorrow that was not shared by the non-Jewish majority of Americans. This new motion picture, straight from Hollywood with a panoply of stars, changed that. So that despite whatever [director] Stanley Kramer was saying in interviews, . . . we had our own conviction of what *Judgment at Nuremberg* was "about."[24]

The 1978 miniseries *Holocaust: The Story of the Family Weiss* (NBC), arguably the single most influential American telecast dealing with this subject, inspired a similar anticipation among American Jews of a public event of definitional value. A feature on the miniseries in *Moment*, a popular American Jewish magazine, stated that, for its readership, "the watching has about it the quality of a religious obligation."[25] NBC reinforced this association by linking the broadcast to fixtures of the Jewish calendar. The miniseries was presented in three-hour installments on four consecutive evenings during the week before the start of Passover, with its final episode airing on the thirty-fifth anniversary of the Warsaw Ghetto Uprising. Watched, at least in part, by half of all Americans, the *Holocaust* miniseries engendered an extensive public discussion, much of which concerned the propriety of presenting this exceptional subject on such an unabashedly popular medium.

The 130 advertisements aired during the miniseries provoked indignation from many critics, who decried these commercial "interruptions" more than any aspect of the television drama itself. Notwithstanding the fact that advertisements are a mainstay of commercial television, their presence during the miniseries was repeatedly assailed as a sign of the moral failings of the entire enterprise, which, at its worst, was deemed not merely sacrilegious but a virtual perpetuation of genocide. In the *Journal of Reform Judaism,* Martin Bernard characterized the "intrusion of advertisements for so many American products" as nothing less than "of the same technological capacity that produced Zyklon-B gas in Germany for expediting the 'final solution of the Jewish problem.'"[26]

In such critiques, the notion that commercials interrupting a Holocaust drama—as if it were just another television program—constitutes a moral failure not only evinces the sanctity with which the Holocaust has come to be regarded. It also reveals an expectation that popular media can and, moreover, ought to satisfy a public desire for ennobling encounters with the Holocaust through works of entertainment. This notion that America's large, diverse public can be inspired to moral improvement by a mediated encounter with the Holocaust exemplifies what communications scholar James Carey describes as the "ritual" nature of mass communication, in which "a particular view of the world is portrayed and confirmed" through mediations that are "dramatically satisfying."[27]

Rituals

The notion of film, broadcasting, or some other mass medium facilitating rituals of Holocaust remembrance may seem counterintuitive. Such rituals have become common American practices, held in schools, houses of worship, government facilities, and other public settings, usually on officially recognized days of remembrance (19 April, the start of the Warsaw Ghetto Uprising in 1943; 29 April, when American armed forces liberated Dachau in 1945; Yom Ha-Sho'ah, Israel's day of Holocaust remembrance, which occurs in late April or early May; 9 November, the start of Kristallnacht in 1938). Typically these rituals have an austere aesthetic and eschew electronic media, instead consisting of speeches, recitations, songs (often unaccompanied), and the lighting of memorial candles.[28] The "liveness" of these memorial programs has special, if tacit, performative value. The appearance of Holocaust survivors at these events embodies their tenacious defiance of the Nazi genocide, and their descendants' presence evinces Jewish communal endurance. The participation of non-Jewish government officials and clergy in these ceremonies testifies to the respect that authority figures outside the Jewish community accord to Holocaust remembrance.[29]

Through mass media, some of these rituals reach larger audiences, which on occasion are international in scope. Such was the case with the *Papal Concert to Commemorate the Holocaust*, performed at the Vatican on 7 April 1994 and subsequently aired on American television. At the behest of Pope John Paul II, this hour-long "interfaith concert" commemorated the Holocaust and the Roman Catholic Church's official recognition of the State of Israel. Hosted by American actor Richard Dreyfuss, the concert featured performances by the London Royal Philharmonic and the Choir of St. Peter's Basilica, conducted by another American, Gilbert Levine. Musical selections included classical settings of Jewish scripture and liturgy—Max Bruch's *Kol Nidre* for cello and orchestra, Franz Schubert's setting of Psalm 92, excerpts from Leonard Bernstein's Symphony No. 3, "*Kaddish*," and his *Chichester Psalms*—as well as the third movement of Beethoven's Symphony No. 9, a work that has come to be widely regarded in the West as emblematic of universal humanism. In addition to the pope, the chief rabbi of Rome and the president of Italy attended the concert. Among the invited audience of over seventy-five hundred were more than two hundred Holocaust survivors.

Though the Vatican arranged the concert, it was first proposed by Levine, who had met the pope while serving as artistic director of the Cracow Philharmonic. Interviewed during the telecast before the start of the concert, Levine explained that both Jewish and Catholic leaders had agreed straightaway that music was the "proper form" for expressing their "commonality of purpose." Unlike drama, speeches, or a scholarly colloquium, music had the special value of "speak[ing] without words." In fact, music proved strategic in eliding the discursive challenges that such a meeting of Catholics and Jews might prompt. Although the concert was characterized as a ritual of religious reconciliation—in the pope's words, expressing the desire, "with the help of Almighty God, [to] work together to help prevent the repetition of such a heinous event" as the Holocaust— the performance employed the idioms of humanistic culture.[30] Both the decorous protocols of the classical music concert and its musical harmonies modeled accord for Jews and Christians in the face of lingering historical and theological tensions.

The *Papal Concert* exemplifies what communications scholars Daniel Dayan and Elihu Katz term *media events*—"high holidays" in the calendar of television broadcasting, ranging from live broadcasts of coronations and lunar landings to coverage of the Olympics—and their complex engagement with religion. Dayan and Katz note that, as "media events mark holidays of the civil religion," they "perform some of the same function as religious holidays." These broadcasts often involve religious rites and leaders, which lend "aura to the state" and can "blur the boundary between the sacred and the profane," especially through "clashes of symbols." The media event thereby "becomes a new liturgy in itself" as it "blur[s] the limits between religions, promoting an ecumenism of [its] own. . . . The thrust of media events is to stress shared features, to disregard irreducible differences between religions." Instead, these broadcasts "tend to recast specific religions as 'religion' in general."[31] What media events such as the *Papal Concert* espouse and validate is a faith in reconciliation per se, more so than a particular faith doctrine.

The concert broadcast presented the Holocaust as a touchstone for a civil religion that elides, even as it acknowledges, Jewish exceptionalism, while also leaving unaddressed the implications for Christian theology. Historian Alan Steinweis has noted this implicit dilemma in an essay on the way Nebraskans found an array of meanings in Holocaust remembrance during the 1990s. He reports that one of his students,

who described herself as a traditional, conservative Catholic, told me that her interest in the Holocaust was stimulated by the Catholic-Jewish dialogue that has been promoted by Pope John Paul II. She praised the pope for recognizing and attempting to rectify a historic wrong and sees it as her responsibility as a Catholic to participate in the process of reconciliation. Whether such sentiments reflect an acceptance of Judaism as theologically legitimate is hard to say, considering that open discussion of this extremely sensitive dimension of the issue is assiduously avoided by just about everyone.[32]

Sometimes religious rituals provide a rubric for works of Holocaust media that, instead of disseminating or incorporating ritual, interrogate its moral value in relation to the Holocaust. In the 1993 sound recording *Requiem: The Holocaust*, composer David Axelrod employs classical and jazz idioms in a work that juxtaposes the Requiem mass with descriptions of the Holocaust. The four movements link sections of the mass with stages of the Nazi persecution of European Jews—"Introit/Krystallnacht," "Kyrie/Trains," "Sanctus/Auschwitz," and "Dies Irae/Gas Chambers"—and the text ironizes the Latin liturgy through its interpolation into the

composer's Holocaust poetry, for example: "Even the ashes of the victims /
Went into the war effort / As fertilizer // This then was Auschwitz // Sanctus, Sanctus, Sanctus / Dominus, Deus sabaoth."

In this work, a mass medium facilitates a Holocaust ritual that resists,
rather than promotes, accord. Axelrod's use of ironic juxtapositions to
voice moral indignation is rooted in the work's inspiration, as the recording's liner notes explain: "'I was watching the trial of [white supremacist
and Holocaust denier] Tom Metzger on TV,' Axelrod recalls, 'And I got
so upset at what he was saying . . . that I looked at my wife and said,
"I'm going to stop the project I'm working on and write something about
this." And this is the result.'"[33] Axelrod responded to one morally disturbing mediation—a Holocaust denier's invasion of the privacy and comfort of home via the television set—with an unsettling media work of
his own, which also offered a counterritual to the public rite of the court
trial. Axelrod's ironized hybrid of Catholic liturgy and Holocaust imagery
both evokes religious authority and questions it, alluding obliquely to the
issue of Christian indifference to Jewish suffering during World War II.
Whereas the *Papal Concert* draws on established concert repertoire, *Requiem: The Holocaust* offers an original composition of abrupt juxtapositions of disparate sounds, including sung and spoken texts, as well as of
musical styles (jazz, religious chanting, modern classical). Circulated as
an audio recording, it engages listeners independent of the presence of
performers, performance venue, or live audience, all of which are key to
the ritual significance of the *Papal Concert*.

Indeed, the context for presenting media works can be essential to imbuing them with ritual value. Screening films as part of Holocaust commemorations has a considerable history in the United States. For example,
Alain Renais's 1955 documentary *Nuit et Brouillard* was shown at Jewish
summer camps as part of Holocaust remembrance programs held on
Tishah b'Ab in the early 1960s.[34] As the inventory of Holocaust media has
expanded in the postwar decades, so have notions of how these works
might be incorporated into ritual practice. In the early 1980s, Eric Goldman, then director of the Jewish Media Service, speculated that film could
facilitate what amounts to a new Holocaust ritual for American Jews.
Goldman compared the role that these works play in contemporary Jewish culture with that of the Passover haggadah: "Every year . . . we read
in our haggadah that it is the obligation of parents to tell their children
of the affliction of our enslaved ancestors in Egypt. So, now, must each
generation be told of the Holocaust; so, now, must a different haggadah

be prepared. . . . The cinematic medium has begun to provide us with a means for the retelling of this massive story."[35]

Goldman's analogy of cinema and the seder suggests that screening films has the potential to become an annual rite of education and remembrance not only for the American public or the Jewish community but also for individual families. Instead of gathering around the dinner table, parents and children might gather around the television set to watch broadcasts, videotapes, or DVDs to recount, learn, and discuss. This suggestion marks a striking departure from widespread notions of television as a destructive force in family life; in 1956, for example, Gunther Anders dubbed the television screen a "negative family table." But Goldman argued that, far from Anders's fears of "dissolving" and "decentralizing" the family unit,[36] the television set can bring family members together for a shared experience of viewing a definitional narrative, followed by group reflection and analysis.

The use of new media in impromptu rituals of Holocaust remembrance is especially revealing, because audiences, rather than producers or broadcasters, initiate these practices. The decisions to present these works and the responses they engender reveal shared assumptions about their significance and their potential for ritual engagement. These are examples of a popular, rather than official, civil religion of Holocaust remembrance. Consider, for example, a memorial program described in a report published by the American Jewish Congress in the spring of 1961. As the war-crimes trial of Adolf Eichmann, under way in Jerusalem, was being televised around the world, the Hillel Foundation at Purdue University arranged a special screening of *Engineer of Death*, a dramatized biography of Eichmann that had recently been aired on CBS's *Armstrong Circle Theater*. (The kinescope shown included commercials that were part of the original broadcast. These, the report explains, were "greeted with sighs of relief" by the audience at Purdue, who, rather than taking offense at the advertisements, as many people did during the 1978 miniseries, "seemed glad to be returned to everyday reality.")[37]

The campus screening, presented to an audience of Jews and Christians, was followed by a panel discussion on the topic, "Is There a Nazi Personality?" The panelists—a sociologist who had fled Nazi Germany as a child, a psychologist who had formerly lived in Vienna, and an American-born clinical psychologist—debated whether the Nazi persecution of European Jewry was a singular phenomenon or was rooted in more universal impulses. The event's setting further complicated this conjoining of television drama with the insights of medical and social scientists. Presented in the campus's "Hillel auditorium that doubles as a synagogue," the screening fused idioms of American popular culture and secular higher education with those of traditional religious devotion, some of which were spontaneous and perhaps prompted by the setting. "Waiting for the lights to go down," the report noted, the audience "sat pensively, somewhat in the manner of worshippers assembled for the Kol Nidrei service." After the panel discussion, "a young man who had escaped the wrath of the Nazis by hiding as a child with partisans in the Polish woods, and now served the local synagogue, stood up to recite the mourner's Kaddish. . . . During the brief Hebrew chant, the Episcopal minister and others [attending the screening] crossed themselves in silent devotion."[38] While the scholarly panel discussion raised challenging questions, divisive and unresolved, about the human capacity for totalitarianism and genocide, religious ritual offered an ameliorating performance of a pluralistic, mutually respectful reverence for God.

Doubtless the most widespread use of a work of Holocaust media to facilitate rites of moral engagement in the United States are special screenings for high-school students of *Schindler's List*, events that assumed that watching the film "should be treated as a religious experience."[39] As noted earlier, when the film premiered, it was widely discussed as transcending the protocols of entertainment. Moreover, the potential of *Schindler's List* to be ritualized is implicit in the film itself, which is framed by scenes of ritual behavior—opening with the lighting of Sabbath candles and concluding with an elaborate enactment of honoring the dead by visiting their graves.

Many American high-school students attended special, often mandatory screenings of *Schindler's List* shortly after the film's theatrical release in December 1993. Although some of these screenings were impromptu undertakings, Steven Spielberg's production company, Amblin Entertainment, offered the film as "the cornerstone of a nationwide Holocaust education project" in the fall of 1994. The filmmaker explained, "We offer a curriculum and free screenings of the film at a designated theater for program participants. We're working with the organization Facing History [and] Ourselves to put together that curriculum." Spielberg explained why, even though *Schindler's List* was then available on video, the project insisted on screening the film in theaters: "First, it's a field trip, so it's a mini-event. Then, it takes some effort to get there. Next, it takes students out of the classroom and into a strange place. It's dark, and every motion picture theater has all the incumbent magic that when the lights go down anything goes. The students are 'there.' It makes kids feel much more a part of the experience because they themselves don't feel they are on safe, familiar ground."⁴⁰ Spielberg characterizes moviegoing as an adventure somewhat akin to pilgrimage, a journey that transports travelers both physically and spiritually.

Elsewhere, Spielberg positioned the Holocaust as a paradigm with universal implications, stating that *Schindler's List* is "about human suffering. About the Jews, yes, because they were the ones Hitler wanted to annihilate. But it's [also] about AIDS, the Armenians, the Bosnians. It's a part of all of us."⁴¹ However, student screenings of *Schindler's List* did not always facilitate the envisioned expansive, morally transformative experience. In some instances, Americans' productive use of the Holocaust as an analogy for a wide array of social concerns complicated the film's paradigmatic moral value. For example, members of the anti-abortion-rights group Massachusetts Citizens for Life provoked controversy when they attempted to exploit a student screening of *Schindler's List* in Great Barrington to distribute literature about what the organization denounced as "America's Holocaust."⁴²

On another occasion, the failure of this screening ritual became, according to one observer, a national "morality tale" in its own right. During a showing of *Schindler's List* in Oakland, California, on Martin Luther King Jr.'s birthday in 1994, a group of high-school students, most of whom were African Americans, were asked to leave the movie theater after laughing during a scene in which a German officer shot a Jewish prisoner. The students' behavior and their ejection from the theater quickly became the subject of debate in national print and broadcast media. This debate, in turn, engendered its own metadiscussion, as participants considered what in fact was at stake in this incident and the ensuing controversy. Much of the public discussion centered on American identity politics, disparaged in an op-ed in the *Washington Post* as "the current hair trigger mind-set toward anything that might qualify as cultural insensitivity."⁴³ But perhaps the incident was so provocative because it demonstrated a failure to relate the Holocaust's moral stature to that of civil rights leader Martin Luther King Jr. The desired transformative ritual—in which the moral value of the Holocaust would become readily apparent and universally accessible in the forum of American popular culture par excellence, the movie theater—became instead an occasion for exposing disparities in cultural and ethical sensibilities among an American public divided by competing notions of disrespect and sacrilege. Indeed, this incident demonstrates how lessons learned from exercises in Holocaust remembrance are not always what instructors wish to impart—and sometimes can even contravene the envisioned edification.

Moral Instruction

Notwithstanding the challenges in teaching about the Holocaust, morally charged pedagogy has been a mainstay of Holocaust remembrance from early in its history. Over time, the pedagogical agenda has moved beyond an immediate postwar concern with informing the public of the facts of what were then called "Nazi atrocities." This agenda was a high priority in the final days of the war in Europe, as mandated by General Dwight Eisenhower, who regarded the testimony offered by soldiers who had witnessed conditions in liberated concentration camps essential to explaining the war's moral imperative to the American public. This concern also informed the Allies' early postwar commitment to hold war crimes trials in occupied Germany.[44]

As the facts of the Holocaust became well established and organized into a master narrative, forming the basis of numerous public education efforts (textbooks, museum exhibitions, documentary films, and so on), the motives for teaching about the Holocaust have expanded. Beyond offering an exposition of atrocities, Holocaust pedagogy is now often motivated by a desire to engage this subject as a moral paradigm. Arthur A. Cohen observed in 1981 that, to some extent, this development was a consequence of a new generation coming of age, one

> that knows nothing directly of the Hitler years and the immediate shock of their ferocity. To this generation the question of meaning has become critical. It is the generation that bears the scar without the wound, sustaining memory without direct experience. It is this generation that has the obligation, self-imposed and self-accepted (however ineluctably), to describe a meaning and wrest instruction from the historical, while believing (perhaps innocently) that understanding is a shield and buckler against repetition of the same catastrophe.[45]

By the end of the twentieth century, this generational shift in approaches to Holocaust remembrance informed American educational policy on a large scale, including several states' requiring Holocaust education for all public-school students. For example, in 1994, the state legislature in New Jersey approved a mandate that

> every board of education shall include instruction on the Holocaust and genocides in an appropriate place in the curriculum of all elementary and secondary school pupils. . . . The instruction shall enable pupils to identify and analyze applicable theories concerning human nature and behavior: to understand that genocide is a consequence of prejudice and discrimination: and to understand that issues of moral dilemma and conscience have a profound impact on life. The instruction shall further emphasize the personal responsibility that each citizen bears to fight racism and hatred whenever and wherever it happens.[46]

Here, the Holocaust is endorsed as a subject of study in its own right and, even more so, as a paradigm for the study of other genocides and an admonition on the potential consequences of bigotry and intolerance encountered in students' own lives. Thus, Holocaust education straddles more conventional educational objectives of mastering information and developing analytic skills, on one hand, and actively engaging with questions of ethics and values, on the other hand. Facing History and Ourselves, an "international educational and professional development organization" that has provided Holocaust pedagogical materials and teacher training since its founding in 1976, characterizes its mission as

> engag[ing] students of diverse backgrounds in an examination of racism, prejudice, and antisemitism in order to promote the development of a more humane and informed citizenry. By studying the historical development and lessons of the Holocaust and other examples of genocide, students make the essential connection between history and the moral choices they confront in their own lives. . . . Facing History's work is based on the premise that we need to—and can—teach civic responsibility, tolerance, and social action to young people, as a way of fostering moral adulthood. . . . Our materials and our approach help students with a wide range of abilities and learning styles understand that their choices and actions matter, and that young people can, and should, be agents of change.[47]

In such undertakings, the notion of the Holocaust as both a singular and an exemplary episode in human experience informs the call for exceptional pedagogy. These educational projects suggest that it is insufficient, perhaps even unseemly, to teach the Holocaust as one would teach other subjects.

At the same time, historians, such as Peter Novick, question "the usefulness of the Holocaust as a bearer of lessons," in part because of the subject's "extremity, which on the one hand makes its practical lessons of little applicability to everyday life; on the other hand makes anything to which it is compared look 'not so bad.'"[48] Yehuda Bauer problematizes differently the moral edification that one might acquire from studying this subject, noting that "to ask questions relating to theodicy does not require recourse to the Holocaust. Any child that is run over in the street arouses the same questions of evil in the world as the Holocaust does. The murder of millions for no apparent reason makes the issue more dramatic, but in principle there is no difference at all."[49] And Novick cautions against the danger of reductionism when studying the Holocaust in pursuit of moral insight: "If there *are* lessons to be extracted from encountering the past, that encounter has to be with the past in all its messiness; they're not likely to come from an encounter with a past that's been shaped and shaded so that inspiring lessons will emerge."[50]

Despite these dilemmas and caveats, Americans evince an expansive desire to employ the Holocaust to teach moral values in the public sphere. This impulse is epitomized by the large-scale Holocaust museums that have opened beginning in the 1980s in or near major American cities (including Chicago, Cincinnati, Detroit, Houston, Los Angeles, New York, and Washington, D.C.). These institutions negotiate a complex of civic commitments to Holocaust commemoration as well as the interests of particular political, religious, ethnic, and other constituencies. Historian Edward Linenthal notes that the process of planning the United States Holocaust Memorial Museum (USHMM) in Washington, D.C., proved an object lesson in itself, demonstrating that such undertakings "do not solve problems or necessarily heal wounds. The more volatile the memory, the more difficult a task to reach a consensual vision of how the memory should be appropriately expressed."[51]

The various groups committed to establishing the USHMM did agree on museum exhibition as an especially effective medium for engaging Americans in Holocaust remembrance. The museum opened to great fanfare and general acclaim for its architecture and exhibitions; in fact, the USHMM was soon so overwhelmed by visitors that within months of opening it encouraged the public to postpone coming to the museum if possible.[52] Typical of history museums, this and other Holocaust museums lead visitors through a chronicle, articulated through an arrangement of texts, images, and artifacts (and often recorded sound, moving images, and projections as well) installed in an environment designed to integrate these various components into a cohesive narrative. Centered on the activity of walking through an enclosed space, these museums make strategic use of physical configurations in their storytelling. For example, visitors to the USHMM proceed through the three-story main installation from the top downward, evocative of Dante's descent through Hell. By contrast, visitors to the core exhibition of the Museum of Jewish Heritage: A Living Memorial to the Holocaust (MJH), which opened in New York in 1997, traverse its three-story chronicle of modern Jewish history (of which the second floor is devoted entirely to the Holocaust) by rising from the museum's entrance, lined with dark gray stone, to the building's skylit rotunda. The MJH's display of genocide notwithstanding, its installation offers an ascendant journey, evoking the Exodus as a journey from darkness to light.[53] These institutions exemplify a new type of museum practice, based less on the collecting of objects than on providing visitors with an "experience," which, like cinema, centers on "an engagement of the senses, emotions, and imagination."[54]

Beit Hashoah/Museum of Tolerance, which opened in Los Angeles in 1993, also makes extensive use of interactive media, especially in the Tolerancenter, the museum's first section. Devoted to calling visitors' attention to issues of tolerance (or, more accurately, *in*tolerance) in contemporary American life, the Tolerancenter uses interactive media to model an active engagement with the ethical issues, as opposed to what the museum characterizes as "observation at a distance." One installation, for example, situates visitors in "a re-creation of a 1950s diner, red booths and all, that 'serves' a menu of controversial topics on video jukeboxes." As it invokes luncheon counters as strategic sites of the U.S. civil rights movement, this installation "uses the latest cutting edge technology to relay the overall message of personal responsibility. Following scenarios focusing on drunk driving and hate speech, this interactive exhibit allows visitors to input their opinions on what they have seen and question relevant characters. The results are then instantly tabulated."[55]

Such efforts exemplify what Barbara Kirshenblatt-Gimblett terms "the museum effect": "Museum exhibitions transform how people look at their own immediate environs. . . . The museum experience itself becomes a model for experiencing life outside its walls."[56] Sometimes Holocaust museums make this effect explicit by bringing the images and morally charged messages from inside these institutions out to the public sphere. For example, in 2006, the USHMM provided extensive information about the genocide in the Darfur region of Sudan both in its exhibition space and on its website. During Thanksgiving week of that year, the museum transformed its building, prominently located near the Washington Mall, into a billboard, by projecting "wall-sized images of the escalating genocide in Darfur onto its façade," marking the first time that the USHMM's exterior was "used to highlight contemporary genocide."[57]

As Holocaust educators in the public sphere seek to integrate moral and academic instruction, they frequently turn, if tacitly, to religious pedagogical models. Two modes of religious learning prove especially compelling and, at times, provocative: *inspirational communion*, the spiritual value of close association with exceptional teachers, exemplified by traveling to a Hindu guru in order to experience *darshan* (devotional viewing), and *abject simulation*, the pedagogical use of an embodied activity to emulate the suffering of an exemplary figure, such as carrying a cross in a Good Friday procession as an enactment of the Passion. New media often figure strategically in realizing these practices, despite expectations that they proffer an unmediated engagement or embodied experience.

In Holocaust education, the mode of inspirational communion most often involves contact with Holocaust survivors, who emerged as figures of unparalleled authority in Holocaust remembrance in the 1970s. Since then, encounters with survivors have been widely considered a nonpareil in Holocaust memory practices, including pedagogy. With the growing recognition that Holocaust survivors are aging, their testimonies have been extensively recorded on film and videotape, following earlier print and audio documentations. The motives for recording Holocaust survivor testimony are complex. They encompass memorializing both individual survivors and the survivor community as a whole; providing material for scholarly research and the production of other mediations, including documentary films and museum installations; and offering survivors an opportunity to confront traumatic memories within a supportive, sometimes therapeutic, rubric.[58]

The pedagogical value of these testimonies figures prominently in the missions of large-scale documentation projects undertaken since the late 1970s. The Fortunoff Video Archive for Holocaust Testimonies, housed at Yale University since 1981, explains that its collection of some 4,300 interviews offers "crucial documents for the education of students and community groups in an increasingly media-centered era."[59] The Shoah Foundation, established in 1994 by Steven Spielberg, has amassed by far the largest such collection. "Each of the nearly 52,000 testimonies of survivors and other witnesses of the Holocaust, preserved for all time, is invaluable," the foundation, based at the University of Southern California, explains on its website. "However, the full social and educational potential of the Shoah Foundation's archive cannot be realized without creating an effective means for future viewers to search through the tens of thousands of hours of testimony. A team of historians, technology professionals, software engineers, and experts in information management developed [the foundation's] cataloguing and indexing systems, in order to make the nearly 120,000 hours of testimony searchable." In its cataloging guidelines, the foundation explains that "it is through indexing and cataloguing that the archive of life histories can be mined, and through the assembly and contextualization of the testimonies within educational curricula and programs, that the work of the USC Shoah Foundation Institute can be realized."[60] Videos and films of survivor testimony strive to bring viewers into virtual contact with survivors' physical presence by offering a record of their affect of remembrance as much as the substance of their recollections. These recordings also capitalize on a growing facility with these visual media, especially among younger generations. Yet even as they promise fuller and readier access, these recordings require further mediation to realize their pedagogical value, including the use of catalog and index databases, which atomize individual narratives into searchable elements within a master taxonomy.

Besides reposing in archives, these testimonies are remediated in a variety of pedagogical enterprises, including Holocaust museums. Each museum configures the visitor's communion with the survivors' virtual presence differently within the exhibition's narrative: In the USHMM, survivor interviews (typically interviewed in closeup, with little or no background) are projected onto a large screen in a separate room near the conclusion of the museum's core exhibition. In the MJH, by contrast, excerpts of interviews with survivors are shown on small screens scattered throughout its core installation, sometimes juxtaposed with artifacts related to the survivors' words. The former strategy presents survivors as larger-than-life figures who loom over the visitor in a space reserved for this encounter alone; the latter approach configures a more intimate, associative relationship between visitors and survivors, as it positions their recollections in relation to other elements of display.[61]

These museums' use of mediated survivor testimonies follows the precedent of their incorporation into dozens of Holocaust documentaries and news reports, which have provided the most extensive opportunities for Americans to encounter Holocaust survivors and their stories over the past three decades. Occasionally the encounter itself becomes the center of attention in these media works, as was the case in "Survivors," a report aired on *ABC News Nightline* on 29 March 2000. The broadcast follows the visit of Gerta Weissman Klein, a Holocaust survivor renowned for relating her wartime story (including in the documentary *One Survivor Remembers*, which received an Academy Award in 1995), to students in Columbine High School shortly after it became the site of the deadliest high-school shooting in American history. On 20 April 1999, two students at the Colorado public school killed twelve fellow students and a teacher and wounded another twenty-four people before taking their own lives. The incident provoked an extensive nationwide discussion of issues ranging from gun control to bullying in schools, the impact of violent media on American youth to the national decline of moral education.

Klein was invited to the school in January 2000, after students had read about her in a textbook on World War II. She spoke to groups of students, teachers, and parents in Columbine about her experiences as a Holocaust survivor, which she offered to these audiences as a model for how they might cope with the trauma they had experienced. In the ABC telecast, members of the Columbine community characterized meeting Klein as a transformative encounter with an ethical role model. After hearing her speak, one parent commented, "I left . . . with a refreshed soul and a thankful heart." At the conclusion of the broadcast, viewers were invited to chat online with the Kleins by logging on to the ABC News website, enabling the television audience to experience the same inspirational communion, albeit at a distance.[62]

As face-to-face encounters with aging Holocaust survivors grow increasingly less feasible, educators have been exploring new possibilities for moral instruction through mediated survivor testimony. One remediation of the Shoah Foundation's extensive inventory of survivor testimonies models how students might gain ethical insights from these recordings. *Giving Voice: Today's Kids Get Real about Bias* (2004) consists of two documentary films and a printed teacher's guide. The first film offers a forty-five-minute compilation of excerpts from interviews with seven Holocaust survivors and witnesses; the second film presents a twenty-seven-minute documentary in the form of a "reality TV–style video" that demonstrates how seven high-school students responded to these interviews. "Equipped with mini-DV cameras, seven young people document their surroundings at school and at home, with friends and family, and share their responses to viewing survivor testimony," the Shoah Foundation explains. "In so doing, they reveal candid and poignant observations about intolerance and bigotry, and they also offer examples of how each of them strives to take responsibility for building a better, more tolerant world."[63]

The students' engagement with Holocaust testimonies entails multiple mediations: The students watch the survivors on video, and their discussions about the testimony, run by adult facilitators, are filmed. The students are brought into the filmmaking process both as documentarians and as subjects of documentation. They are given video cameras and asked to record themselves and family members at home. Students are not only put in the position of filmmakers but also invited, if tacitly, to become subjects of mediated testimony themselves, like the Holocaust survivors, who also were filmed in their homes—for the students' presence before the camera is strategic for the pedagogical objectives of *Giving Voice*.

The Shoah Foundation validates this complex of mediated and remediated encounters as fulfilling the mission of another media work, which is positioned as the fountainhead of the larger enterprise of filming survivor testimonies. According to the foundation, *Giving Voice* "is the legacy of *Schindler's List*: a vehicle for facilitating a 'dialogue' between students and the testimonies."[64] (The word "dialogue" is appropriately in scare quotes, because the engagement between students and survivors is perforce unilateral. Nevertheless, this encounter aspires to the ideal of face-to-face communion between generations.)

Giving Voice juxtaposes excerpts from prerecorded testimonies, which the students in the film have watched, with their reflections on these stories. The students model several strategies for engaging with these testimonies: In response to survivors' accounts of Nazi intolerance, facilitators ask students for accounts of incidents of bigotry they have witnessed. When survivors discuss being forced to abandon their homes on short notice, the students are asked to imagine which of their possessions they would bring if they had to leave their homes under similar circumstances. Survivors' stories of ethical choices made during the Holocaust become texts on which the students comment, extrapolating connections to their own lives. Just as survivors serve as exemplars of morally charged witnessing, the students in *Giving Voice* are asked to take on the onus of standing up for their moral principles. These students thus inherit the mantle of ethical models from the survivors, offering their own reflections and their own presence on camera as paradigms for the young viewers meant to watch *Giving Voice* in classrooms. The practices of engaging the survivors' testimony through imitation, projection, and self-reflexive commentary are rooted in religious education, more so than in the pedagogy of secular classrooms. Whereas, for example, a Christian religious school might ask students to inquire of themselves, "What would Jesus do?" as a touchstone for making moral decisions, the students appearing in *Giving Voice,* and the students watching them, are offered Holocaust survivor testimonies as models for articulating the students' own moral postures.

By inviting students not only to emulate survivors as moral exemplars but also to imagine being in the same circumstances that they experienced during the war, this exercise conjoins inspirational communion with abject simulation. For several decades, educators have employed exercises that ask students to engage the Holocaust through an embodied experience connected to the suffering of victims of Nazism—including simulations of public stigmatization, loss of civil rights, hiding, confinement in crowded living spaces, chronic hunger, deportation, and imprisonment in concentration camps—even though these practices have often provoked controversy. (For example, in 2006, a local television newscast in central Florida, titled "School's 'Holocaust' Experiment Upsets Parents," reported a father's complaint that his son cried when forced to become a Jew for a day.)[65] Mass media figure as both positive and negative models for these exercises. In a 1980 overview of the popularization of the Holocaust in American culture, historian Paula Hyman questioned the appropriateness of such activities and invoked the words of Elie Wiesel, who "holds the mass media responsible for making these misuses of the Holocaust seem legitimate. When Wiesel asked one teacher why she used simulation techniques, he was told, 'If NBC could do it [in the 1978 *Holocaust* miniseries], if they could create fake gas chambers for their audience, why can't we do it for children?'"[66] Education scholar Simone Schweber argues that critics find such simulations not simply "morally unbearable" but "aesthetically repugnant . . . because of their moral implications"; to simulate the Holocaust runs the risk of reducing it "to Disneyland, or blockbuster . . . television."[67]

Mediations can figure in the execution of simulation exercises, even though they center on an embodied experience of some kind. The USHMM, for example, provides each visitor with an identification card that tells the story of an actual person who lived in Europe during World

War II. The cards offer capsule biographies for a variety of victims of Nazi persecution (Jews, Roma, homosexual men, Jehovah's Witnesses, political prisoners), some of whom survived the war, others of whom did not. Upon entering the core exhibition, visitors can select a card matching their sex and age group. "Designed as small booklets to be carried through the exhibition," the USHMM explains, "the cards help visitors to personalize the historical events of the time."⁶⁸ (In the museum's original plan, the identification cards were to be updated at printing stations as visitors proceeded through different segments of the core exhibition, thereby coordinating the individual's unfolding story with the museum's exposition of the Holocaust's master narrative. This plan proved technically unfeasible; instead, visitors receive cards with the subject's full story before entering the core exhibition.) Student visitors to the museum are encouraged to engage the stories on their identification cards in relation to the museum's rubric of narration: "Imagine which items from the Permanent Exhibition would be included if [the student] were to create a small exhibition about the individual portrayed on the card."⁶⁹

As exercises in simulation, these cards both invite identification with an actual victim of Nazi persecution and facilitate a powerful, if tacit, transformation of this imaginary exercise. Approximately the same size and shape as a passport and featuring the seal of the United States on the front cover, the identification cards provide museum visitors, as imaginary victims of Nazism, with the implicit promise of rescue by the American government. In actuality, this aid was denied many people fleeing Nazi persecution during the 1930s and '40s, including those who directly sought refuge in the United States, as the USHMM explains in its core exhibition. But the identification cards (which often become souvenirs of the museum visit) bracket this experience of abject simulation in an implicit frame of American moral rectitude. This value is expressed elsewhere in the museum, including statements by American presidents etched into its outer walls and the use of American soldiers' liberation of concentration camps as the visitor's point of entry into the history of the Holocaust.

Holocaust simulation exercises tend to invite participants to engage with the suffering of victims of Nazism. In this respect, these exercises are reminiscent of other religious practices that invite participants to experience, to a limited degree, the persecution endured by saints or martyrs. But what is perhaps the best-known example of a Holocaust-related simulation exercise in an American pedagogical setting entails a different kind of moral education, by inviting students to emulate, unwittingly, the conduct

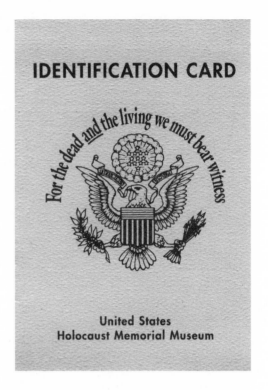

IDENTIFICATION CARD

For the dead and the living we must bear witness

**United States
Holocaust Memorial Museum**

One of a series of identification cards given to visitors to the United States Holocaust Memorial Museum in Washington, D.C., since it opened in 1993. Inside each card is a description of a person persecuted by the Nazis and their collaborators during World War II.

and sensibility of Holocaust perpetrators as a cautionary experience. This exercise exemplifies what anthropologist Michael Taussig has observed about the "magic of mimesis" in religious practices generally: the notion that "one can protect oneself from evil spirits by portraying them."[70]

This simulation exercise also entails an especially complex cascade of remediation. Most familiar as a television film, *The Wave* (ABC, 1981) dramatizes the dangerous appeal of fascism when a high-school history teacher draws his class into a social experiment in which they embrace the empowering possibilities of elitism and totalitarian discipline. At the film's climax, the teacher reveals at a school assembly the leader behind the movement that has galvanized his students—it is none other than Adolf Hitler, represented in an oversized projection of vintage footage, such as students would have seen in documentary films screened in history classes. Students in the television movie (and, presumably, those watching the film, first aired as an after-school special) are shocked to discover not only that they have been misled into an uncritical acceptance of fascist ideology and practice but also that they have, in effect, repeated the errors of history by failing to learn from them, a watchword of Holocaust education. The television drama is based on the eponymous young-adult novel by Todd Strasser, which is itself a fictionalized account of an actual teaching experiment conducted in a history class in Palo Alto, California, in April 1969.[71] Both the book and film have, in turn, inspired other teachers to stage similar simulation exercises with their students, thereby reiterating the cycle of remediation that, in its very repetition, relies on the failure of students to have learned the lessons of the Holocaust from textbooks, documentary films, and other mediations.

Pilgrimage

The quest for moral edification through an embodied, chimerical encounter with the Holocaust is realized most elaborately in pilgrimage practices. Travel to locations where the Holocaust took place or other sites of its remembrance, such as museums and monuments, has become an increasingly prevalent practice for Americans, beginning with visits to the Anne Frank House in Amsterdam, which opened to the public in 1960. Other sites associated with the Holocaust in Western Europe, especially Germany, have also been accessible to foreign visitors for decades (for example, the former concentration camp in Dachau, dedicated as a public memorial in 1965). The end of communist rule in Poland in 1989 enabled an array of Holocaust tourist practices to flourish, centered on sites of mass ghettoization (especially Warsaw) and extermination (especially Auschwitz). Anthropologist Jack Kugelmass terms these trips "secular rituals," noting that they frequently emulate religious pilgrimage. For example, giving blank index cards to Jewish students visiting the memorial at Treblinka and telling them "to write a note to someone who died in the camp [is] an act clearly copied from the Hasidic custom of writing *kvitlekh* [notes]" to a deceased leader of a hasidic community, notes that disciples leave at his gravesite. These trips and the rites that they have evolved, however, are more often undertaken "to express solidarity between the living and the dead" or to address some other social agenda, rather than to engage the numinous.[72] In particular, Kugelmass argues for a political reading of American Jewish travel to Poland:

By evoking the Holocaust dramaturgically, that is, by going to the site of the event and reconstituting the reality of the time and place, American Jews are not only invoking the spirits of the tribe, that is, claiming their martyrdom, they are also making the past time present. Moreover, in so doing, they are symbolically reversing reality: They are transporting themselves from what they are currently perceived as—in America as highly privileged and in Israel as oppressive—and presenting themselves as the diametric opposite—as what they in fact were. It is this image of the self which remains central to the Jewish worldview.[73]

Although the embodied experience is central to Holocaust travel, as it is to pilgrimage generally, media practices figure strategically in realizing these visits. Travelers turn to brochures, guidebooks, videos, and websites before and, occasionally, during their trips and undertake various documentary efforts while traveling and afterward: taking photographs and videos, sending postcards, buying souvenirs, writing diaries, emails, or weblogs during their visits and then, after returning home, creating scrapbooks, slide shows, web pages, and other compilations of materials accumulated while traveling. Moreover, as Holocaust travel has become increasingly institutionalized and professionalized, the journey itself has become a mediation in the form of a tourist production. Although visiting the grounds of former ghettos and death camps may seem an unlikely example of leisure travel, these trips are shaped by the protocols of tourism, which situate places identified as attractions—including such "egregious sights" as "the ovens at Dachau"—within a rubric that assigns meaning to the encounter with these locations, even as they are touted as venues of authentic, unmediated experience. As Dean MacCannell noted, in his seminal study of tourism, "usually the first contact a sightseer has with a sight is not the sight itself but with some representation thereof."[74]

The mediating properties of tourism are most elaborate in regularly scheduled, organized trips for large groups, such as the March of the Living, a two-week trip to Poland and Israel for Jewish youth. Since 1988, the March has been held annually in the spring, coinciding with the Israeli holidays of Yom Ha-Sho'ah and Yom Ha-Azma'ut (Independence Day). Created by Jewish educators in North America and Israel, March of the Living has brought over 50,000 Jewish teenagers from some sixty countries (the preponderance from the United States) on a "mission," in which group travel forms the foundation for "a revitalized commitment to Judaism, Israel and the Jewish People."[75] Participants visit sites in Poland that are, for the most part, landmarks of Jewish mass murder during World War II, followed by locations in Israel intended to showcase a "country that is striving valiantly to keep the age-old flame of Jewish nationhood alive."[76] This itinerary situates visiting these two countries within an established Zionist narrative, which characterizes the destruction of diaspora Jewry as redeemed though the birth of a Jewish state and uses the ritual time of Israeli national holidays to position participants in a mythic journey that enacts Jewish rebirth.

The symbolic centerpiece of March of the Living is the eponymous three-kilometer walk from Auschwitz I to Birkenau. The organizers' website informs potential participants that

> as one of the Marchers you will retrace the steps of the "March of Death," the actual route which countless numbers of our people were forced to take on their way to the gas chambers at Birkenau. You will experience Jewish history where it was made. This time, however, there will be a difference. It will be a "March of the Living" with thousands of Jewish youth, like yourself, marching shoulder to shoulder.[77]

Like the USHMM's identification cards, this activity proffers both an "experience" of history and that history's undoing. In mediating the disparity between its young participants and the genocide of European Jewry that took place decades before they were born, this tourist production assigns a group walk with definitional value, an act of solidarity not only with one's cohort but also with preceding generations of Jews. A letter addressed to participants in March of the Living informs them that "We are all survivors of the Holocaust . . . whether we were there or not, even if we had not yet been born when it all happened. The Holocaust left its mark on us, on our collective and individual being."[78] Just as a traditional homiletic teaches that Jewish souls of every generation were present at the giving of the Torah on Mt. Sinai, the Holocaust is configured as a formative, panhistoric event for all Jews.

As March of the Living's foremost concern is promoting Jewishness conceived primarily in political Zionist terms, religion figures in the trip in complex and inconsistent ways. The two-week visit to Poland and Israel accommodates and sometimes imposes religious practice (such as serving kosher food and restricting activities on the Sabbath), although the program accepts Jews of any religious denomination as well as those who are secular. The March also fosters its own rituals, such as wearing Israeli flags draped over one's shoulders, in the manner of prayer shawls, and lighting memorial candles while visiting death camps. These practices exemplify religion's role in March of the Living, invoked selectively to promote an agenda centered on Jewish communal continuity and political solidarity, irrespective of participants' religious convictions. (In this respect, March of the Living conforms both to the history of the Holocaust—in which Jews were persecuted on racial, rather than religious, grounds—and to political Zionism, which was dominated by a secular leadership in its formative years.)

While the March's organizers tout it as a life-altering experience, they also seek to forge enduring links between the trip's singular nature and the lives its young participants resume upon returning home. Organizers extend the travel experience both before and after the trip itself through pedagogical practices, such as offering preparatory seminars in advance of departing for Poland. Some groups of participants publish collections of writings, photography, artwork, or music reflecting on their experience of the March. The organizers' website posts photographs of past trips submitted by participants and registers these "alumni," who are encouraged to extend the value of their experience by funding "scholarships" for future participants.

During the trip itself, however, the March of the Living employs the tourist encounter to mediate between participants' awareness of their own Jewishness and a shared sense of historical destiny by linking travel with personal coming of age and with entering into modern Jewish history on a grand scale. The medium of travel is vaunted as an unrivaled means of achieving this synthesis. Consider the testimonial of one alumnus posted on the organization's website:

> Almost all Jewish teens learn about the Holocaust, reading books and articles in Hebrew School. . . . I read the books, looked at the pictures, went to the Holocaust Museum in Washington, D.C. numerous times, watched the movies and still, I had no understanding of the Holocaust and what it really was. When I entered Majdanek, it all became real. I cannot explain how I felt but I will never forget the time I spent in that death camp. In those few hours, I started to comprehend the reality of the Holocaust, impossible to do without seeing this firsthand in Poland. Also, Israel took on a whole new meaning for me. Would we have Israel today without the Holocaust? What if it happened again? Why did it have to happen?

Participating in the March of the Living was one of the best choices I have made thus far in my life. While it is extremely intense, mentally and emotionally, going to Poland is a choice we should all make. . . . Unfortunately, the concentration camps will not remain intact forever. It is our responsibility to go and see what happened and pass it on to others.[79]

March of the Living offers participants visions of Jewish life at its fullest, in the destroyed culture of European Jewry and the contemporary State of Israel. Each is characterized as an "'authentic' Jewish experience" that, implicitly, these young Jews do not find at home. Jewish educators value trips to Israel in particular, historian Rona Sheramy reports, because they provide students with "exposure to 'a living Jewish society' operating on 'Jewish time.'"[80] Moreover, these trips serve as a prototype for adult fundraising missions to Israel, which are not only a mainstay of American Jewish philanthropy but also "a source of prideful identification" for many adult American Jews.[81] The organizers of March of the Living promote participation in its trips as vital for the future of organized Jewry: "Many of the future world Jewish leadership will have participated in the March, which will strengthen their connection to each other."[82] March of the Living thus models a self-reflexive future for American Jews, centered on remediating and reproducing the March experience itself.

While the concerns of American Jewish identity politics engendered March of the Living, works of popular media have inspired other Holocaust pilgrimages. In addition to a self-guided walking tour of locations in the Tuscan town of Arezzo, where Roberto Begnini's 1998 film *La Vita è Bella* was shot,[83] there are several guided tours of Cracow and its environs to visit sites associated with the making of *Schindler's List*. Movie tourism is a complex cultural genre, a hybrid of two kinds of mediation: the feature film and the tourist production. These tours evoke the power of pilgrimage by traveling to a site where a well-known story, often valued as a definitional narrative, originates.

The tours in question are not created by the films' producers but have arisen independently, responding to the films' popularity and to public curiosity about their making or the stories they tell. By transforming the locations where films were shot into tourist destinations, movie tours complicate the significance of historical sites implicated in the films' narratives. More than merely juxtaposing the virtual world of the film with the actual world of the tourist site, the movie tour deliberately destabilizes distinctions among the times, events, and locations belonging to the cinematic experience, the tourist experience, and the historical events revisited by both. Movie tourism thus opens up new possibilities for the chimerical experience of entering a film's virtual world. Conversely, the movie tour's attention to a film's production process can enhance viewers' ability to see it as a constructed work of art in relation to historical or geographical actuality.

Schindler's List tours offer a range of sites to visit and various configurations of their significance. Promoters sometimes characterize these tours as occasions for moral inspiration or for virtual communion with the victims of Nazism as well as with an inspirational figure (Oskar Schindler, Steven Spielberg, or both). One tour invites visitors to "find magic and secret places," including "the street tableau in memory of the little girl who inspired Oskar Schindler to acts of altruistic courage."[84] Another tour concludes with "Tea and Polish Conversation at 'Alef's,'" a Jewish-style restaurant in Kazimierz, the former Jewish quarter of Cracow: "Step back in time and immerse yourself in pre-war Kazimierz. Situated in the middle of ancient Szeroka square, Alef has managed to recreate the feeling of days gone by, through original pre-war décor, turn-of-the-century antiques, and carefully selected Jewish klezmer music. Stephen [*sic*] Spielberg frequented this café during the making of *Schindler's List*."[85]

In these expansive efforts to exploit *Schindler's List* as a point of entry into Holocaust history, the tours sometimes challenge the protocols of Holocaust remembrance. Among sites visited on one tour was a road to the labor camp in Płaszów paved with simulated Jewish tombstones, fabricated especially for *Schindler's List* and left in place after filming was completed. (Roads paved with actual Jewish tombstones desecrated during German occupation can still be found in Poland.) These fake tombstones were eventually removed, their presence deemed offensive both to the memory of the Jewish dead and to the destroyed Jewish culture of Poland.[86]

Schindler's List tours offer a provocative conjoining of celebrity culture and Holocaust pilgrimage, in which the tours' celebrities, Schindler and Spielberg, are also commingled. Other visitors and I have observed tour guides easily confuse the two names in their remarks to sightseers, a telling conflation of the mediated and the mediator.[87] Celebrity provides both an organizing principle for the tours (Schindler's wartime exploits, Spielberg's filmmaking experiences) and a moral exemplar, in whose footsteps tourists might follow (Schindler, the "good German"; Spielberg, the

FRANCISZEK PALOWSKI

Śladami "Listy Schindlera"
Retracing "Schindler's List"
Auf den Spuren von "Schindlers Liste"

GUIDE   REISEFÜHRER

PRZEWODNIK

Cover of booklet promoting a tour of landmarks associated with the filming of *Schindler's List* in and around Cracow, mid-1990s. The road paved with fake tombstones depicted on the booklet's cover was fabricated for the 1993 feature and left behind after it was released. The road attracted tourists until its presence provoked protest and was removed.

keeper of Jewish memory). What may well disturb the Holocaust historian in these tours as problematic slippage between actuality and popular representation becomes for the tourist a productive and engaging act of mediation, which compounds the experience of compelling, morally galvanizing storytelling with the pilgrim's desire to inhabit the "legendary topography" of a sanctified site. (As sociologist Maurice Halbwachs notes in his seminal study of Christian pilgrimage to the Holy Land, "sacred places . . . commemorate not facts . . . but rather beliefs.")[88]

Celebrity and Holocaust travel converge differently in telecasts that Americans encounter at home, enabling them to follow well-known figures vicariously on their visits to memorial sites. These broadcasts juxtapose Holocaust remembrance against the significance of the celebrity's public career, as they define the moral value of the Holocaust in relation to the occasion for the celebrity visit. A case in point is the television coverage of President Ronald Reagan's appearance at Bergen-Belsen, where he read from Anne Frank's diary, before making a controversial visit to a

West German military cemetery in Bitburg on 5 May 1985. On this occasion, Holocaust remembrance was galvanized by a conflict between Cold War political exigencies and the politics of remembering World War II, igniting a crisis around Reagan's public image.[89]

Earlier in the year, the announcement that Reagan was going to visit the cemetery—in which soldiers who had fought in the Wehrmacht and several SS officers were interred—had met with vehement protest from American veterans' groups and Jewish organizations. Criticism of Reagan's decision climaxed on 19 April at a White House ceremony in which the president awarded the Congressional Gold Medal of Achievement to Elie Wiesel, who had been an outspoken detractor of Reagan's plan to visit Bitburg. At the ceremony (which had been scheduled prior to the controversy), Wiesel admonished Reagan, "That place, Mr. President, is not your place. Your place is with the victims of the SS."[90] Refusing to cancel the trip to Bitburg, Reagan instead added a stop at Bergen-Belsen. Thus, a ceremonial visit meant to celebrate America's reconciliation with West Germany, as well as their shared military and economic interests, came instead to be freighted by the ethics of Holocaust remembrance, represented by two of its most famous figures: Anne Frank and Elie Wiesel.

Wiesel's own visit to a Holocaust memorial site is the centerpiece of a more recent telecast, one concerned less with the Holocaust's historical significance in relation to current affairs than with engaging its moral force expansively. His appearance on a pair of special broadcasts of *The Oprah Winfrey Show*, aired on 24 and 25 May 2006, entailed a complex of mediating strategies in an elaborate exposition of the Holocaust's paradigmatic value for the talk show's extensive American audience. The first telecast follows Wiesel and Winfrey on a visit to Auschwitz. Throughout the hour-long broadcast, which featured limited commercial interruptions by sponsor AT&T, the two celebrities walk the snow-covered grounds of the death camp (the program was taped in January 2006) and tour its museum. In contrast to other broadcasts or documentary films that follow a Holocaust survivor on a visit to this or another site of mass murder, this telecast placed less attention on recounting the history of the survivor's personal experience or the camp's operation in general than on the Holocaust's affective power and ethical challenges.

Both Wiesel and Winfrey characterize the death camp as imbued with supernal power. Toward the beginning of the telecast, Wiesel refers to Auschwitz as "hallowed ground," and Winfrey asks him, "Do you think the ground carries its own energy, . . . the voices of the dead?" As Wiesel describes his recollections of what took place at Auschwitz, Winfrey voices awe at the daunting challenges that the Holocaust poses ("I have no answers. . . . All these years later, you have no answers"), while asserting its moral importance ("In spite of everything, you still must believe"). At one point, striving to explain the extreme nature of inmates' existence in the camp, Wiesel comments, "Nothing mattered. Fame mattered nothing." This statement is less significant to his own wartime experiences than to his return visit with Winfrey—for it is their current fame, which occasions their visit to Auschwitz and its telecast to millions of Americans, that would have been meaningless in the *univers concentrationnaire*.

Although Wiesel and Winfrey's shared celebrity status occasions this visit to Auschwitz, they play complementary roles in mediating the Holocaust and its significance for the television audience. During the broadcast, Winfrey narrates several brief documentary sequences, explaining over archival footage the history of the rise of Nazism and the operation of Auschwitz. Wiesel is heard reading several excerpts from his memoir *Night*, as the text appears on the screen. The conversations between Wiesel and Winfrey as they tour the camp constitute a meeting of two kinds of Holocaust remembrance: the written recollections of a Holocaust survivor and the image-driven narrative of an American, born after the war, with no familial ties to the event.

The telecast's complex remediation of Wiesel's wartime experience and his stature as a Holocaust survivor of unrivaled prominence also offered a tacit response to controversies involving both Winfrey and Wiesel during the preceding months. In January 2006, *The Oprah Winfrey Show* announced that *Night*, having just been reissued in a new English translation, was the next selection of the talk show's book club, renowned for engaging a large nationwide readership in conversation about the selected titles. Press reports soon characterized the news as "likely to extend the debate over the nature of memoir and truth" prompted earlier that month by the book club's previous selection, James Frey's *A Million Little Pieces*, a memoir of drug addiction, which subsequently proved to be substantially fabricated by its author. Winfrey responded to this revelation by asserting that "the underlying message of redemption in James Frey's memoir still resonates with me."[91] An article in the *Forward*, a nationally distributed Jewish weekly, characterized the arrangement between Winfrey and Wiesel as something of a quid pro quo between celebrities: on one hand, "Winfrey's imprimatur" promised the author of *Night* "a fresh financial success"; on the other hand, in the wake of the controversy over the Frey memoir, Winfrey would benefit from "rehabilitation" in the form of "a trusted voice—a true survivor."[92] In fact, Wiesel's *Night* has a complicated history of its own, including questions about the book's generic status, located uneasily somewhere between memoir and autobiographical novel.[93]

The stature of *Night* was further aggrandized, and its value further complicated, on the talk show's next telecast. On 25 May, *The Oprah Winfrey Show* announced the winners of its "first-ever National High School Essay Contest," in which students were invited to submit entries responding to the question, "Why is Elie Wiesel's book 'Night' relevant today?" Fifty winning essays were selected from some 50,000 entries. The telecast profiles some of the winners, excerpting their essays and interpolating their reflections among comments from Wiesel and Winfrey. In introducing the winners, Winfrey stresses both their diverse backgrounds and their common level of accomplishment: "They are . . . from 22 states. Together, they speak 13 languages, three are class presidents. All of them are honor students. Three have relatives who survived the Holocaust. Some have even survived genocides themselves. And each one of them is eloquent and passionate."[94]

Excerpts from the students' essays heard during the telecast demonstrate how many of them related *Night* to personal trials, including the challenges of living in a crime-ridden neighborhood, being a new immigrant, homelessness, and sexual abuse. Propelled by the contest's question of "relevance," students read Wiesel's experiences in Auschwitz as an analogous, rather than unparalleled, ordeal. The read experience becomes, in effect, a rubric for articulating one's own history; the distinction between the two is elided. As one contest winner comments, "A book pulls you into the world you're reading about. You become that person, you live that life, and it becomes part of your memory because it happens to you."

This broadcast also enables Winfrey to make an analogy to the Holocaust in her own medium. In her remarks, she calls attention to recent genocides in Bosnia and Rwanda, as well as ongoing mass murder in Sudan; then she introduces two contest winners who survived the genocide in Rwanda and now live in the United States. After they relate their wartime experiences, Winfrey asks one young woman about her family—who survived the massacre and still lives in Rwanda—whom she has not seen in twelve years. Winfrey announces to the young woman, "We have flown your family here." Then, as if taking a page from *This Is Your Life*, the young contestant is reunited with her family on camera, in what Winfrey describes as "one of the most amazing moments I've ever experienced on television." The broadcast concludes with other surprise announcements: each contest winner receives a $10,000 college scholarship from *The Oprah Winfrey Show* and contest sponsor AT&T, and Winfrey announces a $50,000 award to the Global Fund for Children, which "creates multicultural books for boys and girls around the world," donated in honor of *Night*.

This second of the talk show's broadcasts devoted to Wiesel and his memoir complements the first one. Winfrey and Wiesel's visit to Auschwitz centers on the Holocaust's singularity as an event testing the limits of human experience and understanding. There, Winfrey repeatedly responded to the sights and Wiesel's recollections by saying that they are "unimaginable, just unimaginable." By contrast, the essay-contest winners appear in the studio where *The Oprah Winfrey Show* is taped; they fill the screen with stories of how readily Americans of all backgrounds can forge personal bonds with Wiesel's narrative. The awe that Winfrey evinces at Auschwitz gives way to celebrating the possibilities of human creativity, extended beyond the telecast in the form of plans for the future (scholarships, publications). The protean nature of television offers viewers a series of surprises: the broadcast opens with scenes of contestants being told that they are winners, climaxes with the reunion of the family separated during the genocide in Rwanda, and concludes with awards for the contest winners. As the wintry chill and solitude of Auschwitz—where Wiesel famously wrote that his life had become "one long night"[95]—gives way to the collective warmth of American daytime television, the singularity of the Holocaust yields to a universal, life-affirming celebration— albeit one that situates surviving genocide at its core.

In a profile of Winfrey published in *The New Republic* shortly after these telecasts, Lee Siegel contemplates "the strange genius of Oprah" as emblematic of a national character that, with these telecasts, effects an extraordinary transformation of the Holocaust as a source of inspiration:

Winfreyism is the expression of an immensely reassuring and inspiring message that has, without doubt, helped millions of people carry on with their lives. . . . On her way to Auschwitz, sitting in her hotel room in Krakow, thinking about the masses of people who were murdered in the death camp, Oprah wrote in [her monthly magazine] *O*, "I have never felt more human." Her empathy and moral growth seem to require human sacrifice. Yet watching Oprah does fill you with hope. It also plunges you into despair. She has become something like America itself.[96]

The 5 and 12 June 2006 cover of *The New Republic* questioned the significance of Oprah Winfrey's visit to Auschwitz with Elie Wiesel, for a special broadcast of her eponymous television program, by spoofing the cover of *O: The Oprah Magazine.* Artist: Drew Friedman.

Monuments

Even as Holocaust travel is centered on physical sites associated with the deportation, confinement, and extermination of the victims of Nazism, erecting memorial structures—including statues, plaques, gardens, and museums—has expanded the landscape of Holocaust remembrance to sites in Israel, the Americas, and elsewhere. These memorial structures both draw on and react against the precedents of religious monuments, such as tombstones and shrines, and the monuments of civil religion, notably war memorials. The practice of erecting monuments to victims of Nazi persecution extends beyond the physical installations themselves, as literary scholar James Young has demonstrated, to include the planning and debating of these projects in advance of their construction, as well as all manner of responses to them upon completion, in conversations, in print and broadcast media, and even, at times, in the form of graffiti or other vandalism. Consequently, Holocaust monuments have become exemplary sites for discussing the nature of public memory practices.

Frequently these discussions problematize the very enterprise of monuments. Young argues that

> the traditional assumption of the monument's timelessness has nearly relegated it as a form to the margins of modern discourse. For once it was recognized that monuments necessarily mediate memory, even as they seek to inspire it, they came to be regarded as displacements of the memory they were supposed to embody. Even worse, by insisting that its memory was as fixed as its place in the landscape, the monument seemed to ignore the essential mutability of all cultural artifacts. . . . "Monumental" was, after all, Nietzsche's disdainful epithet for any version of history calling itself permanent and ever-lasting, a petrified history that buried the living.[97]

Nevertheless, just as monument making remains a mainstay of Holocaust remembrance, the monumental—with its implications of the immutable and triumphant, by dint of forms that are typically conspicuous and gigantic—is often embraced as an idiom appropriate to the task. This tendency is not confined to physical structures. The most popular works of American Holocaust film and television are large-scale works: *The Diary of Anne Frank* (running time 180 minutes), *Judgment at Nuremberg* (186 minutes), the *Holocaust* miniseries (475 minutes, over four evenings), and *Schindler's List* (195 minutes). American Holocaust museums also regularly engage the monumental—indeed, some of their names indicate that they were erected, in part, as shrines: The United States Holocaust *Memorial* Museum, The Museum of Jewish Heritage: A Living *Memorial* to the Holocaust, The Zekelman Family Holocaust *Memorial* Center (in Michigan). Other projects employ similar language in their mission statements, such as the Fortunoff Archive, described as "a living memorial to counteract forgetfulness, ignorance and malicious denial."[98] These and other institutions of Holocaust remembrance are monumental not only in function but in form. The museums, in particular, tend to be in prominently located buildings, and their installations are executed on a grand scale. In addition to memorial sculptures or gardens outside their buildings, these museums frequently employ the monumental as a strategy in their installations, thereby materializing the Holocaust's enormity and, therefore, presenting the event as incomprehensible in its entirety. As literary scholar Susan Stewart notes, "the gigantic represents infinity. . . . we know the gigantic only partially."[99]

A frequent approach to demonstrating the Holocaust's monumental significance is the massing of like elements. Although massing is evident elsewhere—videotaping projects, for example, constitute virtual monuments by accumulating thousands of hours of Holocaust survivors' recorded testimony—it is most readily apparent in museums. The USHMM makes especially elaborate use of the monumental idiom by displaying large numbers of similar items—whether the lists of hundreds of first names of victims of Nazi persecution, etched into the building's glass walls, or the heaps of several thousand shoes taken from prisoners at Majdanek, displayed in the core exhibition.

The best-known example of this display strategy is the museum's Tower of Faces, in which over one thousand photographs of Jews who lived in the Lithuanian town of Eishyshok before World War II are reproduced in enlarged format and displayed on the walls of a tower, several stories in height, that twice intersects the narrative flow of the museum's core exhibition. In this installation, photographs that were once tokens of intimate, personal remembrance among family and friends become archetypal images of a representative lost community. The remediation of photographs that are similar in form to those found in many of the museumgoers' own family albums exploits the intimacy associated with this genre of photography; literary scholar Marianne Hirsch describes the encounter as being "situated right inside" the "domestic space of a family album."[100] At the same time, the installation masses and aggrandizes the images, stripping them of their specific provenance and idiosyncratic value. The placement of many of the photographs in the Tower of Faces, situated either much higher or lower than the visitor's range of viewing, makes it impossible to look at them as one usually views photographs. Their value is rather as part of a large-scale monument, whose many components cannot be seen in their entirety, thereby materializing the visitor's inability to take in completely the destruction of even one community of European Jews. As Stewart observes, "The partial vision of the observer prohibits closure of the object. . . . The gigantic becomes our environment, swallowing us as nature or history swallows us. In the representation of the gigantic within public space it is therefore important that the gigantic be situated above and over, that the transcendent position be denied the viewer."[101]

Perhaps more than any other single example of Holocaust remembrance in turn-of-the-millennium America, the Paper Clips project of the

Whitwell Middle School in rural Marion County, Tennessee, exemplifies a national facility for inventing new forms of civil religion. Including elements of redemptive drama, ritual, moral education, and pilgrimage, the project centers on monument making. The Paper Clips project began in the spring of 1998, when Linda Hooper, the school's principal, decided to institute a voluntary course on the Holocaust in an effort to teach students how to deal with the diversity of Americans beyond Whitwell (population approximately 1,600): "We are all alike," she explained in a book on the project. "White, Anglo-Saxon, and Protestant. You can count the minority families on one hand. There are no foreigners in Whitwell—and no Catholics, no Muslims, no Jews. . . . One day, our kids will leave the sheltered life in Whitwell . . . and they will encounter people who are not 'like us.' How will they handle intolerance or rejection?"[102]

The course was taught by Sandra Roberts, an eighth-grade language arts teacher with no special training in Holocaust history or literature or in Holocaust education. When introducing the subject to her students, she encountered disbelief at the number of Jewish victims. The students' incredulity was not a questioning of the Holocaust's veracity but arose out of the inability to "imagine a number as large as six million." Roberts asked her class to suggest how they might address this problem, and one student proposed that they "collect six million of something and pile it up." It was soon decided to collect paper clips, as this seemed feasible and also proved to be historically resonant. One student discovered that non-Jewish Norwegians had worn paper clips on their lapels to protest Norwegian Jews' being forced to wear yellow stars following the Nazi occupation of Norway.[103]

After gathering paper clips from their homes and from relatives and neighbors, students began soliciting donations of paper clips, writing to "sports heroes, politicians, film stars, and industry leaders" for assistance. Although the preponderance of donations came from "regular folks," the students received paper clips and letters from an array of celebrities, including "former president Bill Clinton, actor Tom Hanks, director Steven Spielberg, and football players from the Tampa Bay Buccaneers and the Dallas Cowboys."[104] Many donations came with letters, which students inventoried. To expand their collection effort further, they created a website, which generated hundreds more donations.

While still far from the goal of six million paper clips, the collection effort began to attract international attention in fall 1999, when Dagmar and Peter Schroeder, German journalists based in Washington, D.C., learned of the project and publicized it in German newspapers, inviting readers to send paper clips to Whitwell. The Schroeders soon heard from many Germans who were moved by the story, prompting the journalists to write a book on the Paper Clips project, which was published in Germany the following year.[105] The book received attention in the *Washington Post* in spring 2001, and then national print and broadcast media picked up the story.[106] As the donations of paper clips continued, the students soon realized that they might surpass their goal of six million. When asked what the students should do if that happened, the Schroeders advised, "Keep on collecting and counting. . . . The Nazis didn't murder only Jews."[107] The students set a new goal of collecting eleven million paper clips, based on a widely accepted figure for the total number of victims of the Holocaust.

The challenge of housing the students' burgeoning collection became more pressing and also entailed symbolic implications. Roberts explained, "We started the project because we wanted to have an idea what six million lives means. . . . It's not decent to leave all the paper clips lying around. We need a memorial for them." Students thought of melting down the paper clips and using the metal to cast a memorial sculpture, but this was rejected as too similar to cremating the corpses of the people murdered in death camps. The students reportedly told their teacher that each paper clip represented a victim of Nazi persecution and "We can't burn them again!"[108] Instead, Roberts and the Schroeders decided that a vintage German cattle car, such as one on display in the USHMM, would make an appropriate memorial to house the paper clips. After an extensive search, the Schroeders found a car resembling the ones used to transport people to concentration camps and death camps. Moving the car from Germany to the United States entailed considerable negotiations, fundraising, and publicity. Meanwhile, residents of Whitwell volunteered to ready the grounds outside the school for the car's installation. As preparations were under way, a group of Holocaust survivors from suburban New York who had heard about the Paper Clip project visited Whitwell in spring 2001 to meet with students and other community members.

The cattle car arrived in the United States in early September 2001 and began the final leg of its journey to Whitwell on 11 September. The coincidence of the arrival of this "symbol of tolerance" with terrorist attacks in New York, Washington, D.C., and Pennsylvania proved meaningful to the students. One student commented, "If I had not known why we were building a memorial, . . . I would know it now."[109] The car arrived in Whitwell on 5 October 2001, bearing the label "Holocaust Mahnmal der Kinder/The Children's Holocaust Memorial." The students installed eleven million paper clips behind glass partitions inside the cattle car, and residents of the town landscaped the surrounding grounds. A local artist created concrete butterflies to serve as stepping stones leading up to the cattle car; the motif invokes a poem by Pavel Friedmann, an inmate of Terezín, "The Butterfly," one of the most famous works of children's writing from the Holocaust era.[110] The Children's Holocaust Memorial was dedicated on 9 November 2001, the anniversary of Kristallnacht.

In the ensuing years, school groups from around the country have visited Whitwell to learn about both the Holocaust and the Paper Clip project on student-led tours. Other schools have contacted the Whitwell Middle School for guidance on their own Holocaust memorial projects. The project's website offers information on visiting the memorial, video of its interior and exterior, and instructions on how to donate to the project or purchase necklaces featuring the paper-clip motif, proceeds of which also support the project.[111] In 2004, the Schroeders published a children's book in English on Whitwell's Holocaust memorial, and a documentary film, titled *Paper Clips*, was aired on HBO and subsequently shown in theaters and at film festivals internationally, garnering several prizes. The Whitwell Middle School has also continued to receive donations of paper clips. A second eleven million were placed in a sealed steel container, eight feet tall, decorated with "a big, shiny paper clip and metal statues of a girl and boy catching butterflies." An additional eight million paper clips are made available to other schools "who submit project proposals."[112]

By the late 1990s, teaching the Holocaust as an exemplar of the consequences of intolerance had become a fixture of public school education in other parts of the United States. This practice seemed especially valuable in Whitwell, as no one there is perceived as Other. Rather, intolerance was characterized as an imaginary problem, and the implications of difference had to be conjured. This challenge to the imagination was compounded by the Holocaust's vastness; conceiving of six million victims apparently tested the limits of residents of this small, remote community. In fact, the ability to imagine this large number (or simply accepting how daunting it is to do so) was insufficient—the number needed to be experienced through collecting six million of some item. (According to the Schroeders, students explained that "we started the whole project because we wanted to see, to feel, and to touch such a big number.")[113] The need to experience six million of anything soon developed into a priority in itself, quite apart from the ethical or historical lessons that initiated this project. The act of collecting took on a life of its own, as evidenced by the decision to expand the collecting to a goal of eleven million (a number whose accuracy as the total count of victims of Nazi persecution is questioned by scholars of the Holocaust)[114] and to continue collecting another eleven million and beyond.

Indeed, the Paper Clips project became a different kind of pedagogical exercise: a test of the students' and their school's resourcefulness, creativity, and drive. The measure of the project's success moved beyond evaluating the students' knowledge of Holocaust history or imparting the lessons in tolerance that Holocaust remembrance is meant to model. Rather, success was measured by the growing inventory of paper clips, the expanding public attention that the project garnered, and the proliferation of memorial efforts that it inspired. And instead of engaging students with fellow Americans whose difference from Whitwell's residents had inspired the Holocaust course in the first place, the Paper Clips project brought the class into contact with Holocaust survivors, journalists, and, largely by means of correspondence, German citizens and American celebrities.

The students at Whitwell and their teachers evinced a ready attraction to the legitimizing power of celebrities (including the aura of Holocaust survivors) and of mass media, as well as a predilection for monumental projects. Besides amassing paper clips and the letters that accompanied them, as well as the eventual installation of two monuments on school grounds, the students created a "pyramid of shoes," displayed in their school, "to recall the millions of shoes left behind by those who perished in the death camps."[115] The Whitwell community also displayed a facility for adopting and combining Holocaust icons—paper clips, cattle cars, butterflies—and for endowing them with meanings that reinforced the value of their project. (For example, the middle school's website explains that eighteen sculptures of butterflies were placed on the grounds around the memorial, the number symbolic in Hebrew "for life," the butterfly "the Christian symbol of renewal.")[116]

The ease with which the Paper Clips project began and expanded is echoed in the project's cascade of mediations, including a website, a documentary film, and a children's book, as well as extensive print and broadcast press coverage. Through reiterations in these various forums, the project's narrative coalesced and took on a validity of its own. Endorsements from so many admirers—Holocaust survivors, German citizens, journalists, educators, religious leaders, politicians, Hollywood celebrities, film festival audiences, media critics—seems to have discouraged any interrogation of the choices the students or their teachers made.

Peter W. Schroeder and Dagmar Schroeder-Hildebrand's 2004 children's book chronicling the Paper Clip project of the Whitwell Middle School in Tennessee is one of a cascade of mediations engaged in the project, including a documentary film promoted on the book's cover.

But the Paper Clips project does raise questions worth probing. The focus on gathering paper clips has disquieting resonances: Is it, if unwittingly, a reenactment of Nazi Germany's rounding up Jews and other stigmatized civilian populations? By representing victims of Nazi persecution with something so small, inanimate, and mass-produced as a paper clip, has their humanity and their individuality been compromised? Paper clips have other resonances in the history of the Third Reich that trouble their association with resistance to Nazism; Operation Paperclip was the code name that American intelligence and military used during and after World War II for a covert project to bring German scientists, including Nazi Party members, to the United States. Was this fact overlooked by the teachers at Whitwell? Is placing the paper clips in a cattle car a problematic evocation of deporting Jews to extermination sites? Is the enclosure of paper clips en masse in the car and in the metal monument the symbolic equivalent of interring so many Holocaust victims in mass graves? The students and their teachers evolved their own symbolic ethos for the collection project—for example, resisting the idea of melting down the paper clips, as this seemed equivalent to cremation—and characterized the cattle car as "a symbolic resting place for millions of victims who have no graves."[117] But why did some concerns emerge and not others?

Indeed, the project as a whole raises larger questions: How does a lesson about intolerance become a large-scale collection effort, expanding to engage celebrities and the mass media, to make monuments, and ultimately to become a pilgrimage destination? And what are the implications of this string of developments?

The Paper Clips project was founded on a practice, widely familiar to American educators at the turn of the twenty-first century, that conjoins "teaching tolerance" with learning about the Holocaust. In doing so, the primacy of studying the event's singular, complex history gives way to an expansive, affectively driven approach to engaging the Holocaust as a moral exemplum. (In this respect, the Paper Clips project resembles *The Oprah Winfrey Show*'s essay contest on *Night*.) In Whitwell, this practice seems to have served as a model for making a series of leaps: from teaching about the Holocaust as a lesson in tolerance to teaching a lesson in enormity; from this new pedagogical concern to the desire to experience the number 6,000,000; from this desire, which engendered the collection effort, to a new objective centered on promoting the project; from this objective to engaging with celebrities; from this engagement to communing with Holocaust survivors; from the ongoing accumulation of paper clips and, moreover, of public validation, to the imperative to make a monument (which, as its name intimates, is both a testimonial to the young creators of the Paper Clips project and a memorial to victims of the Holocaust); and from the creation of the monument to its becoming a pilgrimage site, its value further enhanced by the attention of others.

Why, then, has what appears to be a well-intentioned lesson that went far afield from its original goal continued to receive validation from so many sources, including professionals committed to Holocaust remembrance? Perhaps it is because the students and teachers at Whitwell were emulating the Holocaust remembrance practices of other Americans. They not only embraced the Holocaust's value as a moral paradigm but also adopted widely familiar means of engaging this subject: the importance of publicity, the centrality of affectively charged experience, the attraction to the aesthetics of monumentalism. The tagline used to promote the documentary film *Paper Clips*—"It began as a lesson in prejudice, what happened next was a miracle"—acknowledges the project's transformations and validates them in terms that invoke the numinous. But what exactly is understood as miraculous about this undertaking? Perhaps it is the embrace of the Holocaust as a moral touchstone among such improbable candidates—not Jews, living in a major city, with personal connections to the genocide's victims, but Christians, remote from both the Holocaust and its sites of commemoration. (The Anti-Defamation League, which promotes the documentary and has developed an accompanying educational curriculum, lauds the Paper Clips project as "one of the most inspirational and profound lessons in tolerance, in the least likely of places.")[118] Whitwell implicitly redeems the failures of Holocaust remembrance to galvanize others in America or to effect satisfying responses internationally to more recent genocides in Yugoslavia, Rwanda, Chechnya, or Darfur. The people of Whitwell, by demonstrating the extent to which they would dedicate themselves to the civil religion of Holocaust remembrance in its many forms, validated the great investment that educators, clergy, politicians, and others have made in the Holocaust as a moral touchstone for all Americans.

In the decades since the end of World War II, Americans have developed a set of Holocaust memorial practices that, despite their focus on events that took place far from this land and that directly involved few of its citizens, are as much an indigenous product as other mainstays of the nation's civil religion identified by sociologist Robert Bellah in the 1960s: the American Revolution, the Civil War, and the civil rights movement.[119] America's civil religion of Holocaust remembrance is distinguished by a prevailing sensibility that also informs the nation's public remembrance of these and other events, a sensibility that emphasizes affect over intellect, the generic over the specific, the redemptive over the disturbing, and the integration of competing or dissenting ideologies into a consensual commitment to the importance of belief at its most abstract.

At the same time, American practices of Holocaust remembrance stand apart from other observances of the national civil religion in some respects and thereby indicate what Holocaust remembrance contributes to American public culture. Indeed, Americans' approach to recalling the Holocaust relies heavily on an aesthetics of exceptionalism, manifesting the singular nature of this subject and its value through an array of practices that signify the Holocaust as a limit case. As discussed in this chapter, these include feature films with special screening protocols; commercial television broadcasts whose interruption by advertisements is deemed unseemly; courses with pedagogical goals of moral engagement quite unlike those of other curricula; tourist productions centered on experiencing the abject; and exhibitions that overwhelm visitors with what is, by the standards of museum practice, a surfeit of information, images, and objects. Having situated the Holocaust as an event whose importance is indexed by its singularity, Americans frequently engage it as a site for investigating the extremes of representation and remembrance.

America's civil religion of Holocaust remembrance is especially provocative in its engagement of religiosity. Even as it readily draws on the rubrics of religious practices to realize its own cultural idioms—ecumenical services, memorial concerts, monuments to the dead, and so on—it diverges from the concerns of theology. These commemorative practices are largely humanistic, directed toward questions of social ethics, on one hand, and awe at the event's enormity, on the other hand. In both of these trends the issue of theodicy, so central to theological engagement with the Holocaust, is largely absent. At the same time, the civil religion of Holocaust remembrance is at odds, albeit in a different way, with the profession of history. The desires that this civil religion demonstrates for redemptive narratives, moral edification, and transformative encounters defies most historians' insistence on the Holocaust as an unredeemable episode of human experience, much as these desires obviate theologians' concerns with challenging questions of faith.

This particular configuration of America's civil religion of Holocaust remembrance is not inevitable. The Holocaust could be a subject avoided by most Americans, save for a few scholars or individuals with direct personal connections to the subject. Or this nation's public might readily accede to the authoritative responses to the Holocaust by religious leaders, historians, or philosophers, instead of forging their own understandings of the topic. But American Holocaust remembrance should not be dismissed as ill informed or venal, nor should it simply be disparaged as promoting an "*evasion* of moral . . . responsibilities that *do* belong to Americans as they confront their past, their present, and their future."[120] Rather, Americans' extensive and wide-ranging commitment to engaging with this disturbing history is worthy of attention as an indigenous practice in its own right.

The primacy of mediation, and especially the ready embrace of new media, in Americans' engagement with the Holocaust is central to understanding how so many of this nation's citizens feel that they bear, in Arthur Cohen's words, "the scar without the wound, . . . memory without direct experience." Marianne Hirsch, identifying this kind of engagement with the past as "postmemory," writes that this is "a very particular form of memory precisely because its connection to its object or source is mediated."[121] In American Holocaust remembrance, mediation is essential, even as it is deemed inherently problematic, because it is so widely understood as engaging a subject considered incomprehensible, inapproachable, inaccessible, or unimaginable. As a consequence, Holocaust memory practices regularly raise questions about the implications of mediation, sometimes sparking extensive discussions of public memory culture. At the same time, the ineluctable reliance on mediation in American Holocaust remembrance has prompted solutions to the challenges that the subject poses from within the protocols of American media, often at its most unabashedly popular, exemplified by the widespread importance of celebrity in these practices. Celebrities—be they renowned Holocaust survivors, politicians, journalists, media artists, or simply high-profile personalities—are key to positioning the Holocaust as meaningful to Americans generally. Perhaps because the Holocaust exists for Americans in mediated forms, the celebrity, who also exists for them by dint of mass media, is the appropriate guide to this forbidding subject.

So many discussions of mediating the Holocaust characterize it as an untenable undertaking, yet the examples from American public culture discussed here (and many others not included) testify to a common readiness to take on this daunting task. Its purported impossibility seems to be, if anything, a source of inspiration—by confronting the Holocaust and, therefore, the challenge of its remembrance, drawing on whatever mediating resources are available, Americans test their abilities to bring a national ethos that is itself understood as historically and morally exceptional to redress an extreme failure of civil society. Therefore, even as these efforts engage daunting historical questions and lofty theological dilemmas, they are ultimately self-reflexive, seeking reaffirmations of faith in America.

4

Observant Jews

Elsewhere in this book I examine media that is professionally produced and mass marketed. But American Jewish religious life also
engages media works created by amateurs and small-scale professionals,
typically for a limited audience. Indeed, the audience for these works is
often confined to the creators themselves. Far from diminishing the significance of these media works, their intimate scale of production, circulation, reception, and inventory can facilitate intense engagement with the
nexus of media and religion. Perhaps nowhere else are American Jews so
thoroughly involved in issues arising from this interrelation than in these
works of personal media. Indeed, I begin this chapter with an example
drawn from my own experience, which first got me thinking about this
phenomenon.

"We Want to See How It Looked"

In 1994 I went with my partner, Stuart, to attend the naming ceremony
for his infant niece, Mollie, at a Reform synagogue in Washington, D.C.
When we arrived, Stuart's father came over to us, holding a video camera.
He was planning to record the ceremony but had just learned he would be
taking part in it, and so he asked if one of us would do the taping. I agreed
to do so—even though I had never used a video camera before—after being shown what to do and assured that anybody can operate one easily.

I soon realized that, as the videographer, my attention to the celebration was not the same as that of a family guest and was also different from
an ethnographer's. I became especially aware of this difference when I
heard people whispering behind me. I knew I had to resist the impulse to
turn around, whether it be to ask them to be quiet (which I might have
done as a family guest, concerned with maintaining ceremonial decorum)
or (as an ethnographer in pursuit of "thick description") to listen to and

perhaps even join in the conversation. Even though I had been given no guidelines and had never videotaped anything before, nor had I ever seen a videotape of this or any other sort of ritual, I *did* have an automatic understanding of my task: to serve as an ideal viewer, whose gaze remains fixed continually on the celebrants. In fact, the presence of other observers is only implicit in the video I made.

When the ceremony was over, there were refreshments and chatting with guests for about an hour (which I did not record); then Mollie's family headed home, Stuart and I with them. No sooner had we entered their house than everyone demanded to see the video—everyone, that is, except for Stuart, who found this request very surprising: "Why do you want to see it now?" he asked. "You were just there!" But the others insisted on watching the tape; one of them said, "We want to see how it looked." And so we sat down in the living room, put the cassette in the VCR, and watched the entire video (which runs about twelve minutes). The family, including Mollie's three-year-old brother, remained attentive throughout, commenting intermittently as they watched.

Afterward, Stuart and I talked about his family's insistence on seeing the video so soon after the ceremony, a response that he still found puzzling. I, too, thought it very curious, though I suspected it was not unusual. I wondered, what would an anthropologist, rather than a family member, make of it? Mollie, her brother, and their parents and grandparents had just taken part in the naming ceremony as its celebrants. But standing in the synagogue with the rabbi before relatives and friends somehow did not constitute the entire event. For the ritual to be complete, they also felt the need to see, a little more than an hour after the ceremony had been enacted, "how it looked." Even though its documentation had not been planned in any particular way (including my last-minute role as videographer), the videotape was not adventitious. Rather, its making and viewing were, albeit implicitly, part of the ritual itself.

Baby-naming rituals such as the one just described are a recent innovation in Jewish life but are not without precedent. Historian Ivan Marcus notes that "there is no single standard Jewish naming ceremony for a newborn boy or girl"; as is true of all Jewish life-cycle events, customs of observance vary considerably over time and from one community to another.[1] Among Jewish baby-naming practices, perhaps the most unusual is the ritual known as Hollekreisch, practiced among Ashkenazim in Western Europe beginning in the late Middle Ages and continuing into the modern era. Now an obsolete practice, Hollekreisch is known from various documentary sources, including rabbinic responsa, memoirs, and works of visual art.[2] The ritual itself required no documentation as part of its execution (conducted at home by families, with young children chanting around the infant's cradle; no clergy were involved) but was understood as self-sufficient. Mention of Hollekreisch in documentary sources is typically part of a larger running narrative and is usually generic.

Videotapes of baby-naming ceremonies reflect a different understanding of the relationship between ritual and documentation. Such recordings exemplify what media scholar Michael Renov terms *domestic ethnography*, which is distinguished from conventional ethnographic filmmaking by the "complexity and the interpenetration of subject/object identities."[3] In the instance of ritual videos such as the one described earlier, this interrelation extends beyond that of the people on either side of the camera, informing the relationship between the documentation and the rites enacted before the camera.

Since the mid-1970s, the technology of making and viewing personal videos has become readily available to members of the middle class internationally, transforming the way many millions of people engage with the production and circulation of moving images. The medium's impact is wide-ranging, from matters of surveillance and legal procedures to such activities as medicine, pedagogy, athletics, fundraising, and tourism. Personal videography has also had a significant impact on religious practice, effecting profound changes in the nature of experiencing, witnessing, and remembering rituals. Beyond merely enhancing the observance or documentation of religious practice, this new medium's distinctive characteristics and the cultural protocols it engenders both alter the nature of religious practices and prompt new meanings for them.

Videos of American Jewish life-cycle rituals are of interest in themselves and as part of larger phenomena. These recordings might be examined in relation to the videodocumentation of other rituals—including seasonal holiday celebrations and other subjects connected to religious life, such as travel to holy sites—not only among Jews, in America or elsewhere, but also among other religious groups. The medium of video might be considered within the history of personal photography, starting in the mid-nineteenth century with studio portraits and extending through snapshot photography and motion picture film and beyond videotape to the contemporary use of digital images, still or moving, which can be stored as computer data, transmitted via cell phone, or displayed on the Internet.

Much of what analyzing videos of American Jewish life-cycle rituals reveals is relevant for personal videography in other religious and ethnic communities. For example, although Jewish religious prohibitions limiting photography are culturally specific, their implications resonate with other religions' protocols and how they are negotiated. Similarly, the video-documentation of rituals is often clearly indebted to other photographic practices. At the same time, the relationship among these various media, from daguerreotypes to Internet II, is complex. There is no simple progression from one new photographic medium to the next. Indeed, some earlier media practices appear, in retrospect, to have anticipated attributes of later media. (For example, Barbara Levine characterizes the complex compositions of photographs and captions in early-twentieth-century photo albums as "pre-cinematic.")[4] And not only does the use of different media overlap—sometimes even within the documentation of the same event—but one medium is frequently employed to remediate another—for example, incorporating still photographs into videos or websites. Although this chapter considers this wide range of phenomena, it focuses on video in relation to ritual. This medium's distinctive attributes have especially powerful implications for planning, remembering, and, most of all, experiencing rituals, testifying to the power of a new medium to transform religious life, especially the ways that religion articulates the course of a person's life.

The videotape of Mollie's naming ceremony prompted larger questions about the relation of the ritual's videodocumentation to "the ritual itself": Was the videotape regarded by at least some members of the family as enhancing their experience of the ritual? Could watching the video be understood as an extension of attending the ritual or as a substitute for it—if, say, a copy were sent to a relative who had not come to the ceremony? Conversely, might someone regard making or viewing the videotape as interfering with the ritual or undermining its significance? Or, if the video is understood as part of "the ritual itself," how does it figure in the overall engagement with ritual?

Scholars offer diverse understandings of how rituals relate to mediating practices. Some theoreticians of religion tend to stress as definitional certain aspects of ritual that seem inimical to mediation: ritual's temporal and spatial immediacy, the separating of ritual activity from quotidian experience. Jonathan Z. Smith, for example, insists on "the role of place as a fundamental component of ritual." Discussing rituals engaged in unconventional ways, including through photography, Ronald Grimes terms them "rites out of place."[5] Anthropologists Barbara Myerhoff and Clifford Geertz, by contrast, call attention to the "virtual magic" of rituals, wherein "the world as lived and the world as imagined [are] fused," suggesting an affinity of rituals with mediation.[6] Some communications scholars, such as Eric Rothenbuhler, suggest a similar compatibility, arguing that "ritual is one of the strongest forms of communicative effectiveness. . . . Whatever else it may be, ritual is always also a way of saying."[7] Rather than either contrasting or analogizing ritual and media, let us consider the implications of mediations as part of ritual practice itself, understood as processual and contingent—what religion scholar Catherine Bell terms "ritualization."[8] In this regard, mediations can extend and complicate conventional notions of what constitutes ritual time, space, community, and experience.

This approach to analyzing the photodocumentation of rituals raises a series of questions about the nexus of religion and media. First, there are questions about the relationship of videotaping (or photographing or filming) to rituals as understood by their celebrants. How have the planning, making, viewing, and archiving of these documents become part of religious ritual practice, preceding and following "live" rituals as well as being integrated into them? What symbolic investments do people make in the media documentation of their rituals? Why do they see it as a desirable, even necessary part of religious activity? How has media documentation informed the nature of experiencing rituals? For example, how does knowing that one is being photographed or filmed during a ritual inform one's engagement in it?

Next, there are questions about the protocols these practices have engendered: What sort of requirements, restrictions, recommendations, and so on have religious authorities established for creating these mediations, and how do these protocols relate to those for the rituals themselves? What aesthetic protocols inform photographing, filming, or videotaping rituals? Are these documentations influenced by the ways that other motion pictures (home movies generally, documentaries, Hollywood dramas, music videos) or other cultural forms (novels, diaries, theater, art photography, figurative painting, advertising) tell stories or situate viewing?

These questions, in turn, raise more questions about the agency of ritual photodocumentation: Who are the people who create these mediations: relatives and friends, or hired professionals? How do amateur and professional mediations of rituals differ from one another? How do photographers and videographers shape the rituals they document? Especially when these are professionals, to what extent are they regarded as authorities on not only the documentation but also "the ritual itself"?

Finally, what is the afterlife of these media documentations once they have been produced? How are they viewed, archived, distributed, incorporated into other media? How is the experience of viewing them related to the experience of the rituals that they document?

My ability to create, impromptu, a suitable documentation of Mollie's baby-naming ritual suggests a widely shared photographic culture at work. I was drawing, if unwittingly, on my command of what anthropologist Richard Chalfen terms "Kodak culture," which he defines as "whatever it is that one has to learn, know, or do in order to participate appropriately in . . . the home mode of pictorial communication." Chalfen characterizes the home mode as "interpersonal and small group visual communication centered around the home," including the intimacy of domestic life beyond a physical residence (for example, on family outings and vacations).[9] As manifest in snapshots, videos, and other family photography, the home mode "conforms to folkways," notes media scholar James Moran, to the extent that these practices are highly conventionalized, rooted in preexisting behaviors and values. Moreover, home mode photographs constitute "symbolic statements of consensus"; their "structured redundancy" expresses "conformity to certain cultural ideals," recognizing "personal progress" through "images acknowledg[ing] that the next step in life has been taken in a proper and successful manner."[10] This characterization suggests that the making of home mode photographs has a strong formal and functional affinity for the rituals—birthday parties, graduations, anniversaries, and the like—that are frequently their subject.

Similarly, the automatic nature of how Mollie's family engaged with the videotape of her naming ceremony indicates that this widely shared cultural mode extends to these images' reception. A rabbi in New York City told me of a comparable occurrence: "I was called upon to officiate at a baby-naming in someone's home. The ceremony was videotaped by a relative or friend, and immediately upon its conclusion the tape was rewound and watched. It seemed more important to 'live' the experience via the tape . . . than to have actually witnessed it live!"[11] The implications of this familiar sensibility for ritual practice are very provocative, as the rabbi's comments suggest: Does the desire, while performing a ceremony, to see "how it looked" evince a heightened attention to one's appearance in public generally? Is this more specifically a consequence of the extensive opportunities that photographic technologies provide for fulfilling what Moran characterizes as "a desire to record and observe oneself"—so much so that it seems one can "live" an experience through its videotape? Moran notes that a distinctive feature of video is that it "closes the gap between production and reception. Its images may be viewed, in fact, while the event being recorded is still in progress, imbuing its artifacts with a self-conscious reflexivity foregrounding the theatricality inherent in the home mode itself."[12] Moreover, is performing a ritual, at least sometimes, considered an incomplete experience without viewing its photodocumentation? If so, then does the desire to watch the video of the ritual so soon after performing it constitute a more expansive notion of ritual experience or a more attenuated one?

The behavior of Mollie's family suggests that they were completing the ritual experience by becoming witnesses of themselves, sharing vicariously in the community of the ritual's watchers. At the same time, Stuart and I, observers of the original "live" ritual, were moved closer to the celebrants' experience by joining them in watching and discussing the mediated ritual. (As videographer, I could now watch how I had observed the ritual; I was also in the unique position of watching my own documentation from the vantage of an observer whose attention was now free of the camera.) The family's attentive gaze conformed to the ritual's ideal viewer that I had modeled for them—but my ideal view in turn reflected the ritual's protocols. The ceremony was held in a Reform synagogue, which places a rather high value on decorum, in a sanctuary that clearly articulates the separation of celebrants and observers, the former standing on an elevated platform facing the latter, seated in rows of pews. Viewing the video thus both reaffirmed and challenged the ceremony's fixed boundaries between celebrants and observers. Such behavior supports documentarian Jean Rouch's argument that ethnographic film can create a "participating camera," facilitating a "shared ciné-anthropology,"[13] and Myerhoff's observation that people generally come "more completely alive" in response to the attention of "a camera, a tape recorder, or . . . any indication that a record [is] being made of their existence."[14] Video thus complicates the notion of what it means to "experience" a ritual by enhancing its meaningfulness and fostering more extensive—and different—engagement in the process, centered on the act of watching.

An explanation readily offered for making photographs, films, or videos of rituals is that they are reminders of persons, places, or events that one wishes to recall and are treasured as keepsakes in themselves. Thus, photo albums are frequently inscribed with the word "Memories" on the cover, and a common inscription on old family photographs reads, in various languages, "as a remembrance." Manufacturers of camera equipment, film, and videotape regularly promote their goods as instruments of remembering (exemplified for decades in the United States by the phrase "Kodak memories"). Yet scholars of photography and of memory regularly problematize this facile connection. "Scientists agree that the brain does not operate like a camera," notes psychologist Daniel Schachter, who cautions that memory does not work "like a video recorder, allowing us to replay the past in exact detail." Rather, he argues, "memories are built from fragments of experience" in what psychologists term "an encoding process—a procedure for transforming something a person sees, hears, things, or feels, into a memory."[15]

Cultural critics have seized on the disparity between photography and memory as strategic for understanding the workings of remembrance. Susan Sontag famously characterized every photograph as a "memento mori," an assertion with challenging implications.[16] If, for example, a photograph of a newborn baby serves as a reminder of death, it does so by displacing memory from the photograph's referent—that is, whatever or whoever was situated before the camera when rays of light reflecting from this subject were exposed to film (or, in the digital age, to a process of encoding reflected light in bytes of information). Thus, art critic John Berger argues, "every photograph presents us with two messages: a message concerning the event photographed and another concerning a shock of discontinuity. Between the moment recorded and the present moment of looking at the photograph, there is an abyss."[17] Marianne Hirsch similarly argues that "photographs, ghostly revenants, are very particular instruments of remembrance, since they are perched between memory and postmemory"—a kind of remembering that is "distinguished by generational distance and . . . deep personal connection" and is "mediated not through recollection but through an imaginative investment and creation."[18] Rather than simply indexing subjects of the past, these writers argue, photographs have a significance of their own, inherent in the medium itself, which complicates the viewer's relationship to their subjects and their remembrance. Indeed, these analyses of photography suggest that this medium, by its very nature, facilitates a way of remembering quite different from what the mind does independently or in relation to other media, such as written texts.

Developments in photographic technology have further complicated the distinctive role of the photographed image (whether still or moving) in remembrance, notably by dint of the recent ability to view images immediately after their recording. Indeed, video can be viewed on a monitor as images are being recorded. Still photographs can be seen either minutes after their taking (with Polaroid cameras) or as soon as the shutter has been open and shut, in the case of digital cameras. These developments have transformed the nature of still photography, not only allowing photographers to scrutinize their work on the spot but also enabling subjects to participate in evaluating the images, deciding whether they should be saved or destroyed (both videotapes and the memory cards used in digital cameras can be erased and rerecorded) and whether additional poses or footage need to be shot. Consequently, photographic images of events are less often first viewed—and first become objects of remembrance— days or weeks after their recording and are more frequently scrutinized by photographers and their subjects in situ, prompting greater self-consciousness of creating documents of memory as integral to the event to be remembered.

Viewing the videotape of Mollie's naming ceremony so soon after the synagogue ritual took place was therefore less an instrument of remembrance, as this is conventionally understood, than an instrument of the ceremony's consolidation and validation, functioning somewhat like the repetition of words or gestures that often occurs in ritual performance. Unlike the original ritual, however, this "repetition" took place in a different setting (a private home instead of a synagogue) and without the presence of either clergy or congregants. Viewing the video of a ritual in this manner does not simply "repeat" ritual behavior but elaborates and redirects it as an occasion of observing rather than enacting. Although it is distinct from the act of remembering, this redirection of experiencing the ritual as a mediated, self-reflexive act of witnessing will also continue to inform the celebrants' remembrance of the ritual as an event that they observed, especially to the extent that they re-view the video as an act of recollection.

Indeed, Mollie's family's viewing of the videotape of her naming ceremony shortly after returning home from the synagogue assured them that the ritual had been documented for future watching. This tape then joined their inventory of other photodocumentations of birthday parties, vacations, soccer games, dance recitals, and the like. It is an inventory that, I think, typically is only seldom revisited. Several years after the ceremony took place, when I wanted to discuss home videos with students, I asked Mollie's father if I could borrow this videotape. I learned then that the family had not looked at it again since the day of the ceremony; moreover, this tape (until recently, the only copy) remained in my possession for years. Nevertheless, its existence as a record of the ceremony *is* of value to the family; were I to tell them that I had lost or damaged it, they would doubtless be upset, as I am sure they would have been if something had gone wrong with the video camera during the ceremony and it failed to record the event.

Knowing that the event is being recorded has become key to experiencing "the ritual itself," as is knowing of the potential for the documentation's repeat viewing (even if it is seldom, if ever, actualized), for this double awareness secures the event's remembrance. Chalfen observes that taking pictures as *aides de memoire* is occasionally characterized as "making an investment," suggesting that "home mode images gain in interest when people make investments in creating a memory bank."[19] The very decision to photograph or videotape a ritual marks it as a memorable event, for the act of making this photodocumentation implies future acts of looking back, which, as in the case of Mollie's naming ceremony, will revisit both the actual ritual and the first viewing of the videotape shortly thereafter. As part of "the ritual itself," photography looks forward to retrospection; by anticipating future rites of the ceremony's contemplation through viewing, the medium further attenuates and complicates the ritualization process.

"In Keeping with Good Taste and Decorum"

Videotaping a baby-naming ceremony is but one example of a generally heightened attention to documenting a newly arrived life. This practice has flourished in the era of photography, growing more extensive as a series of new media has facilitated greater possibilities: professional studio portraits of babies, snapshots of infants in home mode, 16 mm and 8 mm home movies of newborns arriving home from the hospital or in maternity wards, videotapes of births.[20] Indeed, media documentation of new life now extends beyond even this threshold; photographing or videotaping sonograms of the fetus *in utero* facilitates prenatal surveillance not only for obstetricians but also for expecting parents and their family and friends.

Interrogating the desire for such extensive photodocumentation of a new life and of childhood more generally shifts attention from the camera's subject to the adults who produce, circulate, and display these images. Home movies, according to Heather Nicholson, "may disclose as much about the adults in charge of making and showing the film as the children framed by the camera"; at the same time, these films "also hint at the film-maker's belief in children as the future." And herein, Nicholson argues, lies a paradox: "the expanding capacity to record childhood experience [has] coincided with renewed debate about the disappearance of childhood." Does "the production and consumption of idealized family memories and childhoods" in the form of home movies, she asks, "represent either a form of wish fulfillment . . . or a surrogate vision of childhood as modernizing pressures continue to erode traditional notions of childhood and family experience?"[21] And are these films staged to produce an image of an ideal childhood, or, within their staging, does their subjects' behavior manifest the ineluctable child, who cannot be completely restrained?

These questions acquire additional significance when the photodocumentation centers on a ritual that is itself freighted with symbolic value and, for many people, challenging implications—namely, the *berit milah* (circumcision ritual) or, as it is more commonly known in the United States, the *bris* (the Yiddish term). Unlike baby-naming ceremonies, circumcising infant Jewish boys, usually eight days after they are born, is among the oldest and most widely observed Jewish practices, its origins traditionally rooted in biblical narratives of Abraham (Genesis 21:4) and Moses (Exodus 4:25). In recounting the ritual's origins, modern books on the Jewish life cycle also note the prehistoric roots of circumcision, dating back to the Stone Age.[22]

Rabbinic law governing other Jewish life-cycle rituals requires some form of documentation as part of their enactment—the *ketubbah* (wedding contract) for a marriage, the *get* (writ of divorce) for a divorce— or they involve textual or visual documentation as part of longstanding custom (such as erecting an inscribed tombstone within a year following burial). The *bris*, however, makes no such requirement, though there are some local customs for documentation, including record books kept by the *mohel* (circumciser) in some communities and making a decorated Torah binder from a cloth used during the circumcision, once common among Western Ashkenazim. Indeed, the Jewish circumcision rite is understood as semiologically self-sufficient; the circumcised penis is both the signifier of the covenant of Abraham and its signified fulfillment.[23] Although the ritual once inspired an elaborate material culture—ornamented and inscribed circumcision tools, decorative cloths and plaques adorned with blessings recited during the ceremony, special ceremonial chairs—circumcision is, by and large, no longer a site of such cultural creativity. Unlike other Jewish celebrations that have engendered an elaborate material culture, the *bris* has become visually more austere. What, then, prompts photographing or videotaping this ritual?

Although indigenous visual documentation of the *bris* was, until the advent of video, limited and often oblique, the ceremony is a longstanding fixture of Christian art. The circumcision of Jesus is depicted frequently in European church decoration and illustrated editions of the New Testament, often reflecting some awareness of contemporary Jewish practice of the ritual. In these works, as well as in ethnographic representations of Jewish custom as early as the seventeenth century, the viewer's attention is typically focused on the baby amid the assembled family or community and on the rite that is about to be performed. The circumcision is observed from a perspective centrally positioned in relation to a formally arranged tableau and yet at a remove from it—offering, in effect, a "gentile's-eye view."

Bris videos that I have seen configure witnessing the ritual quite differently, and they also differ from the videodocumentation of the baby-naming ceremony described earlier or from other rituals, such as a bar or bat mitzvah, that are usually held in a synagogue. Though a *bris* can be performed in a synagogue, it is often held in the home of a family member. In such cases, the improvised transformation of private living space into a semipublic ritual space (and a temporary operating theater) creates a more compressed, fluid configuration of the physical boundaries between observers and celebrants. Not only does the *bris* destabilize the use of space; the gaze of observers during this ritual is also problematic. It can be difficult to witness a *bris*, and observers often avert their gaze during the actual surgery.

Videodocumentation evinces this problematic gaze in the very subjective, contingent protocols of *bris* photography. Some *bris* videos that I have seen concentrate very closely on recording the circumcision procedure; others avoid it altogether. In some instances, the video camera was on during the circumcision ritual but photographed only the observers' reactions (though the various benedictions and the baby's cries can be heard off-screen). Still photographs taken at a *bris*, by contrast, seldom

Circumcision: the gentile's-eye view. "Le circoncision des Juifs Portugais," in Bernard Picart, *Cérémonies et coutumes religieuses de tous les peuples du monde*, 1723. (Library, Jewish Theological Seminary of America)

document the ritual itself. This difference in use of the two media appears to hold true when both photographs and video are shot at the same event, suggesting that the different media themselves inspire separate photographic protocols and aesthetic sensibilities. Moran notes that video's distinctive properties—notably, its ability to record extended sequences at lower light levels—"increase the potential range and volume of events and behaviors recorded during home mode production." He argues that video's "less self-conscious presence on the scene of domestic living tends to relax some of the artificial conventions imposed by home movies, even when camcorders are appropriated to document special events."[24] Thus, video cameras enable the user to zoom in discreetly on a subject from a considerable distance, filming events that center attention on small-scale action, as is the case with the *bris*. Indeed, although these rituals are now frequently documented by amateur photographers on videotape, such was apparently not the case with 16 mm or 8 mm film, which requires setting up lights for interior filming; moreover, the length of a reel of film limits shooting sequences to a few minutes, whereas video enables continuous recording for two hours or longer.

The challenging nature of *bris* photography and videography is sometimes discussed in the course of the ritual itself. At Eli Oz Berliner's *bris*, held in a Manhattan synagogue in 2004, the *mohel* invited guests with cameras to step forward as the ritual was about to begin; at one point, he quipped, "There are a lot of paparazzi here today." At the same time, he asked photographers to refrain from taking pictures while the baby was undiapered, "in keeping with good taste and decorum," and he also cautioned that flash photography could distract the *mohel.* Eli is the son of documentary filmmaker Alan Berliner, who has made innovative and thought-provoking use of home-movie footage in *Family Album,* his 1986 documentary about these films, and in a series of documentaries about himself and his family: *Intimate Stranger* (1991), *Nobody's Business* (1996), *The Sweetest Sound* (2001), and *Wide Awake* (2006). At his son's *bris,* Berliner explained that he was having the ritual filmed in part because of his own "obsessions" but also so that, should his son some day want to make a documentary film about fathers and sons, or about rituals, he would have some "interesting footage" to work with.[25]

Berliner regards home movies as raw material for future cinematic self-exploration, their potential realized in the work of a second filmmaker. "Reusing selected images and sounds links all of my films—as if they're all part of the same 'genealogy,'" he explains. "I sometimes think of it as a metaphor for the idea of recombinant DNA." The implications of this observation are telling, especially in relation to what Berliner, among others, characterizes as the "father-dominated" nature of home movies. Through the processes of selection and juxtaposition inherent in montage, parental authority is subverted, and the father's gift of images to the son is reconfigured, as genetic material is in biological reproduction. Having worked these kinds of transformations on home-movie footage (both of his own family and of other, anonymous ones), Berliner is alert to the constructed nature of these films themselves: "Home movie images are lies. . . . They frame the family (for posterity) as a source of perpetual joy and fun."[26] For Berliner, the filmmaker's task is to unpack, reframe, and interrogate the ideal vision of the parent—or, as Renov writes of domestic ethnography film generally, "to enact a kind of participant observation that illumines the familiar other while simultaneously refracting a self-image."[27]

Berliner notes that shooting video entails considerably less planning than shooting film requires. Amateur filmmakers, like professionals, need to think "cinematically" in advance of shooting—planning the moments to be filmed, their duration, staging, illumination, and so on—whereas video has become increasingly spontaneous, especially as lightweight, portable cameras enable automatic focus, exposure, and other technical settings.[28] As a result, shooting video becomes more indiscriminate. It is more akin to looking, albeit with a purpose; it thus becomes more ethnographic. In fact, *bris* videos usually offer a very self-conscious ethnography. The question of what (not) to film—in addition to sometimes avoiding the circumcision, *bris* videographers choose whether to record family members crying or otherwise displaying emotional distress—may reflect the videographers' relation to the subjects or to the event, sometimes evincing an ambivalence about circumcision and even about Jewishness more generally. In this respect, the camera may imitate the avoidant eye of the anxious spectator (in contrast to the ideal, unwavering spectator of the baby-naming ceremony discussed earlier).

Much of the attention of *bris* photodocumentation is directed away from the circumcision itself with regard to both time and subject. Whether or not *bris* videos record the surgery, they, like still photos, typically document the assembled family and friends before and/or after the circumcision. During these sequences, the video camera often roves about the space, informally recording various groupings and (if there is audio) conversations. Similarly, still photographs of a *bris* are typically taken before or after the surgery and show not only the baby but also his parents and others in attendance. The *mohel* is not usually included in these still images, indicating that the photographers' attention centered on family and community rather than the ritual bringing them together. Such is the case with the hundreds of *bris* photos posted on the website onlysimchas.com. "Only simchas" references a Yiddish saying, *nor af simkhes*, "[may we meet] only at joyous celebrations." On this website, mostly young, modern Orthodox American Jews post images of recent life-cycle celebrations (also including bar mitzvahs, betrothals, and weddings) and exchange greetings. In this venue, images of circumcisions and other life-cycle celebrations enter a communal inventory, validating these individual rituals' affirmation of Jews' continuity as a people.

This concern figures prominently in the ritual's language, which anticipates the baby's future as a member of the Jewish community, to which, it is wished, he will contribute by entering "into the Torah, the nuptial canopy, and into good deeds" and, implicitly, by eventually fathering children of his own. (This is forthrightly manifest by the Western Ashkenazic Torah binder, which commemorates the *bris* as the first step in a Jewish male's life through images that often project his future as an adult.)[29] In contrast, the attention of *bris* photos and videos is often retrospective, directed back on those who more immediately bear the responsibility of Jewish continuity, especially the boy's parents and their new awareness of this onus. This perspective underscores the *bris* as a significant event not so much for the infant—who, though at its center, is an involuntary and unaware participant—but for the assembled adults, for whom this is a definitional (and, especially for new parents, transformative) moment. As anthropologist Vincent Crapanzano notes of circumcision rituals among Muslims in Morocco, this archetypal rite of passage is also, perhaps more so, a rite of return for adults witnessing the circumcision, especially for the boy's father: "he too is submitting now as he did then to the manifest message of the rite, to custom and tradition, ultimately to the will of God."[30]

Who, then, is meant to watch the *bris* video, and when? The notion of the boy eventually seeing it provokes no little anxiety. Anthropologist Jonathan Boyarin reports the following anecdote about the videotape of his son Jonah's *bris*: "When . . . Jonah was born a cousin (not at our request) decided to videotape the *bris*. For some reason, when Jonah was about four (!) we were watching the videotape at home. Just as the video reached the critical moment, Jonah (watching) shouted, 'No! Don't do it!'"[31] For the child, the *bris* video documents not only what appears to be a painful act but also an infant's struggle against adult control, by dint of the rite itself and its photodocumentation. Watching a video of one's own circumcision could well invite rebellion rather than affirmation.

Then what sort of observing is the *bris* video meant to facilitate? With an ethnographic eye on the proceedings in their full complexity, the video offers a gaze at some remove from this ritual of communal affirmation. At the same time, these videos are often a very intimate form of ethnography. Unlike other life-cycle videos (of bar/bat mitzvahs and especially weddings), *bris* videos are more likely to be amateur efforts by acquaintances of the celebrants. These videographers' choices regarding what to record and how to record it reflect close insiders' perspectives on the event's local significance. At the same time, customs of the ritual suggest another possible understanding of witnessing the *bris* implicit in these videos, though it is unlikely a conscious one. According to Jewish

tradition, the biblical prophet Elijah attends, unseen, every *bris* and pro-
tects the child during the ceremony. The prophet is invoked as the ritual
begins; the *mohel* places the child on a seat and declares, in Hebrew, "This
is the chair of Elijah," and there are various customs for symbolically accommodating Elijah at the ceremony with a special chair, which remains
empty throughout the ritual. Perhaps the video of a *bris* provides a way of
imagining the gaze of Elijah as universal surveyor of these proceedings or
of extending the desire for this enhanced witnessing of the *bris* from the
folkloristic imaginary to modern technology, linking the individual ritual
with an enduring, intergenerational, national collective.

"Maybe Families Are Better Off Not Having a Recording!"

The camera's "watchful eye" can "transform activities into spectacles,"
Nicholson observes. "Cinematic childhoods become performative," and
the camera becomes an "adjunct to other forms of parental control."[32]
Perhaps nowhere in the videotaping of Jewish life-cycle events does the
relationship between generations become more charged than in the documenting of bar and bat mitzvahs. These coming-of-age rituals engage the
interrelation of parent and child at a crucial moment of transition for
both. As documenting these rituals has grown more elaborate with the
advent of videotape, they articulate tensions not only between generations
but also between the protocols of religious authority and the sensibilities
of popular religion. Indeed, these mediations both testify to and facilitate
transformations of the meaning of bar and bat mitzvah for some Jews, for
whom the rituals' traditional significance has been inverted.

In popular usage, the terms *bar mitzvah* and *bat mitzvah* refer to both
the celebrant and the ceremony, at which a young man or woman, respectively, typically thirteen years old (though often twelve for young women),
marks the assumption of adult status in Jewish religious life by reading
from scripture during communal worship for the first time in his or her
life. Like the *bris*, this ritual does not traditionally require any documentation, but with the advent of studio photography, portraits commemorating the bar mitzvah became a common practice on both sides of the Atlantic. (Photodocumentation of the bar mitzvah pre-dates that of the bat
mitzvah by several decades, the latter ritual being largely a post–World
War II phenomenon and, moreover, one not observed by many Orthodox Jews.)[33] In the early twentieth century, bar mitzvah photography was

typically confined to a studio portrait of the celebrant dressed in a prayer shawl, traditionally worn by adult Jewish men during prayer; the similarity of these portraits suggests the establishment of an iconographic rite of passage in the photographer's studio parallel to the ceremonial one in the synagogue.[34]

These early photographs were taken at a time and place separate from the bar mitzvah ritual. The advent of portable cameras for making snapshots, home movies, and videos has, over the decades, prompted growing desires to extend photodocumentation to the celebration that usually follows the synagogue service and to the service itself. This is problematic, however, as most bar/bat mitzvah rituals (and many postritual celebrations) take place in synagogues on the Sabbath, and so the desire to photograph these rituals conflicts with rabbinic tenets regarding what acts are permitted on the Sabbath generally and in the synagogue specifically. Like other questions of Jewish law prompted by new technologies, this issue has engendered debate and rulings among the rabbinates of different American Jewish denominations, especially the non-Orthodox.

Across these different movements, rabbinic discourse typically characterizes photography, still or moving, as inherently at odds with religious experience, quite apart from the issue of when rabbinic law permits photography. The Reform movement's Central Conference of American Rabbis offered a ruling on videotaping in the synagogue in 1986, which "generally discourage[s] it as it is often intrusive," noting an array of rabbinic assertions, from the Talmud to early leaders of the American Reform movement, that "nothing may distract the worshipper from worship."[35] Among Conservative rabbis, this issue generated a series of responsa, beginning in the early 1980s (and invoking earlier discussions of photographing and audiotaping Sabbath services, dating back to the 1950s). On the whole, members of the Committee on Jewish Law and Standards of the movement's Rabbinical Assembly either ruled against videotaping on the Sabbath or condoned it only under certain conditions (for example, "when the camera has been pre-focused, preset, attached to a timer, and placed in a location where its presence will be unobtrusive and perhaps even hidden from the view of the worshippers"), ultimately leaving the decision up to individual rabbis.[36] Similarly, the executive director of the Reconstructionist Rabbinical Association reports that, rather than there being an official institutional position, the issue is left to the discretion of individual rabbis, who tend to "focus more on whether video interferes with the event rather than on halakhic [i.e., rabbinic legal] issues," and of individual congregations, some of which "have a no-photo/no-video policy" for the entire Sabbath, whereas others "allow [photography] at [the] reception but not during the service, some allow [videography] at the service as long as [there are] no lights, no mikes that interfere, etc."[37]

Conservative rabbis' legal arguments largely center on whether videotaping violates Talmudic prohibitions against work on the Sabbath. Key concerns are whether videotaping is the equivalent of writing, a traditionally forbidden form of work (with some rabbis arguing for both possibilities, based on differing understandings of the science of magnetic tape), and whether the impulse to fix recording equipment (another form of prohibited work), should it malfunction, is equivalent to similar temptations, which traditionally prohibit playing musical instruments, among other activities, on the Sabbath. Quite apart from legal issues, both Reform and Conservative rabbis raise other concerns in their debates about videotaping, evincing varied understandings of the medium's transformative impact. One question Conservative rabbis have asked is whether videotaping a worship service in any way "enhances" the Sabbath—that is, contributes to spiritual engagement with the holy day's "tranquility and dignity"—or, conversely, whether mediation interferes with this experience, for example, by encouraging worshippers to "play to the camera."[38] Similarly, the Reform ruling asserts that "it is essential to keep the videotaping as a recording of what has occurred and not 'stage' the service for the taping."[39] At the same time, the mediating potential of videotape has special appeal for some rabbis. One Conservative rabbi proposes that "providing a tape of . . . services to those hospitalized or confined to their homes or in nursing homes is an important mitzvah [here meaning "good deed," though resonant with another meaning of the term, "religious precept"]. . . . All too often family members are absent from significant events due to chronic illness, temporary incapacity, or the difficulty of taking a long trip. . . . For these family members, a tape enables those not physically present to share the excitement of the event."[40] But another rabbi argues that "tapes destroy the 'mythic quality' that a ceremony would otherwise assume in people's memories. Tapes indiscriminately record the mistakes and limitations of events along with their positive features. Human memory, in contrast, blessedly enables us to filter out the miscues so that we can remember such events as being better than they actually were. Maybe families are better off *not* having a recording!"[41] Although both rabbis understand video as informing memory practices, their concerns for the medium's implications diverge.

These rabbis also debate what contribution the media documentation of a bar or bat mitzvah celebration might make to the "enhancement of the family's Jewish life" beyond the ceremony itself.[42] Some Conservative rabbis have advocated for this position, including an early argument presented in 1953 by Jacob Agus, who proposed that "there is a positive value for Judaism in recording [on audiotape] a bar mitzvah or similar occasion, since Jewish piety today is not coextensive with a person's life. It is now found in certain strong points, of which the bar mitzvah observance is one of the most important. The more this ceremony is recalled at family gatherings, the better it is for Judaism."[43] More recent discussions have affirmed that, "with the continuing development of technology, [Agus's] argument is even more cogent."[44] But other Conservative rabbis have dissented, acknowledging the larger concern about a decline in observance while disputing the power of photography to effect piety: "A tape of a child chanting her Haftarah [a selection from the Prophets or Writings read following the weekly Torah reading] [is] not likely to encourage a family to observe Shabbat [the Sabbath] or attend services without the motivation of a special occasion. . . . Do we really believe that photographs . . . or a tape of the service will do years later that which the ceremony itself has failed to do?"[45]

Aesthetic concerns run throughout these discussions, relating, on one hand, to the larger question of enhancing the Sabbath, a traditional occasion for engaging certain aesthetic pleasures, and, on the other hand, to the artistic protocols of videography. Thus, one proposal for permitting videodocumentation of Sabbath worship under certain circumstances suggests that, following the practice of varying actions from the way they are usually performed during the week so that they can be done on the Sabbath, "the recording equipment should be hidden from view. . . . The camera should be as inconspicuous as possible and remain stationary and unmanned. The camera, through its wide angle lens, will record everything that occurs on the pulpit, and the family can edit the resulting tape as it sees fit."[46] Here and throughout this rabbinic debate, a tension is manifest between halakhic efforts to regulate modern technology and the investments that many Jews have made in video as enhancing remembrance, communal experience, and even piety.

In order to fulfill congregants' desires for a photographic record of the bar/bat mitzvah ritual, some congregations that ban photography on the Sabbath do allow the ceremony to be simulated for the camera (despite some admonitions against "playing to the camera"). Typically, this is done at the synagogue a day or two before the ritual. What the camera records as a remembrance of the bar/bat mitzvah ceremony is, therefore, a *preen-actment* of the actual ritual. As is the case with screening a baby-naming video shortly after the ceremony was performed, this videodocumenta-tion of the bar/bat mitzvah complicates the ritual's relationship to time—here, documenting for future recollection an event that anticipates "the ritual itself." The slippage between the actual ritual and its preenactment is sometimes manifest in these videos, which vary in the extent to which they simulate the ceremony, especially when they record both audio and video. For example, when reciting prayers or blessings, a choice will be made to utter either the Hebrew names of God or their substitute forms—*Adoshem, Elokeynu*—as is traditionally done when uttering divine names outside of actual worship.

This dislocation of the ceremony's documentation from its actual cele-bration—creating a simulacrum of an event to facilitate its remembrance before the event has, in fact, taken place—is emblematic of a larger shift in meaning of the bar/bat mitzvah ritual for many American Jews (who are represented disproportionately, I believe, among those who commis-sion these more elaborate mediations). Rather than commemorating the beginning of adult responsibility regarding Jewish religious observance, with the first of future occasions when the young man or woman will par-ticipate in synagogue rites of reading scripture, the ceremony more likely celebrates for those Jews in question the end of a childhood of Jewish learning and the beginning of a Jewish adolescence (rather than adult-hood) often marked by religious nonobservance. In such circumstances, the bar/bat mitzvah constitutes what Crapanzano terms a "disjunctive" rite, which offers the celebrant not the official, promised transition from one stage of life to another but rather "a series of contradictory messages that remain unresolved, at least in the ritual immediate. What resolution, if any, may come with time." The ritual itself offers only "the illusion of resolution," but "the illusion of ritual must be denied; the ritual illusion must be taken as real."[47]

Reconfiguring the bar/bat mitzvah as a meaningful landmark in the Jewish life cycle is now often effected by the frequent practice of present-ing, usually at festivities following the synagogue service, a mediated life review of the celebrant. Typically, this presentation consists of a slide show or videomontage of photographs and, sometimes, clips from home movies or videos of the celebrant's life from infancy to the present, of-ten with musical accompaniment and, occasionally, intertitles or recorded narration. This presentation, whether assembled by family members or produced professionally, implicitly situates the bar/bat mitzvah ritual as the culmination of a childhood narrative.

This inversion of the bar/bat mitzvah's traditional significance—configuring it as a culmination rather than a beginning—and the disparity between the modern concept of adolescence and the traditional Jewish concept of adulthood has opened up possibilities for associating these coming-of-age rituals with the modes of parody and kitsch. The notion of a bar mitzvah film as a meaningful documentation of a rite of passage was lampooned in Canadian author Mordechai Richler's 1959 novel *The Apprenticeship of Duddy Kravitz* (and became a memorable sequence in the book's 1974 film adaptation). In one of Kravitz's more outrageous schemes to make his fortune, he serves as "executive producer" of a bar mitzvah film. Richler recounts the film's screening for the family of the celebrant, Bernard Cohen, in the form of a screenplay, punctuated by the family's often irreverent comments ("Look at Sammy, stuffing his big fat face as usual"). The author conjures up a film, ostensibly created by Kravitz's business partner, a pretentious cineaste, that is composed of a wide-ranging montage of images ("Lightning. African tribal dance. Jungle fire. Stukas diving. A jitterbug contest speeded up. Slaughtering of a cow. Fireworks against a night sky. More African dancing."), narration ("As solemn as the Aztec sacrifice, more mysterious than Helen's face, is the pregnant moment, the meeting of time past and time present, when the priest and his initiate reach the *ho'mat*"), and music ("Elgar's 'Pomp and Circumstance' . . . the drinking song from 'La Traviata' . . . Al Jolson sings 'Eli, Eli'"), constituting a film that parodies ethnographic documentary, art film, and home movies ("A smiling Rabbi Goldstone leads Bernard up the aisle of the temple. In the background second cousins and schoolmates wave and smile at the camera."). But the ultimate target of Richler's satire is Bernard's arriviste father, who has bankrolled this extravaganza and embraces its wild excess: "Mr. Cohen, sitting in the first row . . . , thought, it's worth it, every last cent or what's money for, it's cheap at any price to have captured my family and friends and foolish rabbi."[48]

Today, American video artists routinely refer to overly flashy, computer-generated special effects as the stuff of "bar mitzvah videos"—the awkward overreaching of the adolescent exemplifying an aesthetics of overindulgence. This sensibility is not limited to bar/bat mitzvah videos, which typically include (and often concentrate on) the parties following the synagogue services; it can frequently be found in the parties themselves, which have become extensively thematized events. In recent decades, bar/bat mitzvah parties are often conceptualized around a comprehensive theme, articulated in invitations, décor, food, music, clothing, favors, and activities. (Some of these elements entail photography, such as renting a machine that will print photographs of guests on souvenir items.) Thematized bar/bat mitzvah parties suggest that the celebrant is meant to distinguish him- or herself not through a traditional display of Jewish erudition but through an elaborately conceptualized, self-styled performance of "an imaginary world" that will "transport the guests to their wildest fantasies for one night only, be that the chicest of nightclubs [or] the toniest of beach resorts."[49]

The coincidence of these extensively thematized parties and the advent of videotaping these celebrations in the 1970s is telling, for this kind of celebration—the party as *Gesamkunstwerk*—is conceived as an event to be experienced in cinematic terms. In recent decades some bar/bat mitzvah celebrations have featured celebrity impersonators (for example, Michael Jackson in the 1980s), and some of these events take their themes from Hollywood genres, such as the western or jungle adventure film. More than simply providing a record of the celebration, the bar/bat mitzvah video constitutes the ultimate fulfillment of the event's cinematic sensibility.

This sensibility extends to the profile of bar/bat mitzvahs in late-twentieth-century American popular culture, as they have become frequent subjects of television dramas and comedies (in which the bar/bat mitzvah figures in a variety of plots that use the ritual to explore some aspect of adolescence) and the occasional feature film (including the 2006 comedy *Keeping Up with the Steins*, which satirized elaborately thematized bar mitzvah parties). The videotaping of bar/bat mitzvahs has also engendered a subgenre of documentary filmmaking, in which an extraordinary ritual—such as an American boy's bar mitzvah celebrated in communist Poland (*Spark among the Ashes*, 1986) and especially rituals celebrated by young people with disabilities (*Eugene*, 1995; *Best Man*, 1997; *Mayor of the West Side*, 2003; *Praying with Lior*, 2007)—becomes the film's centerpiece. In these documentaries the rituals' extraordinary circumstances seem to demand extraordinary mediation, which fuses elements of conventional videodocumentation of the synagogue ceremony or party with an extended portrait of the celebrants, their families, and the elaborate efforts made to perform the ritual.

A generation after the advent of the thematized bar/bat mitzvah party, some of its first cohort of celebrants have scrutinized these events,

Bar mitzvah of Joshua Speisman, Roslyn, New York, 1989. Thematized bar and bat mitzvah celebrations sometimes take their inspiration from popular film genres. (Courtesy of Bar Mitzvah Disco)

centering on their mediation, through a self-reflexive remediation. With the publication of *Bar Mitzvah Disco: The Music May Have Stopped, but the Party's Never Over* in 2005, a segment of American Jewish gen-Xers now approaching middle age have revisited their bar/bat mitzvah celebrations and thereby confront the end of a prolonged adolescence. This threshold is typically marked by having achieved career success and decisions to "settle down" (generally understood in heteronormative terms: marrying, having children), developments that invite this cohort to reappraise its relation to Jewishness.

As the book's title indicates, attention centers not on the synagogue service but on the partying that follows and the epiphenomena this engenders, including invitations, favors, T-shirts, decorations, and extensive photodocumentation. Although lavish bar mitzvahs have been the subject of rabbinical admonition for generations,[50] gen-Xers perceive their celebrations as having achieved an unprecedented level of ostentation about which they feel ambivalent. Indeed, the authors of *Bar Mitzvah*

Disco characterize this ambivalence as emblematic for their generation, described as having come of age "in contradictory times. . . . We believed the labels we wore said as much about us as the words that came out of our mouths. We did our damnedest to get to third base despite the backdrop of the deadly scourge of AIDS. Greed was good yet we still learned all the words to 'We Are the World.'"[51]

This ambivalence runs throughout the book's response to looking back at the bar/bat mitzvah, enabling self-critique and a reevaluation of these rituals and their significance. The photodocumentation of these bar/bar mitzvah celebrations and its remediation are central to facilitating this self-reflection. *Bar Mitzvah Disco* offers a selection of brief reminiscences about bar/bat mitzvahs by the likes of author Jonathan Safran Foer, cultural critic Josh Kun, and comic Sarah Silverman, interspersed among hundreds of color photographs of these celebrations. Dozens of contributors submitted photographs to the authors of *Bar Mitzvah Disco* through an appeal posted on the Internet; the project began as a website before becoming a book, and plans have been initiated for a documentary film on the topic.[52] The collection effort also gathered material culture (T-shirts, invitations, etc.) and videotapes, some of which are shown on the project's website. The book's structure follows the narratives of bar/bat mitzvah celebrations as articulated in the videos and photo albums that families (or the photographers they hired) created to commemorate these events, proceeding from formal family photographs (with extensive discussion of the clothes selected for the occasion) to parting shots of the celebrant waving good-bye to the camera. The assembled materials constitute a hybrid of nostalgia, arch celebration of kitsch, and popular autoethnography.

Perhaps the ultimate remediation that *Bar Mitzvah Disco* engages is the faux mitzvah—a celebration that simultaneously re-creates and spoofs the parties of lost youth. The project's website offers a downloadable guide to staging a faux mitzvah and notes that one need not have had a "real" bar/bat mitzvah—or be Jewish—to have one of these celebrations. In addition to reenactments of party rituals (such as a ceremonial lighting of thirteen candles on the bar/bat mitzvah cake), enhanced by retro clothing and period music, faux mitzvahs sometimes also include self-reflection facilitated by screening the video from the original bar/bat mitzvah that is being both recalled and mocked.[53] The faux mitzvah is the ultimate subversion of this life-cycle ritual, in which simulacrum prevails, transforming a rite of passage into a retreat back to childhood.

This mode of reengagement with the bar/bat mitzvah through acts of remediation is self-critical of its limitations even as it embraces them. It evinces a larger desire for engagement with Jewishness that does not simply evade or deride the subjects' past—nor does it simply adopt this past on its own terms. As this cohort was trained by their own bar/bat mitzvah celebrations to be self-styled, their acts of self-directed authoring and designing are key here. Style is not the enemy of substance but is regarded as being substantial, even essential. And acts of mediating and remediating do not take one further from a threshold experience in one's life; indeed, they are expected to bring one closer to it.

"Pass the Tissues, Please!"

Some Conservative rabbis opposed to videotaping bar/bat mitzvah celebrations on the Sabbath have also bemoaned the video camera's presence at weddings, but they concede that on these occasions "we must unfortunately tolerate it."[54] Indeed, weddings entail the most elaborate involvement of videography in American Jewish ritual. As is the case in many other religious and ethnic communities, weddings are the most lavishly celebrated and, consequently, most extensively professionalized of life-cycle rituals among Jews, often serving as occasions for demonstrating parents' prosperity as well as celebrating their children's marriage. These elaborate celebrations are frequently regulated at least as much by photographers, caterers, and professional event planners as they are by clergy or the celebrants' families. Consider, for example, the negotiation between longstanding religious custom and newer protocols of wedding photography in Marcus's description of the start of a typical "modern Orthodox/ traditional wedding in the United States":

> Before the guests arrive, the bride or the groom and each of his or her families are taking turns with the photographer in the room where the wedding will take place. [In keeping with traditional practice,] some couples are fasting on the day of their wedding and do not want to see each other prior to the ceremony at the huppah [wedding canopy]. This means that the photographer has to settle for separate bride-party and groom-party shots until after the ceremony. Friends of the bride and groom serve as look-outs in the hallways and signal one then the other that the coast is clear so the bride and groom can emerge and be photographed

with his or her family. This also means delaying the arrival of the bride and groom at the wedding celebration because the bride and groom are photographed together only after the ceremony.[55]

Wedding photography, both still and moving, can also structure the proceedings by inspiring ritual innovation. Photographers regularly pose the bride, groom, and others in the party in conventional poses (for example, the couple photographed in profile, toasting each other with glasses of champagne, their arms interlocked) or stage activities in which the wedding party and, sometimes, guests take part. For example, films made in the 1950s of weddings celebrated by the Dushoffs, a Jewish family in Philadelphia, document a ritual of male and female guests kissing the bride that appears to have been staged, at least in part, with the camera in mind.[56]

Photographers' regulation of the wedding is implicated in the responsibility they have assumed for the event's recollection. "For many couples the Wedding Day goes by so fast. It's difficult to remember what actually happened," Gabriel Solomon Photography of New York City informs potential customers on its website. "We facilitate a way for you to relive the moments of your wedding day so you can remember what your wedding was all about."[57] So strong is the imperative to photograph the wedding in order to remember it—indeed, in order to experience it—that photographers are routinely turned to during preparations for the celebration, and sometimes during the celebration itself, for instruction. In addition to giving wedding parties directions on staging the ritual during rehearsal, photographers are known on occasion to ask couples and their relatives during the ceremony to repeat what they have done for the camera, to ensure that it is properly recorded.

Such "retakes" of ritual behavior are called for (and complied with) because professional wedding videos are typically highly produced media pieces, with narration, titles, music, and special effects added by the videographers, in contrast to the relative spontaneity and formal simplicity of amateur videos. In professionally produced wedding videos, footage of the event is extensively edited, in order to create a continuous narrative. The aesthetic owes more to the cinema than to amateur home-movie making, which, as film scholar Patricia Zimmermann notes, typically eschews editing and other conventions of narrative cinema.[58] Thus, the website for Simchavision, wedding photographers catering especially to Orthodox Jews in Lakewood, New Jersey, vaunts "state-of-the-art digital cameras and editing equipment to custom create your story," aided by "Emmy nominee, television trained videographers."[59] Professionally produced videos of rituals facilitate a distinct mode of mediated witnessing, which is modeled not on the gaze of an amateur insider, recording in "real time," but on cinematic notions of observing, directed by the protocols of filmic storytelling, articulated by montage.

As is the case with bar/bat mitzvah celebrations, video producers can also situate the wedding as the culmination of life narratives told through the compilation of images. Simchavision, among other production companies, offers to create for clients a "family history/photo montage" of "pictures of the bride and groom from childhood to engagement set to music interspersed with video footage of the bride and groom telling their own special story. We live in a video age where old film and video footage of the couple's childhood can be added to their story. This unique piece will be projected at your wedding for your guests to enjoy. (Pass the tissues, please!)"[60] Here, video producers take over the role of the *badkhn*, or wedding entertainer, of traditional Yiddish-speaking culture, whose task is to offer guests an emotionally moving and aesthetically regulated performance in the form of rhymed couplets, intoned to instrumental accompaniment. The *badkhn*, too, customizes his performance to suit the bride and groom and their families, though typically his verses address hopes for the couple's future, rather than narrating their past.

Moran, who was himself a professional event videographer, notes that wedding videos entail a complex relationship between videographers and their clients: although this relationship "may hold out the potential for a genuine collaboration . . . , [it] may be fraught with power relations." He argues that, "although technically a biography in production," the wedding video "should function as an autobiography during reception."[61] As client-driven works, wedding videos situate the bride and groom in the role of executive producers, invited to select from among an array of photographic styles and storytelling strategies an aesthetic that suits their own sensibilities: "Whether your style is formal and elegant or sleek MTV, we go the road you want," Simchavision promises. "Hollywood special effects, slow-motions, wide screen, black and white, filters, glide cam, crane cam."[62] In the open marketplace of wedding videography, professional photographers promote competing aesthetics on their websites as they vie for clients. Hollywood genres are not the only possibilities offered as suitable for wedding videos. The Jerry Meyer Studio of New York City touts its approach to event videography as "photojournalism."[63] Similarly, Notowitz

Productions of Southern California stresses its distinctive "documentary" style. "We like it real. So no cheesy effects, and we don't cover everything with music. . . . We are the driving force in what some call wedding video journalism, also known as . . . documentary wedding video production, an exciting, personal way to have your wedding video become a real, lasting heirloom for your family." David Notowitz assures potential clients that his videographers are "top professionals" who are "calm under pressure, unfalteringly reliable, unobtrusive, and technically highly skilled. . . . Your finished wedding video will be a rare gift . . . that will last forever—a video that will touch your heart, entertain your children, and rekindle your love. I know personally how important a video is because my wife and I watch our video every anniversary. I'm sure glad 'Cousin Joey' didn't shoot it!"[64] Note the multiple investments made in the video: it is variously a work of professional reportage, a family keepsake, and even something of an aphrodisiac. Notowitz positions the wedding video as essential to the value of a ritual understood as a life-defining event, with implications that extend well beyond the ceremony itself. At the same time, he addresses the challenge inherent in the event's ephemeral nature: "You will not get a second chance with your video. Words of congratulations and best wishes from relatives beautifully celebrating while they're healthy, strong, and able to share in the joy of your special day . . . a kiss and warm hug from your father . . . a laugh shared as you cut your cake . . . These moments are priceless and you want your videographer to have the experience and talent to expertly capture these memories on video."[65] Failure to commission proper, professional photodocumentation of the wedding, he warns, will result in an event that cannot be effectively recalled.

On occasion, a bride and groom conceptualize their wedding as an original work of art of their own making, in which mediation defines the structure of the celebration as forthrightly as religious protocol. Such was the case when media/installation artist Melissa Shiff and her husband, art historian Louis Kaplan, planned their wedding, which took place in Toronto on 12 October 2003. Shiff describes the ceremony as a reinvented ritual, using "postmodern artistic strategies" that negotiate "between contemporary performance art and the customs of the traditional Jewish wedding." The ritual made extensive use of digital and electronic visual media, which Shiff characterizes as having become "an active participant in the conveyance of aesthetic, cultural and even religious meaning instead of merely standing outside as a documentary witness." During the ceremony, both bride and groom walked down the aisle in white clothing,

Wedding of Melissa
Shiff and Louis Kaplan,
Toronto, 2003. During
the ceremony, artist
Shiff projected portraits
of her and Kaplan's
ancestors onto the *hup-
pah* (wedding canopy).
(Courtesy of Melissa
Shiff)

onto which Shiff projected sacred texts written in Hebrew. The centerpiece of the ceremony was the *huppah*, traditionally a square of white
cloth suspended over the bride and groom by four poles. Shiff tilted the
cloth at a forty-five-degree angle, positioning it halfway between the usual
horizontality of the *huppah* and the verticality of a movie screen. During
the ceremony, a series of texts and images were projected onto the *huppah*, including a sequence of "ancestor portraits," inspired by a traditional
prayer inviting the souls of deceased relatives to attend the wedding. Here,
the *huppah* becomes a kind of family photo album that is monumental
in physical scale and, at the same time, evanescent as a presence. Shiff
explains that "instead of merely conjuring up the memory of those that
have left us in the mind's eye, we decided to create a visual representation
of our respective family members who had passed away, . . . so that their
larger-than-life images hovered above us, watching over our celebration,
if only for a moment, and then receded back into the void."[66]

Just as the *huppah* and movie screen were fused in the Shiff-Kaplan
wedding, so were traditional ritual and photographic practices of remembrance. Their wedding (which Shiff arranged to be videotaped in anticipation of making a documentary film about the ceremony) was not simply a
ritual documented through photographic media or even one conceived in

cinematic terms. Rather, Shiff and Kaplan engaged various photographic and ritual practices as equally valid, compatible resources for the crafting of an event that honored religious and artistic conventions as well as problematized them. Here, religious lore and observance both motivated and challenged artistic creativity, and media technology was invested with the power to facilitate spirituality and interrogate tradition.

"Everyone Wants Their Own Reality Television Show"

Until recently, funerals seemed to be the exception to this proliferation of engagements with life-cycle rituals through photography. For most Jews, refraining from taking pictures or video at funerals seems as automatic as the impulse to document other rituals. Earlier in the history of still photography, the medium's association with death, at least among many Christians, was extensive: deathbed photographs and images of the deceased lying in coffins became popular in Western Europe and North America in the latter half of the nineteenth century. That moment also witnessed the advent of embellishing photographs of the dead with elaborate frames, text, paint, embroidery, and an array of objects—including the hair of the deceased—to create mementoes of lost loved ones. And at the same time, photography was employed by occultists on both sides of the Atlantic Ocean to fabricate images of the spirits of the dead.[67]

By contrast, in 1987 Chalfen reported that, among Americans generally, "the actual end of life is seldom documented" in home mode photography and that most people do not consider funeral rites or interment to be "appropriate subject matter" for the camera.[68] This view may be in keeping with the general principle, noted by filmmaker Michelle Citron, that home movies tend to focus very selectively on happy occasions, codifying what she characterized as "the 'good' memory."[69] Among Jews, this absence would also conform to the protocols of their funerals, which are traditionally quickly planned events, eschewing spectacle: the dead are buried, usually within twenty-four hours of expiring, in plain wood boxes (when state law forbids the more traditional practice of burying corpses wrapped in plain cloth shrouds); bodies are not embalmed or made up for viewing, coffins are closed, and there are usually no floral displays or other pageantry in the funeral procession. This visual austerity extends to the mourning period. At home, mourners cover mirrors during *shivah* (the first week of mourning), a time of limited activity. Mourners observing traditional restrictions during *shivah* refrain from working and from other activities—ranging from putting on makeup to watching television—which suggests that posing for pictures or screening videotapes would be unacceptable.

There have been occasions when Jewish funerals, both in America and elsewhere, were photographed, though these are exceptional cases. First, there are funerals of famous Jews, such as Yiddish writer Sholem Aleichem. His funeral in New York on 15 May 1916 became an impromptu Jewish national pageant—stretching from the author's Bronx home down the length of Manhattan and proceeding to his burial in a Brooklyn cemetery—the day-long event serving as the equivalent of a state funeral for a patriarchal literary lion. (Between 100,000 and 250,000 people are estimated to have lined the streets to watch the cortege, making this the largest funeral in New York City history until that of actor Rudolph Valentino in 1925.) Souvenir albums of photographs of Sholem Aleichem's funeral, documenting the orderly masses who turned out to honor the writer with the dignity befitting a national hero, were published shortly thereafter, in order to raise funds for the publication of his collected works.[70] Second, there are funerals of Jewish victims of anti-Semitic violence, especially those murdered in pogroms in the Russian Empire during the early decades of the twentieth century. Photographs of these corpses were published in the press and distributed by Jewish self-defense organizations internationally. Here, the transgressive act of displaying dead Jews parallels the moral outrage over their murder and may also have served as part of radical Jews' rejection of traditional Jewish mourning practices.

A more prevalent role for photography in Jewish mourning practices finds it displaced from the deceased and the time of death to the erecting of tombstones at the end of the period of mourning. Photographing tombstones or mourners at graveside—typically taken when the stones are erected, about a year after the date of death—was a common practice in Eastern Europe during the early twentieth century. Often these photos were sent to relations who had emigrated, showing them that family members back home had been properly buried and allowing immigrants to experience vicariously the traditional rite of visiting the graves of one's ancestors. Sometimes immigrants making return visits to their East European home towns had themselves photographed at their relatives' tombstones toward this same end.[71] Similarly, visiting the graves of revered figures long dead—hasidic leaders buried in Eastern Europe, sages interred in Morocco, or ancient landmarks in or near Jerusalem, such as Rachel's

Tomb—are often documented with still or moving pictures as part of pilgrimage practices today. In some Jewish communities, photographic portraits of the dead appear on tombstones, following local non-Jewish practice. Small enameled plaques with portraits of the deceased are sometimes affixed to tombstones in Europe and the United States, a practice dating from the late 1800s. In the post–World War II era, Soviet Jewish tombstones are frequently etched with large portraits taken from photographs, as are some tombstones of Jews from the former USSR in American cemeteries, following Soviet practice.

Videotape also engages Jewish mourning rites at a distance by providing instruction. Following the precedent of books on these subjects, educational videos inform Jews how to observe traditional burial and mourning practices and, indeed, how to grieve. Recent examples include *From Life to Life: Death and Mourning in Jewish Tradition*, "a sensitive documentary" that addresses the topic "with care and feeling." The film depicts "the preparation for burial, the simple pine coffin, the muslin shroud, the ritual of Taharah [cleansing of the corpse], the burial, sitting shiva, and the need for a tombstone." Touted by its distributor as "a realistic and illustrative undertaking with strong human interest," the medium's pedagogical value is enhanced by its capacity to be emotionally engaging as well as informative.[72] Other videos advise Jewish mourners on articulating their grief, such as *Generation to Generation: Jewish Families Talk about Death*, which offers "personal stories of loss" plus "commentary from religious leaders and bereavement counselors" to demonstrate how "open and honest dialogue can help heal the pain of loss."[73] There are even videos that explain how to prepare a corpse for burial according to rabbinic law. *The Ultimate Kindness: Chevra Kadisha* [local burial society] *and Tahara*, offers guidance for "the individuals in communities who have the responsibility of providing tahara for the deceased" and is also recommended as "a valuable educational tool for those who may be considering the formation of a Chevra Kadisha," which prepares corpses for burial.[74]

Such a video proved crucial for Carol Abadi, who found herself suddenly obliged to prepare the body of her aunt for burial. In a 2006 feature for an online Jewish magazine, Abadi explains that, having to "learn how to perform a *tahara* in the next few hours," she was taken to a funeral home for "a *tahara* crash course," which consisted of instructions in the ritual from a rabbi and a video, which she watched repeatedly, "until exhaustion," including one last time immediately before carrying out the procedure itself. Despite her great anxiety at having to perform this ritual,

Abadi reports, "As soon as we started the ritual, I went into a daze and started feeling a special love. . . . Everything flowed perfectly. It seemed as if my soul had taken over and knew exactly what to do."[75] Beyond the video's informational value, it offered Abadi reassurance, especially through repeated viewings, which perhaps modeled for her the ritual's "perfect flow" and even the sense that her soul "knew exactly what to do."

But now video no longer serves only as a tool for rehearsing or reflecting on rituals of death. In recent years, video cameras and recordings have begun to appear at Jewish funerals, though this practice has been seldom and provocative. "I recently received a brochure from a Jewish funeral home offering a service I find appalling," begins an anonymous letter to Wendy Belzberg, whose advice column "Ask Wendy" appears in the online magazine *Jewish World Review*, in 2003. "A personalized video of the deceased that can be viewed at the funeral and on demand whenever you visit the gravesite. Surely this cannot be in keeping with Jewish law?" Wendy replies,

> Against Jewish law? No. Against any semblance of good taste, religious or secular? Absolutely. Tacky. Embarrassing even. Are there special effects? Serial rights? Are the producers members of the Writers Guild of America? This is the kind of thing that makes the Dark Ages look good. And with good reason. Tempting though it may be to immortalize your loved one this way, a family picture album, sprinkled with babka crumbs at the kitchen table, is probably a more tasteful way to go. No one needs a posthumous Emmy, after all.[76]

Here, the ludic anxiety engendered by the very idea of video recordings at funerals (as opposed to another use of photography—the photo album—to facilitate remembering the dead) is compounded by the discomfort that, apparently, Jewish law does not forbid what seems to be a flagrant violation of the decorum, if not the laws, of the rites of mourning. Yet when the Star of David Memorial Chapel in West Babylon, New York, installed video cameras and Internet servers in 2006 "so that funeral services could be put on line," the innovation was characterized as enhancing the ritual's purpose: "According to Jewish tradition, a funeral allows people to deal with the loss and honor the dead by listening to the retelling of that person's life," explained Rabbi Irwin Kula, president of the National Jewish Center for Learning and Leadership, to a journalist reporting on this development, the first instance of a Jewish funeral home in the New York metropolitan area offering to record and transmit funeral services. "The more people that get to hear that, the better."[77] Rabbi Jeffrey Astrachan of nearby Temple Beth Elohim in Bethpage noted that funerals were joining other Jewish life-cycle events that were videotaped for later viewing. "In moments of extreme emotion, be it grief or joy, sometimes the moments pass and we are not able to moderate our emotion enough to focus on the experience," he explained. Although he thought video cameras at the funeral home "provided a valuable service," Astrachan cautioned that it ought not "replace coming to a funeral." Kevin Gray, one of the owners of the Star of David Memorial Chapel, agreed, noting, "You can't hug someone over the Web."[78] Nevertheless, he explained that making funeral services available for simultaneous viewing on the Internet or for later viewing on a DVD addressed the problem of getting to a funeral within the short amount of time that Jewish tradition affords and enabled those incapable of traveling because of ill health to view the ritual. (Other cultures have adopted videodocumentation of funerals to fulfill religious obligations challenged by the limits of time and space. Grimes reports that Ghanaian immigrants in Canada regularly videotape funeral rites and send the recordings back to families in Africa, "because tradition requires inheritors to participate in funerals, and video participation is one way of discharging that duty across the ocean.")[79]

More than a convenience, then, recording a funeral service can be understood as facilitating a different kind of relationship to "the ritual itself," affording a more attenuated and even contemplative emotional engagement. The funeral home providing this service acknowledges the distinction between the unmediated event and its online or video version by circumscribing the funeral's mediation, offering limited views of the proceedings ("a panoramic view from the back and a close-up focusing on the speaker and the first few rows of seats") and not bringing cameras to the graveside service.[80] Access to the webcast of the memorial service requires viewers to log on with a password, so as "to help fend off intruders."[81]

Whereas the Star of David Memorial Chapel offers family members a DVD of the funeral service as transmitted online, "as a keepsake," others offer the possibility of a more elaborate production. Jo-Ann Stokes, a local videographer, will create, "upon request, footage of the receiving line at a funeral home, the eulogy, the procession and the family saying goodbyes to the deceased at the cemetery, along with 40 to 50 photographs taken during the person's lifetime, all set to music." Such a videotape integrates documentation of the funeral with a life review of the deceased through photomontage, similar to compilations of images regularly presented at bar/bat mitzvahs and weddings. This practice brings death rituals into the home mode of personal photography and, conversely, integrates the ritual screening of life review through one's inventory of snapshots and home movies into funeral rites. Screening life-review videos in memorial services has become a "burgeoning trend" in America, according to Robert J. Biggins, the president of the National Funeral Directors Association, who suggests that these videos, shown both during and after funerals, "may be a very strong tool in the healing process" of mourning and "may ultimately be replayed more often than wedding videos."[82]

Indeed, the cemetery may become the final repository of one's photographic personal history as well as one's bodily remains. Such is the promise of the seven cemeteries affiliated with the Forever Network, a business venture inaugurated in the late 1990s, which brings together funeral homes, burial grounds, and video services. The brainchild of brothers Brent and Tyler Cassity, who are descended from "a long line of undertakers" in St. Louis, the Forever Network provides families with funeral services combining traditional burial and new media practices of remembrance. "The best way to remember someone is by seeing not their body but their body of work—in photographs, film and video clips," explains Tyler Cassity in an interview published in *Daily Variety*, and his brother characterizes "the cemetery of the future" as "a library of lives that's not just for the famous, but for the famous to family and friends."[83]

On the Forever Network website, clients are offered the opportunity to create LifeStories, personal histories of themselves or a loved one: "Forever LifeStories are made by working with our specially trained Biographers. They may include photos, spoken descriptions, text, video clips, old film reels, awards, or other memorabilia. These items are captured digitally at one of our Forever Studios locations, and preserved as a permanent part of the Forever Memorial Archive . . . , maintained by the Forever Endowment Care Fund."[84] Access to these personal histories is provided both online and on touchscreens at the cemeteries where their subjects are interred, provided that these cemeteries are part of the Forever Network. The network includes two Jewish cemeteries, Beth Olam in Hollywood, California ("founded in 1899 as a separate Jewish Section of the original Hollywood Cemetery"), and its namesake, Beth Olam St. Louis, a newly created burial ground in Creve Coeur, Missouri. The latter cemetery "also proudly features a Shoah Memorial LifeStories touchscreen giving visitors access to [a] multimedia Shoah archive which includes videotaped testimonies from

Video touchscreen set in stone at the Beth Olam Cemetery in Hollywood, California, under the management of Forever Network. This and other screens located in the cemetery enable visitors to watch videos of loved ones interred there.

Shoah survivors, rare sound recordings, and letters from lost loved ones."[85] LifeStories are meant to be "interactive," both in their creation (involving family members collaborating with the staff of Forever Studios) and in their use as vehicles of mourning and remembrance. "More people visit our online cemeteries to view archives than . . . come visit loved ones who are buried," reports Tyler Cassity. Via the computer, "they talk to them, many of them talk on a weekly basis, tell them how they're doing."[86]

Although LifeStories proffer a personalized, intimate form of memorialization, this means of recalling dead relatives and friends is modeled on practices associated with memorializing the famous (as was the case, over a century ago, with deathbed photographs). Tyler Cassity explains that "back in the '80s, it was shocking [for his clients] to have these big video cameras set up in their living rooms. Now, it's easier, because everyone wants their own reality television show."[87] A *Time* magazine feature on the Forever Network concurs, arguing that its success is due to the realization that "many Americans would love to have their own A&E *Biography*."[88] (The Forever Network similarly promotes Beth Olam Hollywood Cemetery as a site of celebrity memorialization: "The final resting place of hundreds of Hollywood luminaries, as well as scores of significant Rabbis, early Hollywood settlers and other community leaders, Beth Olam has become a cultural landmark, and was recently added to the National Register of Historic Sites.")[89] Just as professionally produced wedding videos emulate various Hollywood genres, thereby shaping the nature of the wedding celebration as well as its recollection, self- or family-produced memorial videos promise to transform mourning practices and remembrance of the dead. This transformation includes how individuals might anticipate their own deaths and what they might offer to grieving friends and family, as well as to future generations of descendants seeking to learn about their familial past.

In this respect, memorial videos have something of a Jewish precedent in the ethical will, a personal statement intended "to leave moral exhortation for [one's] children's guidance" after the author's death.[90] Following biblical models, the ethical will was a longstanding oral practice, with examples described in the Apocrypha and Talmud, and eventually became a Jewish literary genre (with the earliest extant examples dating to the mid-eleventh century). But the organizing principle of memorial videos, even when created by their subjects, is not didactic, offering life lessons to the next generation. Relying primarily on their subjects' photographic history, these videos inspire less moralizing than they do narrating, in which the life of the deceased, as it has been presented to a series of cameras, is the center of attention, much like a celebrity biographical film.

The Cassitys characterize their venture into memorial videos not as inimical to traditional burial practices but rather as compatible with the brothers' efforts to create "eco-friendly" cemeteries, in which "green burials" are enhanced by technology (absent of stone or metal grave markers, visitors will locate the graves of loved ones using a global positioning system).[91] Striving to liberate the rites of death from mainstream practices that Tyler Cassity characterizes as the "commercialization of denial," the Cassitys envision burials that use biodegradable materials and digital technology to create rituals that are self-styled, nonexploitative, and emotionally engaged.

By contrast, Moran characterizes memorial videos as a hybrid of home video, funeral management, and event video that constitutes an uneasy mix of the private, the professionalized, and the commodified. He argues that, rather than assisting family and friends in confronting the actuality of death, these media works "may actually counteract their intended therapeutic benefits by reinforcing contemporary notions of the corpse as a cultural taboo." Unlike nineteenth-century deathbed photography, these videos never represent "the deceased as corpse." Moran also attributes the limitations of memorial videos to the nature of their medium, in contrast to still photography: "irreversible suspension of time, the violence to our sense of duration . . . , these qualities [that] still photography shares with death are in effect reversed, timeshifted by video. Whereas photography arrests, video reanimates. Video's capacity for the instant replay . . . reconceives of life as something that can be rewound indefinitely."[92]

And yet this property of reanimation is central to these videos' appeal, enabling a relationship with the dead that defies, or at least sidesteps, the finality of loss. The notion of sending emails to deceased loved ones, posted at the site where their memorial video reposes, conjures up images of Jews visiting the graves of ancestors and speaking to them (or, in the case of the graves of famous sages, leaving written notes for them), and yet the relationship is different, in large measure due to the media being used. At the center of these new online remembrance practices is a narrative video, in which a lifetime of photodocumentation—and of responding to the protocols of engaging with cameras—is integrated into a story shaped by the conventions of the documentary and the biopic. Memorial videos have the potential to become the ultimate organizing principle for all preceding photographs, serving as the final resting place of a lifetime of photo opportunities.

In 1971, anthropologist Roy Rappaport argued that "in technologically advanced societies . . . the relationship between sanctity and authority changes," to the detriment of "true sanctity." For, "whereas in the technologically undeveloped system authority is contingent upon sanctification, in the technologically more developed societies sanctity becomes an instrument of authority."[93] The videography of American Jewish life-cycle rituals does evince considerable changes in relationships between notions of the sacred and religious authority (whether it be clergy, canonical texts, or received traditions). These media practices, however, have not compromised practitioners' experience of sanctity as valid and authentic. On the contrary, through their photographic practices, they have effected an expansive opening up of the boundaries delineating ritual time, place, community, and practice, as well as religious authority.

This breaking down of borders delimiting ritual's sanctity is borne out not only in the videos' form and content but also in the distinctive circumstances of their viewing. The very act of screening videotapes or DVDs of personal rituals on one's "home entertainment center" is a noteworthy departure from the rites of viewing home movies in the era of 16 mm and 8 mm film, which entailed waiting for days for the film to be processed, as well as the special effort of setting up the projector and screen and transforming one's living room into a temporary cinema. Videotapes and DVDs routinize the viewing of these rituals by situating them within the same frame that surrounds the watching of cartoons, music videos, quiz shows, prime-time dramas, vintage movies, and so on. This imbrication of religion and entertainment positions viewing personal life-cycle celebrations in relation to other media rituals that communications scholars have identified—both the televisual "high holidays" of the Super Bowl, royal weddings, and presidential inaugurations[94] and the quotidian routines of tuning in to soap operas, favorite situation comedies, or nightly newscasts before bed. Consequently, the different modes of storytelling offered by home mode videos and by commercial entertainment inform one another—indeed, as videos of rituals emulate Hollywood, MTV, or cinéma vérité, while network television airs *America's Funniest Home Videos* (ABC, 1990–present), just how different are these media from one another?

Posting videos on the Internet effects another telling shift in their viewing. Family websites and the password-protected site of a funeral home situate personal videos in a virtual family album. When these images are posted on communal sites, such as the aforementioned onlysimchas. com, they are housed within a larger archive, run by and for a community whose members not only know many of the others directly (searching such sites is usually done by name) but also share a cultural bond. But when these media are posted on general viewing sites, such as YouTube. com, they enter a much vaster inventory, which is given order by a database of keywords. Here, generic terms such as "Jewish" or "bar mitzvah" will locate the material in question within extensive and diverse archival holdings, whereas in a communal Jewish website these search terms would be of limited, if any, use. In the context of a general viewing site, home videos become public curiosities, situated within a universe of subjects seemingly limited only by what has been mediated on digital video. Placing one's personal videos online, especially on such a site, entails new notions of visibility; it locates one's own media (and, moreover, one's own experience represented therein) within a vast virtual collection available to anyone and, possibly, to no one. The potential significance of one's personal video is thereby opened up to untold possibilities—which might, in fact, become documented through commenting and rating devices—in the gaze of complete strangers.

This universalizing of viewing parallels the democratizing impulse to create media. As much as photographing weddings, bar and bat mitzvahs, and other life-cycle rituals has been professionalized, this has not excluded amateur photography at these events. Guests often come with their own cameras to celebrations that they know will be photographed or filmed professionally. Moreover, it has become a frequent practice to place disposable cameras (some of which are manufactured with special festive packaging) on the tables where guests are seated for the banquets following these ceremonies. Encouraged to take pictures of one another or of the surrounding festivities, guests are thereby drawn into the process of documenting the celebration. Although guests' posing for pictures has long been a part of these celebrations, taking pictures has now become a means of structuring guests' social engagement with one another.

These practices of photographing rituals, incorporating photography into rituals, and viewing the photodocumentation of rituals are all exemplary of popular religion, in which "ordinary" people—not clergy, lay leaders, or other elites—fashion their own practices around established religious observances and, in doing so, create alternative meanings for rituals. These innovative uses of photography, film, and videography variously enable those who practice established ceremonies to redefine their roles of participant and observer, to recenter their locus of authority, to reverse their temporal trajectory, to subvert their symbolic value, and to reconceptualize their sense of what constitutes ritual experience. Religious leaders, who generally operate outside these popular practices, are obliged to negotiate with the demands prompted by the desire for ritual photography. In this respect, the engagement of American Jews today with ritual photography should be considered both synchronically, as part of an array of contemporary practices of what Myerhoff terms "religion in the making,"[95] and diachronically, in the history of Jewish popular religion, especially as it engages new media, starting with the printed book.[96]

Anthropologist Bruce Kapferer has argued that ritual not only "moves its participants" and "organizes their emotions and experience" but also "questions . . . taken-for-granted elements of cultural life and holds them up for inspection."[97] Photographs, films, and especially videos of Jewish life-cycle celebrations exemplify all these qualities of ritual, even as they challenge longstanding understandings of ritual practices and their meanings. Beyond complicating how rituals are observed, these new media practices have profound implications for how those who make and watch them experience Jewish life.

5

A Stranger among Friends

One December in the mid-1980s, I received a greeting card unlike any I had ever seen before. On its cover was a photograph of a bagel, adorned with a bow printed with red and green holly sprigs. Inside the card read, "Oy vay [Oh, woe], another holiday!"[1] I soon discovered other, similar holiday cards for sale in card shops, with new ones appearing in subsequent Decembers. At the same time, I noticed a spate of episodes of prime-time television series in which interfaith couples grappled with what has been termed the "December dilemma"—that is, the coincidence of Christmas and Hanukkah during that month.[2] Both phenomena have continued into the twenty-first century, joined by an array of other practices dealing with the juxtaposition of these two religious holidays and their significance for different constituencies, ranging from couples in Jewish-Christian intermarriages to the general American public.

When I first noticed these responses to the December dilemma, they seemed to be unprecedented—not only in their substance but, perhaps even more so, in the forms they took. These phenomena made unusual use of popular media, whether television programs seen by large national audiences, the great majority of whom did not directly experience the issue at hand, or mass-produced greeting cards that seemed to flout the boundary between two discrete holidays and, moreover, to thwart the validity of their celebration. What, then, do these and similar December dilemma practices indicate about changes in the American Jewish community, both demographically and regarding the community's relation to the national public sphere? More broadly, what do these phenomena suggest about changes in American notions of religious pluralism? Of intermarriage and interfaith relations? Of religious celebrations in the public sphere? Of multiculturalism, as it relates to religion? And what is the significance of the various media involved in these phenomena?

While these practices evince recent changes in American Jewish life and American culture generally, they are also part of an intercultural encounter reaching back for generations and out beyond America's borders. Jews' engagement with Christmas has an extensive history, manifest in a remarkable range of undertakings, from rabbinic debates about what to do on the day marking Jesus's birth to various European folkways and recent works of American popular culture.[3] The issue engages Jewish clergy and lay leaders, as well as many "ordinary" Jews, and at times elite and popular Jewish responses to Christmas have clashed. This may be so because Jews have found Christmas to be a productive point of entry into larger questions about the significance that Christianity has for them, not only theologically but also socially, culturally, and politically. By engaging with Christmas, Jews undertake a refracted examination of themselves—as individuals, families, communities, and as a whole people—in relation to another religious doctrine as well as to neighbors, majority cultures, social protocols, economic forces, or government policies. Not surprisingly, then, when Jews talk about Christmas, they often wind up discussing something else: family, assimilation, intermarriage, Hanukkah, anti-Semitism, Otherness, Americanness.

Jewish discussions of Christmas are also more than talk. Frequently they center on behaviors, including those associated with celebrating the holiday—exchanging gifts or greetings, displaying decorations—as well as various counterbehaviors for the holiday, from covering up sacred books to eating in Chinese restaurants, singing Yiddish-inflected parodies of Christmas carols to promoting new winter holidays (un-Christmas, Chrismukkah). Indeed, these discussions themselves can be regarded as an ongoing cultural practice. For Jews, Christmas serves as a catalyst for a remarkable set of definitional behaviors in which the self is realized in relation to others. This encounter readily invites mediation, not only in form—by initiating discussions and disseminating them through print, recordings, broadcasting, or the Internet—but also in substance, by compelling Jews to negotiate their status in relation to America's Christian majority both as fellow citizens and as Others.

The following consideration of Jews' engagement with Christmas traces its dynamic from Old World origins through immigrations to America in the nineteenth and early twentieth centuries and up to the turn of the millennium. More than a journey across time and space, this examination also moves through an array of new media, including newspapers, books, sociological surveys, sound recordings, advertisements, greeting cards, telecasts, emails, and websites. The topic at hand involves Jews across the spectrum of religious observance (including those who are ardent

"Why should Jewish children have to gaze in envy . . . when they have such a rich heritage of their own?" This brochure, promoting a campaign to help Jews "celebrate Chanukah with dignity," was distributed circa 2000 by Awaken, an Orthodox Jewish outreach organization based in Lakewood, New Jersey. Christmas, unmentioned in the brochure but evoked in this cover image, epitomizes both the fear and the allure of assimilation.

secularists) as well as Christians, who are implicated as objects of contemplation and as participants in conversation. From this wide-ranging and protean array of cultural practices, Christmas emerges less as an occasion for American Jews' alienation or withdrawal—the one day of the year above any other when, Jonathan Sarna writes, they "so deeply feel the clash between the country they love and the faith they cherish"—than as one of the most prominent opportunities for Jews to perform definitional rites in the American public sphere.[4]

"The Opposition Festival"

The great majority of Jewish immigrants to America has come from Europe and therefore arrived with some prior exposure to Christian beliefs and practices, including Christmas. The first sizeable wave of Jewish immigration to the United States took place in the middle decades of the nineteenth century. These Jews came, for the most part, from German lands, concomitant with a much larger immigration of Christians from this region. Their arrival coincided with a transformation of the celebration of Christmas in America, described by religion scholar Leigh Schmidt as shifting from "carnivalesque revels and drunken binges of street celebrations" to the "genteel observance" of rituals centered on middle-class domesticity and gift exchanges.[5] Historian Stephen Nissenbaum notes that the Christmas practices widely adopted in mid-nineteenth-century America, epitomized by placing decorated pine trees in homes, "entered American society through the avenues of commercial culture, but did so in the name of precommercial folk culture." He notes that although "it is a commonplace to believe that Christmas trees were transmitted to America by early German immigrants," the practice was in fact "a relatively new tradition in Germany itself" in the early 1800s, and the practice was largely spread both there and in the United States through print culture. Similarly, Santa Claus was popularized in American periodicals during the first decades of the nineteenth century as "a conscious reconstruction of Dutch ritual—an invented tradition."[6]

German Jews were implicated in this transformation of Christmas in America, primarily as merchants selling gifts and other goods for the holiday celebration. This role proved to be symbolic as well as instrumental. In the late nineteenth century, the Jewish merchant had become a frequent target of American humor and was sometimes portrayed as profiting at gentiles' expense during the Christmas season or served as a sign of the holiday's inappropriate commercialism. A cartoon in the humor magazine *Puck* in 1878, titled "Spread of the Christian Religion," depicts a half-dozen dark-haired, hook-nosed men and women presiding over tables laden with small trees and toys, labeled "Christmas Gifts"; below is the caption, "How our Hebrew friends at Tammany Hall utilize the opposition festival."[7] This sort of humor persisted into the early twentieth century. A 1911 issue of *Life* includes a cartoon, titled "The Spirit of Christmas in New York," in which "S. Clausenstein"—a thin man with aquiline nose and long, pointy beard, in a fur-trimmed Santa suit and hat—uses Yiddish-accented English to hawk toys to a group of young children. The cartoon appeared alongside a short feature on "Keeping Up Old Customs" of Christmas, reported as including an "imitation holly wreath," "gas-logs in the fireplace," "electric candles in imitation Colonial sconces," and gifts made of ersatz sealskin, amber, silk, and so on.[8] Jews' role in the commercialization of Christmas was thus obliquely linked with other practices perceived as faux, corrupting customs and lore understood as authentic.

During the nineteenth century, a considerable number of Jews in German lands had adopted aspects of the domestic Christmas celebration (trees, present exchanges) practiced by their Christian neighbors, as part of a larger trend toward Jewish integration into mainstream German culture. Such a "so-called Christmas Jew" might observe Jewish as well as Christian holidays, regarding "Christmas as a German *Volkfest*."[9] Some German Jews brought these practices with them to the United States or even adopted them after their arrival, for, by the final decades of the nineteenth century, German Jews living in America had begun establishing their own counterpractices around Christmas. Sarna notes that they held pageants, festivals, and other public celebrations of Hanukkah "to counteract the growing allure of Christmas."[10] According to Barbara Kirshenblatt-Gimblett, these Jews' holiday observances "converged with social seasons and shopping cycles. Nowhere was this more clear than in the annual charity fairs held just before Christmas. For Jews these fairs were a response to the December dilemma," she argues, being "concerned less with 'copying' the Gentiles . . . and more with using these fundraising socials for Jewish ends."[11]

Beginning in the 1880s, the much larger population of Jewish immigrants from Eastern Europe brought a different understanding of Christianity, as well as different notions of Jewish-gentile relations, formed by the circumstances of the Russian and Austro-Hungarian empires. East European Jews had some familiarity with their neighbors' Christian practices and occasionally participated in them (for example, Jews who managed rural estates were known to organize Christmas parties for their Christian workers), but adopting Christmas or other religious practices as part of integration into a cultural mainstream had limited possibility or appeal.[12]

Instead, these Jews engaged Christmas at some remove, articulating their relationship with the holiday and with Christians more generally through lore and practices of their own making. They developed a body of folkways around Christmas, including a sizeable inventory of Yiddish terms for the holiday, observances, and explanations for doing them. Together, these practices constitute a counterculture, in which familiarity with Christmas and Christianity informs practices of their subversion.

Remarkably, there are some twenty different terms for Christmas among Yiddish dialects spoken across Eastern Europe before World War II. *Nitl*, the most common and widely reported term, was sometimes regarded as having a "scholarly" connotation. Most other terms were distinctive to a particular region and usually owed their origin to a local non-Jewish language. Thus, *vaynakht* (cf. German *Weinachten*) is reported in Alsace, Galicia, and western Poland; *rizlekh* is found in Ukraine (where Christmas is called *rizdvo*), and *yolkes* was given by informants in Belorussia (cf. *yolka*, Belorussian for "Christmas tree"). Although Jews considered these to be Yiddish words, they also used other terms for Christmas that they characterized as linguistically non-Jewish: *kaleyd* (from the Lithuanian *kaledos*), *vigilye* (from the Polish *wigilia*), *rozhestvo* (from the Bulgarian *rozhdestvo khristovo*) and *koratshon* or *kritshun* (from the Hungarian *karácsony*).

Still other Yiddish terms for Christmas were clearly Jewish inventions. Christmas Eve was known in parts of central and southern Europe as *goyimnakht* (gentiles' night), as well as *tolenakht* and *yoyzlsnakht* (both meaning, colloquially, "Jesus's night"), and in Ukraine and eastern Galicia, it was called *blinde nakht* (blind night), *finstere nakht* (dark night), or *moyredike nakht* (fearful night). In western Poland, the Polish *boze narodzenie* (literally, "divine birth") was transformed into the Yiddish *beyz geboyrenish* (literally, "wicked birthing"). Here, *narodzenie* is translated into a Yiddish word for "birth" but with the ending -*enish* added, which often has a deprecatory connotation, and a bilingual pun transforms Polish *boze* (divine) into Yiddish *beyz* (wicked). Another bilingual pun turns German *Weinachten* into Yiddish *veynakht* (literally, "woe-night").[13] These last examples epitomize the East European Jewish response to Christmas. Like whistling in the dark, they mock the source of anxiety as they acknowledge its existence. The same affective tension is voiced in Yiddish proverbs about Christmas. One such saying, *Nitl iz a bezyer layd* (Christmas is a wicked burden), is parried by another: *Nitl is a beyz lidl* (Christmas is a wicked little song).[14]

This pattern of simultaneously expressing and flouting fear is also manifest in Jewish folkways. Ethnographic sources report a number of customs that East European Jews practiced on Christmas: Children did not go to *kheyder* (traditional elementary religious school), nor did men engage in the study of sacred texts. On Christmas Eve, Jews stayed inside their homes, sometimes shuttering their windows. Children played cards, an indulgence otherwise permitted only on Hanukkah. Protective covers were placed over holy books and on vessels containing liquids and food. Sources for this curious set of customs, collected by folklorists during the interwar years, offer various explanations for these practices:

In our region they had the following superstition: On Christmas Eve all liquids are covered with a piece of iron. It is said that if you didn't cover them, they would become corrupted with Jesus's blood. On Christmas you don't study in *kheyder* because the *tome* [ritual impurity] . . . reigns everywhere.

At one time you didn't study in *kheyder*, *besmedresh* [house of study for adult Jewish men], or yeshiva. We were motivated to do this because Christ was once a great scholar, and if we study on Christmas, he'll demand to be paid tuition.

Children said that "Yosl Pondrik" [i.e., Jesus] flies around. I recall that we didn't study so as not to give honor to "him." An old woman explained it this way: "He" flies around, hides in a holy book, and won't come out; then "he" says that he also taught it. Another explained it this way: when he comes across an open holy book, he "soils" it [i.e., he defecates on it].[15]

These various folkways all address the problematic figure of Jesus. On one hand, he is an ominous bearer of ritual impurity, a concept governing a wide range of behavior in the daily life of traditionally observant Jews, including taboos associated with eating, dressing, sex, body functions, and illness, as well as birth and death. Whereas Christians believe in the redemptive powers of Jesus's blood, this lore characterizes it as contaminating. On the other hand, Jesus is recognized, if begrudgingly, as a formidable figure and deserving of some respect. Some informants referred to Jesus as Christ, but others alluded to him obliquely as "he," the implicit taboo of directly naming Jesus suggesting both fear and esteem; still others called him *Yoyzl* (a slangy diminutive of Jesus, mock-endearing in tone) or *Yosl Pondrik*. Another interwar informant offered an explanation of this name:

Yosl Pondrik . . . comes from the Talmud . . . where he is called . . . "son of Pantura." People surely know this term from the book *Toledoth Yeshu* [History of Jesus], which relates that Jesus's mother Mary found favor in the eyes of the wicked Pantura and became pregnant by him.[16]

Toledoth Yeshu, a medieval Jewish response to the gospels, debunks Jesus's divinity with an alternative biography: he is revealed to be the son of a man who, according to various versions of the text, either seduced or raped Jesus's mother, the innocent Miriam (Mary). *Toledoth Yeshu* attributes Jesus's ability to perform miracles to his having stolen a magic name from the Temple in Jerusalem and discredits Jesus's resurrection by claiming that his corpse was stolen by Judas Iscariot.[17] *Toledoth Yeshu* not only denies that Jesus is the messiah but also implicitly defends his status in the Christian world by explaining how an illegitimate Jewish heretic could come to be so revered. Similarly, East European Yiddish folklore about Christmas acknowledges the awe that Jesus inspires while diminishing his stature. He not only flies around, demonlike, making blood appear mysteriously and spreading *tome*, but he spoils holy books by defecating on them, as if he were an irreverent bird. And when Jesus's prodigious scholarship is acknowledged, it comes with the all-too-human expectation that he will demand payment for the wisdom he imparts. Yiddish speakers' highly ambivalent engagement with Jesus and Christmas thus inspired a rich and imaginative array of responses, in which the resourcefulness of play with language, lore, and custom parried a sense of social vulnerability.

"Vi es goyisht zikh, azoy yidlt zikh"

For the most part, these folkways did not persist among East European Jews after immigrating to the United States, beyond occasional recollections of their past. The American Yiddish poet Mani-Leyb, for example, wrote a sonnet about Christmas, in which he evokes the fears of oppression that the holiday instilled in Old World Jews.[18] Once in America, these Jews not only discovered other ways of celebrating Christmas but also encountered different kinds of Christian communities among their new neighbors and different possibilities for relating with Christendom. Nevertheless, Old World memories continued to inform Jewish immigrants' engagement with Christmas and Christians in America, if only to point up the newness of this relationship. Moreover, ludic Old World responses to Christmas may have inspired new American Jewish ones in the form of word play and parody.

Just as a burgeoning print culture was key to promulgating Christmas traditions in nineteenth-century America, immigrant Jewish responses to Christmas found expression in new media, especially the Yiddish press. Newspapers and other periodicals emerged as major forums for East European Jewish immigrants, much as mother-tongue publications served other immigrant communities arriving from Europe at the time. By 1914, New York City was home to five Yiddish dailies, catering to a spectrum of immigrant readers from religious traditionalists to the ardently secular and politically progressive. The most popular of these papers, the *Jewish Daily Forward*, had a circulation of over 200,000 at its peak in the mid-1920s. The cultural impact of the American Yiddish press was unprecedented. As historian Tony Michels notes, "People who had never seen a Yiddish newspaper in Europe soon became devoted readers, looking to the press for guidance, information, and entertainment." Beyond reporting current events, the Yiddish press "functioned in several capacities at once": it provided information on all manner of subjects for immigrant readers, who often had no formal general education, published works of literature and cultural criticism, and offered a means of learning about and "interpreting American society, politics, and culture."[19]

Within this agenda of enlightening readers about life in the United States, the *Forward* addressed the subject of Christmas regularly, on a seasonal basis, throughout the first half of the twentieth century. Through a variety of approaches and formats—including news reports, features, poems, cartoons, and editorials—the newspaper explored the holiday's complex of implications for Yiddish-speaking immigrants and their children, revealing the dynamics and range of their relationship to mainstream American culture and to Christianity as a worldwide ethos. As a socialist newspaper, the *Forward* often approached Christmas as an opportunity to critique the injustices of capitalism or the backwardness of religion. Such was the case in the 25 December issue of the *Forward* published in 1897, its inaugural year. "Santa Claus," a poem on the front page by the socialist leader and poet Abraham Liessin, describes a poor orphan who asks Santa Claus, in Jesus's name, for help. Santa replies that he cannot help her, explaining that the gifts he carries are for the children of the rich.[20] Other articles in the *Forward* highlighted the disparity between the holiday's lofty, universalist sentiments and the harsh realities of economic hardship and social intolerance, whether reporting on family tragedies that occurred on Christmas ("Santa Claus, the Angel of Death") or cataloging the injustices taking place under the auspices of "Christian civilization," including, in 1901, violence in the Philippines and the Transvaal: "Christmas! What terrible feelings this word awakens! . . . In one's thoughts many generations of superstition and senselessness fly by, of ignorance and darkness. . . . 'Peace on Earth,' sigh the masses of living corpses, who suffer under the yoke of Christendom."[21] This trope continued into World War II; in

December 1940, an editorial began, "Once again, it is Christmas. Once again church bells ring their old, familiar tune: 'Peace on Earth, good will toward men.' . . . It has been over 1,900 years, but everything remains the same. There is no peace in the world and no good will toward men."[22]

Occasionally the *Forward* explained the history of Christmas, especially its pre-Christian origins in Roman winter solstice rites ("Christmas—Older than Jesus," "How Christmas Was Converted into a Christian Holiday").[23] These articles reflect the paper's secularist approach to religion generally as a phenomenon of human social development that should be subjected to rational analysis, historicized and scrutinized for its values (such as promoting ethical behavior) as well as its limitations (resisting scientific advances, encouraging prejudices). This approach informed a 1910 editorial advising Jews how to make sense of Christmas as a phenomenon of contemporary American life. "We should do as Maimonides says Moses did with regard to sacrifices," the anonymous editorialist argued, noting that, according to the medieval Jewish philosopher,

> Moses personally hated the custom of sacrifices, but Jews had become so schooled in the practice by gentiles, that even God and Moses couldn't wean them from it. So they decided to give sacrifices a different meaning, replacing idol worship with devotion to the God of Moses. If this could be done with sacrifices, it can certainly be done with [Christmas] presents given to adults and children—remove the idolatrous meaning and insert a new meaning, the one that all freethinking gentiles give to it.[24]

As the *Forward* negotiated between traditional Jewish suspicions of Christendom and progressive visions of humanistic universalism, it examined the relationship among the religious origins of Christmas, its modern ideals, and the actual practices of its observance, especially giving Christmas presents and exchanging holiday greetings. A 1904 feature scrutinized the widespread practice of Jews' exchanging Christmas presents, identifying this as the epitome of integration into American culture across the ideological spectrum of Jewish immigrants:

> Who says that we aren't Americanizing? . . . Among the thousands of people now filling the big stores are many Jews . . . buying Christmas presents. . . . This has become fashionable among Jews in America; they go about it with a holy fervor. . . . Here in New York, the first thing that shows you're not a greenhorn is buying Christmas presents. . . . The

freethinker ridicules the holiday of Christmas, the pious Jew grieves over it, but both of them buy presents in honor of the occasion.

True to the *Forward*'s socialist sensibility, the article analyzed the socio-economic value of this gift exchange—noting that what matters most is "that you buy someone a Christmas present, not that the present itself is of any use"—and critiqued the compulsion many people felt to buy presents, especially workers pressured to give holiday gifts to their bosses, even if they could ill afford to do so.[25]

By the early 1920s, Jewish observance of Christmas on New York's Lower East Side seemed to a *Forward* reporter to be "just like the day before Passover," as Jews shopped for presents and prepared for holiday parties, which had become "a genuine custom, an institution, among the local Jewish youth." Christmas, the reporter argued, "is not a purely Christian holiday" and perhaps had become a Jewish one as well. The reporter suggested that this development was due to American public schools, where immigrants' children had long been exposed to Christmas celebrations, and was a consequence of a longstanding pattern of Jews' incorporating gentile practices into Jewish life, according to the Yiddish proverb "*Vi es goyisht zikh, azoy yidlt zikh*" (However non-Jews act, Jews follow suit).[26]

Not all the *Forward*'s disquisitions on Christmas accepted the holiday's newly prominent place in immigrant Jewish life as a beneficent or, at least, inevitable phenomenon. In a 1910 essay, author Morris Rosenfeld lamented,

The Jewish child in America is never more deserving of pity than during Christmas. While his Christian friends have something to look forward to, for him, everything is gloomy. The decorated shop windows everywhere charm and wink at passersby. . . . And all of these pretty, attractive things will later be brought into people's homes, where they will adorn the green, grinning Christmas tree. Nor will there be any lack of presents. . . . The Jewish child sees this. And in America he sees this more than any other place. Here the division between Christians and Jews is not as great. Their children go to the same schools, where they sing the same Christmas songs. . . . It is not easy for a Jewish child in Christian surroundings to dismiss from his young, thirsty heart such universal joy, such colorful, glittering happiness, that fills every place, . . . except Jewish houses. . . . He feels lost, that he is not in the right place, that he is a stranger among his friends and does not have a world of his own."

Rosenfeld, the most renowned of the so-called sweatshop poets in turn-of-the-century American Yiddish letters, both voiced the emotional ordeals of immigrant life and championed Jewish nationalism in his writings. In this essay, he articulated American Jews' sense of alienation from their Christian neighbors in relation to the commercial and celebratory pleasures of Christmas. Rather than embrace its merrymaking and universalist spirit, which he dismissed as "a pale, twisted, clumsy idol," Rosenfeld advocated that Jews should celebrate Hanukkah—the equivalent of "a powerful, valiant hero"—as the "cure" that Jewish history has prepared for this "plague."[27]

During World War II, Christmas offered new opportunities for reflecting on Jewish-Christian relations, at home and abroad. In an editorial published during Christmas week in 1941, Abraham Cahan, the *Forward*'s venerable editor in chief, debated the holiday's value for American Jews with another East European Jewish immigrant. Cahan's fellow immigrant was less perturbed by Jews' exchanging Christmas presents than by hearing Jews wish Christians a "Merry Christmas," protesting, "A Merry Christmas? Not for us Jews. . . . If there is a Christian holiday that Jews *absolutely* cannot celebrate, it is Christmas." Cahan argued that "someone who is completely American has absolutely no anti-Semitic feelings, even on this night. . . . He considers Christmas a holiday that celebrates love of humankind. . . . An American wishes Jews a 'Merry Christmas' with all his heart." Cahan contrasted these sentiments with those of Germans, who had created a new anti-Semitism rooted in the medieval hatred of Jews, and he asserted that, if America was not "completely free of anti-Semitism," such feelings largely came from "un-American sources."[28]

Cahan's optimism about the American spirit of Christmas is complicated by other discussions of the holiday in the *Forward* at the time. A letter sent by a reader in 1941 to the *Bintl briv* (literally, "packet of letters"), the newspaper's popular advice column, reported how an immigrant couple discovered, to their dismay, that their son and daughter-in-law had a Christmas tree in their home, which the son justified as being "for the sake of his children, so they won't feel any different than their non-Jewish friends in the neighborhood." Responding to the letter's request for the editor's opinion on the matter, the paper printed the following:

The national American holidays are celebrated here with love and joy by Jews and Gentiles alike. But Christmas is the most religious Christian holiday and Jews have nothing to do with it. Jews, religious or not, should respect the Christmas holiday, but to celebrate it would be like dancing at a stranger's wedding. It is natural that a Jew who observes all the Jewish traditions should be opposed to seeing his son and grandchildren trimming a Christmas tree.

Rather than quarreling with their son, the *Forward* advised, the immigrant couple should "explain the meaning of Christmas to him," and the paper admonished the father for failing to "instill Jewish traditions in his son."[29]

In the immigrant Yiddish press, Christmas served as a proving ground for testing new practices—giving gifts, exchanging holiday wishes, attending holiday parties, displaying decorations—that were emblematic of Jews' relations with Christianity and of their Americanness. Yiddish newspapers offered a forum for discussing these practices and assigning meaning to them as they were taking place. As an annual activity, reading about Christmas in Yiddish constituted a form of engagement with the holiday itself, marked as a Jewish undertaking by dint of a language that served as a bond uniting writers and readers.

"Deck the Hall with Boughs of Chaleh"

In the early decades of the twentieth century, Anglophone American public culture occasionally addressed the subject of Jews and Christmas. The topic figured, for example, in the plots of an early silent film (*The Jew's Christmas*, 1913) and one of Broadway's most popular comedies of the 1920s, *Abie's Irish Rose*, which brings its story of Irish-Jewish intermarriage to a happy resolution around the Christmas tree in the home of Abie Levy and Rose Mary Levy (née Murphy).[30] Rabbis made occasional use of popular American periodicals to address the challenges that Christmas poses for Jews, such as a 1906 essay in the *Ladies Home Journal* by Emil G. Hirsch, a prominent Reform rabbi and a professor of rabbinics at the University of Chicago. Asking what role Jews might have in that "rare hour when differences of station and origin are fused in the consciousness of the equivalence and equality of all men," Hirsch responded that, although Jews must "take exception" to the holiday's "theological associations," the "Christmas sentiment of 'good will to men' is certainly an echo of the convictions and aspirations which the Jewish Festival of Lights [i.e., Hanukkah] emphasizes. . . . The ethics symbolized by Christmas are Jewish."

Poster made by the Morgan Lithograph Company for *The Jew's Christmas*, a 1913 Universal film, in which immigrant Jews learn of the many "instances of the kindness of the gentiles towards the Jews in this country."

Therefore, the holiday "has found welcome in many a Jewish household. Its theological implications have been forgotten in the sweeter melodies which it has dedicated to the universal humanities." Hirsch separated the humanistic ethos of Christmas from its theological foundation and, moreover, positioned Judaism as precedent for the humanism of Christmas, while also suggesting that Christmas is the ultimate fulfillment of Jewish aspiration: "the Jew . . . kindles his less radiant Hanukah lamps, and in their more modest glow reads the prophecy of a more inclusive advent when Peace will prevail on God's earth."[31]

Writing for a largely non-Jewish readership, Hirsch characterized Jews' encounter with Christmas as meaningful for their Christian neighbors: on one hand, reassuring them of Jews' embrace of the holiday's universal value; on the other hand, positioning Jews as the progenitors of this value and therefore worthy of Christians' respect. Similar sentiments were expressed in 1939 by another Reform rabbi, Louis Witt, in an essay for *The Christian Century*. An advocate of promoting relations among Jewish and Christian religious leaders, Witt explained that, no longer seeing Jews' celebration of Christmas as "a shameful aping of alien gods," he had "come to see good in the Jewish observance of Christmas," noting that "the Jew has survived in part by virtue of the force and logic of syncretism" and that, "by virtue of its inherent humaneness and universalism," Christmas had "become too big to be only Christian." In concluding, he asked his Christian readers, "Is it neither treason of Jew nor triumph of Christian but partnership of Jew and Christian in the making of a better world in which the Christ can have part only by energizing and perpetuating and hallowing the partnership?"[32] Jews' embrace of Christmas is thus the ultimate fulfillment of its comprehensive humanistic ideal.

Remarkably, these Reform rabbis' arguments resemble some of those made by secularists writing at the same time in the *Forward*. But the latter were distinguished by their use of Yiddish, which defined their conversation as internal to Jewish, and especially immigrant, readers. Theirs was a public conversation, but one that assumed a common cultural background and shared questions about the future. In the English-language press, Jewish clergy negotiated the sensibilities of a less familiar audience as well as a topic from which both authors and readers were at some distance, each seeking to imagine the other's experience refracted through the prism of their own desires.

On occasion the *Forward* did not merely scrutinize but actually facilitated Jewish Christmas practices. The paper ran advertisements for Christmas sales (one example, probably a direct translation of an English-language ad, features a Yiddish-speaking child writing to Santa Claus) and printed, among recipes that readers regularly submitted, a menu for a complete Christmas dinner (including stuffed turkey, sweet potato casserole, and fruit compote; the meal was awarded the top prize of five dollars).[33] The *Forward* also reported on the role of parody in American Jews' engagement with Christmas. In 1924, a column in the paper's English-language section that invited contributions from readers included the following account:

In our school, which is on the East Side, we taught the children an old
English song for the holiday season, beginning:
> *Deck the hall with boughs of holly*
> *Tra-la-la-la-la-la-la-la-la-la*

> *'Tis the season to be jolly—etc.*
> Our little Jewish children sang it as follows:
> *Deck the hall with boughs of chaleh [bread].*[34]

American Jews' parodic engagements with Christmas verses and folk-ways recall the playfully subversive Yiddish Christmas terms and lore of Eastern Europe, even as these parodies exemplify how immigrant communities employ language play, especially code-switching, to negotiate the disparities between their Old World and New World sensibilities. In 1927, Milt Gross, creator of cartoons captioned in a Yiddish-inflected dialect that spoofed immigrant Jews' mores, published *De Night in de Front from Chreesmas*, a parodic rendering of the famous poem "A Visit from St. Nicholas," attributed to Clement Clarke Moore. Gross transformed this sentimental portrait of an enchanted Christmas Eve in small-town America into a raucous, chaotic night in an urban apartment building, populated by Jews, Irish, and African Americans, in language that pushes dialect humor to dadaist extremes:

> On December two fife witt jost wan ivvning privvious
> Was gung on dere gungs-on extrimmingly grivvious—
> By mine enimizz woist shouldn't be sotch a plight—
> Und we closing witt bast Yooltite weeshes—Goot nite![35]

Moore's oft-parodied poem has inspired other Judaized versions, including "Erev Krismes" (Christmas Eve), a comic Yiddish translation by Marie Jaffe (in which, for example, Santa Claus becomes "Reb [Mister] Nikky"), first published in 1965.[36] Other Jewish spoofs of the poem are rendered in English, peppered with Yiddishisms. Works of folk humor, they have occasionally appeared in print and have long circulated through photocopies or, more recently, emails; several can now be found on the Internet. Typically, these parodies transform the poem into a narrative about the arrival, on the first night of Hanukkah, of either a Jewish analog to Santa Claus ("Schloimay Claus" or "Max Klaus") or of Santa himself (who is sometimes revealed to be a crypto-Jew) in a Jewish home stockpiled with Ashkenazic delicacies:

> And if all of these goodies don't fill up your gatkes [undergarments]
> Last but not least, some Chanukah latkes [pancakes].
> "A latke?" cried Santa, "what is this delight?"

On the outside it's golden and inside it's white.

On the outside so crisp and inside it's yummy
And he gobbled them up 'til he filled his fat tummy.
Then they gave him a dreidel [spinning top] and showed him the plays
And he took a menorah to light for eight days.[37]

These and other Jewish Christmas parodies reflect a different kind of engagement with the holiday from the editorials, poems, and essays in the Yiddish *Forward*. In these parodies, Yiddish—whether employed as a full language or as a limited sampling of isolated terms—figures not as an immigrant Jewish vernacular but as what I have termed elsewhere a "postvernacular" language, its secondary, symbolic level of meaning trumping its primary level of signification as a language of daily life. A distinctive feature of many postvernacular translations into Yiddish is a "reworking of the original work's fictional world into a Yiddish world," suggesting that "inherent in Yiddish is a distinctive cultural sensibility that cannot help but Judaize whatever enters its semiotic field."[38] In Jewish Christmas parodies, the presence of Yiddish is inherently disruptive, voicing an essentialized Jewishness that skews the Christian world of the original verses.

Even when employing dialect humor and stereotypes resembling anti-Semitic humor, these parodies are distinguished by their Jewish agency. Though these parodies' portrayal of Jews is often less than flattering, they are not simply present as the objects of attack. Rather, Jews are actively engaged in creating these polemically motivated acts of imitation, which, according to literary scholar Simon Dentith, define them as parody.[39] Jewish Christmas parodies imitate their Christian sources in order to realize a variety of polemical strategies. Gross's poem is a carnivalesque subversion, assailing the magical domestic charms of "A Visit from St. Nicholas" with explosive force. Similarly, humorist S. J. Perelman's 1936 burlesque "Waiting for Santy: A Christmas Playlet," a spoof of Clifford Odets's 1935 agitprop one-act play *Waiting for Lefty*, mocks both Odets's elevated left-wing rhetoric and the popular image of Santa's workshop as a happy wonderland populated by Old World artisans. Perelman transforms this setting into a sweatshop staffed by oppressed, restive Jewish gnomes (named Rankin, Panken, Rivkin, Riskin, and so on). Their speech is inflected with Yiddishisms, as is that of their employer, the "pompous bourgeois" Sanford (Sam) Claus. Perelman not only portrays the notion of Jewish proprietorship of Christmas as inherently risible but also flouts earnest left-wing critiques of the holiday's corrupting commercialization.[40] In its excesses, "Waiting for Santy" both invokes and mocks anti-Semitic stereotyping of Jews as profiting at the expense of Christmas. (Thus, one gnome complains of Claus, "A parasite, a leech, a bloodsucker—altogether a five-star nogoodnik! Starvation wages we get so he can ride around in a red team with reindeers!")[41]

With this hyperbolic language, Perelman deployed what Dentith characterizes as the "normative corrective function" of parody to offer a critique of the excesses of Odets's style and of Christmastime sentimentality. "Waiting for Santy" also exemplifies what Dentith notes is a "paradox" inherent in many parodies: by dint of their mastery of the texts they are lampooning, parodies can perpetuate and sometimes even validate "just the situation that they seek to resist"—in this case, the cultural power of Christmas.[42] Rather than scrutinizing Christmas at a skeptical distance, these parodies demonstrate their creators' fluency in its lore and aesthetics. But instead of aspiring to embrace Christmas as a universal celebration in which Jewish difference would become irrelevant, these parodies seize the occasion to flaunt Jewishness as ineluctably Other. Judaizing widely known Christmas verses and folkways annuls their felicitous universalism, subverting it with prickly, idiomatic, ethnic particularism. At the same time, though, these parodies suggest the possibility of a Jewish engagement with Christmas, however ironized and problematic it may be.

Whereas some of these parodies are works of American Jewish folklore, anonymously created and largely transmitted through informal social networks, other examples have circulated as mass-produced commodities. Besides Gross's book and Perelman's skit (first published in the *New Yorker*), there are Allan Sherman's musical spoofs, "God Bless You, Jerry Mendelbaum" and "The Twelve Gifts of Christmas," which were heard on some of his highly popular comedy recordings made in early 1960s. These include his best-selling debut album, *My Son, the Folksinger*, on which he offered mock versions of selected folksongs as a kind of antifolklore, their lyrics demonstrating, in Sherman's words, "what would happen if Jewish people wrote all the songs—which, in fact, they do."[43] (Here, Sherman doubtless had in mind, among other examples, Irving Berlin's "White Christmas.") These Judaized Christmas parodies engage the economy of holiday gift exchange even as they mock it in their form (as "gag gifts") and, sometimes, their content. Sherman's "The Twelve Gifts of Christmas" offers an inventory of undesirable presents—such as "a statue of a lady with a clock where her stomach ought to be"—that, in the song's final verse, are all taken back to be exchanged.[44] Parody thus enables a kind of Jewish ownership of Christmas that, though understood as essentially comic, offers a double-edged understanding of the holiday's significance for Jews. Just as these parodies demonstrate a mastery of both Christian and Jewish cultures, the inventiveness that crafting them demands evinces the possibility of responding to the December dilemma through acts of creativity, rather than abstinence or acquiescence.

"Uncle Sam, the Hanukkah Man"

Notwithstanding these parodies' enduring popularity, the predominant Jewish response to Christmas after World War II has centered less on mocking the holiday than on expanding the celebration of Hanukkah, both among Jews and, increasingly, in the general public sphere. Parody was, in effect, superseded by the pursuit of parity. Although there are precedents for this trend in the prewar era, as noted earlier, Hanukkah's transformation into the Jewish parallel to Christmas was realized in the postwar years on a grander scale and largely through consumer practices, including new forms of material culture and new media. Historian Jenna Weissman Joselit notes that Hanukkah, "one of the few Jewish ritual practices actually to grow rather than diminish in popularity, enjoyed an unprecedented burst of attention in the years following World War II, when it emerged not only as the Jewish antidote to Christmas but as its functional equivalent."[45] Joselit notes that Hanukkah gifts for children expanded beyond small sums of money, a longstanding East European custom, to giving a series of presents, one for each of the holiday's eight days. The Hanukkah menorah emerged as a new commodity, including electric and musical versions. Mass-produced paraphernalia for the holiday proliferated, much of it paralleling Christmas items, including chocolates and cookie cutters in iconic holiday shapes, holiday-themed decorations and wrapping paper, and a spate of Hanukkah books, recordings, and games for children.

Although these products were largely meant for Jewish consumption, other new undertakings positioned Hanukkah in relation to Christmas for the Christian public. Early postwar ecumenical broadcasts generally did so obliquely, by explaining Hanukkah to their audiences during the winter holiday season.[46] Consider, for example, *A Time for Valor*, one of a series of short television plays on Jewish holidays produced in 1960 for syndicated broadcast by the Jewish Chautauqua Society, a public educational organization established by Reform Jews in 1893. *A Time for Valor* portrays the relationship of the two holidays through the friendship of two American boys: Jerry, who is Jewish, and Paul, who is Christian. When Paul comes over to Jerry's house to play with his new train set, a Hanukkah present, Paul's lack of knowledge about the holiday initiates an explanation of its history and customs, including "flashback" reenactments of the Maccabean revolt. Jerry's father, who narrates the story, emphasizes its significance for Americans—"If it weren't for the fight of the Maccabees, we wouldn't have the religious freedom we have today"—and for Christians: "Not only Jews, but Christians have reason to rejoice in this holiday, because the bravery of the Maccabees saved Judea, where, about 170 years later, Christianity was born."[47] After Jerry's father lights the menorah, Paul's parents arrive with presents for Jerry's family. As the drama concludes, the two boys exchange holiday wishes and gifts. The symmetry of this ending belies hidden tensions and imbalances: whereas Christmas is self-evident, Hanukkah needs to be explained. At the same time, Hanukkah is vaunted as the moral foundation for monotheism and freedom of religion, enabling the celebrating of Christmas in America.

Some Jews voiced concerns about elevating the celebration of Hanukkah to the status of "a major competitive winter sport" early in the postwar period. Writing in *Commentary* in 1950, Grace Goldin explained, "If Chanukah comes earlier than Christmas, it's an inoculation; if later, an antidote; either way, . . . the character of the holiday has been transfigured by an accident of timing: what used to be a festival of freedom becomes a festival of refuge." When a Christian neighbor visited Goldin's home, decorated for Hanukkah with an "orchard of medallions, plaques and paper chains," and observed that the holiday is "not so different from Christmas after all," Goldin countered that "we have to put up a stiff competition." Moreover, she asserted, Jews "sooner or later have to break the news to their children as to what kind of world this is, and . . . not having Christmas is as good a place as any to begin." As an object lesson in marginality and intolerance, she argued, coping with Jews' remove from Christmas should "condition our children for the future—for the series of small slaps they will some day suffer from . . . some professor, or some classmate, or from the world."[48]

Much of Goldin's concerns for her own children centered on their obligatory participation in their public school's Christmas pageant. These annual performances attracted considerable attention in both Jewish and mainstream publications in the early postwar years, often in conjunction with organized protests by Jewish parents. In a 1954 study of American Christmas as an exemplar of national culture, James Barnett notes that these protests "have been made since the beginning of the present century and show no signs of abating." In response, "a number of schools have attempted to bridge the religious gap between Christians and Jews at this season by presenting joint Christmas Chanuka programs." Conceding that neither Christians nor Jews were unqualified supporters of these programs, Barnett notes that "the latter group, as a minority, has more at stake in continuing them than does the larger Christian majority."[49]

When Jews debated public school holiday observances in the early postwar years, they often articulated their positions in terms of what would be in the best interests of the general public, invoking the American commitment to religiosity and the separation of church and state. In 1949, the Committee on Education of the American Jewish Committee wrote that "the Jewish community of America is deeply concerned with secularistic tendencies in contemporary American life, which, if permitted to grow unchecked, may work great harm to the moral and spiritual basis of American Democracy." The committee insisted, however, that "the maintenance and furtherance of religion are the responsibility of the synagogue, the church, and the home, and not of the public school system."[50]

Joint Christmas-Hanukkah school celebrations seldom proved popular with either Christians or Jews, at least among those addressing the topic in print, perhaps because these events called for compromises that relied on specious criteria. In 1950, Thomas Clemente argued in the pages of *The Commonweal*, an independent lay Catholic journal, that "the desire to promote joint Christmas-Hanukka observances in the public school," however admirable in principle, actually "emphasizes the reason why Catholics insist upon a parochial school education for their children and find public schools inadequate." Their "hyphenated" programs make the two holidays "one and the same," doing each religious community a disservice, by making "cultural oneness or sameness an overriding good," at the expense of "sacred belief."[51] Similarly, a 1961 article in the monthly magazine of the women's Zionist organization Hadassah argued that "the introduction of Hanukah as a counterbalance to Christmas" was "unsound. . . . Two wrongs do not make a right." Moreover, "by linking Christmas and Hanukah, we create a misconception of the nature of both holidays in the minds of the Jewish and non-Jewish child."[52]

Author Grace Paley transformed the challenge that public school Christmas pageants posed to American Jews into a subversive opportunity for Jewish self-realization in her 1959 short story "The Loudest Voice." Here, Jewish children come into their own idiosyncratic ownership of Christmas by commanding all the leading roles in their school's holiday play by dint of their vocal strength, in contrast to their Christian class-mates' "very small voices." Paley's young narrator, Shirley Abramowitz, inverts the anxieties about Christmas of her immigrant parents' genera-tion by expressing concern for the holiday's vulnerable status in their ur-ban Jewish enclave: "On our corner a tree had been decorated for us by a kind city administration. In order to miss its chilly shadow our neighbors walked three blocks east to buy a loaf of bread. . . . Oh, not me. On the way to school, with both my hands I tossed it a kiss of tolerance. Poor thing, it was a stranger in Egypt."[53]

But American Jews more often addressed the challenges posed by Christmas without play or irony, as growing postwar concerns about the consequences of Jewish assimilation superseded fears of gentile anti-Sem-itism. To address this new concern, some American Jews turned to a new medium: the social science study. As Charles Silberman has observed, at the time "Jewish families did not merely see Christmas as a problem; they felt the need to have a *policy* toward it."[54] Stuart Svonkin notes that during World War II American social scientists had "demonstrated their usefulness by devising and interpreting propaganda, waging psychological warfare, working to maintain home front morale, and training recruits. After the war social scientists translated their wartime services into other 'practical' fields, such as market research, public opinion polling, and advertising."[55] In the early postwar years, social science research played a foundational role in developing policies for both secular and religious Jewish organizations, which used this research to evaluate American Jew-ish religious observance and to combat anti-Semitism. Several postwar studies commissioned by American Jewish groups specifically addressed how Jews, especially youth, responded to Christmas.

Sociologist Irving Canter, as National Director of Program and Pub-lications of the B'nai B'rith Youth Organization, undertook a survey of 868 Jewish teenagers in 1960 in order to quantify their engagement with Christmas (how many had Christmas trees in their homes, participated in school holiday programs, exchanged Christmas cards or gifts, and so on) and sought to relate this data to qualitative matters of "religious con-science," "loyalty" to Jewish observance, and the character of "intergroup experiences."[56] Canter's survey followed on the heels of a study by Milton Matz, another sociologist. Matz's survey of second- and third-generation

American Jews on their use of and attitudes toward Christmas trees yielded a complex of responses:

> 79.2 per cent of them never have Christmas trees but . . . 37.5 per cent think that having a tree would "make it easier for their children." 34 per cent of them, regardless of whether they have a tree or not, are concerned with whether they should or should not have a tree. 58.3 per cent feel that their children want a tree. 21.4 per cent indicate that they do not know what they would tell their children were they to ask for a tree. 31.6 per cent would wish that the Christmas tree were acceptable to the Jewish religion.

Matz also detected shifts in attitudes toward Christmas trees among second- and third-generation American Jews. Whereas immigrants' children tended to view the tree as "a non-Jewish religious symbol," immigrants' grandchildren regarded it as a "social" symbol and therefore were more likely to have a tree at home. For the older generation, Christmas trees served "as a hyphen between the two components of [their] identity," whereas the younger generation saw the trees as symbolic of "affirming [their] at-homeness in America." Given the extensive discussion and speculation around Christmas trees, above and beyond their actual use, Matz concluded that they "must be considered as a symbol with some pertinent meaning to the American Jew."[57] Similarly, a study undertaken in the early 1970s by Reform Judaism's Union of American Hebrew Congregations concluded that the presence of Christmas trees in Jewish homes served as a diagnostic tool for determining the extent to which Jews were "ambivalent about their Jewish identity" and were more or less "assimilated." "Christmas tree consumers" were correlated with generational differences, extent of Jewish education, synagogue affiliation and attendance, home ritual observance, and attitudes toward intermarriage.[58] In all these studies, Christmas observance epitomizes Jewish assimilation, understood as an abandonment of distinctive Jewishness in both conviction and action.

Through such efforts as social science studies, public protests, and legal petitions, American Jews in the early postwar years appealed to the rational forces of the U.S. Constitution and social science methodology to resolve the December dilemma. The Bill of Rights would mediate between church and state, while the dispassionate analysis of sociologists would diagnose pathologized behavior and offer insight into its remedy. At this time, the term *December dilemma* emerged in American Jewish discourse, assigning a name to concerns regarding not simply what Jews should do on Christmas but also what informed their decisions, given a perception of expanded possibilities, on one hand, and an apparent lack of satisfactory resolution, on the other hand. Typically, efforts to enumerate Jews' various options regarding the December dilemma characterized them all as "equally undesirable alternatives." Striving for parity between Christmas and Hanukkah tended to raise questions about the limitations of such exercises, which sometimes appear to verge on parody, in the form of a "Hanukkah bush" or giant *dreydl* (four-sided spinning top) as stand-ins for a Christmas tree and "Uncle Sam, the Hanukkah Man" as a Santa analog. Only occasionally did someone defend these cultural innovations as a form of "contra-acculturation." Writing in the *Reconstructionist*, Canter argued that, "rather than being a step toward assimilation," these phenomena "represent the Jewish genius at work in (1) selective borrowing, in which we find resistance to and rejection of Christian theology; and (2) the establishment—in a revived, refurbished and glamorized Hanukkah—of a 'series of counter values' in the face of the American Christmas dilemma."[59]

"I Prefer the Stranger's Ways"

By the mid-1970s, a new kind of mediation of the December dilemma had appeared in print: personal, confessional essays about how individual Jews engaged Christmas. Published in mainstream periodicals and newspapers, these pieces differed from the programmatic exhortations of rabbis, offering instead the idiosyncratic observations of "ordinary" Jews. Unlike social scientists or Jewish community activists, these essayists did not propose either to speak for other Jews or to offer prescriptions for solving the December dilemma. Rather, its exposition served as an end in itself.

Among the first of these essays and perhaps the most controversial was Anne Roiphe's "Christmas Comes to a Jewish Home," published in the Home section of the *New York Times* a few days before Christmas 1978. Roiphe, an author then best known for her feminist novel *Up the Sandbox!* (1970), offered a wide-ranging text, in which her family's observance of Christmas served as a point of entry to family history, the socioeconomic dynamics of American Jewry, ethnic isolation (among not only Jews but also, by point of comparison, the Amish), as well as Yiddish, Hanukkah, the "ghetto," diaspora, Western art, the Holocaust, foodways, and anthropology. The attenuated, hybrid nature of her family's Jewishness was neither explained away nor qualified but taken as a given. Christmas lights reminded Roiphe of the light of a candle that her mother lit in memory of her deceased parents, a longstanding Jewish custom. On recalling when her family awoke one Christmas morning to discover that their Christmas tree had tipped over, she wrote that, as they set it up again, "I thought of the rebuilding of the temples. I wondered if only in Jewish homes did the trees fall." As to why she preferred Christmas to celebrating Hanukkah (whose "story always irritated me"), Roiphe explained, "I suppose it's like deciding to have dinner with an ex-spouse with whom one has old and bitter quarrels or a new friend whose foibles seem more distant and therefore more charming. . . . I prefer the stranger's ways."[60]

Rather than attempting to present a resolution to the December dilemma (a term she does not use), Roiphe suggested that the challenges Christmas poses to Jews are defining, even as they are anything but consistent or rational. In the spirit of the essay as an exercise in probative writing, she offered the act of tracing the dynamics of her engagement with Christmas, as well as where this exercise led her thinking, as being of value in themselves. The dilemma is not to be undone but, if anything, to be embraced, both as a highly idiosyncratic quest and as emblematic of larger cultural needs. "We are trying," she concluded, "to be civilized."[61]

Responses to Roiphe's essay, which she had considered "a small, unimportant piece," were extensive and passionate, as she recalled a decade later:

> The phones rang at the *New York Times*—it seemed as if all the officers of all the major Jewish organizations were complaining to their personal friends at the *Times* about my piece. Housewives, rabbis, lawyers, doctors, businessmen, all but Indian chiefs phoned or wrote in, furious that the paper had published an article that advocated assimilation, displayed ignorance of Judaism, and seemed to express contempt for the Jewish way of life. At our house the phone calls began on Thursday at noon and lasted for weeks.[62]

A week after Roiphe's essay was published, the *Times* printed a response by author Cynthia Ozick, who explained that Roiphe "is not an assimilated Jew, as I am," which for Ozick required "an exchange of study and of knowledge" as "the justice and plain daily decency of reciprocal learning."[63] The *Times* also published replies from fourteen readers, an unusually large number for the paper to publish on such a feature. Almost all were unsparing in their condemnation of Roiphe's article, especially Jewish community leaders: "One of the most sorrowful collections of abysmal ignorance, self-contempt, and tooth-fairy level of theology that I have ever encountered," wrote a rabbi from Flushing, New York; "Mrs. Roiphe's children would do better to study Jewish texts, rather than Frosty the Snowman," advised the president of the Women's League for Conservative Judaism, adding that "to treat Christmas as merely a family event is an affront to Christianity." Especially striking are the various assessments of Roiphe's Jewishness, including a characterization of her essay as "only the latest installment in a 2,000-year-old chronicle of Jewish self-hatred." "I feel sorry for Mrs. Roiphe because she is not Jewish," wrote another reader. "She prefers to celebrate Christmas; which is fine, because she is no longer a Jew." Yet another letter stated that "Mrs. Roiphe, by her own admission, does not maintain a Jewish home, nor, she argues, would she conceive of becoming Christian. She is nothing."[64]

But even as these respondents so roundly denounced Roiphe and her essay, they responded in kind, often relating their own histories of holiday observance (and nonobservance) and assessing the larger significance of these accounts. Like Roiphe's essay, these letters also raised in passing an array of topics related to the subject at hand: the commercialization of holiday celebrations, the Crusades, humanism, Zionism, Karl Marx, Purim. Most of these letters were critical of Roiphe's hybridized engagement with Jewishness and Christmas and, unlike her, were usually quick to propose some remedy to what was perceived as a problem. Nevertheless, they joined Roiphe in the enterprise she had initiated, offering personal reflections on the December dilemma in this forum of mainstream journalism—even the author who advised Roiphe that she should confine her thoughts on the topic "to the privacy of her rabbi's office or analyst's couch and not make [them] a matter of public forum."[65]

The afterlife of Roiphe's 1978 essay is also remarkable. The vehement responses it engendered led the author to reassess her relationship to being Jewish, resulting in her 1981 book *Generation without Memory*. In this memoir, Roiphe elaborated on her family's connections to Christmas (noting that it also was a way of celebrating her birthday, as she was born on 25 December), and she reflected on the holiday's significance for them and for American Jews more generally as "a kind of checking point where one can stop and view oneself on the assimilation route."[66] Readers have frequently characterized *Generation without Memory* as a kind of cultural *t'shuvah* (repentance and return to religious observance) that is emblematic of other Jews in the author's cohort. In 1985, Silberman asserted that the fact that "the Roiphe family now celebrates Chanukah," as a consequence of her *New York Times* article and all that ensued, "exemplifies an important trend, in which lighting Chanukah candles increases, generation by generation, among secular as well as religious Jews."[67]

Roiphe's "Christmas Comes to a Jewish Home" has come to mark a watershed, still referenced a generation later in young authors' works on the December dilemma.[68] Since then, moreover, the end of each Roman calendar year has witnessed the publication of similar confessional essays (as well as ethnographic reportage and advice columns) on the December dilemma in regional and national newspapers and magazines.[69] Such articles are no longer so likely to provoke outrage, reflecting recent cultural developments—including changing attitudes toward family life, intermarriage, and cultural hybridity—as well as being a consequence of these essays' frequency. For some American Jews, writing, reading, and responding to introspective reflections on the December dilemma in the public sphere now constitute a seasonal rite in itself.

MixedBlessing

Not long after Roiphe's essay appeared in the *New York Times*, Jews began to engage with Christmas in yet another medium. Starting in the 1980s, American greeting card companies began issuing holiday cards such as the one described in this chapter's opening. These cards do not mark the celebration of either Christmas or Hanukkah per se but rather address their seasonal coincidence and its implications.[70] Part of an expanding inventory of yearly occasions for sending greeting cards (including Oktoberfest, Ramadan, Diwali, Day of the Dead, Black History Month, Pulaski Day, St. Urho's Day, Administrative Professionals Day, and National Day of Prayer, among others)[71] and markets for buying them, these cards do not merely acknowledge but formalize the December dilemma. Bringing it into the matrix of greeting cards configures the seasonal confluence of Jewish and Christian holiday calendars as an occasion in itself, acknowledges the anxieties associated with it, and at times even proffers a resolution through what Leigh Schmidt terms a "consumer rite."[72]

December dilemma cards engage both of these holidays and religions from a perspective centered on Jewish rather than Christian experience.

Greeting card, ca. 2000. Inside: "Ah. The joy of sects." Created and written by Adrienne E. Gusoff. Published by Recycled Paper Greetings, Chicago. (Courtesy of Adrienne E. Gusoff)

The cards iterate some of the humorous strategies found in Jewish Christmas parodies that have appeared in the United States since the 1920s in books, on sound recordings, and more recently on the Internet. And, like newspaper and magazine articles on the topic, these cards appear anew each year, serving at once as a barometer that measures the pressure of the December dilemma and as a calibrator of its changing meanings. However, December dilemma cards are a media practice of a different kind, for it is only when they are circulated that their artfulness is fully expressed; they must be given and received in order to realize the social relations between Christians and Jews represented in the cards' words and images.

Those relations reflect the range of American Jewish responses to the December dilemma, from alterity to parity. As was typical of earlier Jewish Christmas parodies, these cards often express alterity by using Yiddish. Here, too, comic transformations of Christmas verses into Hanukkah verses through Yiddish (or, as is usually the case in December dilemma cards, by selectively integrating Yiddish elements into English) produce an incongruity that marks Hanukkah (and, by extension, Jews) as Other. Thus, a parody of the "Twelve Days of Christmas" on one such card begins, "On the Eighth Day of Hanukkah, my true love gave to me: 8 maids a-milkhik [dairy], 7 swans a-shvitzing [sweating], 6 geese a schmoozing [chatting]."[73] Other cards employ Jewish alterity so as to let non-Jews position themselves as knowledgeable outsiders in relation to Hanukkah's celebrants. "Happy Hanukkah from your Gentile friends," reads one such card on the outside; inside: "GOYS [gentiles] 'Я US."[74]

Many December dilemma cards exploit the humorous potential of postulating parity for the two holidays, suggesting that "Hanukkah bushes" and other Jewish analogs to Christmas customs created in the mid-twentieth century can no longer be taken seriously, even as threats to the integrity of Hanukkah. Some cards play with punning fusions of Christmas and Hanukkah (or more generally Jewish) iconography—for example, a six-pointed Star of David made out of striped candy-canes or a reindeer whose antlers become a menorah. Other cards carry the Christmas/Hanukkah analogy to its illogical conclusion: one such card depicts a couple in a lot where Christmas trees are sold loading a giant menorah onto their car.[75] Similarly, several cards pair Santa Claus with an iconic Jewish figure, usually a portly bearded man in hasidic garb, but sometimes a fiddler on the roof. Conversely, there are cards that subvert Santa's iconic stature, much like earlier Jewish parodies of "A Visit from St. Nicholas," by either landing him, through the chimney, in a Jewish home or revealing him to be a crypto-Jew.

These analogies are often tellingly asymmetrical, if not competitive. Whereas the menorah, the central ritual instrument (and icon) of Hanukkah, appears frequently in the designs of December dilemma cards, the birth of Jesus is rarely portrayed (a card depicting the Nativity and inscribed, "It's a goy!" is an exception).[76] Similarly, the occasional appearance on these cards of the Star of David to represent Jews or Judaism is, apparently, never juxtaposed with its parallel religious icon, the cross. Rather, Christmas is most frequently indexed by symbols of popular custom, especially decorated pine trees and a red-and-white-suited Santa Claus. Similarly, the frequent use of Yiddish and images such as bagels and shtetl fiddlers invokes Jews as an ethnic, rather than religious, community. As has long been the case in American Jewish engagements with Christmas, December dilemma cards sidestep the holiday's theology while foregrounding what has been variously termed its "social," "national," "cultural," or "folk" aspect.

In the spirit of competition, one card offers a definition of Hanukkah as a "festive holiday when people of Jewish ancestry joyously celebrate not having to put a large dead pine tree in their nice clean living rooms."[77] But when Christmas prevails, it is not without considerable Jewish angst. Another card depicts a conversation between a Jewish boy, who requests a Christmas tree, and his grandmother, who replies, "Go get a tree. And after the holidays, don't throw it away. Just plant it on my grave."[78]

Multiple variations of this inventory of ludic strategies recall earlier Jewish responses to the December dilemma, some dating back to the turn of the twentieth century. Their persistence suggests a widespread understanding of both holidays' iconography and an enduring predilection for their mockery and parody. And yet these cards express a wide range of responses to the December dilemma, some of which reflect distinctly late-twentieth-century sensibilities. In particular, some examples delight in harmonizing the holidays, most often by depicting a Christmas tree and a menorah together in domestic comfort; others, however, seem to take equal pleasure in subverting the seasonal notion of interfaith accord and good will toward all. Indeed, some cards address forthrightly the challenge of finding a politically correct response to the December dilemma: "Every year my entire family gathers for the holiday season," reads the outside of one such card, which depicts a large, diverse, and not especially harmonious family (among them a jock, a punk, and a vegetarian lesbian couple) standing before a fireplace hung with stockings, a menorah on its mantel, and a decorated Christmas tree nearby. "We try to set aside differing religious affiliations, lifestyles, preferences, and political views to come together in joyous reunion." Inside, the card reads, "Can I come to *your* house?"[79]

These various strategies both propose Jewish cultural possibilities and challenge them, as they demonstrate that to play with holiday iconography is to engage with the December dilemma. Like the ludic folklore and parodies of previous generations, as well as more recent personal, confessional essays, the designing, marketing, and sending of these cards may be seen as creative cultural activities in their own right. Yet not long after December dilemma cards first appeared, they met with official opprobrium. In 1989, they were the subject of a press release issued by the American Jewish Committee, in conjunction with the National Conference of Christians and Jews:

To combine the religious and cultural symbols of Hanukkah and Christmas in greeting card art is to diminish the sacred symbols of each faith and is an affront to Judaism, to Christianity, and to serious interfaith relations. While both of the festivals contribute to an annual season of celebration, each is totally distinct in origin and purpose. True interreligious relations require respect for the integrity of distinct faiths and a repudiation of syncretism. . . . We appeal to the publishers of such cards to refrain from future editions, and we urge the public to reject equivocally [sic] anything that blurs the distinctions between our unique and cherished holidays.[80]

These sentiments were reiterated a decade later, as December dilemma cards began appearing in the form of electronic greetings on the Internet. "It is mistaken and misguided to synthesize the distinct symbols of our two traditions," commented Christopher Leighton, executive director of the Institute for Christian and Jewish Studies, who attributed the practice to "an American vision that tries to advance tolerance by pretending that differences don't matter that much." Neoconservative advocate Elliot Abrams told a *New York Times* reporter that these cards are "a terrible sign of intellectual and religious confusion. These are separate religions, and if Judaism is to survive it will be by marking these separations emphatically."[81] By invoking more general tropes about American religious pluralism and Jewish continuity, these statements situate December dilemma cards within larger concerns of religious leaders and organized interfaith movements. For these advocates, the cards challenge foundational tenets of engaging religion in the American public sphere—namely, that respect for religion requires recognizing not only the existence of different creeds but also their integrity, as well as the importance of paying them equal respect in the public sphere. The notion of "separate but equal" has been superseded in American public discourse by the virtues of integration, with regard to race, and multiculturalism, with regard to ethnicity; the same does not appear to hold true for religion. Religions are, in effect, widely understood as parallel lines that must not cross, whether in enmity or in syncretism. Violation of this separation is deemed disrespectful, even destructive, confusion, rather than productive fusion.

Censure, however, has not stopped December dilemma cards from being produced, bought, and sent. Indeed, the number and variety of these cards has grown since their advent in the 1980s. One e-card website reported that about one in ten of the "10 million free holiday cards sent via computer from its site" in 1999 were "interfaith."[82] If anything, these cards mark a trend that is normalizing their prevailing sentiments of accommodation and inclusiveness. December dilemma cards are now produced by the Jewish divisions of such major companies as Hallmark (Tree of Life) and American Greetings (L'Chayim To Life!). Smaller, independent companies also produce these cards, including one, MixedBlessing, which specializes in addressing the December dilemma, as the company's website explains:

> In December 1988, Elise and Philip Okrend pondered over what kind of holiday greeting card to send to their friends in interfaith relationships. Instead of sending two separate cards or one non-denominational card, Elise doodled a card with a Star of David merging with a Christmas tree, that would go well for both faiths. Their friends loved the card and the idea so much that MixedBlessing was born.[83]

Testimonials posted on MixedBlessing's website position its cards as appropriate realizations of the authors' own understandings of interfaith relations. "We have sent out your cards the last few years," writes Ariana Raines of Reston, Virginia. "They wonderfully represent us and many of the people we send them to and always generate very positive reactions from recipients." Bob Schultz of Ledgewood, New Jersey, explains, "Our family has been buying your cards for years and they are wonderful. [They show] everyone how close we are as a family and how much we care about each other's religion." And Meredith Pechter of Atlanta, Georgia, comments, "It is always hard to find the right card because I was raised Christian and my husband Jewish—these cards give justice to both [religions]."[84] Rooted in the writers' personal experiences, these testimonials position December dilemma cards as appropriate socially and ethically.

The notion that these cards offer resolution, comfort, or acceptance distinguishes them from a provocative series of greeting cards by the American Jewish artist Martha Rosler. Created and mailed by the artist during the years 1974–1978, Rosler's series *X-Mas Cards or From Our House to Your House* employs mass-produced card stock, onto which holiday greetings are printed alongside a personal snapshot. Rosler created troubling juxtapositions among the cards' preprinted text ("seasons greetings from our house to your house"), photographs of herself in incongruous or uncomfortable poses (for example, standing in her crowded kitchen while wearing a wedding dress), and her own additional captions (to the aforementioned image, Rosler added, "5'4" x 119 lbs. / framed & reframed"). The artist conceived of these cards as a critique of sending

Christmas cards, which she has described as "an American custom . . . , like watching every year the same . . . Christmas shows [on television]. . . . I would be sitting there and looking and thinking: Christmas. Not my holiday."[85]

By contrast, December dilemma cards embrace the protocols of holiday card exchange and the cultural economy in which this mass medium thrives. Even when some of these cards offer a social critique not unlike Rosler's, their meaning depends on the histories of both Christmas cards and Jewish holiday cards. Americans began sending one another Christmas cards in the 1860s, but until the final decade of the nineteenth century, notes historian William Waits, the cards were costly and were "exchanged by only a small number of prosperous Americans." Christmas cards became a mass phenomenon beginning in the 1890s; as they became more affordable, they began to replace the earlier practice of exchanging among friends small, inexpensive, manufactured items, known as "gimcracks." By the turn of the twentieth century, these extensive gift exchanges had come to be seen as an economic burden, and gimcracks' low-brow nature was deemed incompatible with the proper celebration of a religious holiday. Gradually, gift giving was confined to a small circle of relations and close friends, while the extensive exchange of gimcracks among a larger circle of acquaintances shifted to the practice of mailing Christmas cards. Regarded as "a less substantial type of remembrance," cards were held "to be honest and rational symbols of most friendship relations." By the 1910s, greeting card manufacturers advertised their wares as "the ideal item for exchange between friends," and Christmas cards also came to be seen as appropriate tokens of exchange among business associates (as opposed to gifts, which were regarded as being too much like bribes). Seen as lacking in "economic weight," Christmas cards, in effect, dematerialized holiday gift exchanges.[86]

Around the turn of the twentieth century, Jews in Europe and America began sending holiday greeting cards to one another on Rosh Hashanah, as an extension of traditional oral wishes that God grant the recipient a good year and continued life. Some Rosh Hashanah cards also voiced other sentiments, from romantic love to love of Zion. These cards offered greetings in the form of original verses in Yiddish, rather than conventional Hebrew wishes, and the cards' secular nature was often echoed in playful imagery, including such modern phenomena as airplanes and movie theaters. Here, the novel medium of the holiday card transformed an oral practice into a commodity and traditional wishes for divine beneficence into expressions of contemporary, and often secular, Jewish hopes and desires.[87]

The repertoire of Jewish holiday cards has expanded slowly: Hanukkah greeting cards began to appear in the United States in the mid-twentieth century, especially in the form of billfolds for giving gifts of money.[88] Passover cards are a more recent and less widespread innovation. The limited number of Jewish holidays for which cards are manufactured reflects, in part, the narrow range of religious practice of most American Jews. This phenomenon also indicates that those who do observe the full inventory of Jewish holidays do not regard them as requiring greeting cards, even though these Jews have elaborated the material culture and media practices of some of these holidays (notably Purim and Succoth) in other ways.[89]

The recent advent of December dilemma cards coincides with other signal shifts in Jews' profile as an American religious community, in which Hanukkah figures as a strategic opportunity for Jews to engage the public with unprecedented prominence. Beginning in the 1980s, the display of Hanukkah menorahs as part of winter holiday decoration in public spaces received unprecedented attention. During that decade, Lubavitcher hasidim began to erect and light large menorahs, some several stories tall, in prominent outdoor locations in cities across the United States and around the world, often attracting local coverage in print and broadcast media. In a commemorative volume documenting this activity, Lubavitch characterized these displays with rhetoric recalling statements liberal Jewish organizations had made a generation earlier, championing the celebration of Hanukkah as "a lesson in religious freedom" that

> confirms the basic beliefs of America's first settlers, themselves victims of religious persecution. . . . The First Amendment to the Constitution guarantees individuals the right to practice their religion without fear, and prevents the government from favoring any particular faith. . . . The public menorahs symbolize this spirit of liberty and have thus won a place not only in Jewish life but also in the life of the American people.[90]

In fact, these displays have proved a contentious emblem of America's guarantee of freedom of worship. They have been the subject of several court cases, including one brought before the U.S. Supreme Court in 1989 (*County of Allegheny v. American Civil Liberties Union*), which resulted in a ruling permitting menorahs as part of public holiday displays that include symbols of other holidays. Therefore, juxtaposing what are regarded either as unambiguously religious objects, such as a crèche, or as having "both religious and secular dimensions," as in the case of the menorah, endows these symbols with new meaning as signifiers of the American civic values of religious freedom and cultural pluralism. Noted one journalist covering the impact of the Supreme Court's ruling on more recent local cases concerning the display of holiday decorations in Colorado, Florida, New Jersey, and Tennessee, "Context is everything."[91]

The notion that publicly acknowledging Judaism exemplifies America's commitment to religious freedom would seem to have informed the decision by the United States Postal Service (USPS) in 1996 to issue a stamp for Hanukkah, the first non-Christian religious holiday to be so recognized. (The United States has issued Christmas stamps annually since 1961, and in 2001 the USPS issued a stamp for the Muslim holidays Eid al-Adha and Eid al-Fitr.) The Hanukkah stamp "represents the Postal Service's respect for the cultural and ethnic diversity that is fundamental to the American people," stated USPS governor S. David Fineman.[92] "The story of Hanukkah . . . speaks to celebrants around the world—and to millions of Americans—telling a story of triumph over adversity, strength in conviction, and belief in the possibility of miracles. . . . [The Hanukkah stamp] reminds us, as Americans, that at the heart of our diversity we are joined together by a network of common needs and values."[93] Remarkably, the USPS discourse avoids characterizing Hanukkah as a religious celebration—just as Christmas is officially commemorated as a national holiday—for to do otherwise would raise questions of the separation of church and state. Rather, the national discourse reflects popular avoidance of theology in favor of an abstract "belief" of universal value, on one hand, and the distinction of a particular culture and ethnicity, on the other hand.

Affixed to a greeting card envelope, a holiday stamp links the personal scope of the enclosed message with a nationally recognized occasion and incorporates personal relationships into religious, ethnic, or national solidarities. Holiday cards sent by individuals frequently come with photographs or letters reporting on the past year's activities, linking a more intimate socializing among family and friends with wishes for "peace on earth" and "good will to all men." The annual exchange of holiday cards, though practiced on a vast scale, offers the individual sender a means of inventorying and regulating a sense of communal solidarity among scattered family, friends, and colleagues. This annual practice is complicated by the card's status as a modular commodity that offers consumers both stylistic novelty and generic familiarity in a competitive marketplace. As items of exchange, holiday cards imply social reciprocity and create a need for balance; everyone should have a card to send to everyone who sends him or her one. The wide range of December holiday cards available to the consumer not only offers abundant options but also poses the challenge of finding appropriate cards for the relationships between the sender and an array of recipients.

December dilemma cards articulate a distinctive set of social relations through card exchanges: between Christians and Jews, from or to interfaith families, and even between Jews, especially those who might not take their common religion for granted. ("To my love at Hanukkah," reads the front of one card, depicting a man and woman lighting a menorah. Inside: "I'm glad that we have each other, and that we share the same beliefs.")[94] These cards also offer various responses to conventional Christmas greetings, some affirming the spirit of all-embracing good wishes, others questioning the universalist implications of "Seasons Greetings," as was the case in articles published decades earlier in the Yiddish press. Thus, a card bearing the title "A True Story for the Holidays" shows a woman in a coat and scarf sitting on a bench, surrounded by holiday shoppers and decorations. "Every year when Christmas rolls around," the front of the card explains, "Margo doesn't get all stressed out from worry about Christmas shopping, Christmas decorating or Christmas with the relatives. Her secret?" Inside: "She's Jewish."[95]

The ambivalence that inheres in the December dilemma, including not only religious differences but also distinct notions of how to engage them, is sometimes articulated in the format of these cards. Typically, these holiday cards are what their publishers term a "studio card"—that is, "a long card with a short punch line"—which became popular in the mid-twentieth century and thereby "firmly establish[ed] the popularity of humor in American greeting cards."[96] These bifold cards juxtapose the cover image and text with what appears inside. In December dilemma cards, the transition from outside to inside can be deployed provocatively or ironically, creating a tension between a convivial medium and a confrontational message. For example, the outside of one card, showing a smiling figure wearing a Santa hat and lighting a menorah, reads, "I sincerely wish that you may enjoy the holiday and/or celebration of your religious, ethnic, or socio-political choice over the coming weeks whenever it/they may fall and whatever it/they may be so named. . . ." Inside: "Now, if this card still pisses someone off—fuck 'em."[97] This example finds edgy humor in the impossibility of resolving the December dilemma, understood (and mocked) as the etiquette of political correctness. The card makes explicit that hypersensitivity to the dilemma is itself part of the dilemma; the un-anticipated expression of outrage inside the card both voices and defuses the anxiety.

The Merry Mish-Mash Holiday

Even as the December dilemma inspires a protean array of responses, it seems to be a delimited occasion for addressing interfaith concerns. Pass-over's proximity with Easter, for example, has engendered little in the way of parallel (April angst?) phenomena. Rather, in the past quarter century or so, the December dilemma has inspired a proliferation of practices that variously celebrate or interrogate American multiculturalism. Perhaps nothing better exemplifies this development on a grand scale than sea-sonal broadcasts on the December dilemma in television series aired on national networks since the mid-1970s. Sketches on the comedy-variety series *Saturday Night Live* (NBC, 1975–present) have occasionally found humor in Jews' engagement with Christmas, often iterating well-estab-lished parodies. These include Jewish versions of Christmas carols; the ap-pearance of Hanukkah Harry (played by Jon Lovitz), a comic Jewish Santa analog; and, perhaps most famously, Adam Sandler's "Hanukkah Song," first performed on the show on 3 December 1994, in which the comedian offered a roster of Jewish celebrities to comfort alienated Jews on Christ-mas.[98] Echoing the widespread practice in public schools, some Christ-mastime variety broadcasts include segments devoted to Hanukkah. One of the more provocative examples was aired on 29 November 1997, when African American drag queen RuPaul invited actress (and celebrity stu-dent of Kabbalah) Sandra Bernhard on his eponymous variety show (VH-1, 1996–1998) to explain the mystical significance of Hanukkah. As Bern-hard explained the holiday's customs and lit the menorah with her host, multiple cultural boundaries were crossed—race, gender, sexuality, reli-gion, ethnicity—along with those between the sacred and the secular, the reverent and the playful. During the segment, RuPaul appeared atypically shy about entering into the celebration of Hanukkah, asking repeatedly whether it was "sacrilegious" for a drag queen to participate. But Bern-hard, expansively inviting, insisted that the spiritual force of the holiday transcended all boundaries.

The advent of December dilemma episodes as a staple of situation comedies and drama series in the 1980s entails a more elaborate integration of the subject into ongoing plots and the lives of continuing characters.[99] Typically aired in December, these episodes link the calendar of the series' virtual worlds with that of their audience. These programs also locate the December dilemma in settings familiar to viewers, such as the workplace (for example, an episode of NBC's *ER* aired on 12 December 1995) or school (*Beverly Hills 90210*, Fox, 14 December 1994), but most frequently situate it in the domestic sphere of an intermarried family.

The dramatic series *thirtysomething* (ABC, 1987–1991) examined the emotional conflicts that the December dilemma provoked in one such couple, Michael Steadman and Hope Murdoch Steadman, in two broadcasts, aired 16 December 1987 and 20 December 1988. For the series's creators, Marshall Hershkovitz and Edward Zwick, these broadcasts addressed multiple interests, including an ongoing effort to use the television series as a vehicle for an oblique kind of self-portraiture. Discussing their motives for dramatizing the December dilemma, they explained, "We are both Jews" who "are also both married to non-Jews. As religion goes, we are skeptical when it suits us, ardent when we need to be, and mostly uninterested in the observance of anything more than the benchmark holidays." In planning a second broadcast on the December dilemma, Hershkovitz and Zwick sought to extend the complex engagement with the topic of their first effort, which they characterize as having been "the only consciously ambivalent holiday show on network television." By electing to "talk about a problem we had talked about before," they sought a way to "say something about the nature of all problems—that you solve them, and they don't go away."[100]

The second broadcast's self-consciousness extended to Hershkovitz and Zwick's attention to their medium: "We wanted something silly to say something serious. . . . And so we chose the sitcom, the most frivolous of TV forms, to tell the story of Michael Steadman's crisis of faith. We also wanted to talk about TV itself—how its shopworn constructs taught us, for better or worse, a way of seeing the world."[101] The episode embeds into the drama a vintage situation comedy, shot in black and white, as the vehicle for Michael's fantasies (wherein he and his family star in a parody of the 1960s sitcom *The Dick van Dyke Show*). This episode also suggests the appeal of magical solutions—here, in the form of Santa Claus (played by Jack Gilford), who also appears to be a local rabbi—to the messiness of real life.[102] Michael and Hope's fraught negotiations over holiday observances are similarly offered a kind of miraculous resolution: After suffering mild injuries in an automobile accident, Hope discovers that she is pregnant with their second child. The experience of catastrophe and its apparent "happy ending" galvanizes Michael to reflect on his sense of faith, made more complicated but also more urgent in light of his own religious skepticism and his intermarriage. At the episode's conclusion, Michael enters a synagogue, located across the street from the lot where he has bought a Christmas tree for his family, and recites Kaddish in memory of his father.

Although December dilemma episodes tend to treat the subject earnestly, often centered on affirming familial bonds at their most sentimental, the topic is occasionally the subject of satire. An early episode of the animated comedy series *South Park* (Comedy Central, 1997–present), first aired on 12 December 1997, spoofed the efforts of public institutions to avoid offending religious sensibilities by presenting a "politically correct" winter holiday school program reduced ad absurdum to gray minimalism. More provocatively, this episode also both evokes and lampoons the messages of spiritual uplift typically offered in television's holiday specials for children. The creators of *South Park* ridicule such presentations of miraculous faith in the supernal by having Kyle Broflovski—South Park, Colorado's self-proclaimed "lonely Jew," who is alienated from his classmates' celebration of Christmas—encounter the miraculous in the form of a talking turd, who only speaks to Kyle.

The task of crafting a self-styled, hybrid holiday celebration in response to the December dilemma was a recurring subject on *The OC* (Fox, 2003–2006). On its 3 December 2003 episode, the dramatic series popularized the term *Chrismukkah*, ostensibly the invention of Seth Cohen, the son of an upscale interfaith family in California's Orange County. In the following season, Seth introduced the "yarmuclaus," a cap that fuses the *yarmulke* (skull cap traditionally worn by religious Jewish men) and Santa's hat, as an innovative artifact that materializes the family's solution to the December dilemma. "I'm also overseeing licensing and merchandising, O.K.? T-shirts, mugs," Seth informed his family, insisting, "If my sense of the cultural zeitgeist is accurate . . . , this is the year that Chrismukkah sweeps the nation." Notwithstanding the series's trademark arch "self-referentiality," the episode makes "a case for hybrid vigor," notes critic Virginia Heffernan. "Seth's pluck, after all, is founded in his sense that unless he invented something, his parents wouldn't give him any traditions at all. By persuading his family and friends to give the Chrismukkah goof a try, he persuades them to continue to imagine new habits and rituals—ones that might make them happier than the ones they pace through out of grim obligation and false cheer."[103]

For many American Jews, Christmas has become a definitional occasion that demands some kind of action, resulting in an array of self-styled annual rites involving an interrelation of new media, social interests, and material culture. These practices range from privately planned events, such as "un-Christmas" parties, at which Jewish friends gather for dinner and the exchanging of "un-Christmas" presents,[104] to institutional activities, including special programs offered on 25 December by Jewish museums and community centers. Some Jews make a point of volunteering on Christmas, either working in a soup kitchen to feed those in need or taking shifts on the holiday at hospitals, police stations, and other workplaces, so that Christian co-workers can spend the day with their families. Joshua Plaut describes in his dissertation on contemporary American Jewish responses to Christmas the evolution of Jewish volunteerism on Christmas from individual undertakings to institutionalized efforts such as Project Ezra, run by the Synagogue Council of Massachusetts since 1986.[105]

This attention on action—on having something to do, and, moreover, something understood as meaningfully Jewish, on 25 December—distinguishes many responses to the December dilemma in recent decades. These new practices have emerged at the same time that the extent of Jewish-Christian intermarriage has become commonplace in the United States within little more than a generation, increasing from less than 10 percent in the 1960s to over 30 percent two decades later.[106] To a considerable extent, these new ways of engaging with the December dilemma respond directly to this demographic development and to signal changes in how some American Jews perceive intermarriage.

Among more liberal American Jews, discussions of intermarriage expanded in the 1980s beyond what had previously been widespread condemnation and toward greater acknowledgment of intermarriage as a common practice with which the Jewish community should engage in some way. In these discussions, the December holidays often exemplify the challenges that religion poses to intermarried couples and their families. Sociologist Egon Mayer's 1985 study of American Jewish-Christian intermarriages observed that, whereas "Jewish holidays appear to mark the holiday calendar of intermarried families at least as much as if not more than Christian holidays," Christmas "enjoys a very wide appeal in intermarried homes." At the same time, some "60 percent [of intermarried families' homes] had a menorah," whereas only 40 percent had "objects of Jewish art" or "Jewish books, including a Jewish Bible or prayer book."[107] In a 1989 book on intermarriage, Susan Weidman Schneider noted theological issues at stake in the December dilemma but focused on its challenges as they pertain to lived experience. For example, she described a Jewish man who "'allowed' his [Christian] wife to have a Christmas tree in their house and then refused to hang anything on it himself and wouldn't approach it or touch it. The tree was a taboo object to him." Suggestions Schneider offered for addressing the December dilemma similarly focused on cultural practices: "To avert confrontation, there should be ways the non-practicing partner can become part of the celebration; with Hanukkah, for example, a Christian father can learn to play *dreidel* (spinning top) games with the children, a traditional holiday pastime that will keep him part of the action yet not force him into religious participation."[108]

These studies suggest that, even as many American Jews have developed a new discussion of intermarriage in recent decades, their responses to the December dilemma in this context are often indebted to previous generations' engagements with Christmas. Here, too, it would appear that, from a theological perspective, Jews' problems with Christmas might pose more of a challenge for Christians' universal aspirations than the holiday does for Jewish beliefs. From a cultural, social, or political perspective, however, the need for a distinctive response to Christmas is a decidedly Jewish concern. Schneider noted more generally that, among intermarried couples, "Christians often express feelings of wanting to make the two traditions one, restoring them to what they think of as a primary unity. The Jews want to acknowledge their distinctiveness."[109] Notwithstanding expressions of interfaith accord that many December dilemma practices articulate, these practices originate in this Jewish concern for distinctiveness. As linguist Max Weinreich noted, this concern is a fundament of Jewish culture, even when it appears to resemble non-Jewish life: "The very existence of a division" between Jewish and non-Jewish cultures, he argued, "is much more important than the actual location of the division line."[110] Sending December dilemma cards, watching Christmas/Hanukkah episodes of television series, and other rites of "being Jewish at Christmas" evince both a continuation of this longstanding concern for distinctiveness and a relatively new desire to see it expressed through mass media and in public forums.

A telling development among recent American Jewish responses to Christmas, exemplified by December dilemma cards but not limited to them, is the proliferation of a new material culture. These items include materializations of the December-holiday syncretism that has long been the subject of jokes and parodies, as well as goods that are part of an ever-expanding inventory of Hanukkah analogs for the material richness of Christmas. These items are sometimes fabricated in relation to media works; for example, a website for fans of *The OC* offers Chrismukkah merchandise, including the yarmuclaus featured on the series in 2004, as well as wrapping paper, recorded music, and a photo album for the holiday.[111] More December dilemma goods are offered at chrismukkah.com, including greeting cards, coffee mugs, T-shirts, and a cookbook, *Chrismukkah: The Merry Mish-Mash Holiday Cookbook*, which features such comic fusions of Christmas customs and Jewish foodways as "Gefilte Goose," "Kris Kringle Kugel," and "Blitzen's Blintzes."[112] In addition to these mass-produced items are do-it-yourself projects. In a 2002 book of Jewish handicrafts, *Judaikitsch: Tchotchkes, Schmattes, and Nosherei*, authors Jennifer and Victoria Traig offer guidelines for making a "Hanukkah Headband," which features nine felt "candles" radiating from the top of the wearer's head, as a riposte to Christmas festive attire: "One December we were out shopping and noticed that everyone else was wearing a silly holiday headband. We saw reindeer antlers, holly, and Christmas tree branches. But where were the menorot? It didn't seem fair. . . . So we scurried home and whipped this up."[113] At the turn of the millennium, Jewish museums and other institutions that host public programs on 25 December frequently offer crafts workshops, especially for children, in which participants can make menorahs or Hanukkah gift-wrapping paper, paint murals, or decorate craft items for the holiday.[114]

All these undertakings are offered as productive responses to the December dilemma. They are productive in two senses of the term: a tangible product is made, and the effort this entails is understood as productive—that is, as beneficial—in itself. For people troubled by the December dilemma, these acts of inventing, manufacturing, marketing, and consuming are offered as positive responses to a phenomenon that has long been associated with a lack of possibilities for celebration, communion, or consumption and that has instead inspired a sense of unhappiness, anomie, or envy. Thus, whereas Christmas cards were regarded as having *de*materialized large-scale holiday gift exchange, December dilemma cards materialize solutions to a problem of popular religious practice.

Not surprisingly, then, these cards have occasionally figured in promotions for products. In 1997, a card from Tanqueray spirits relativized

Happy Holidays Menorah Christmas Tree, designed in Israel by Sahar Batsay and made in China for Decor Craft, Inc., of Providence, Rhode Island. This ritual object, purchased in 2007, materializes fusions of the Christmas tree and menorah that have been depicted in cartoons since the turn of the twentieth century.

seasonal celebrations in a menu of interchangeable options: "Mr. Jenkins [the company's fictional spokesperson] wishes you a most enjoyable/pleasant/frictionless/mischievous . . . Hannukah/Christmas/Kwanzaa/non-denominationally committed celebration . . . , as well as a happy/salty/spicy/naughty . . . New Year."[115] Virgin Mobile cell phones championed religious and ethnic syncretism in the company's offer of discounts in the spirit of Chrismahanukwanzakah, a "completely madcap mix of holiday traditions" that sought in December 2004 to deploy this mélange not only to push product but also to ameliorate "the nation's post-Election obsession over the supposed 'morality gulf' between the Red states and the Blue states." Here, the communion implicit in religious syncretism, evoked through a provocative hybridization of ethnic and religious iconography (for example, a card with Santa Claus sitting in a lotus, holding a sitar and a *dreydl*), serves as a model for healing a politically divided country.[116]

Conjoining material culture and media practices in response to the December dilemma appears to be a singularly American phenomenon, in part because it exemplifies what is widely regarded as a national propensity for consumerism.[117] Schmidt argues that the advent of consumer rites around religious and public holidays in mid-nineteenth-century America "was made possible by the ever-widening scope of the commercial revolution" that had begun during the previous century. This new consumer culture was distinguished by endless "novelty and abundance," imbricated with "the fantastic play of dreams and passions. In the increasingly democratic world of consumption, luxury and self-fulfillment countered thrift and frugality, and protean self-fashioning subverted the fixedness of hierarchy."[118] According to historian Andrew Heinze, encountering this consumer culture proved a defining experience for immigrants to the United States: "If the American people has been characterized by a peculiar faith in the principle of a rising standard of living, then the adaptation of immigrants to the 'perspective of abundance' must be considered an essential part of Americanization." Heinze sees Jews as doubly exemplary of this principle: "As consumers, Jews sought important elements of American identity more quickly and thoroughly than other groups of newcomers. As entrepreneurs in consumer-oriented trade, they, more than others, enriched the potent environment of urban consumption which had become such a distinctive feature of American society."[119]

Despite frequent condemnation, especially by religious elites, of consumer-driven holiday celebrations, consumerism may also be seen as providing opportunities for creating and sharing new cultural possibilities in defiance of official privations and restrictions—or even as an act of faith in America. In this regard, the media works and other cultural practices of the December dilemma are exemplary of popular religion, typically privileging cultural and social concerns over theological ones. These practices do not merely reflect consumerist propensities for the self-styled but also participate in a larger American project, exemplified by Christmas, that seeks a place for religiosity in the public sphere that is somehow also compatible with national values of disestablishment and freedom of worship. In addition, as Jewish definitional rites, December dilemma practices engage longstanding practices for asserting Jewish difference in response to a Christian majority culture, bringing other concerns and modes to the center as they marginalize theology: First, over the course of the past century, American Jews evince an ever-growing investment in realizing their encounters with Christmas in public spheres, especially through mass media and consumer goods. Second, these practices frequently give pride of place to play, through ludic use of language and iconography, as a valued idiom for negotiating the disparities between Jews and Christians, Hanukkah and Christmas, definitional Otherness and universalist aspirations. Third, Jewish mediations of Christmas are frequently concerned with productivity, responding to the December dilemma, if often unwittingly, in the idiom of consumerism that figures so prominently in Americans' celebration of Christmas.

The December dilemma's many practices all offer structures for engaging in conversations about challenging notions of religion, community, and public culture and for relating these large-scale social issues to the intimacy of home, family, and friends. These practices are also mediating agents, seeking to articulate a variety of strategies for accommodating and confronting challenges that a diverse American population faces as it experiences signal shifts in its understandings of difference and commonality, during a season that idealizes optimism. In the face of longstanding celebrations of the miraculous, the practices of the December dilemma make the case for celebrating the problematic.

6

The Virtual Rebbe

In the final decades of the twentieth century, one of the most exceptional of the world's many Jewish communities became one of the most visible. The followers of Lubavitch hasidism, also known as Chabad, were estimated at the end of the twentieth century to number upward of 100,000 worldwide, including some 40,000 in the United States, about half of whom live in the community's center in Crown Heights, Brooklyn.[1] Chabad is thus much smaller than American Jewry's major religious denominations (the largest, Reform Judaism, reported over 1,500,000 members at the turn of the millennium) or nonreligious organizations (Hadassah, the largest Zionist membership organization in the United States, has over 300,000 members).[2] In fact, Chabad has fewer followers than Satmar, the largest of the American hasidic communities in the post–World War II era. And yet, as sociologist Samuel Heilman argues, the influence of Chabad should not be measured "by the number of guys they have in black hats" but rather "in the number of Jews they've had an impact on, and that is far in excess of their actual number."[3]

To a considerable extent, this renown is deliberate—indeed, it has been a fundament of Chabad hasidism for decades. This commitment to visibility in the public sphere distinguishes Lubavitch not simply from other hasidim or *haredim* ("ultra-Orthodox Jews," including both those who are hasidim and those who are not) but also from other Jewish religious communities generally. Chabad's approach to publicizing its mission of fostering increased Jewish religious observance and promulgating its particular vision of Jewish messianism is quite unlike efforts at self-promotion that other American Jews have undertaken, such as the Jewish Theological Seminary's ecumenical broadcasts of the mid-twentieth century (see chapter 2). In postwar America, Lubavitcher hasidim have evolved a culture distinguished not only by its singular spiritual vision but also by its uses of media, especially new media, to realize this mission. These engagements with new media have become defining practices for Lubavitcher hasidim and have been instrumental in extending their sense of purpose globally. Chabad's media practices have enabled its followers to negotiate daunting challenges posed by the Holocaust to Jews generally and, more recently, to respond to a crisis of continuity specific to this community—the death of the seventh Lubavitcher rebbe, Menachem Mendel Schneerson, in 1994. Some observers predicted that his death would lead to the demise of Chabad; the rebbe had left no successor, and many of his followers believed that he was the messiah. Instead, the community continues, expanding its presence in the public sphere and forging a new spiritual relationship with the leader they refer to simply as the Rebbe, largely through media practices that are remarkably innovative and provocative.

"Communicating the Infinite"

As exceptional as Chabad appears now, it has distinguished itself among hasidic communities from its inception, even as its origins are rooted in the foundation of hasidism. This movement transformed religious life for many East European Jews, beginning in the mid-eighteenth century, by popularizing Jewish mysticism and establishing the rebbe (literally, "teacher, master"; plural, *rebeyim*) as a figure who "mediated between this world and the other" on behalf of his disciples, "drawing down . . . the divine effluence for the benefit of the community." These innovations were manifest in new forms of "worship through corporeality," in which the rebbe "sacralized . . . worldly endeavors," and in new social formations, in which *rebeyim* assumed important public roles in Jewish communal life.[4] Chabad hasidism was established in the late eighteenth century by Shneur Zalman of Liadi, one of the youngest followers of Dov-Ber of Mezritch, who was, in turn, the primary disciple of the progenitor of hasidism, Israel ben Eliezer, known as the Baal Shem Tov (miracle worker). Chabad hasidism had its beginnings in small towns in the Lithuanian provinces of Vitebsk and Mogilev in the northwest of the Russian Empire: Liozna, Liadi, and especially Liubavichi, where the movement flourished for over a century and from which it derived its name. Located far from the centers of hasidism in southern Poland and Ukraine, Chabad offered a distinctive approach to hasidic thought and practice, while embracing such key tenets of hasidism as the popularization of Jewish mysticism as a key to personal and communal spirituality and the importance of a rebbe as a charismatic leader and spiritual mentor. This distinction is indicated by the movement's use of the appellation *Chabad*—an acronym for the Hebrew words *hakhmah* (wisdom), *binah* (understanding), and *da'at* (knowledge)—to signify its conceptualization of hasidic practice, which gives pride of place to the intellect. Outside observers of the movement readily noted Chabad's distinctive ethos. Historian Simon Dubnow characterized Chabad as "rational Hasidism," which "strove to adapt the emotional pietism" of the founder of hasidism to the "intellectualism" of rabbinic Judaism, especially as practiced in its stronghold in Lithuania. In the hands of the founder of Chabad hasidism, "the ecstasy of feeling is transformed into ecstasy of thinking." However, even though Chabad challenged prevailing hasidic teachings and practices, Dubnow noted that its "pantheistic doctrine"—his characterization of hasidism's expansive approach to engaging Jewish mysticism—was anathema to the *mitnagdim*, or rabbinic opponents of hasidism.[5]

In *Communicating the Infinite*, Naftali Loewenthal argues that fundamental to Chabad's hasidic theology is its "communication ethos," born out of a commitment to making "some aspect of the highest levels of Jewish mystical experience . . . accessible to the Jewish people at large" and not just a learned elite schooled in the texts and textual practices of Jewish mysticism. This aspiration "led to the definition of Habad as a clearly distinguished branch of Hasidism with a unique emphasis on the goal of communication." Loewenthal suggests that this commitment can be discerned in the origins of Lubavitch hasidism. He notes that Shneur Zalman's career as a hasidic leader began when it was decided that he, alone among a group of disciples of Dov-Ber of Mezritch based in Lithuania, would remain in the region when the others left for Palestine in 1777—a decision prompted by a concern about how "Hasidic thought and attitudes [would] be communicated to society if the leadership were thousands of miles away."[6] This decision appears to have prefigured both the incipient movement's commitment to a region of Eastern Europe that was otherwise a redoubt of *mitnagdim* and a defining concern for Chabad about communicating hasidic teachings at a distance.

Such practices were in tension with the importance that hasidim placed on *yehidut*, a private meeting between an individual hasid and his rebbe, regarded as an encounter of extraordinary affective and spiritual intensity. Loewenthal notes that Shneur Zalman, as the first Lubavitcher rebbe, was concerned that, "because of the large number of people, new followers are finding it difficult to see him in *Yehidut*." Shneur Zalman wrote that "it is absolutely essential to speak to them in *Yehidut*, and no alternative is possible." Resolving this problem led to the publication in 1797 of Shneur Zalman's most important work, *Likkutei Amarim* (*Collection of Statements*), commonly referred to as *Tanya* (*It Was Taught*). Making innovative use of the print medium in hasidic culture, this foundational text of Chabad theology was "intended to provide direct guidance to the reader, like a manual, and is a substitute for the *Yehidut* interviews with the author, in which he had given direct spiritual advice to his followers."[7]

From the beginning, Chabad hasidism might be seen as a series of visionary efforts to negotiate the geographic dispersal of East European Jewry, to reach across cultural divides within the Jewish community, and to offer an approach to Jewish spirituality that strives for comprehensive engagement with the numinous through diverse practices, including the study and application of rabbinic law as well as esoteric mysticism and popular ecstatic practices. These ongoing efforts, entailing a commitment to exploring innovative approaches to communicating Chabad's multivalent approach to religiosity, have provoked controversy both among other hasidim and among nonhasidic Jews.

Chabad's pattern of innovative approaches to hasidic practice proved strategic to the community's relocation to America in the 1940s, with the arrival of the sixth Lubavitcher rebbe, Yosef Yitzhak Schneerson. At the time, the United States was home to only a few hasidim, including a small Chabad community that had settled in Brooklyn in the mid-1920s. After the Holocaust, the United States—in particular, neighborhoods in Brooklyn—soon emerged as the center of hasidic life for many surviving communities of hasidim, including Lubavitch. Other new centers of hasidism were established in Montreal, London, Antwerp, Jerusalem, and Melbourne, among other cities. This geographic reconfiguration prompted new kinds of engagement both among different hasidic communities and between them and their neighbors. These new forms of contact were also shaped by new communications media, as anthropologist Jerome Mintz notes in his study of hasidim in New York: "With telephones in every household and a fax machine in every office, gossip moves at an electronic gallop. Today a dispute may range from Jerusalem to New York, but allies and antagonists are joined instantaneously by wire, satellite, telephone, fax, the daily press, and television."[8] Writing in the early 1990s, Mintz does not mention cell phones or the Internet, but by the end of the twentieth century these, too, were part of the array of new media with which hasidim have grappled in the post-Holocaust era.[9]

Under the leadership of the sixth Lubavitcher rebbe, Chabad pioneered using new media to reestablish hasidic life in these new circumstances. Shortly after arriving in New York, Yosef Yitzhak Schneerson inaugurated a monthly magazine, *Hakeriah Vehakedushah* (*Reading and Holiness*), in 1941, followed by another periodical, *Kovetz Lubavitch* (*Lubavitch Collection*), in 1944. The founding of the Kehot Publication Society in 1942 was linked to the establishment of Merkos L'Inyonei Chinuch, a central Chabad organization for Jewish education. In 1944, Chabad also instituted Nigunei Chassidei Chabad, an organization for collecting and disseminating on long-playing records traditional melodies sung by Lubavitcher hasidim.[10] Following the death of Yosef Yitzhak Schneerson in 1950, his son-in-law, Menachem Mendel Schneerson, who was himself a descendant of this dynasty of *rebeyim*, assumed leadership of Chabad. The new Lubavitcher rebbe expanded on his predecessor's commitment to renewing the Lubavitch community through institution building and innovative use of new media on an unprecedented scale.

"Tapping G-dly Forces"

Observers have regularly noted Chabad's expansive use of media for promotion and outreach under Menachem Mendel Schneerson's leadership. A 1957 profile observed that "though mysticism lies at its core, the Lubovitcher movement has been blessed with a flair for organization and public relations that has enabled it to strike firm roots in environments as diverse as Communist Russia, North Africa, and the United States."[11] Several years after Menachem Mendel Schneerson's death, another observer characterized the community as "undoubtedly the most dynamic, most outgoing and at the same time most self-publicizing . . . of all the Hassidic groups."[12] Often thought of as a postwar innovation, this commitment to public visibility builds on precedents that predate both the seventh Lubavitcher rebbe's tenure and Chabad's move to America.

Consider, for example, Chabad's use of portraits of its leaders, beginning in the nineteenth century with reproductions of paintings of the first and third Lubavitcher *rebeyim*, followed by photographs of more recent leaders. Chabad employed these images as instruments of establishing authority, consolidating community, and facilitating spiritual engagement.[13] Art historian Maya Balakirsky Katz notes that, whereas these images were first circulated in order to consolidate followers of Chabad during a period of contested leadership, later portraits were published to facilitate disciples' spiritual communion with their rebbe. During the interwar years, photographs of Yosef Yitzhak Schneerson played a strategic role in maintaining devotion among the widening diaspora of his followers and during periods of unprecedented challenges, including his arrest and exile by Soviet authorities in the 1920s. Katz argues that a widely reproduced photograph of the sixth Lubavitcher rebbe at work in his study employed this familiar Western visualization of political power and scholarly authority to counter the visual strategies used in revolutionary portraits of Lenin and Stalin, depicting them as proletarian heroes. According to Katz, Yosef Yitzhak Schneerson also collected portraits of disciples while in exile from Soviet Russia. She posits that he "used his photograph collection to maintain his role [as spiritual leader] from afar," enabling him to negotiate "the role of absent rebbe" and thus to "hold virtual court" with these images, in the form of an "extended family album."[14]

During Menachem Mendel Schneerson's tenure as Lubavitcher rebbe, which lasted forty-four years until his death at the age of ninety-two, the number and variety of images of Chabad's spiritual leader proliferated. Moreover, they became part of new social practices both within the Lubavitch community and in its efforts to engage others. These new practices began shortly after Yosef Yitzhak Schneerson's death, when his successor urged followers to gaze upon a picture of the late rebbe as a spiritual aid. Beginning in the 1960s, photographs of Menachem Mendel Schneerson began to circulate widely, concomitant with the expansion of Chabad's campaign of sending emissaries to live in communities around the world and promote Chabad hasidism among less observant Jews. Both still and moving images of the seventh Lubavitcher rebbe became vital components of these outreach initiatives.

Katz notes that Menachem Mendel Schneerson preferred, instead of the formal portraits of his predecessor, photographs that showed him "going about his day as a religious and political leader," often "surrounded by his Hasidim, actively performing the rituals of civic and religious duties: praying, waving, greeting, listening, and speaking." Over time, the range of photographs of the Rebbe proliferated, and they have been put to many uses. In addition to appearing in all manner of publications, including leaflets and cards distributed by Chabad emissaries, portraits of the Rebbe are incorporated into a variety of three-dimensional, functional items, including "key chains, cuff links, watches, clocks, kippot [skull caps], tzedakkah [alms] boxes, and decorative plates," and his face has appeared in oversized format on large signs, posters, and even blimps and giant billboards.[15] Katz argues that this new, expansive visual culture was instrumental in transforming Menachem Mendel Schneerson "from a beloved scion of the Chabad dynasty into *Melekh HaMashiach*, the King Messiah." While he was still alive, some Chabad messianists believed that "their leader's growing visual presence might hasten his anointment as the King Messiah." And after the Rebbe's death, Katz asserts, "Habad success-fully transformed itself into a community of loyal disciples *sans* rebbe" thanks to this visual culture.[16]

As much as photographs and their uses burgeoned during Menachem Mendel Schneerson's years as Lubavitcher rebbe, his leadership is distin-guished even more so by Chabad's use of television and video, and these media play a crucial role in the community's continuation since the Reb-be's death. Like still photography, Chabad's use of television and video builds on earlier media practices and established teachings; even so, these newer media have offered the community distinct opportunities and chal-lenges. To begin with, most stringently observant Jews consider the me-dium of television to be inherently problematic. Whereas hasidim gen-erally make selected use of still photography, provided that it conforms to their mores (especially with regard to modesty of one's appearance in public), most hasidim completely shun television, at least officially. So do many other *haredim*, who equate the technology with its broadcast con-tent, which they consider incompatible with their values and sensibilities, and so regard the act of watching television as inherently pernicious. In a 1992 essay for the *Jewish Observer*, a magazine published for nonhasidic Orthodox Jews by the Agudath Israel of America, Rabbi Shimon Schwab denounced television as "a wide-open window to immorality." Much like media-wary scholars of the Frankfurt School decades earlier, he argued that television, by its very nature, "leaves a much deeper impression than reading a newspaper or book does. Sitting in front of the screen, you no longer think for yourself: the thinking is done for you. . . . The assimi-latory influence is thus much more insidious than that of other media, when our critical faculties are in full function."[17]

Among hasidim, the moral campaign against television starts at an early age. A Yiddish primer published in 1977 by Satmar hasidim includes a story in which a young hasidic girl learns that watching television is "a great sin," accompanied by an illustration of a television set with the words "*Men tor nisht*" (It's not allowed) inscribed on the screen.[18] Simi-larly, *Handl erlikh* (Deal Honestly), a Yiddish board game created by

An Orthodox Jewish group based in Toronto distributed this audiocassette at the turn of the millennium as part of a campaign to combat the adverse impact of television on Jewish youth. A video-tape of the panel discussion recorded on this tape is also offered. The figure, a "TV-head" wearing a skullcap, is reading the Pentateuch in Hebrew.

Hungarian hasidim in the 1970s, features a penalty card for watching television, admonishing the player (who loses three turns), "You have rendered your eyes impure! [Television] leads you astray from the proper Jewish path! . . . To atone for this great sin, you must do genuine penance!"[19] (Mintz notes that television "nonetheless manages to surface in [hasidic] community life in one way or another," and he offers several anecdotes of hasidim who stash television sets under the bed or in secret cabinets.[20] I have also been told of appliance stores, in Brooklyn neighborhoods with a large ultra-Orthodox Jewish population, that offer to deliver a television to the home of a *haredi* customer by placing the set inside a carton for a dishwasher or some other appliance, lest the purchase elicit censure from neighbors.)

Notwithstanding this ban, Chabad's avid engagement with television does not distinguish it from other hasidic communities by dint of an interest in technology generally. Despite the popular image of hasidim as embodiments of a bygone era, especially as portrayed in American works of fiction and feature films, these Jews are not Luddites.[21] As Heilman observes, hasidim are not all strangers to the personal computer or the fuel-injected automobile engine, and in no way do they see their traditionalism as "backwardism." Indeed, Heilman suggests that, for hasidim, "technology often represent[s] what [is] best, perhaps all that [is] good, in the outside world."[22] Even so, Menachem Mendel Schneerson is distinguished among hasidic leaders for the way in which he situated technology within his view of humankind's relationship to God and to the universe.

In public addresses, the Rebbe occasionally expounded on the significance of technology. In one discourse he sanctified the advent of modern science as having been predicted in the Zohar, the foundational work of Jewish mysticism, noting that this medieval text teaches that "in the six-hundredth year of the sixth millennium after Creation [i.e., the year 1839/1840], there will be a great advance in the secular sciences, in order to ready the world for the arrival of the seventh millennium,"[23] which will witness the advent of the messianic age. Setting aside the issue of whether the Zohar actually forecasts such phenomena, it is worth noting that this date marks the advent of both the still photograph (which Louis Daguerre made public in 1839) and the telegraph (Samuel Morse applied for his patent in 1840), two technological innovations that paved the way for television and other new communications media of the twentieth century. Scholars of Western culture and philosophy have also characterized the moment of these technological discoveries as a watershed, though of course they conceptualize it quite differently. Michel Foucault identified this moment of technological and epistemological development as "the threshold of our modernity."[24] And Jonathan Crary argues that during this period there occurred a signal shift in the Western conceptualization of visual perception, reflected in the writings of Goethe and Schopenhauer, as a subjective, physiological phenomenon that "endowed the observer with a new perceptual autonomy" and enabled the fabrication of "new forms of the real."[25]

The Rebbe's conjoining of the history of technology with Jewish cosmology epitomizes Chabad's predilection for bridging seemingly disparate epistemologies and, at the same time, reflects his own singular intellectual background. Before he was selected to lead the Lubavitch community, Menachem Mendel Schneerson had studied at a technical college in Paris, where he received a diploma in electrical engineering in the late 1930s.

Lubavitcher hasidim do not characterize this experience as detracting from his qualifications as the leader of their community; rather, they vaunt the Rebbe's schooling in science as evidence of his comprehensive acumen, which extended beyond his training in rabbinics and hasidism and, at the same time, enhanced his commitment to their supreme validity. A biography of Menachem Mendel Schneerson published by Chabad explains that, as rebbe, he "found various uses for [his knowledge of mathematics and physics] in defending Judaism from scientific attack. He would also explain the mystical meaning of certain mathematical concepts."[26]

In the Rebbe's teachings, he conceptualized technological advances not as inherently corrupting distractions but as containing—as do all aspects of this world—the potential to be integrated into Jewry's spiritual mission. "Developments such as television," he explained, are "instances of tapping and understanding G-dly forces that are manifested in nature. Man has been charged with tapping these resources to refine and civilize the world, to transform our material surroundings into a proper home for spirituality and G-dliness."[27] Television, then, is understood as but one means of realizing Chabad's ongoing commitment to making esoteric principles of spiritual transformation accessible and meaningful to the entire Jewish community.

Publicizing the Miracle

Under Menachem Mendel Schneerson's leadership, Chabad embraced radio, television, video, and the Internet, always doing so on its own terms, and thereby further distinguishing itself from other hasidic communities. Similarly, whereas other hasidim tend to circumscribe contact between members of their communities and less observant Jews, Chabad has made outreach to potential *ba'alei-t'shuvah* (Jews not raised in traditionally observant homes who decide to follow Orthodox religious practice) central to its mission. Even more singular and provocative is Chabad's very public insistence that the messianic age is imminent and, according to many of his followers, that the Rebbe is the messiah. New media have been instrumental in realizing both of these commitments, and Chabad's innovative uses of these media underscore the exceptional nature of its convictions.

An early example of these innovations during Menachem Mendel Schneerson's tenure began in 1960 with weekly classes on *Tanya* aired on the New York radio station WEVD. Shortly thereafter, other Orthodox Jews criticized these broadcasts as sacrilegious, and the Rebbe came to their defense, explaining that "radio is a comparatively new technology. Only recently has it been utilized by Jews for holy purposes such as learning Tanya, whereas before that it had been used for secular and even unholy purposes. On this basis, say some Jews, Tanya should not be learned on radio, for radio is intrinsically evil. Such a claim is not only wrong, but totally contradicts Torah and the Jewish faith." On the contrary, the Rebbe argued,

> Learning Tanya on the radio is a manifestation of the dissemination of the wellsprings of Chassidus to the outside. Through the radio, the actual wellsprings of Chassidus are spread *instantly* to every place in the world, engulfing the "outside" in the wellsprings—and thereby purifying the "outside." It is the preparation to the fulfillment of the promise, "The earth shall be full of the knowledge of the L-rd as the waters cover the sea" [Habakkuk 2:14], for, as was promised to the Baal Shem Tov, Mashiach will come "when your wellsprings shall spread forth to the outside."[28]

Journalist Sue Fishkoff reports that in 1970 "Chabad congregations in London, Israel, and Melbourne were connected to Crown Heights by telephone hook-up for the first live, intercontinental version of one of the Rebbe's *farbrengens* [communal gatherings]." By the decade's end, "Schneerson's *farbrengens* were telecast live via satellite and cable TV, and in 1988, several years before the creation of the World Wide Web, the late Rabbi Yosef Kazen used Fidonet, an on-line discussion network distributed on several thousand nodes internationally, to spread Yiddishkeit [here, 'Judaism']."[29] Since the Rebbe's death, Chabad's pioneering use of media, especially the Internet, has continued to attract attention in the mainstream press. A 1995 report in the *Village Voice* explained that, during the previous year, Chabad's mandate of "*uforatzto* [And you shall spread out (Genesis 28:14)] was extended to Jews in cyberspace. With three access points, a host, and a Web home page, thousands of wired Jews the world over hit Chabad House each day." Besides serving as a virtual gathering place, Chabad's website remediates its extensive corpus of cultural works. There, in addition to lessons in *Tanya*, inventories of the Rebbe's writings, and information on holiday celebrations, the reporter explained, "I heard plaintive *niggunim* (religious melodies) and viewed online galleries of work by Hasidic painters."[30]

In this cascade of new media, television and video came to figure strategically in two key components of Chabad culture during the last decades
of the twentieth century, continuing into the present. First, these media facilitated the community's expansive contact with outsiders, both Jews and
non-Jews, in new ways. Second, television and video helped strengthen
and elaborate the spiritual relationship of Lubavitcher hasidim with the
Rebbe, especially since his death. Despite the importance the Rebbe gave
to these and other new media, there has been no single, unified policy
within Chabad on their use. Rather, various individuals and organizations
within the movement have created a range of media works and institutions, both with and without the sanction of Chabad leadership, addressing different constituents through a range of media, genres, formats, and
venues. Affiliate organizations of Chabad, such as the American Friends
of Lubavitch and the children's group Tzivos Hashem (Army of God),
have produced and distributed videos. Others, created by individuals or
small, independent production companies based in Crown Heights, are
sold in neighborhood bookstores, by mail order or, more recently, on the
Internet. Some special broadcasts, such as the annual Chabad telethon
produced in Los Angeles, are disseminated via a variety of cable and satellite feeds across North America.

In some instances these undertakings are the initiative of a single
member of the Chabad community. For example, Rabbi Yosef Katzman,
a Lubavitcher hasid, began his own weekly television series in 1992 under
the title *A Cable to Jewish Life*. He explains that, "while born out of the
wisdom of the most recent Lubavitch Rebbe," whose approval Katzman
secured before initiating the series, "*A Cable to Jewish Life* is an independent production." Since 1996, it has aired on Brooklyn Community Access
Television and also appears on National Jewish Television, which dissemi-
nates the series to some 400 other public access stations across the United
States. In addition to Jewish beliefs and practices, the range of topics discussed on the series resembles those addressed on other American talk
shows, from health ("The Physician and Torah") to business ("The Rebbe
and Wall Street"). *A Cable to Jewish Life* offers these discussions as points
of entry into "some of the secrets you missed out on in Hebrew school,"
thereby indicating a target audience of (potential) *ba'alei-t'shuvah*.[31] Katzman extends his broadcasts' reach on a companion website, where visitors can subscribe to an email newsletter, find local stations carrying the
series, and order copies of past broadcasts.[32]

Although most of Chabad's television broadcasts and videos address adult viewers, some are intended especially for children. In 1994, Tzivos Hashem created *Professor Pellah's Place: A Chanukah Adventure*, a pilot for an unrealized series intended to teach young viewers about Jewish traditions.[33] This pilot was produced by the creators of *Shalom Sesame*, a children's series about Israeli life and Jewish culture for American audiences, modeled on American public television's *Sesame Street*. The cast of *Professor Pellah's Place* includes a "terrific teenage mitzvah [here, "religious commandment"] mission force"—that is, four young teenagers— a wise-cracking goldfish puppet named Bernie, and Professor Pellah (in Hebrew, *pele* means "marvel"), who is a kind of cybercreature, appearing to the teenagers as a talking head on a computer screen.

Professor Pellah's Place assumes a young audience with perhaps limited knowledge of Jewish history and ritual, but which is well versed in mainstream American television. As on *Sesame Street*, the cast presents a series of short, individual segments: animated stories, person-on-the-street interviews, music videos, and media parodies of *The Tonight Show*, *COPS*, and MTV (which here becomes "Maccabee TV"). The program takes self-conscious delight in the powers of modern media—for example, the teenagers communicate via computer with the Professor about short films they have made. To its target audience of Jewish youth, *Professor Pellah's Place* demonstrates the possibility of being both traditionally observant and engaged in the technologies and idioms of modern culture.

This celebration of technology to promote traditional piety also serves as the program's point of entry to teaching about Hanukkah. Together, the various segments of *Professor Pellah's Place* constitute an extended lesson in the "mitzvah of *pirsum ha-nes* [publicizing the miracle (of Hanukkah)]." The program transforms the traditional realization of this religious obligation—which simply consists of displaying a lit Hanukkah menorah in the window of one's home—into a multiform, mass-media enterprise addressing a global audience. Thus, one sequence of *Professor Pellah's Place* includes footage from NASA of a Jewish astronaut spinning a *dreydl* (Hanukkah top) within the gravity-free confines of the space shuttle.

The elaboration of this simple religious obligation exemplifies Chabad's larger emphasis on the value of publicity. Chabad also teaches the importance of *pirsum ha-nes* to celebrating Hanukkah in its Jewish Children's Museum, which opened in a building opposite the movement's central headquarters in Crown Heights in 2004.[34] The museum's Hanukkah installation, one of a series of Jewish holiday displays, invites children to play the role of a television reporter covering the historical origins of Hanukkah during the Maccabean revolt of 165 BCE as if it were unfolding in the present. The museum's website informs prospective visitors, "Video monitors will feature a news anchor reporting on the 'breaking news' of the Maccabees' revolt against the Syrians. He will then cut to field anchors for reports. Museum visitors will then be prompted, with easy-to-follow instructions, to record their own 60-second reports, which they can make up or read from a monitor. These segments will then be integrated into the 'newscast.'"[35]

Chabad further extends publicizing the miracle of Hanukkah through the well-promoted lighting of large, outdoor menorahs in cities around the world. Local news telecasts often cover these lighting ceremonies, usually on the first evening of the holiday. In 1992, Chabad further elaborated this practice by producing *Chanukah Live*, an hour-long telecast featuring simultaneous lighting ceremonies in Washington, D.C., Moscow, Paris, Jerusalem, and Brooklyn."[36] These efforts not only transform a private, domestic ritual into a large-scale, public spectacle with universal implications; they also establish acts of publicizing the miracle of Hanukkah as integral to the miracle itself, essential to realizing its spiritual significance.

Chabad's focus on publicity as vital to spirituality is by no means limited to celebrating Hanukkah or other holidays. The regular appearance of religious proclamations on billboards, bumper stickers, subway posters, and full-page announcements in major newspapers (many featuring toll-free telephone numbers and, more recently, Internet addresses) is part of Chabad's commitment to exploiting the full range of communications media to exhort all Jews to perform acts of piety and thereby bring about the messianic age. Yet even as Chabad's outreach efforts to other Jews make innovative use of media, they build on foundational notions of hasidic communication. Hasidism first spread through the teachings of itinerant charismatic leaders, exemplified by the Baal Shem Tov, who circulated among Jewish communities throughout Ukraine and Poland. As the movement attracted growing numbers of followers, this dynamic changed. Hasidic leaders established courts, to which they attracted followers from surrounding communities. As these *rebeyim* became more stationary figures, the locations of their courts—the towns of Bobowa, Góra Kalwaria, Munkács, and so on—became synonymous with their particular teachings and their dynastic leadership. The most popular *rebeyim* attracted followers from across Eastern Europe, who identified as Bobover, Gerer, or Munkacher hasidim according to their devotion to their rebbe, regardless of where these disciples lived.

In this respect, Menachem Mendel Schneerson remained a conventional rebbe; he almost never left Crown Heights during his leadership of Chabad, except to visit his father-in-law's grave in Queens. The international extent of his followers and, beyond them, his general renown worldwide depended largely on Chabad's use of communications media. Lubavitcher hasidim celebrate this phenomenon as a sign of the Rebbe's unprecedented spiritual impact. Yet even as his disciples have regularly flocked to Crown Heights from around the world (continuing to do so since the Rebbe's death to observe Jewish holidays or attend conventions of teachers and emissaries), Chabad has altered the dynamic of hasidic disciples in relation to their rebbe. Under Menachem Mendel Schneerson's leadership, Chabad adopted an expansive approach to the centrifugal dissemination of hasidic teachings that was a hallmark of earlier generations of *rebeyim*, which their followers realized by circulating manuscripts, print publications, stories, and songs. Supported by a wide-ranging use of communications media, Chabad extended this outward movement of information further, seeking the attention of Jews generally (and occasionally, non-Jews as well). The Rebbe repeatedly charged his followers with this task as a fulfillment of their community's ultimate destiny, which amounts to nothing less than ushering in the messianic age.

Chabad's use of new media for outreach is epitomized by its telethons. The brainchild of Rabbi Boruch Shlomo Cunin, director of the West Coast Chabad in Los Angeles, the first telethon was aired in 1980. Originally produced to help rebuild Chabad's Los Angeles headquarters after a fire destroyed it, the annual event is now televised nationally (and, since 2000, streamed live on Chabad's website) and raises millions of dollars each year, "supporting the largest network of educational and nonsectarian social services under Jewish auspices on the West Coast."[37]

These broadcasts generally follow the conventions of the American charity telethon genre: over several hours, appeals for funds are imbricated with celebrity appearances, entertaining performances, and testimonies to the worthiness of the charitable causes being supported. These include institutions of special interest to Lubavitcher hasidim, such as "Chabad houses" (outreach centers) and religious schools, as well as Lubavitch-run social welfare programs for substance abusers and the homeless in Los Angeles. The telethon also acknowledges its donors' largesse by running a strip along the bottom of the screen listing the names of contributors,

Poster advertising the Chabad telethon, December 1994, indicating the channels on which people in the New York metropolitan area could view the broadcast.

their home towns, and the amounts of their gifts. When pledge totals are periodically announced, the number of dollars raised is celebrated by a group of hasidic men dancing a lively hora, sometimes joined by one of the celebrities lending support to the cause.

The telethons exemplify Chabad's command of American public relations and celebrity culture. Cunin explains that the nonsectarian social programs that Chabad runs, using funds raised on the telethons, are "very important for public relations. . . . People see we are in this community." The community in question being Los Angeles, the participation of celebrities in this public relations effort is of prime importance. Among the array of actors, athletes, musicians, comedians, and popular "personalities" who have appeared on the telethons are Kareem Abdul-Jabbar, Dom Deluise, Whoopi Goldberg, Elliot Gould (who has participated in every telethon), Bob Hope, Anthony Hopkins, Jack Klugman, Lois Nettleton, Edward James Olmos, Regis Philbin, Jon Voight (another regular participant who, though not a Jew, has found Chabad hasidism an important resource in his "spiritual seeking"), and Michael York. As with other telethons, celebrity-sighting has become an important incentive for watching this broadcast; Fishkoff reports that "the show has become so hip that it has engendered a rash of telethon-watching parties in certain L.A. circles." And in a remarkable example of reciprocal remediation, "one year the cast of [the NBC situation comedy] *Friends* filmed a special segment for the telethon . . . [as] a return favor for Cunin's permission to rebroadcast an earlier *Friends* episode that showed several *Friends* regulars watching actual telethon footage."[38]

In keeping with the expansive aesthetic of telethons generally, these annual broadcasts test the limits of Chabad's celebrated high degree of engagement with others. Throughout the telethon, audiences can observe considerable interaction among hasidic and nonhasidic Orthodox Jews, Orthodox Jews and those who are more liberal, Jews and non-Jews, as well as the mingling of modern social problems with traditional Jewish values and religious devotion with popular entertainment. In the telethon aired on 6 December 1994—the first one broadcast after Menachem Mendel Schneerson's death—Cunin's solemn tributes to the Rebbe appeared alongside the jocular spiel of the telethon's emcee, veteran Borscht-Belt comedian Jan Murray. All this took place before a small but enthusiastic studio audience, who were not themselves Lubavitcher hasidim, as evinced by their dress and the seating of women and men together.

Appearances by well-known performers from mainstream American popular culture alternate with an array of Jewish performers, from Israeli vocalist Ron Eliran to entertainers best known in Orthodox enclaves, such as singer Mordechai Ben David. These Orthodox musicians fuse traditional piety with demonstrations of enthusiasm that draw on the aesthetics of American popular music and dance. The 1994 telethon, for example, featured performances by the Argentine-born Yehuda Glantz, who bounded on stage, sporting a brightly colored poncho and *peyes* (sidelocks) that dangled below his shoulders, energetically wielding an electric guitar as he sang the Richie Valens hit "La Bamba" in Yiddish. Routines performed by the Miami Boys Choir, an Orthodox choral group established in 1977, accompanied upbeat songs with disco-inspired dance steps, enhanced by flashing color lights on the backdrop behind the singers, even as they were dressed in costumes—black caps and knickers with white shirts and stockings—that evoked Jewish boys' clothing in an early-twentieth-century shtetl.

From the inception of Chabad's telethon as a reaction to a crisis, it has demonstrated a distinctive facility for improvisation. During the telethon aired on 21 August 1999, Cunin explained that, in response to a recent local tragedy—the shooting of Jewish children at a Los Angeles day camp—the telethon's producers decided to do something "special" and "unique" by presenting a *siyyum ha-torah* (ritual completion of a Torah scroll) during the telethon. As the scribe penned the final letters onto the parchment, with the Rebbe's portrait displayed in the background, Cunin invited both the studio audience and viewers "at home" to rise and cover their heads as signs of reverence. Mordecai Ben David sang "Ani ma'amin" ("I Believe") a traditional avowal of Jewish faith, including redemption by the messiah; actor Mike Burstyn (who later in the telethon performed the vaudeville chestnut "Mammy" in the manner of Al Jolson) delivered a narration about the Torah in relation to the continuity of the Jewish people. Finally, Cunin, holding the Torah scroll, spoke passionately about the desire for the messiah to "bring Jews out of *goles* [exile]." This remarkable sequence exemplifies the elasticity of Chabad's approach not only to these broadcasts but to spiritual innovation more generally: incorporating a traditional ritual within an effort to capture the attention of a larger public, relating the ritual's significance both to past suffering and to future aspirations, extending the sanctity of witnessing the ritual to a vast, unseen audience, and situating this entire hybrid sequence under the aegis of Chabad's worldview, embodied by the Rebbe's portrait.

Amid the telethons' energetic, expansive performances, Chabad also exercises tacit control over the propriety of public appearances made in its name. Notably, women neither sing nor dance during the broadcast, in keeping with hasidic notions of the modesty of women's appearance in public. Similarly, the breasts, arms, and legs of female celebrities who address the television audience are well covered, even if their dresses are often flashier than those worn by Lubavitcher women. An extensive and rich cultural performance, the telethon celebrates Chabad's sense of the compatibility of its spiritual mission with the modern world. This performance of outreach is complemented by one of virtual ingathering, manifest in the streaming list of donors from across the country as well as in the motley assortment of entertainers, Jewish community leaders, and recovering addicts who make appearances throughout the telecast. Within Chabad's cosmology, this ingathering has teleological implications. Believing that the messianic age will arrive when a requisite number of religious commandments have been performed, Lubavitcher hasidim regard each act of support, each dollar raised for charity, as a contribution toward this sum. The joyous dancing when pledge totals are posted during the telethon celebrates the anticipation of this ultimate transformation, toward which Chabad has advanced the world by that many increments.

"Your Eyes Will Watch Your Guide"

Even though the telethons and *Professor Pellah's Place* conform to Chabad's notions of propriety and devotion, these media works are primarily intended for viewing outside the community. This intent becomes more apparent when they are compared to other broadcasts and videos made primarily for internal audiences. For example, *Hakhel II: A Year in Lubavitch*, a ninety-minute video produced in 1994, proffers "a treasure of unforgettable moments" from the year 5748 (1987/88). Beginning in 1980, Chabad revived—and reinvented—the ancient practice of *hak'hel*, a communal gathering in Jerusalem following the year of *shemitah* (the "sabbatical year," when fields lay fallow).[39] Within the movement's larger goal of enhancing Jewish communal spirituality and thereby hastening messianic redemption, Chabad promoted its revival of *hak'hel* as a step toward realizing the "ultimate *Hakhel*, when, together with all our brothers and sisters, we will assemble in the Third *Beis HaMikdash* [the ancient Temple in Jerusalem, which is to be rebuilt in the messianic age] and eagerly quench our thirst with the Torah teachings of *Mashiach*."[40] During the *hak'hel* year of 5748, Chabad convened a number of special gatherings to promote scholarship and devotion in the spirit of the ancient *hak'hel*. Besides footage of these events, *Hakhel II* features scenes documenting the annual cycle of holiday celebrations as well as some singular, unanticipated events. These range from local television coverage of the funeral of Chayah Moussia Schneerson, the Rebbe's wife, to shots of construction on Eastern Parkway, the central esplanade in Crown Heights. In its form, *Hakhel II* resembles a home video compilation. With no voice-over narration and minimal titling, it presents a sequence of discrete segments in chronological order. The video assumes an audience of community insiders who can provide their own commentary about persons, places, and events that they recognize, much like the viewers of home movies.

In chronicling a year in Lubavitch Crown Heights, *Hakhel II* demonstrates the Rebbe's salient presence. He is the only individual for whom the camera shows sustained interest, and his singular presence is repeatedly juxtaposed against his massive number of followers. Many sequences show the Rebbe engaged in official activities: delivering discourses at *farbrengens*; distributing to lines of followers dollar bills for charity or food and drink at holiday celebrations; praying; blessing the Torah; drawing well-water for baking matzo, burning leavened foods forbidden during Passover; and, with sweeping gestures of his arms, exhorting large groups of men at *farbrengens* to sing with greater enthusiasm. The Rebbe's presence is also felt more obliquely, in scenes of men reciting blessings during Succoth with the Rebbe's *lulav* (ritual bundle of palm, willow, and myrtle branches), in glimpses of his portrait displayed in shops and homes, or shots of the large, Tudor-revival building at 770 Eastern Parkway that not only is Chabad's central headquarters but also has become a metonym for the Rebbe.

Sometimes the presentation of Chabad's media works reveals telling differences in how insider and outsider audiences are conceptualized. *Farbrengen: An Evening with the Lubavitcher Rebbe—Yud Shevat 5732*, a gathering at 770 Eastern Parkway of Lubavitcher hasidim with Menachem Mendel Schneerson filmed on 26 January 1972, was issued on videotape in 1997, one of several releases of recorded *farbrengens*. The packaging for this two-cassette set (the recording lasts four and a half hours) features explanatory texts in both English and Hebrew that are parallel but not identical. (The *farbrengen* itself was conducted, as usual, in Yiddish; the video provides no subtitles.) The Hebrew explanatory text assumes a more culturally knowledgeable audience, listing the Rebbe's name along with a series of honorific acronyms and using scholarly terms such as *pardes ha-torah* (referring to different levels of meaning that can be found in a scriptural passage), which are simply omitted in the English text. The English explanation, conversely, describes the Rebbe as applying the "timeless truths" of traditional Jewish scholarship to "issues of contemporary social and ethical concern"; this universalizing language does not appear in the Hebrew text. Moreover, the two texts proffer different viewing experiences to their respective audiences. The English reader is told that "to experience a Farbrengen with the Rebbe is to glimpse the unity of higher and lower worlds, a meeting of the Divine and the human, the mystical and the mundane, the timely and the timeless." But the Hebrew reader is offered a more direct promise of theurgy (that is, an engagement with the divine that advances one's pursuit of spiritual perfection), which can be experienced—not merely "glimpsed"—through the act of viewing the video. This act is characterized as the equivalent of partaking in the actual communal event: "Those who watch this video can rise up from profane life into another world, a spiritual world, and experience the numinous awakening in matters of divine worship and the holy illumination felt by those who participated in the *farbrengen* itself."[41]

From the late 1970s to the early 1990s, videotapes and satellite broadcasts produced for Chabad's widely dispersed followers expanded on the community's established modes of internal communication through print publications, sound recordings, and traveling emissaries. At the same time, these new media practices facilitated new communicative experiences, especially with regard to how hasidim might relate to the Rebbe. Broadcasts and videotapes have allowed followers around the world to engage the Rebbe's presence, and the spiritually transformative properties this encounter entails, without leaving their homes. To some extent, this use of media follows the precedent of *Tanya* as a proxy for face-to-face communion with one's rebbe, though broadcast television and video configure this mediated engagement with a spiritual leader differently. Through these newer media, Lubavitcher hasidim could experience this virtual encounter collectively and simultaneously with other communities in Chabad's diaspora while watching live broadcasts, which were often shown communally on large screens, or could do so either in small groups or individually at a time of their own choosing by viewing videotapes. In these mediations, the Rebbe's teachings are tied to his visual presence, which is both more attenuated than in actual encounters—being a two-dimensional, virtual image of a figure known by viewers to be, in fact, somewhere else—and more (apparently) imminent. Whether by dint of the large-scale image of a video projection in a communal setting or by virtue of the intimacy of television watching, especially within the privacy of home, the Rebbe, especially his face, could be seen in greater detail than is typical of public events and is more akin to the intimacy of *yehidut*. And whereas a rebbe is traditionally most accessible to adult male disciples, videos and broadcasts provide women and children in Chabad families with closer views of the Rebbe than they were likely to have had in large public gatherings, where they were segregated and usually positioned peripherally.

These mediated encounters with the Rebbe occasionally prompted innovations in traditional hasidic practice. For example, a colleague of mine recalls attending a live satellite telecast of a *farbrengen* from Crown Heights when he was in Michigan during the 1980s. Among those present at the screening was the rabbi of the local Chabad house, who came dressed in his *kapote* (traditional robe), *gartl* (sash), and fedora, as if he were attending the actual event taking place in Brooklyn. However, the rabbi also took notes on the Rebbe's discourses, something that would not be done at the *farbrengen* itself. Such behavior indexes this virtual encounter with the Rebbe as something close to, but not identical with, attending the actual event.

In at least one instance, Chabad used video technology to facilitate communication to the Rebbe from his disciples. During a visit to the Soviet Union in the 1970s, Chabad emissaries videotaped Soviet Jews' personal petitions to the Rebbe, which were addressed directly to the camera as if speaking to him. Upon their return to Crown Heights, the emissaries played the videotape for the Rebbe.[42] But Chabad's primary use of videotape and broadcasting has been to send communications from Crown Heights outward. Schneerson's charisma remains central to these mediations; they extend the possibility of being in a rebbe's revelatory presence, which has long been a fundament of hasidism. As Dubnow wrote of the Baal Shem Tov, his "personality . . . impressed the people far more than his doctrine, which could be fully grasped only by his nearest associates and disciples."[43] Indeed, the Rebbe's appearance on broadcasts and videotapes might be construed as more in keeping with the Baal Shem Tov's charismatic, affective—and, in its day, revolutionary—appeal to a mass following than the much more circumscribed public presence of other late-twentieth-century *rebeyim*.

In the mid-1990s, the most extensive collection of media documentations of the Rebbe was available at Merkaz Shiduri Chabad, the World Lubavitch Communications Center (WLCC). From its modest storefront headquarters in Crown Heights, the WLCC, also known more informally as the Duplicating Center, produced and sold copies of recordings documenting Menachem Mendel Schneerson's appearances at public gatherings of his hasidim dating back to the mid-1980s on videotape and the early 1950s on audiotape.[44] In addition to holiday celebrations and *farbrengens,* there are videotapes of long lines of visitors to 770 Eastern Parkway receiving one-dollar bills from the Rebbe. The recipient was expected to give the money to charity, but these bills were often saved as mementos of one's brief encounter with the Rebbe, and other money was donated to charity. Beginning in the late 1980s, these distributions of dollars were videotaped; those who remember the date on which they received their dollar could order a copy of the videotape and thereby revisit this brief moment of close communion with the Rebbe.

Texts on the cover of the WLCC's catalog of audio and video recordings offer this inventory as an extension of the Rebbe's teachings and locate its value within hasidic discourse on the significance of viewing one's spiritual mentor. The catalog's front cover features two short citations in Hebrew from *Toras Menahem* (*The Teaching of Menachem*), a compendium of public discourses delivered by Menachem Mendel Schneerson during his first months as the Lubavitcher rebbe in 1951, in which he discussed the spiritual value of photographs of the previous rebbe:

> Imagine the rebbe's face as if you were meeting with him in private; those who have not seen the rebbe should imagine the rebbe's face by means of a picture. A picture of the rebbe is like a vision of his face. . . .
>
> When you are . . . in a state of low spirits, you are advised to connect with the rebbe by means of a picture of his holy face. From time to time it is necessary to imagine the rebbe's holy face, and to remember the words heard from the rebbe.[45]

These citations implicitly characterize watching a videotape of Menachem Mendel Schneerson as an extension of his teaching that visualizing his predecessor, facilitated by a photographed image, enhances the hasid's spirituality. In *Toras Menachem,* this principle is, in turn, rooted in the teachings of the Zemah Zedek, grandson of the founder of Chabad and the third Lubavitcher rebbe, who had traced the concept back to Talmudic sources: "Whoever invokes a teaching in the name of its author should visualize that teacher as if he were standing before him."[46] And the ultimate source of this principle, a passage from Isaiah—"Your eyes will watch your Guide" (30:20)—appears, in Hebrew, on the back cover of the WLCC catalog.

But viewing a video of the Rebbe is, of course, different from looking at his portrait or photograph, as it is from imagining his visage or beholding his actual, live presence. Unlike still photographs of the Rebbe, video portraits offer the viewer images not only of the Rebbe's face but also of his body—and both of these in motion—as well as of the environments in which he moved, his interactions with others, and their responses to him. Some videos also provide audio of the Rebbe's words, and so these recordings can function like texts, providing documentation of the Rebbe's teachings that can be reexamined by followers searching for insights into his instruction, much as they do with his printed teachings. These videos link the authoritative power of the Rebbe's teachings with the transformative power of being in his presence. Since the Rebbe's death, moreover, this corpus of videodocumentation enables him to seem present for his followers, doing so in ways unlike any other means that hasidim have had to connect spiritually to deceased *rebeyim*—whether through legends about their wondrous deeds, printed collections of their teachings, gravesite shrines, or living descendants and disciples.

"Moshiach Has Become a Major Media Event"

During the late 1980s, as the photo- and videodocumentation of the Rebbe was at its most profuse, Chabad messianism intensified. Insistence that the messianic age was approaching and that Lubavitcher hasidim had a special obligation to hasten its arrival was not new to Chabad, nor did these convictions originate with Menachem Mendel Schneerson's leadership. However, the messiah was a subject of ongoing concern in the Rebbe's public discourses, and he identified recent world events—including the fall of the Soviet Union and Israel's escaping extensive harm from Iraqi missile attacks during the Gulf War—as signposts of the messiah's advent.[47] In April 1991, the Rebbe proclaimed the messiah's arrival was imminent and, moreover, depended on the will of his followers: "All that I can possibly do is to give the matter over to you. Now, do everything you can to bring moshiach, here and now, immediately."[48]

The Rebbe's proclamation inspired Lubavitcher hasidim to intensify their outreach efforts and to promote messianism in conjunction with appeals to Jews to become more observant of traditional religious practice. A print advertisement produced in the early 1990s proclaimed, "It's OK to get excited about Moshiach," thanks to the Rebbe's announcement that "the Time of the Redemption has arrived." The ad exhorted less observant Jews to action not only by increased religious practice but also by engaging with the advertisement itself. This engagement included filling out a coupon and mailing it to Chabad's headquarters with one's name, address, and an indication of which of a list of commitments one will make to the Rebbe "to do something extra to be more ready for Moshiach," including "studying the Torah regularly," "keeping kosher," and "doing more to treat my neighbors kindly." The ad also listed a toll-free number (1-800-4MOSHIACH) to call to request literature or a guest speaker on this issue, and a notice at the bottom of the ad explained that, "due to the urgency of this matter, we permit and recommend newspapers, organizations and individuals to reprint the above for distribution."[49] Responding to the ad and even remediating it were themselves implicit acts of hastening redemption.

Most provocatively, the advertisement explained that "many prominent rabbinic authorities" had identified Menachem Mendel Schneerson as "the Presumed Moshiach," an idea that was publicly embraced by growing numbers of Lubavitcher hasidim. Historian David Berger has recounted how, during the early 1990s, messianist Chabad rabbis argued that the

Blank CD, early 1990s, imprinted with a photograph of the seventh Lubavitcher rebbe, Menachem Mendel Schneerson, above a stylized landscape of Jerusalem. The Hebrew text reads, "Redemption immediately." The CD is meant to serve as an amulet, hung by a thread from the rearview mirror of one's car.

Rebbe's achievements as a communal leader and teacher fulfilled the criteria for identifying the messiah established by the Jewish philosopher Maimonides in the twelfth century. Berger notes that the Rebbe's response to these claims was ambivalent: "He vigorously proclaimed the imminence of the redemption . . . , strongly implied that he might be the redeemer, and certainly did not stop the messianist campaign. At the same time, he refrained from any open, explicit proclamation of his own messianic identity, taught that public relations must be conducted in a manner that would win acceptance, and continued to encourage leadership roles [in Chabad] for people who were known to oppose the messianists."[50]

In March 1992, the Rebbe suffered a stroke, leaving him unable to speak and limiting his ability to move. This development fueled the convictions of followers who believed him to be the messiah. "The fact that the Rebbe cannot speak is a sign that redemption is near," one Lubavitcher hasid explained a year later, when interviewed in a popular American Jewish magazine. He offered as a prooftext Isaiah 53:3—"He was despised, shunned by men, / A man of suffering, familiar with disease"—a key text in Jewish messianic theology that, as Berger has observed, has a complex history, also playing a central role in Christian doctrine and figuring in Jews' explanation of their exilic suffering.[51] In the months following Menachem

Mendel Schneerson's stroke, Heilman commented that the Rebbe was, in effect, "alive and dead at the same time. . . . He is with his followers but he is no longer verbal. . . . Everything he does is subject to interpretation."[52] Indeed, the Rebbe's stroke prompted a heightened scrutiny of his smallest gestures and increased attention to his silent appearance at public events. As occasions for seeing the Rebbe grew increasingly infrequent, due to his declining health, Lubavitcher hasidim took to carrying pagers, known as "Moshiach beepers," which notified them when the Rebbe (referred to as M H M, meaning "*Melech ha Moshiach*") made a public appearance at 770 Eastern Parkway.[53] The Rebbe was thus becoming more like his widely familiar presence in photographs, visible but silent and immobile, displayed in places of honor and as the focus of reverential gazing.

By the early 1990s, Chabad's growing attention to the Rebbe as the messiah had become known outside the community, sparking heated discussion among other Jews and eventually attracting attention from the general public. Some Orthodox Jews denounced Chabad's claims that Menachem Mendel Schneerson is the messiah, arguing that such claims are incompatible with traditional messianic beliefs; other Jews speculated that Lubavitchers' messianism would damage their effectiveness in the wider community. Rudy Boschwitz, a former U.S. senator and longtime supporter of Chabad, commented, "The messianic fever does not help the movement at all. I'm not sure how the messianism will affect my donations. . . . Anointing the Rebbe the messiah will turn people away." And Jewish studies scholar Lawrence Schiffman admonished Chabad: "If you turn yourself from an outreach movement into a false messiah movement, many of those who have gained so much spiritually and religiously from your work will find themselves unwilling to follow you further."[54]

In New York, the issue attracted ongoing interest in the local mainstream press. In January 1993, the *New York Times* reported on escalating tension among factions within Chabad, divided over their certainty that the Rebbe was the messiah. This dispute was reportedly approaching a "showdown" over a planned "coronation" of the Rebbe as messiah, to take place at 770 Eastern Parkway and "televised on the worldwide Lubavitch satellite hook-up."[55] (This plan was never realized.) A year later, *New York* magazine featured a cover story on the Rebbe's declining health and the question of Chabad's future, which the magazine sensationalized as a "Holy War" and a "tale of human frailties with Old Testament dimensions."[56] As observers outside Chabad contemplated the Rebbe's eventual death, they often predicted its demise, and some even feared the possibility of mass suicides among the Rebbe's followers.[57]

In the days following the Rebbe's death on 12 June 1994, his hasidim were the subject of intense public scrutiny as, in the words of a reporter for the *Washington Post*, "one of the century's grand-scale examples of how a religious movement struggles to redefine its faith in the face of failed prophecy."[58] *New York Newsday* featured the Rebbe's death on its front page and ran several stories covering his funeral, reactions by his followers in New York and Israel, as well as reports on the Rebbe's life and the question of Chabad's future. Besides comments from Chabad leaders and ordinary members of the Lubavitch community, *Newsday*'s reports featured assessments of the state of the community by academics in the United States and Israel.[59]

In the earliest responses of Lubavitcher hasidim to the Rebbe's death, they turned to media practices with which they were familiar. The Rebbe's funeral procession was broadcast live via satellite, enabling an international audience of Chabad communities to watch some of their fellow hasidim in Crown Heights "dancing and singing in anticipation of [the Rebbe's] resurrection and the imminent redemption."[60] Mediations of the Rebbe quickly began to play a new role in the community. "From a portable tape player, the voice of Grand Rabbi Menachem Mendel Schneerson filled the Lubavitcher Jewish sect's cavernous hall in Crown Heights," recounted one report, published a week following the Rebbe's death. "They were listening for clues in his words . . . , trying to figure out how to persevere."[61]

By the end of 1994, a new set of practices evolved at the Rebbe's grave in Old Montefiore Cemetery in Queens, where he is buried beside his predecessor. *New York* magazine reported that hundreds of followers sent personal petitions to the Rebbe via fax, which, in keeping with established hasidic practice, were read aloud and placed at the gravesite. Chabad purchased a house near the cemetery to serve

> as a kind of 24-hour visitor's center and decompression center, where the faithful can either prepare for their time at the grave or come down afterward. One room is used for study. Another chamber . . . is now a video room. Tapes of Schneerson play continually on a lone television surrounded by some chairs. . . . There's also a room with a long table and writing materials where believers can sit and compose the notes they leave on the rebbe's grave. . . . And of course, there are the fax machines

that regularly print out, along with all of the expected messages and requests, wedding invitations for the rebbe.[62]

Press coverage of Chabad in the wake of the Rebbe's death continued to discuss rifts among members of the community, divided over their convictions that the Rebbe is the messiah, the nature of the Rebbe's existence, and the future leadership of Chabad. These internal conflicts were also disputed through Chabad's established media practices. Different factions within the community used print, broadcast, and recorded media, previously deployed in outreach efforts, to advocate in the general public sphere for their positions on messianism.

The Rebbe's status as the messiah was proclaimed forthrightly in *Melech HaMoshiach Is Here and He Will Redeem Us*, a video by singer Moshe Yess, produced and sponsored by Yechi Hamelech (Long Live the King) Productions. Recorded in Miami Beach "in front of a live, culturally-diverse audience" in June 1995, the video promotes Chabad messianism through a series of musical performances. In the first song, performed in a "country-music" idiom, Yess refers to hearing about the Rebbe through mainstream media, including *Time* magazine and evening news telecasts on ABC. Yess uses Chabad's large, heterogeneous audience of potential *baalei-t'shuvah*, occasional supporters, and well-wishers to inform the style of his message and to link outreach with messianism. Yess implies that his ability to communicate the messianist message to so many different people in diverse idioms demonstrates its universal validity.

Opponents of the messianic movement within Chabad have used video both to assert their authority as official spokespersons for Lubavitch following the Rebbe's death and to articulate their position on his legacy. Here, too, the presence of the community's sizeable penumbra of outside supporters is strategic. *Living the Legacy*, a video produced by the American Friends of Lubavitch in Washington, D.C., chronicles a tribute to the late Rebbe offered on 28 June 1995 by American political figures and Jewish leaders from around the world. On this occasion, the U.S. Congress awarded the Congressional Gold Medal posthumously to the Rebbe, "the only rabbi ever to receive America's highest civilian award." Offering a series of tributes to the Rebbe were members of Congress—including Speaker of the House Newt Gingrich, Representative John Lewis, and Senator Joseph Lieberman—the chief rabbis of Israel, Russia, Morocco, and Australia; Itamar Rabinovitch, the Israeli ambassador to the United States; and George Stephanopoulos, senior adviser to President Clinton, appearing on his behalf. Others honoring the Rebbe's achievements included philanthropist Ronald Perelman, national chairman of the American Friends of Lubavitch; Nobel laureate Elie Wiesel; Talmudic scholar Adin Steinsaltz; and violinist Itzhak Perlman, who performed a medley of Jewish songs "that were cherished by the Rebbe."

Chabad was represented at this tribute by leaders from Lubavitch communities around the world and members of the Agudas Chassidei Chabad, the international movement's umbrella organization. Significantly, they spoke of the Rebbe in the past tense throughout the proceedings. Near the beginning of *Living the Legacy*, Rabbi Moshe Herson, a member of this governing body, articulated its conceptualization of the Rebbe's posthumous presence for his followers: "The Rebbe is not physically and visibly with us, although unquestionably his spirit is now in this room." Although this and similar statements made throughout the program were not without ambiguity (commenting on Menachem Mendel Schneerson's legacy, the chief rabbi of Morocco stated that "no one has the right to say that [the Rebbe] is dead"), they clearly avoided speaking of the Rebbe as living or as the messiah. Nor did they address Chabad's messianic hopes in general or, indeed, Chabad's future. Significantly, these remarks were made before prominent religious and political leaders outside of Lubavitch, who echoed these sentiments in their own remarks about the Rebbe's legacy. This strategy facilitated Chabad leaders' self-presentation to their "American friends" as these leaders wished to be seen by others of authority in the larger American and Jewish worlds and demonstrated the extent to which Chabad leaders depend on outsiders for the movement's continued existence. Beyond an ongoing reliance on financial support from people outside Chabad, the movement requires continued engagement with others through its outreach efforts in order to fulfill its ultimate goal of ushering in the messianic age.

As these examples demonstrate, a telling element of media works created by Chabad since 12 June 1994 is how they conceptualize and articulate the Rebbe's existence. What may seem straightforward and self-evident to people outside the community has been a fraught issue within Chabad, because the Rebbe's viability has powerful implications for the community's messianism and, therefore, for its sense of purpose. As Berger wrote shortly after the Rebbe's death, a fundament of traditional Jewish messianic belief is that the messiah "will not die before completing his mission," an argument Jews have made for centuries against Christian claims that Jesus of Nazareth is the messiah. In keeping with mainstream Orthodox

Judaism, Berger argued that, when Menachem Mendel Schneerson was alive, "Messianic claims made for him were ill-advised but well within the boundaries of normative Judaism. . . . But the persistence of such a claim after his death is beyond the pale of Judaism."[63]

In the months following Menachem Mendel Schneerson's death, Lubavitcher hasidim responded in a variety of ways to the theological challenges his death posed, reflecting a diversity of convictions about the Rebbe as messiah. Some Lubavitchers acknowledged that the Rebbe was dead and did not bring about redemption, but they remained vague about his status as the messiah. Explaining that in his final months the Rebbe was in fact preparing his followers for his death, one Lubavitcher hasid commented, "The Rebbe was able therefore to decide on the path to be taken after he had ceased to live. He could have ushered in the Redemption if he had chosen to do so, but he had taken another course." Others argued that the Rebbe's teachings about messianism are still valid and the onus of fulfilling Chabad's mission of effecting the messianic age is incumbent upon his followers. In these remarks, Lubavitcher hasidim tended to avoid speaking directly of the Rebbe as either alive or dead and spoke instead of "the words of the Rebbe" or "the rebbe's instructions."[64] Responses varied among Chabad's unqualified messianists as well. Some accepted the Rebbe's death as "a physical passing [that] represents a temporary stage" before his resurrection and revelation as the messiah, in defiance of longstanding Jewish doctrines about the messiah.[65] Yet other Lubavitcher hasidim claimed forthrightly that the Rebbe is not dead and therefore poses no challenge to the protocols of traditional Jewish messianism. Rami Antian, treasurer of the International Campaign to Bring Moshiach, asserted that the Rebbe "is physically alive" and "is living in 770," although "we can't see him," because "it's an optical illusion." Shmuel Spritzer, a member of the board of *Bais Moshiach* magazine (a messianist Lubavitch weekly), agreed, explaining that the Rebbe is invisible because *rebeyim* "have two bodies, one in which they physically live and another in which they move around. They can be in more than one place at once. . . . The rebbe will reveal himself, no question."[66]

As different groups within Chabad presented their positions on messianism in public, they sometimes made striking use of media practices with which they were familiar. Especially remarkable is a live, international broadcast on 31 January 1996, marking the date when Menachem Mendel Schneerson assumed leadership of Chabad in 1951. Promoted with a full-page advertisement in the *New York Times* and other newspapers, this broadcast linked Lubavitch communities around the world with Chabad's central headquarters in Crown Heights "to declare the Rebbe as King Moshiach and to pray for his immediate revelation."[67] Following the protocols of a live news broadcast, the hour-long program is anchored by "news correspondent" Jeffrey Weiser, who is clean-shaven, unlike the hasidim seen in the broadcast, though he wears a skull cap, as he is "reporting" from inside the Chabad synagogue at 770 Eastern Parkway. Weiser introduces Rabbi Shmuel Butman, chairman of the International Campaign to Greet Moshiach, an especially active messianist movement within Chabad. (In the mid-1990s, Butman presided over a "Moshiach store" in Crown Heights, selling messianist literature and media as well as a variety of promotional materials.) Butman describes what is taking place: "Central to the *khosid* [hasid] is a *farbrengen*. . . . And there's no *farbrengen* without the Rebbe. . . . Here 770 looks like it hasn't looked in a long time. Everyone is here to this great *farbrengen*. Everyone is waiting for the Rebbe. The Rebbe's table is here. The Rebbe's chair is here. And everyone is waiting—any moment—for the great revelation when we will meet with the Rebbe again." Butman explains that the chairman of the rabbinical court in Crown Heights is now in the synagogue and is "inviting the Rebbe to this great *farbrengen*." The broadcast then cuts to a brief clip of vintage footage of the Rebbe entering the same space amid a crowd of hasidim. On the soundtrack, the Rebbe is heard speaking about the messiah's imminent arrival. Then the broadcast returns to Butman and Weiser for continued coverage of the event, which offers a series of live connections to Chabad congregations in Russia, South Africa, Israel, France, Australia, and the United States, where local rabbis exhort their communities to call for the revelation of the Rebbe as the messiah. These live, remote segments alternate with sequences of vintage audio and video of the Rebbe, starting with his first *farbrengen* as the seventh Lubavitcher rebbe, in which he articulated tenets of Chabad messianism before enthusiastic crowds of followers. At the program's culmination, multiple images on a split screen present Chabad communities around the world joining in the simultaneous chanting of the messianists' proclamation, "Yechi Adoneinu Moreinu V'Rabbenu Melech Hamoshiach L'olom Vo'ed!" (Long live our lord, our teacher, our master, king messiah forever and ever). This chant, Butman explains, is meant to "bring life" to the messiah and effect his imminent revelation.[68]

This telecast exemplifies the facility with which Chabad messianists draw on their established media practices and extensive media inventory to foster a new kind of spiritual communion among widely scattered fellow hasidim. The broadcast articulates a crucial juncture between the diachronic axis of the Rebbe's leadership of Chabad and the synchronic axis of contemporary international devotion to him. Whereas *farbrengens* broadcast when the Rebbe was alive extended devotional attention to his charismatic leadership to followers worldwide, this broadcast centered their attention on a shared conviction that the Rebbe is the messiah and that, through Chabad's existing institutional and communications infrastructure, they can unite in prayer for his reappearance. The telecast's imbrication of live broadcast with vintage footage of the Rebbe was not meant to present the Rebbe's return as an actuality but rather offered a simulation of his followers' shared aspirations. For those who believe that the Rebbe is the messiah and anxiously await his reappearance, this montage of live and vintage video rendered their imagination of the Rebbe's redemptive return in the form of a mediated experience of communal viewing. Drawing on the familiarity of Lubavitcher hasidim with video images of the Rebbe, especially in the context of watching a *farbrengen*, this broadcast demonstrated new ways of engaging with these images. In the face of the Rebbe's continued absence, this broadcast gave a new sense of purpose to a virtual gathering of believers around the world, validated by its enactment before an international general audience.

During the week following this telecast, Agudas Chassidei Chabad responded with a full-page announcement of its own in the *New York Times*, denouncing such "recent statements and declarations by individuals and groups concerning the matter of Moshiach and the Lubavitcher Rebbe, Rabbi Menachem M. Schneerson, of sainted memory"—thereby clearly speaking of him as deceased—and advising "the public to exercise discretion when confronted with unauthorized public statements in the media or otherwise, concerning the Rebbe and his teachings."[69] Even as this statement addressed the general public—responding, perhaps, to antimessianist censure from other Jews, especially in the nonhasidic Orthodox community—it also asserted the authority of Agudas Chassidei Chabad within the Lubavitch community. Undaunted, the International Campaign to Bring Moshiach organized another special broadcast on 31 March 1996, the Rebbe's birthday, with messages aired in multiple languages (including Chinese, Japanese, and Arabic) on mainstream cable television stations from the Weather Channel to TV Food Network. In a full-page advertisement in the *New York Times*, the broadcast's producers informed readers that "today, your TV will finally broadcast something of value." The ad exhorted readers to celebrate the Rebbe's birthday by focusing on his "revelation that 'Moshiach is on the way,' ushering in the era of Redemption," and to order a "Redemption book and video package."[70] Here, broadcasting and video acquire legitimacy as they assume the Rebbe's traditional role of revelation, and properties of these media, especially television—visibility, simultaneity, liveness—inform the discourse of the Rebbe's current state of being. In Butman's words, "Moshiach has become a major media event."[71]

This contest between factions within Chabad was not only conducted in mainstream media but scrutinized therein as well. The *New York Times* reported in February 1996 that some Lubavitch leaders, including rabbis who served on the executive committee of Agudas Chassidei Chabad, found the activities of the most outspoken messianists in their community "embarrassing" and undeserving of the extensive attention they had attracted, being the work of a "fringe" movement within Chabad. The *Times* also explained that "when the rebbe died, many expected Rabbi Butman and his followers to desist and accept his death as proof that they had been wrong. Instead, they gradually stepped up the campaign."[72] Several observers of Chabad characterized these developments as exemplifying the findings of *When Prophecy Fails*, a 1956 sociological study of how a contemporary community coped with the consequences of an unfulfilled prophecy—in this case, the failed prediction that beings from outer space would destroy the Earth, as claimed by a group in the suburban Midwest of the United States shortly after World War II. This prophecy's failure led not to the group's disillusionment but rather to "increased fervor" and especially to increased efforts at "publicity seeking" on behalf of their beliefs. The study's authors theorized that this response constituted an effort to resolve the "cognitive dissonance" between expectations engendered by prophecy and their failure to materialize. *When Prophecy Fails* claimed that the fervor of belief can become so strong that "it may . . . be less painful to tolerate the dissonance than to discard the belief and admit one had been wrong." In addition to efforts to rationalize the apparent failure of prophecy, proselytizing becomes a key activity for the disappointed believers: "If more and more people can be persuaded that the system of belief is correct, then clearly it must, after all, be correct."[73]

In analyses of Chabad's activities since June 1994, some scholars have argued that the responses of Lubavitcher hasidim to the Rebbe's death afford an opportunity to nuance the conclusions of *When Prophecy Fails*. Anthropologist Simon Dein posits that "even such an intense religious group as Lubavitch are not a group of fanatics who follow doctrine without question," but rather they have tried "to reason their way through facts and doctrine in the pursuit of understanding." Followers of Chabad, he claims, "coped with this failed prophecy by appealing to a number of rationalizations which not only preserve, but enhance, their commitment to messianic prophecy." A central strategy for Chabad members, which Dein terms a "process of spiritualization," entails a shift from "the empirically testable belief that the Rebbe is the messiah" to "a superrational unfalsifiable belief that he is more powerful in the spiritual world."[74]

Lubavitcher hasidim articulate this spiritualization most readily in terms of the Rebbe's visibility or presence. Dein reports that shortly after the Rebbe's death, many of his followers "expressed the idea that he would be resurrected. Most emphasized that he still had a major presence in the world and that, without the hindrance of his physical body, his spiritual presence was even greater."[75] In a study of responses to the Rebbe's death among Lubavitcher hasidim in Canada, sociologist William Shaffir notes how Chabad leaders offered prooftexts to model this new understanding of the Rebbe's place in the world, and how his hasidim might engage it, by recalling Menachem Mendel Schneerson's own account of how the first Lubavitcher rebbe cited the Zohar: "'A Tzaddik [sage] who departs from this world is present in all the worlds more than he was during his lifetime." To which one hasid commented, "The leader remains a leader even now and even though not seen physically still remains a leader. . . . Even after his death, his presence can be felt more than even before, not being limited to the physical body."[76]

It was not inevitable that discussions of the Rebbe's existence after 12 June 1994 would center on visibility, but neither is it surprising. Seeing the Rebbe—not only in person but, much more widely, through an array of mediations of both still and moving images—had become a hallmark of Chabad hasidim under Menachem Mendel Schneerson's leadership. Portraits of the Rebbe have functioned at times like a brand for Chabad, at times like a devotional icon; both the Rebbe himself and his followers characterized contemplating his image as having spiritual value, drawing on precedents within Chabad teachings that are, in turn, rooted in rabbinic and biblical prooftexts. In his final months, the Rebbe had become more and more like a portrait—silent and immobile, displayed with special reverence. His stillness enabled followers to project onto him their own understandings of his significance independent of his agency.

At the time of the Rebbe's death, author Chaim Potok suggested that "the media-conscious orientation of the Habad movement, starting with the arrival of Yosef Yitzak in the United States, may have been a key factor in its promulgation of a strongly messianic ideology. Messianism may have been seen as a device to attract more media attention to the movement and its outreach goals."[77] I would argue, conversely, that Chabad's elaborate media practices have enhanced the community's ability to imagine the Rebbe as the messiah: a figure with worldwide renown and impact, exhorting his followers to make unprecedented use of the divine gift of technology to advance redemption. In some ways, the Rebbe was like the "miracle of television"—able to be in more than one place at the same time, widely seen and yet immaterial.

The extensive inventory of moving images of Menachem Mendel Schneerson has acquired new significance since his death. Many videos link the Rebbe's image with his words and provide opportunities to recall his performance as communal teacher and inspirational leader. His discourses at *farbrengens* have been transcribed and published, like the teachings of generations of hasidic leaders, but videodocumentation of the Rebbe at these gatherings provides a record of the performance and reception of his spiritual instruction as well as the instruction itself. Punctuated by the enthusiastic singing of disciples, these recordings model for the viewer an experience of the Rebbe as a charismatic leader quite apart from the content of his discourses. Other films and videos of the Rebbe, often recorded without sound, document the Rebbe's activities as a public figure: leading prayers, meeting with visitors, overseeing ritual practices, greeting long lines of followers. Even amateur footage of the Rebbe simply walking along Eastern Parkway attracts attention, offering a reminder of his powerful, active presence among his followers. This video inventory can both remind viewers of the Rebbe's absence and suggest ways to compensate for it—even by transforming the Rebbe's physical absence into an advantage. Valued during his lifetime as means of extending the enlightening encounter with the Rebbe to followers far from Crown Heights, these images now can enable imagined engagements with the Rebbe for those who remember him and those who can only know him through his virtual presence. Indeed, as some of his disciples have argued, the Rebbe may be a more powerful spiritual leader as an invisible, dematerialized presence—or rather, as a virtual reality—for his followers, exemplified by his legacy of mediations and media practices.

"We Look at Your Picture, We Feel That You're Here"

In the years since Menachem Mendel Schneerson's death, dire predictions of Chabad's dissolution and despairing masses of followers have not come about. Despite some reports of instability within the community, especially among its youth, Chabad vaunts its expanded infrastructure and strengthened sense of purpose.[78] Notwithstanding internal struggles over leadership, practice, and policy—and quite apart from external castigations of its messianists—Chabad has established new ways of maintaining the community and its mission that accommodate the Rebbe's absence. Having left his followers without either a designated heir or an explicit alternative, Menachem Mendel Schneerson continues to be referred to as the Rebbe and continues to serve as the central source of spiritual inspiration for his hasidim. Shortly after his death, some observers of Chabad predicted that "the availability of a vast library of videotapes" of the Rebbe might serve to "preserve a sense of the departed Messiah's physical presence."[79] In fact, an array of media works and practices created during the Rebbe's leadership now serve as the basis for much of Chabad's operation. As means of maintaining a spiritual relationship with the Rebbe, they have become vital to the very existence of Lubavitch, and it appears that they can and will continue to be for the foreseeable future.

Since June 1994, Lubavitcher hasidim have produced numerous new broadcasts, audio and video recordings, and expanded their presence on the Internet. Some of these media works directly address the Rebbe's absence and its implications for his followers. A case in point is the 1998 sound recording *Oh Rebbe: The Rebbe Lives*, a selection of ten songs in English by various lyricists. These songs express the difficult emotions provoked by the Rebbe's absence ("It's been so long now / The Rebbe is hidden from our eyes . . . / The pain of concealment tears our heart and soul") and model how parents might explain the Rebbe's continued significance to their children ("Dear son, you must understand / The Rebbe is only concealed / But the truth is that he is alive / And needs only to be revealed").[80] One lyric validates the power of the Rebbe's mediated presence by relating a story of a childless couple who, seeking God's help to have a child, turn to a poster of "Melech HaMoshiach": "Rebbe, oh Rebbe, fulfill our need / We look at your picture, we feel that you're here / Looking after your children with care." Soon, the couple has a son, who is named Mendele, after the Rebbe.[81]

Other media works demonstrate how the vast inventory of audio and video recordings of the Rebbe can serve as sources of instruction and inspiration for new generations of Lubavitcher hasidim. The 1996 video *Hand in Hand: Children Learning from the Rebbe* provides young children with instruction in "the Rebbe's middos tovos [good behavior]." Lessons in conduct—including praying with proper concentration and observing religious obligations joyously, as well as the importance of politeness, tolerance, sharing, and punctuality—are related to stories about the Rebbe, who appears in an array of still and moving images. Children in the video are seen looking at photographs and videos of the Rebbe, as a song explains, "I close my eyes and see the Rebbe's picture in my mind. / The Rebbe is the best example of how I would like to be, / And as I follow in his ways, his smile follows me." The video's packaging explains, "We constantly look up to the Rebbe as our teacher. The way he davens [prays] is a lesson. His simcha [joy], chayus [vitality], and devotion to hiddur mitzvah [enhancing the observance of religious commandments] are lessons. From everything he does, we can learn."[82] Here, video enables mimetic learning from the Rebbe and fosters a devotional bond with him centered on encounters with his image. Similarly, *Davening with the Rebbe*, a video and companion audio recording issued in 2000, offers the Rebbe reciting routine prayers and blessings as a means of teaching the listener how to recite them according to the particular practice of Lubavitcher hasidim. In addition, these recordings enhance the listener's worship through imitation of the Rebbe that constitutes an implicit communion with him.[83]

Even for hasidim who had met the Rebbe, audio and video recordings of him acquire new value as they are remediated and figure in new media practices. Videos of the Rebbe play as an ambient presence in a variety of settings, from Chabad's outreach booth in Ben Gurion International Airport in Israel to a kosher restaurant on Manhattan's Upper West Side. Hasidim also engage these recordings more deliberately in conjunction with traditional ritual. Heilman reports that, following the conclusion of the Sabbath, some Chabad congregations will play a video of the Rebbe's discourse on that week's Torah reading. In such instances, the sociologist notes, video recordings are endowed with a "power that goes beyond the image."[84] Attributing enhanced significance to these recordings can include practices that might be termed *videomancy*—that is, assigning divinely guided meaning to a seemingly chance encounter with a moment in a videotape, just as bibliomancers open books to random passages in order to seek answers from the supernal.

Heilman recalls observing a version of this practice while at the visitors' center that Chabad established near the Rebbe's gravesite. A Chabad emissary from a Latin American country was also visiting the Rebbe's grave at the time. The emissary

talked about an encounter that the current president of that country had had with the Rebbe when he was the ambassador. . . . At that time the Rebbe said to him, "You will some day be president." And he became president, and since that time he sends little notes . . . to Chabad . . . to bring to the cemetery. . . . As I walked out, . . . they have a running [video] loop [showing the Rebbe with a line of visitors]. . . . I stopped . . . and I said, "Who's he [the Rebbe] talking to now?" And the man who was taking me out, his face got white, and he ran into the office to pull out the emissary. That moment was exactly the moment when the Rebbe was speaking to this particular person who would become the president of that Latin American country. And therefore, the fact that I had seen that moment at that time was a message from the Rebbe to me that he was acknowledging my presence there at that time. So the video image is not just a picture. . . . It is a vehicle for making the dead Rebbe—or the occluded Rebbe—present and communicating with you.[85]

The value that Lubavitcher hasidim ascribe to audio and video recordings of the Rebbe is further enhanced by a central archive for all this media documentation, which has been established under the auspices of Jewish Educational Media (JEM). Originally founded in 1980 as a production company to create documentary and educational media for the Chabad community, JEM accumulated an extensive inventory of film footage, photographs, audio recordings, and videotapes in the course of production. In 2006, JEM acquired the holdings of the WLCC, and JEM's director, Rabbi Elkanah Shmotkin, realized that with this acquisition came the onus of inventorying and preserving thousands of hours of images and recordings. Much of this media is, like other films and videotapes of its vintage, in danger of deteriorating in the near future.[86] In an appeal for funds to help underwrite JEM's preservation costs, Shmotkin explained, "We have undertaken this effort for the benefit of every Chosid—every Jew, really—including you and your children. The Rebbe is dear to every one of us, and these archives have the ability to help us connect with him and learn from him. . . . This archive is a priceless treasure which, for all of our sakes, must be saved and preserved. We need to keep the

Rebbe's image and voice a part of our lives."[87] The following year, JEM presented some of its "vital treasures in need of preservation" at an "exclusive screening" for Chabad emissaries and supporters. One emissary explained that the screening was "a moving reminder of what we are missing since Gimmel Tamuz [the date of the Rebbe's death, according to the Jewish calendar], and how important the videos are to keeping the Rebbe a part of our lives." Reporting on the evening's success, JEM quoted one avid supporter: "I learned just last week, that everything in the world is created to serve G-d. . . . Now I know beyond any doubt why multimedia was created. This collection will create generations of learning and scholarship for the Jewish people."[88]

In a feasibility study outlining its preservation needs, JEM conceptualized its media archive as the epitome of Chabad's mission in the wake of the Rebbe's death. Characterizing its holdings as the Rebbe's "visual legacy," JEM warned that the mutable condition of these images and recordings poses a "crisis" for the community: "If [we] do not act quickly, these precious images and sounds will forever be lost. . . . This could mark a historic turning point for JEM and the Lubavitch movement." The challenge of preserving deteriorating media parallels the larger challenge that Chabad faces of continuing a mission centered on the charismatic leadership of an absent figure. JEM's plan to organize and digitize its holdings will not only maintain these fading images and words of the Rebbe but also facilitate greater access to the collection, enabling it to "become an important resource with a much broader appeal than it currently has." Preservation thus serves Chabad's longstanding commitment to outreach: "More people have learned about the Rebbe and have been inspired by his words via film, video and audio broadcasts and recordings than have seen him in person. If these moving images are preserved, his wisdom and teachings will continue to reach around the world each year, for generations to come."[89]

JEM's productions remediate material from its extensive inventory of vintage recordings and images in a variety of new works, including educational recordings, historical documentaries, and interactive CD-ROMs. Among JEM's educational recordings is *Living Torah,* a series of compilations of vintage video clips coordinated with weekly Torah readings, which provides an opportunity to "experience the thrill of learning Torah directly from the Rebbe." Each program includes a selection of the Rebbe's teachings on the weekly reading of scripture, with subtitles available in several languages; a "Special Moment" of the Rebbe "captured on

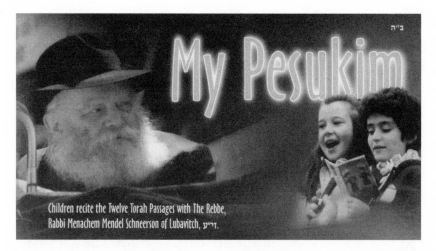

Children recite the Twelve Torah Passages with The Rebbe,
Rabbi Menachem Mendel Schneerson of Lubavitch, ז״ע.

My Pesukim (*Torah Passages*), a video produced in 2002 by Jewish Educational
Media, featuring "Twelve Torah Passages as recited by young boys and girls in
the Rebbe's presence. WATCH as the Rebbe affectionately observes the children
recite the Pesukim. . . . HEAR a short explanation from the Rebbe on each of the
Pesukim." Using vintage footage of the Rebbe, this and similar videos teach a
new generation of Lubavitch children basic religious texts and practices in conjunction with the mediated presence of the Rebbe as an inspirational figure.

video" (such as blessing a glass of wine at a *farbrengen* or celebrating the
completion of a Torah scroll); a "personal conversation with the Rebbe"
(in which he discusses topics ranging from the need to support Israel's
national bank to the best time of year to move into a new home); and a
Hasidic melody "sung in the Rebbe's presence" at a *farbrengen* or a "personal story of an encounter with the Rebbe." The *Living Torah* series (of
which there are over 150 programs) links the traditional ritual of reading
scripture in the synagogue with a new kind of practice, centered on the
mediation of scripture through the Rebbe's teachings, which are themselves remediated by video. Here, the communal, public character of the
Torah reading service is complemented by the customized intimacy of
watching a video (which promises instruction "in your language—at your
level" with "many playback options"), and the primacy of scripture is tied
to the centrality of the Rebbe.[90]

JEM's documentaries relate episodes in Chabad's history (for example,
the 2000 film *Embers* tells how "the Rebbes of Chabad-Lubavitch risked

their lives to keep Yiddishkeit alive across the Soviet Union") and present the biography of Menachem Mendel Schneerson as both a singular leader and an epitomizing figure for Jewish experience in the twentieth century. The series *My Encounter with the Rebbe* narrates his life history through a compilation of vintage images and personal remembrances collected for JEM's "oral history project," in which interviewees "share their experiences, the guidance they received, the lessons they learned and the impact of the Rebbe on their lives."[91] With this endeavor, JEM links conventional practices of documentary biography filmmaking with hasidic practices of hagiographic storytelling, in which recollections of a rebbe's life are conjoined with imparting ethical or spiritual lessons, thereby reinforcing the centrality of one's rebbe as a source of inspiration even in his absence.

JEM uses CD-ROM technology to provide opportunities for interactive learning, especially through play. CD-ROMs produced for Jewish holidays not only offer video games (such as "Help David the Dreidel Snowboard down the Mountain," a Hanukkah game), alongside holiday songs and recipes, but are themselves playfully conceived—whether as "Virtual Chanukah Gelt [money]," "Virtual Shalakh Manos [gifts of food]" for Purim, or a "Virtual L'Shanah Tovah" greeting card for Rosh Hashanah—as ludic variants on traditional forms of exchanging holiday gifts and wishes.[92] Through its website, JEM offers opportunities to watch video clips, download podcasts of the Rebbe, purchase audio CDs, DVDs, and CD-ROMs, contribute to its preservation project, or offer one's own personal recollections of encounters with the Rebbe, thereby suggesting multiple points of entry into Jewish religious life through Chabad's media practices. So comprehensive is this vision of Chabad's spiritual culture as centered on new media that it even informs JEM's vision of the messianic age. At the conclusion of a recent announcement to Chabad emissaries concerning plans for the media archive, Shmotkin wrote, "May we merit Moshiach's coming, when we will once again be broadcasting from Beis Chayenu ["the house of our life," a term used by Lubavitcher hasidim to refer to 770 Eastern Parkway], live."[93]

Notwithstanding the pride of place accorded to broadcasting in this eschatological vision, Chabad's pioneering use of the Internet may surpass all of the movement's previous engagements with new media. Individual Lubavitcher hasidim explored the possibilities of communicating in cyberspace early in the medium's history. Yosef Kazen's first ventures into cyberspace in the late 1980s, noted earlier, eventually led to the creation of the website chabad.org, which went online in 1993. The website provides access to an array of other media—texts (including download-able versions of *Tanya* and other key works of Chabad hasidism), images, audio and video recordings—available in multiple languages and target-ing different audiences (including special sections for women and chil-dren). Alongside information about Chabad philosophy and history are resources on Jewish holidays and life-cycle celebrations, as well as reli-gious practices of daily life, presented according to Lubavitch protocols. Exploiting the Internet's interactive capacities, the website invites visitors to locate a Chabad campus center, visit the Rebbe's grave or send a prayer to be read there, submit a news story, donate to support the website, shop on linked book, media, and Judaica websites, or post questions on Jewish practice and philosophy to "Ask the Rabbi"; questions of special interest to women can be sent to "Dear Rachel."[94]

In a self-reflexive indication of the Internet's importance to Chabad, the website offers extensive information on its own history, mission, and reception. Praise for chabad.org from the *Washington Post*, the *Tennes-sean*, and *Wired* ("At the vanguard of harnessing technology to promote Judaism"), among other mainstream media institutions, punctuates pages that delineate the site's vision and scope. Chabad.org reports that it "cur-rently serves close to one million people a year. . . . Our rabbis and staff responded to more than 108,000 email queries this year. We currently of-fer 9,000 pages of information, 2,400 audio classes and 120 video clips." Interspersed throughout this presentation of the website's history are tes-timonials from non-Orthodox, nonobservant, and isolated Jews. One en-thusiast who lives on the "tiny island of Curaçao" writes, "You are my link to the outside world and, as far away as I am, I feel connected to my Jewish roots!" The website characterizes the range of its mission, like that of Cha-bad itself, as comprehensive: "Chabad Online transcends all boundaries, serving the religious and the non-observant, affiliated and non-affiliated, young, old and all in between."[95] Like the West Coast Chabad telethons, chabad.org realizes the movement's vitality by demonstrating the extent of its interface with people beyond its community. In an interview with Jeff Zaleski, author of *The Soul of Cyberspace*, Kazen explained: "Our setup was never for our own group. On the contrary, this was set up strictly to deal with the outside world. . . . Getting a message of Judaism to the Jew who doesn't know much, to the Gentile who is interested in finding out what Judaism has to offer."[96]

Chabad.org offers links to sites beyond its own extensive resources, in-cluding affiliated publishers of books and media as well as a directory of

Chabad centers and institutions located around the world, many of which maintain their own websites. These links exemplify Chabad's ongoing efforts to make new connections as part of its agenda to promote behavior that will bring the messianic age closer—in Kazen's words, to "utilize the power and reach of the Internet to raise the moral and ethical barometer of our planet."[97] At the same time, Kazen was quick to clarify the Internet's limits regarding Jewish religious life. The medium cannot simulate material, embodied practices: a ritual meal, a Torah service, private prayer. When Zaleski asked why a *minyan* (quorum of ten adult male Jews traditionally required for group worship) could not be convened in cyberspace via a chat room, Kazen explained, "Because there's no physical presence. We don't necessarily see the spiritual reality of what is happening at the time, but certain things have to be done with physical people. . . . The quorum of ten people requires ten physical bodies. Each individual person has a spark of godliness within them, which is the soul."[98]

Notwithstanding the convictions of some people that the Internet "is somehow going to free us from the tyranny of the body,"[99] Kazen insisted on the notion, long a fundament of hasidism, that the spirit is rooted in the human body. This concept had especially charged implications at the time of his conversation with Zaleski, during the years immediately following the Rebbe's death, when messianic claims made by some Lubavitcher hasidim were at their most fervid and provocative. The connection of the spirit to the body posed a daunting challenge to those Chabad messianists who insisted that the Rebbe was alive by demanding that they offer some exceptional, arcane possibility for his viability and visibility.

The persistence of Chabad's messianism in the wake of the Rebbe's death has engendered an array of comparisons, mostly by other Jews observing this phenomenon with opprobrium. Some of them invoke the specter of Sabbeteanism—Jewish devotion to the seventeenth-century self-proclaimed messiah Shabbetai Zevi, which endured even after his decision to convert to Islam rather than become a martyr—or characterize Chabad as having, in effect, become "a new form of Christianity."[100] Others suggest that, as there is no heir to follow the seventh Lubavitcher rebbe, his hasidim might become *toyte khsidim* (literally, "dead hasidim")—like the disciples of Nahman of Bratslav, who also left no successor after his death in 1811—and that the Rebbe's writings and media documentation might become, like Nahman's teachings, the focus of his followers' devotion and study.[101] This last comparison shifts from controversial matters of theology to issues of mediation that are, in their own way, no less provocative. Devotion not merely to the Rebbe's words, written or spoken, but also to the Rebbe as a virtual presence both maintains and transforms a fundament of hasidism, which has been distinguished for over two centuries by the primacy it assigns to followers' devotional engagement with a charismatic leader.

And yet the notion that Chabad might continue to flourish in the absence of a rebbe is not entirely new. Herbert Weiner, a Reform rabbi who wrote a profile of Chabad in the late 1950s, argued that the key to the community's success in reestablishing itself in post–World War II America was that "Lubovitch depended less on its Rebbes than did other sects. . . . The meticulous concern for organized study, for well-edited textbooks, for public relations and good business procedure—all so apparently incongruous in a sect of mystics—was actually a key to Lubovitch's special history." Is Chabad's present ability to sustain its community and sense of purpose by relying heavily on new media practices simply a continuation of what Weiner characterized as its distinctive use of "these 'vessels' of thought and organization" with which it had already transformed hasidism?[102] Might some Lubavitcher hasidim come to regard their embrace of new media during Menachem Mendel Schneerson's leadership—which began just as television emerged as a mass medium and ended as the Internet was becoming a ubiquitous presence—as preparation for Chabad's fulfillment of its spiritual agenda, which would not be possible without these media and the virtual community that they enable?

Chabad's use of new media, may, in fact, constitute a test of the limits of the virtual as a mode for Jewish (or, indeed, any other) communal spirituality. In the mid-1990s, just as Lubavitcher hasidim were first grappling with the loss of the Rebbe, the classicist Walter Burkert pondered the future of religion at the conclusion of his study of its origins, in which he characterized religion as a "biological" response to anxieties about the unseen and unexplainable. Burkert suggested that humankind is now on the verge of "the most crucial changes" in its engagement with religion since the invention of writing. As a consequence of the "electronic network" of our "computerized society," he argued, "the individual finds herself or himself in the solitude of arbitrariness while being controlled by new and ineluctable dependencies so subtle and efficient that the older forms of communication look awkward and antiquated by comparison." As a result, "religion, stuck between nature and network, might cease to function," and "collective ritual may be supplanted by self-engendering games within the brave new world of virtual realities." Moreover, "'real' reality will make itself felt" in response to its "virtual counterfeits," resulting in the increased "likelihood . . . of regression, of fundamentalism, or even primitivism revived."[103]

Chabad's media practices today suggest something other than the possibilities either that religion will disappear in the wake of cyberspace or that cyberspace and its discontents will fuel religious primitivism. There is a fundamental tension in Chabad's uses of new media: on one hand, they facilitate a proliferation of points of entry for both Jews and non-Jews internationally; on the other hand, they reiterate a common, ostensibly inevitable, spiritual end-point. Rather than resolving this tension, Chabad's new media practices appear, in fact, to complicate and intensify it further. In light of the tenacity of Lubavitcher hasidim both before and after Menachem Mendel Schneerson's death, this tension promises to animate their future as followers of a leader whose presence (and absence) as a virtual Rebbe may prove to be not untenable but definitive.

Indeed, the virtual mode may be regarded as a fundament of the Rebbe's legacy. Not simply reckoned in hundreds of hours of audio and video recordings, it is also a consequence of his ideological commitment to the use of new media as vital and divinely sanctioned components of Chabad's spiritual project. There is no human successor to continue the leadership of Chabad, and Menachem Mendel Schneerson's status as messiah remains a provocative and unresolved question for many Lubavitcher hasidim. And yet his followers' devotion to the Rebbe in the virtual mode is not merely a matter of default. Rather, by embracing these new media practices, they affirm his life and teachings.

New Media/New Jews?

An Afterword

While working on the preceding chapters—emailing queries to colleagues, combing the Internet for resources, listening to music downloaded onto my iPod, ignoring my cell phone—I have also had contemporary questions about the impact of new media on the religious life of American Jews very much in mind. The case studies examined in *Jews, God, and Videotape* will, I hope, offer insights into how to analyze this unfolding phenomenon. Here, in closing, are some thoughts to that end.

So often, the first responses to new media tend toward extremes and frequently use religious imagery in doing so. These new technologies are readily hailed by some observers as "miracles" promising utopian social reforms or, just as easily, denounced by others as the "devil's work," dooming humankind to utter ruin. When confronted with a new technology's daunting transformative possibilities, people seem less inclined to call for nuance, and it seems untenable to suggest simply waiting to see what happens.

I remember visiting a professor in his office in the early 1990s, as he was trying out a newly released CD-ROM of the Talmud. "This will change everything," he said, eyes glued to the screen. "It's the end of erudition. Our professor of Talmud will be out of a job." I was not sure he was right then, and the ensuing years have, in fact, proved him wrong—even though publishers of that and other canonical Jewish religious texts in digitized, searchable form often tout their wares as providing something akin to instant expertise. (One such advertisement boasts that its product is "designed for maximum ease of use and efficiency by even the most novice of users! Gone are the days of lengthy, time consuming searches through piles of books, that would leave you with the feeling that you didn't adequately cover all the necessary sources on a subject. Now . . . , you can bring up all references to any subject in [hundreds of] books in seconds!")[1]

The Talmud is now also available in searchable form online, in the original Hebrew/Aramaic and in translation. In the latter form, it frequently turns up, through Internet searches, on an anti-Semitic website, to the consternation of Jewish scholars—an unanticipated consequence of this new facility.[2] Having the Talmud in a digitized, searchable format has indeed challenged its traditional pedagogy, which is rooted in committing the extensive text to memory. (Doing so entails visual as well as textual recall, as the place on the page where a Talmudic passage appears is key to understanding its significance in relation to other passages—hence the yeshiva tradition of the "pin test": a pin is inserted at random into a page of the Talmud, and the scholar being tested must name the word that the pin passes through on the pages following.) At the same time, knowing how to read the Talmud's highly elliptical language, which rests on its foundation as "oral law," as well as what to look for within the Talmud's vast, abstrusely organized contents, remains difficult, if not impossible, to master without training. Professors of Talmud are not obsolete as a result of digital technology, but it will compel them to develop new methods of teaching and evaluating their students, just as the advent of print transformed Talmudic scholarship, organized around a standard printed page.[3]

Hyperbolic responses to a new medium, especially positive ones, often reveal desires to forge new connections between technological innovations and an established way of life. In *The Talmud and the Internet*, Jonathan Rosen savors similarities in their form ("doorways through which visitors pass into an infinity of cross-referenced texts and conversations"), style of engagement (an "interrupting, jumbled culture"), and social implications (offering users "a virtual home"), explaining, "I take comfort in thinking that a modern technological medium echoes an ancient one."[4] Sometimes the desires to interrelate Jewish life and new media include affirming one's connection to the numinous. In the 1998 book *Judaism Online: Confronting Spirituality on the Internet*, authors Susan Zakar and Dovid Kaufmann explain how the Internet served as a strategic point of entry into Orthodox Judaism for Zakar, in the course of a spiritual journey that also traversed fundamentalist Christianity, agnosticism, and Conservative and Reform Judaism. Zakar's encounter with Orthodoxy started by encountering Kaufmann, a rabbi, when "she raised the question of women's role in Judaism on the Internet." The book's dust jacket reports that currently Zakar "is a familiar presence on the Internet," maintaining several Jewish organizations' websites. Besides running a web-design company with her husband, "she is frequently called upon to offer online support and guidance to others who are in the process of converting [to Judaism] or becoming more observant." Noting that Zakar met her husband thanks to technology (as neighbors, her Apple II was interfering with his television reception), Kaufmann remarks, "Divine Providence works even through computers!"[5]

People who create Jewish resources for the Internet frequently characterize them as transformative undertakings, sometimes on a grand scale. The creators of the Open Source Haggadah, which enables the user to "build a Haggadah for yourself," offer their project as a prototype for similar online compilations of texts for worship, which "may very well revolutionize the way in which Jews engage with Judaism."[6] At the same time, many of these media innovations rely on older technologies, canonical works, and traditional media practices, as does the haggadah project (which, even as it strives to facilitate self-styled ritual, largely follows the traditional structure of the Passover ritual and its centuries-old text). Similarly, the Internet facilitates Talmud study in a number of rubrics, including podcasts of a daily *gemara shiur* (Talmudic study session) available for downloading at dafyomi.org, which brings to cyberspace the practice of communal daily study of a page of Talmud, a "program initiated by Rav Meir Shapiro in 1923 at the First World Congress of [the international Orthodox organization] Agudath Israel in Vienna."[7] Other Jewish websites employ new technology to facilitate traditional communal rites in the actual world, including synagogue worship (for example, shulshopper.com, "the premier online service for finding and reviewing congregations that you help create") and Jewish marriages (such as jdate.com, which bills itself as "the modern alternative to traditional Jewish matchmaking" and boasts that "countless marriages begin right here").[8]

This indebtedness to established Jewish media, literacies, and cultural practices haunts even those Jewish online undertakings vaunted as being on the frontier of cyberculture at its most comprehensive and openended. Nowhere is this relationship more strikingly evident than in the Jewish presence on Second Life (secondlife.com), "a 3-D virtual world entirely built and owned by its Residents." First made publicly accessible in 2003, the site now claims over thirteen million "residents," also referred to as "avatars," worldwide.[9] Among the many ventures realized in this "world of endless possibilities" are the undertakings of virtual Jews, dubbed "Javatars" by Julian Voloj (who assumes the persona of Kafka Schnabel in

Second Life). A journalist, Voloj both reports on virtual Jewish phenomena and (as Schnabel) edits *2Life*, the Second Life Jewish community's
online magazine.[10] Javatars have established several virtual synagogues, a
Jewish museum, and a Holocaust memorial, as well as yeshivas and "virtual versions of Tel Aviv and Jerusalem" (the latter including a simulation of the Western Wall), among other sites in Second Life. There, virtual
Jews must also grapple with the presence of anti-Semitism, including "virtual neo-Nazis."[11]

The creators of *2Life* vaunt their community as "more diverse in age,
religious affiliation and R[eal] L[ife] geographical origin than any [Jew-
ish] community could be in the real world. . . . Second Life Judaism is
therefore a unique intercultural dialogue, . . . a mélange of different identities, in which age, origin, gender, and even religious affiliation are unimportant. It is an experiment with an uncertain outcome, but with obvious
potential for new and creative ways to explore culture, heritage and identity."[12] As characterized here, the relationship between Second Life Judaism and actual Jewish life is complex. The former is implicitly deemed
superior to the latter, even as the merits of Second Life Jews are measured
in "RL" terms (including geography)—while, at the same time, characterizing such defining elements of "RL" existence as "unimportant." An open-
ended experiment, Second Life Judaism looks forward to innovation yet
does so while pursuing inherently retrospective interests in Jewish "culture, heritage and identity."

Some of the Jewish phenomena in Second Life exploit opportunities
that the medium of computer animation provides for fabricating beings,
environments, and situations that could not exist in actuality. For example, there is Matzohenge, "a building entirely built out of . . . matzoh,"
which, according to *2Life*, "feels like a Pesach [Passover] theme park"—
perhaps because it also features, among other things, "swimming gefilte
fish." Its creator, known as the avatar Crap Mariner, explains, "I wanted to
create something impossible."[13] Matzohenge is indeed that (at least in "RL"
terms), but its significance, especially as a work of Jewish culture, relies
on knowledge brought to Second Life from without. In particular, as a
parodic work, its effectiveness assumes multiple cultural literacies and an
understanding of their interrelation as provocatively amusing.

The same issue of *2Life* features advertisements for actual engagements
in Jewish life, including a matchmaking service: "Want to meet someone
who shares your love for Jewish heritage in RL and S[econd] L[ife]?"[14]
Like other online Jewish dating services, this one poses a challenge that a

traditional Jewish matchmaker is unlikely to face: are the SL Javatars who are seeking (real? virtual?) Jewish partners also "RL" Jews themselves? Creating a Jewish virtual persona when one is not, in actuality, a Jew is not only possible but apparently welcome (or at least not discouraged) in Second Life Judaism. Voloj notes that among Second Life "residents" are some who "study Torah and so on who are not even Jews." In Second Life, "because you're just a computer animation, you can basically do whatever you want," he explains and also observes that "you can't tell if someone is Jewish or not."[15]

To some extent, Second Life Judaism resembles another form of "virtual Jewishness" found today in European countries, especially Germany and Poland. There, non-Jews play klezmer music, act in Yiddish theater troupes, run Jewish restaurants, and so on, realizing what Ruth Ellen Gruber characterizes as "a form of Jewish culture . . . minus the Jews." In these practices, "memory of Jews is employed as a vehicle for self-discovery and self-exploration" not only (or even primarily) for Jews but also for Germans, Poles, and other Europeans, especially those born after World War II. This "virtual Jewish world is a realm . . . in many senses constructed from desire rather than from memory or inherited tradition," Gruber writes. "'Jewish' thus can become a label with a life of its own."[16]

Second Life Judaism engages similar practices of questing and role-playing, but it does so within the new medium of online gaming. Voloj, among others, distinguishes Second Life from MMORPGs (massively multiplayer online role-playing games), as it "gives its users a huge amount of autonomy, so they can create whatever they want." He observes that "most of the 'residents' refer to Second Life as an alternative reality and not as a game."[17] Indeed, one Second Life resident explains: "When a person . . . on the screen stops being a game tool and starts being a part of you, perhaps that is when you begin looking for the place that really matters to you in Second Life." Another observes that, unlike online chat rooms, "in Second Life you are not anonymous; you create a different identity. . . . You reinvent yourself in Second Life."[18] Yet even as it offers the opportunity to "reside" in a separate milieu that aspires to be comprehensive in scope (much vaster than, say, the week-long Jewish culture festival held each summer in Cracow's former Jewish quarter of Kazimierz), Second Life Judaism is inevitably centered on the individual, sitting alone at his or her computer. The virtual Jewishness that Gruber describes centers on visiting established cultural sites and participating in shared literacies. By contrast, one's point of entry into Second Life is the invention of an avatar, and institutions (such as Temple Beth Israel, the first Second Life synagogue) can be fabricated by a single person. These creations rely largely on each individual's resources and imagination.

At the same time, Second Life Judaism resembles the virtual Jewishness enacted in contemporary Europe, in that both disrupt a relationship, long thought of as indelible and tautological, among an individual person, an intergenerational collective, and some notion of Jewishness. This identity is understood as primarily an inheritance (whether it be the traditional rabbinic principle of Jewishness as a matter of matrilineal heritage or the broader notion of ethnicity as acquired "by descent"), which is realized in terms of cultural practices (rituals, language use, folkways, and so on). By contrast, Second Life proposes a Jewishness that is not only freed from physical embodiment but also brimming with endless possibilities.[19] And yet so much of Second Life Judaism iterates actual Jewish life: synagogue worship, traditional seasonal holidays, Chabad outreach activity, Holocaust commemorations, Zionism, even online Jewish periodicals. Promoting *2Life*'s Aufbau Café as a virtual venue for Javatars to engage one another, Voloj/Schnabel recalls the "culture of European Coffee Houses, the loss of which I still bemoan—where people met, discussed openly and contributed in developing civil society. We do not intend to bring nostalgia into SL, but we absolutely want to recreate a platform . . . to enable the Jewish debate."[20]

In a milieu in which reinvention has limitless potential, why is this virtual Jewish world so indebted to the actual one? Beyond serving the interests of individual spiritual seekers or the ambitions of groups envisioning Jewish communality in more ideal circumstances than real life affords, Second Life Judaism seems to be motivated by a desire to validate Jewish actuality through a largely faithful replication in virtual reality. Innovation is mostly limited to playfulness that relies on established Jewish cultural literacy. Second Life resident Avram Leven explains, "I am not someone who lives his life any differently in RL (real life) versus SL (second life), so being Jewish in SL is a natural thing for me. My 'virtual Judaism' is simply an extension of my RL practices and beliefs."[21] Building these virtual Jewish innovations and environments, even creating a Jewish avatar for oneself, might therefore be thought of as new acts of faith for some, whereas for others it affords an opportunity to perform a Jewish self without parallel in real life.

Second Life Judaism seems to support, if unwittingly, those scholars who challenge the widespread discourse on virtual reality rooted in "the perception of new electronic media as abstract, disembodied, and de-contextualized information" and consequently as portending "the end of humanity." Mark Hansen instead argues that these new technologies "alter the very basis of our sensory experience and drastically affect what it means to live as *embodied* human agents." According to Hansen, "media convergence under digitality actually increases the centrality of the body as framer of information: as media lose their material specificity, the body takes on a more prominent function as selective processor in the creation of images."[22] In Second Life Judaism, actual Jews intensify their engagement with "RL" Jewishness by processing the many challenges and possibilities that Second Life poses to them as Jews—including its highlighting the performative nature of Jewishness, "embodied" by non-Jews' Jewish avatars.

Some Internet users have reflected on the implications of this new configuration of virtuality and actuality for Jewish life early in the history of this new medium. In 1994, anthropologist Jonathan Boyarin noted a paradox in playing "Jewish geography"—which he defined as "the social activity of establishing links with fellow Jews, usually upon first meeting them, by elaborating with them an informal account of shared family, friendship or community ties"—on the Internet: "The game depends on finding people who were in the same place at the same time. But playing it via computer requires neither. . . . Since one can communicate via electronic mail with anyone from anywhere, the point is less establishing new and lasting links than renewing one's sense of being a part of a network that will follow you wherever you go, if you continue to help maintain it."[23] Even as the Internet liberates users, it demands new responsibilities from them.

If there is one key, overarching insight that emerges from the case studies examined in this book, it is the importance of looking for the most telling consequences of new media on a community's religious life not at its extremes but somewhere in the middle. True to the multiple meanings of the term *media*, new technologies effect their most significant innovations in religious life by establishing new connections and thereby creating new in-between loci. These are situated not on the frontier, looking into a limitless void, as Second Life intimates, but rather at some new interstice, and so they look back and forth among known options.

The preceding chapters demonstrate how diverse are the ways that new media can facilitate novel connections that enable innovative cultural prospects somewhere in the middle: Cantors use an array of media to negotiate between artistic celebrity and serving as a community's conduit to the supernal. Ecumenical broadcasts offer something akin to, yet distinct from, a religious rite and respond to specifically Jewish concerns as they seek to address common public interests. Public works of Holocaust remembrance avoid theology even as they invoke religiosity and strive to situate their subject as both a paradigm of universal importance and a nonpareil. Individuals invest new value in the act of witnessing the photodocumentation of themselves performing a religious ritual as its ultimate fulfillment, thereby breaking down simple distinctions between participant and observer, experience and remembrance. Hybridized December holiday celebrations champion a syncretism that both embraces and interrogates two religious traditions. And followers of a charismatic religious leader maintain their devotion to him despite his physical absence, thanks to their investment in the spiritual value of his virtual presence.

In all these examples, some new cultural midpoint emerges and is perceived not as unsatisfactory compromise, illegitimate syncretism, a state of impurity, or being lost between two worlds but rather as hybrid, protean, revelatory. From this perspective, the affinity of religious life and media practices can be best appreciated by the religious skeptic and media detractor as well as by the devotee. In the pursuit of something new, people at the intersection of religion and new media revisit religiosity at its origin—the effort to connect the limits of the human condition to a larger unknown. By adopting or even merely considering new mediating practices, they may discover (and we who study them may observe) new possibilities of engaging this unknown emerging not somewhere far off but here, in our midst.

Notes

NOTES TO THE INTRODUCTION

1. This joke (or a variant) appears on Jewish humor websites, e.g., www. haruth.com/jhumor52.html; http://yanksfansoxfan.typepad.com/ysfs/2004/09/ intercepted_mem.html (accessed 21 Aug. 2007).

2. Michel Marriott, "Nothing to Watch on TV? Streaming Video Appeals to Niche Audiences," *New York Times*, 6 Aug. 2007, C1.

3. Lisa Gitelman and Geoffrey B. Pingree, "Introduction: What's New about New Media?" in *New Media, 1740–1915*, ed. Lisa Gitelman and Geoffrey B. Pingree (Cambridge, Mass.: MIT Press, 2003), xii. See also Carolyn Marvin, *When Old Technologies Were New: Thinking about Electric Communication in the Late Nineteenth Century* (New York: Oxford University Press, 1988).

4. Diane Zimmerman Umble, "Sinful Network or Divine Service: Competing Meanings of the Telephone in Amish Country," in Gitelman and Pingree, *New Media*, 139.

5. Jo Ann Koltyk, "Telling Narratives through Home Videos: Hmong Refugees and Self-Documentation of Life in the Old and New Country," *Journal of American Folklore* 106, no. 422 (fall 1993): 435–449; Linda Dégh, "Tape-Recording Miracles for Everyday Living: The Ethnography of a Pentecostal Community," in *American Folklore and the Mass Media* (Bloomington: Indiana University Press, 1994), 110–152; Daniel Wojcik, "Polaroids from Heaven: Photography, Folk Religion, and the Miraculous Image Tradition at a Marian Apparition Site," *Journal of American Folklore* 109, no. 432 (spring 1996): 129–148.

6. L. Honors, "Radio–Phonograph: That's the Bone of Contention in Jewish Families These Days," *Jewish Daily Forward*, 3 Aug. 1924, English sec., p. 3.

7. Reboot, "About Us," www.rebooters.net/aboutus.html (accessed 17 Sept. 2007).

8. Anna Greenberg, *"Grande Soy Vanilla Latte with Cinnamon, No Foam . . .": Jewish Identity and Community in a Time of Unlimited Choices* [report] ([New York]: Reboot, [2006?]), 3, 32.

9. See, e.g., J. Hoberman and Jeffrey Shandler, *Entertaining America: Jews, Movies, and Broadcasting* (Princeton, N.J.: Princeton University Press, 2003).

10. Melville Herskovits, "Who Are the Jews?" in *The Jews: Their History,*

Culture, and Religion, vol. 2, ed. Louis Finkelstein (Philadelphia: Jewish Publication Society, 1949), 1168.

11. Michael L. Satlow, "Defining Judaism: Accounting for 'Religions' in the Study of Religion," *Journal of the American Academy of Religion* 74, no. 4 (Dec. 2006): 842.

12. Lynn Schofield Clark, "Overview: The 'Protestantization' of Research into Media, Religion, and Culture," in *Practicing Religion in the Age of Media: Explorations in Media, Religion, and Culture,* ed. Stewart M. Hoover and Lynn Schofield Clark (New York: Columbia University Press, 2002), 8, 9.

13. Jeremy Stolow, "Religion and/as Media," *Theory, Culture and Society* 22, no. 4 (2005): 119, 125.

14. Joseph B. Soloveitchik, *Halakhic Man,* trans. Lawrence Kaplan (Philadelphia: Jewish Publication Society, 1983), 3, 4, 32, 39.

15. Melvin Konner, *Unsettled: An Anthropology of the Jews* (New York: Viking Compass, 2003), 108.

16. See Alain Finkielkraut, *The Imaginary Jew,* trans. David Suchoff (Lincoln: University of Nebraska Press, 1997); Jack J. Cohen, "Toward an Ideology for Post-halakhic Jews," *Jewish Civilization* 2 (1981): 127–144.

17. Isaac Deutscher, *The Non-Jewish Jew and Other Essays* (New York: Hill and Wang, 1968), 36.

18. See Mikel J. Koven, "'You Don't Have to Be Filmish': The Toronto Jewish Film Festival," *Ethnologies* 21, no. 1 (1999): 115–132.

19. See Barbara Kirshenblatt-Gimblett, "The Electronic Vernacular," in *Connected: Engagements with Media,* ed. George E. Marcus (Chicago: University of Chicago Press, 1996), 34.

20. Lisa Lipkin, "Long Live American Heroes: God Places Fourth behind Seinfeld, Sandler, and Howard Stern," *Forward,* 22 Nov. 1996, 13.

21. Raymond Williams, *Keywords: A Vocabulary of Culture and Society,* rev. ed. (New York: Oxford University Press, 1983), 203.

NOTES TO CHAPTER 1

1. Sholem Aleichem, *The Nightingale; or, The Saga of Yosele Solovey the Cantor,* trans. Aliza Shevrin (New York: Putnam's Sons, 1985 [1886]), 31–32.

2. On the early history of the cantor, see A. Z. Idelson, *Jewish Music in Its Historical Development* (New York: Tudor, 1944), 101–109; Mark Slobin, *Chosen Voices: The Story of the American Cantorate* (Urbana: University of Illinois Press, 2002), 4–8.

3. For a modern example of rabbinic law on cantors, see "Who Is Fit to Stand before the Ark," in Walter Orenstein, *The Cantor's Manual of Halakhah* (New York: Cantorial Council of America, Yeshiva University, 1965), 19–37.

4. Israel Abrahams, *Jewish Life in the Middle Ages* (Philadelphia: Jewish Publication Society, 1896), 91.

5. As reproduced in Jacob R. Marcus, *The Jew in the Medieval World* (Philadelphia: Jewish Publication Society, 1938), 217.

6. Mark Slobin, "Some Intersections of Jews, Music and Theater," in *From Hester Street to Hollywood: The Jewish-American Stage and Screen*, ed. Sarah Blacher Cohen (Bloomington: Indiana University Press, 1983), 29.

7. Richard Dyer, *Stars* (London: British Film Institute, 1979), 6ff., 22, 30.

8. American cantorial recordings are listed in the inventory of Jewish recordings in Richard K. Spottswood, *Ethnic Music on Records: A Discography of Ethnic Records Produced in the United States, 1893 to 1942*, vol. 3, *Eastern Europe* (Urbana: University of Illinois Press, 1990), 1293–1552, passim.

9. Kathy Peiss, *Cheap Amusements: Working Women and Leisure in Turn-of-the-Century New York* (Philadelphia: Temple University Press, 1985); Andrew Heinze, *Adapting to Abundance: Jewish Immigrants, Mass Consumption, and the Search for American Identity* (New York: Columbia University Press, 1990), 159; Susan L. Braunstein and Jenna Weissman Joselit, eds., *Getting Comfortable in New York: The American Jewish Home, 1880–1950* (New York: Jewish Museum, 1990), 36–38.

10. "Pathé Frères Phonograph Company" [advertisement], *Jewish Daily Forward*, 24 April 1920, 4; "Columbia Gramophone Co." [advertisement], *Jewish Daily Forward*, 22 Aug. 1917, 2; "Columbia Gramophone Co." [advertisement], *Jewish Daily Forward*, 24 May 1918, 7; "Pathé Frères Phonograph Company" [advertisement], *Jewish Daily Forward*, 10 Sept. 1920, 4.

11. On the nature of early recordings, see, e.g., Timothy Day, *A Century of Recorded Music: Listening to Musical History* (New Haven, Conn.: Yale University Press, 2000); David J. Steffen, *From Edison to Marconi: The First Thirty Years of Recorded Music* (Jefferson, N.C.: McFarland, 2005).

12. R. Murray Schafer, *The Soundscape: Our Sonic Environment and the Tuning of the World* (Rochester, Vt.: Destiny Books, 1994 [1977]), 91.

13. Pinkhas Minkovski, *Moderne liturgye in undzere sinagogen in Rusland* [Modern liturgy in our synagogues in Russia] (Odessa: Druk fun Kh. N. Byalik un Sh. Burishkin, 1910), 1ff., my translation; see also Slobin, *Chosen Voices*, 60.

14. Judd L. Teller, *Strangers and Natives: The Evolution of the American Jew from 1921 to the Present* (New York: Delacorte, 1968), 71.

15. Samuel Vigoda, *Legendary Voices: The Fascinating Lives of the Great Cantors*, vol. 1 (New York: [Samuel Vigoda], 1981), 576–577.

16. Mark Slobin, *Tenement Songs: The Popular Music of the Jewish Immigrants* (Urbana: University of Illinois Press, 1982), 19.

17. On "Eyli, Eyli," see Irene Heskes, *Passport to Jewish Music: Its History, Traditions, and Culture* (New York: Tara, 1994), 203–205. On "Afn pripetshik," see

James Loeffler, "'The Musical Nation': Jews, Culture and Nationalism in the Late Russian Empire" (Ph.D. diss., Columbia University, 2006), 116–123, 230–238.

18. Spottswood, *Ethnic Music on Records*, 3:1466.

19. The song was recorded by Cantor Maurice Ganchoff (Asch, 1941), Cantor Mordechay Hershman (Victor, 1923), William Robyn (Brunswick, 1933), Cantor Shloimele Rothstein, as Cantor W. Rosenthal (Columbia, 1920).

20. "Der Chazen Un Gabbe" (Victor, 1927); "A Chazon Oif Probe" (Victor, 1928, not issued); "A Probe Oif Chazonim" (Brunswick, 1928); "A Chaz'n's Debut In A Klein Shtedtele" (Victor, 1921); "A Chazen A Shiker" (Brunswick, 1928); "A Chazan Auf Der Elter" (Columbia, 1924); "Der Chasendl (The Cantor)" (Victor, 1928).

21. See Spottswood, *Ethnic Music on Records*, 3:1386, 1297, 1395–1400.

22. Morris Goldstein, "Owinu Malkeinu" (Columbia, 1920); Kalman Juvelier, "El Rachem Vechanun" (Columbia, 1915); Simon Paskal, "Al Tashlicheno" (Victor, 1911); William Robyn "V'shomru" (Victor, 1922); Rose Herringer, "Ahawas Oilom" (Columbia, 1915, not issued); Dorothy Jardon, "Rachem" (Brunswick, 1922); Delphine March, as Delphine Marx, "Al Tashlichenu" (Emerson, 1919); Estella Schreiner, "Al Tashlichenu" (Brunswick, 1921); Regina Prager, "Kol Nidre" (Zon-O-Phone, 1909).

23. "Kaddish, fun 'Yeshiva Bocher'" (Columbia, 1921); "Rachem, fun 'Der Golem'" (Pathé, 1926); "Ovinu Malkeinu, fun 'Dem Chazen's Tochter'" (Columbia, 1928); "Mismore Ledovid, from 'Gott, Mensch & Taifill'" (United Hebrew Disc and Cylinder, 1905).

24. See Slobin, *Tenement Songs*, 169.

25. "A Chasen'dl Oif Shabes, Sung by the Famous Cantor Rev. Joseph Hoffman," arr. William Scher (New York: S. Schenker, 1932); "A Chasen'dl Oif Shabos, As Sung by Cantor Hershman," arr. Leo Low (New York: Jos. P. Katz, 1921); "A Chasen'dl Oif Shabes, Sung by the Famous Cantor Rev. Rabinowitz," arr. William Scher (New York: S. Schenker, 1932).

26. "Eili Eili, Lomo Azavtoni, Sung by Cantor Josef Rosenblatt," arr. H. A. Rusotto (New York: Hebrew Publishing Company, 1916); "Eili, Eili, As Sung By Rosa Raisa," arr. Josef Bonime (New York: Metro Music, 1927); "The Original Eli-Eli, Originally sung by . . . Sophia Karp," arr. R. A. Zagler (New York: S. Schenker, 1919); "The Original Eli-Eli, sung . . . by Belle Baker" (New York: J. & J. Kammen Music, 1946 [1919]).

27. "Eli, Eli, as Arranged and Sung by Cantor Josef Rosenblatt ([Loose-Wiles Biscuit Company], n.d.).

28. Slobin, *Chosen Voices*, 51ff.

29. Jonathan Sarna, introduction to *People Walk on Their Heads: Moses Weinberger's Jews and Judaism in New York*, ed. and trans. Jonathan Sarna (New York: Holmes and Meier, 1982), 13.

30. Shmuel Goldblum, "Der poet fun khazones" [The poet of cantorial singing], *Jewish Morning Journal*, 21 Aug. 1925, 4.

31. Bernard Kwartin, "The Cantor and the Vocal Art," in *Chazanuth: 40th Anniversary Journal* (New York: Jewish Ministers Cantors' Association of America, 1937), 16–18.

32. Slobin, "Some Intersections of Jews, Music and Theater," 29.

33. See, e.g., Ted Merwin, *In Their Own Image: New York Jews in Jazz Age Popular Culture* (New Brunswick, N.J.: Rutgers University Press, 2006); Michael Rogin, *Blackface, White Noise: Jewish Immigrants in the Hollywood Melting Pot* (Berkeley: University of California Press, 1996); Mark Slobin, "Putting Blackface in Its Place," in J. Hoberman and Jeffrey Shandler, *Entertaining America: Jews, Movies, and Broadcasting*, 93–99 (Princeton, N.J.: Princeton University Press, 2003).

34. Hoberman, "On *The Jazz Singer*," in Hoberman and Shandler, *Entertaining America*, 80.

35. *The Jazz Singer* [souvenir program], reproduced in Hoberman and Shandler, *Entertaining America*, 83.

36. Hoberman, "On *The Jazz Singer*," 77.

37. "When Yossele Rosenblatt Used to Pray . . ." [advertisement], *Jewish Daily Forward*, 8 Sept. 1947, 3.

38. "Yossele Rosenblatt: Tribute to a Legend" [advertisement], *Forward*, 20 Nov. 2003, 3. The concert was staged by the nonprofit organization Cantors World, which promotes Jewish interest in cantorial art.

39. Discographies of Rosenblatt's recordings appear in Samuel Rosenblatt, *Yossele Rosenblatt: The Story of His Life as Told by His Son* (New York: Farrar, Straus and Young, 1954), 369–372, and Spottswood, *Ethnic Music on Records*, 3:1472–1480.

40. Rosenblatt, *Yossele Rosenblatt*, 221.

41. "Rabbi [*sic*] Rejects $1,000 Fee to Sing in Opera," *New York Times*, 15 April 1918, 13.

42. See, e.g., "Yosele Rozenblat, der bavuster khazn, vet efsher vern an opera zinger" [Renowned cantor Yossele Rosenblatt may become an opera singer], *Jewish Daily Forward*, 19 April 1918, 1, 4; Y. Kirshenboym, "Der omed iz im tayerer vi $1000 a nakht in der opera" [The pulpit is worth more to him than $1,000 a night at the opera], *Jewish Morning Journal*, 18 April 1918, 4; B. Botwinik, "Bay Yosele dem khazn in shtub" [At home with Yossele the Cantor], *Jewish Daily Forward*, 28 April 1918, 4.

43. S. Dingol, "Yosele Rozenblat vert a talmid fun Karuzo" [Yossele Rosenblatt takes lessons from Caruso], *Yidishes Tageblat*, 28 April 1918, 7.

44. Lola, "Yosele khapt dem makhzer un loyft in shul arayn!" [Yossele grabs his prayer book and runs into the synagogue!] [cartoon], *Der groyser kundes*, 3 May 1918, 7.

45. See also Morris Clark, "'Inner Voice' Told Cantor Rosenblatt to Shun Opera Stage," *Musical America* 28, no. 8 (22 June 1918): 33–34, a source Samuel Rosenblatt cites in his biography of his father.

46. Rosenblatt, *Yossele Rosenblatt*, 261–262.

47. Teller, *Strangers and Natives*, 71.

48. Arline De Haas, *The Jazz Singer: A Story of Pathos and Laughter, Novelized . . . from the Play by Samson Raphaelson, Illustrated with Scenes from the Photoplay . . .* (New York: Grosset and Dunlap, 1927), 95–96. On Rosenblatt's role in the film, see also Jeffrey Knapp, "'Sacred Song Popular Prices': Secularization in *The Jazz Singer*," *Critical Inquiry* 34 (winter 2008): 313–335.

49. Alfred A. Cohn, "The Jazz Singer: Adaptation and Continuity, from the stage play by Samson Raphaelson," in *The Jazz Singer,* ed. Robert L. Carringer (Madison: University of Wisconsin Press, 1979), 86–88.

50. Ibid.

51. Rosenblatt, *Yossele Rosenblatt*, 289–290.

52. "Cantor Rosenblatt's Voice for 'The Jazz Singer,' via Vitaphone," *Moving Picture World* 86, no. 4 (28 May 1927), 273.

53. According to Spottswood, *Ethnic Music on Records*, 3:1479.

54. Carringer, *The Jazz Singer*, 140.

55. Rosenblatt, *Yossele Rosenblatt*, 287.

56. A. J. Bloome, dir., *The Dream of My People* [videocassette] (Teaneck, N.J.: Ergo Media, 2003 [1933]).

57. Rosenblatt, *Yossele Rosenblatt*, 337.

58. Sidney M. Golden, dir., *The Feast of Passover* [DVD] (Waltham, Mass.: National Center for Jewish Film, 2005 [1931]).

59. *A khazn af probe* [videocassette] (Waltham, Mass.: National Center for Jewish Film, 2002 [1931]). Translation by Cantor Murray E. Simon.

60. J. Hoberman, *Bridge of Light: Yiddish Film between Two Worlds* (New York: Schocken Books, 1991), 262.

61. Ibid., 265.

62. "Second Avenue Theatre" [promotional pamphlet] (New York, 1935), RG 112, YIVO Archives, n.p.

63. As cited in Hoberman, *Bridge of Light*, 263.

64. Max Nosseck, dir., *Overture to Glory/Der vilner shtot khazn* [videocassette] (Teaneck, N.J.: Ergo Media, 1988 [1940]). English subtitles per original film.

65. Slobin, *Chosen Voices*, 94.

66. *Cantor Bela Herskovits: Crystal-Tone Records Present Bela Herskovits, Heroic Tenor, Chief Cantor of Budapest* [sound recording] (Boston: Crystal Tone, [194?]), inside album cover.

67. *Songs by Bela Herskovits, The "This Is Your Life" Cantor* [sound recording] (MGM: E3424, [195?]); Eddie Cantor and Bela Herskovits, *Two Cantors at Carnegie Hall* [sound recording] (Tikva Records T-52, [195?]). Herskovits appeared on *This Is Your Life* on 8 Feb. 1956. On Holocaust survivors on *This Is Your Life*, see Jeffrey Shandler, *While America Watches: Televising the Holocaust* (New York: Oxford University Press, 1999), 28–40.

68. E.g., Yosef Shlisky, who recorded the aria for Vocalion in 1921.

69. "The Aria 'Rachel,'" *Cantors in Yiddish: Arias, Operetta, Folk Songs, and Chassidic Songs by Famous Cantors* [sound recording] (Israel Music, no. ICD 5047, n.d.), band 1. Though undated, the original is apparently an early post–World War II recording. Koussevitzky, a renowned cantor in Warsaw before World War II, immigrated to the United States in 1947; he continued performing into the 1960s and died in 1966.

70. Zalmen Zilbertsvayg, ed., *Leksikon fun yidishn teatr* [Yiddish theater lexicon], vol. 3 (New York: Farlag "Elisheva," 1959), col. 2410.

71. *Kol Nidre Night with Moishe Oysher* [sound recording] (New York: Rozanna Records, [1957?]), album cover.

72. The back of the album cover of *Kol Nidre Night with Moishe Oysher* states, "Radio broadcast rights are administered by TV-Time, White Plains, New York."

73. *The Moishe Oysher Seder* [sound recording] (New York: Rozanna Records, [1956?]).

74. *The Moishe Oysher Chanuka Party* [sound recording] (New York: Rozanna Records, [1958?]), album cover.

75. Ibid.

76. *The Moishe Oysher Seder*, album cover.

77. See J. Hoberman, "*The Jazz Singer*: A Chronology," in Hoberman and Shandler, *Entertaining America*, 84–92.

78. Winthrop Sargeant, "Pagliacci from Brooklyn," *Life*, 3 Nov. 1952, 127.

79. For a discography of Tucker's recordings, see James A. Drake, *Richard Tucker: A Biography* (New York: Dutton, 1984), 279–292.

80. Tucker appeared on *Person to Person* on 12 Dec. 1952.

81. See, e.g., Winthrop Sargeant, *Divas* (New York: Coward, McCann & Geroghegan, 1973), 134–167.

82. "Conversation with Richard Tucker," *The Eternal Light* (NBC), 7 June 1970, T792, National Jewish Archive of Broadcasting, The Jewish Museum, New York.

83. *The Responsa of Professor Louis Ginzberg*, ed. Rabbi David Golinkin (New York: Jewish Theological Seminary, 1996), 75.

84. Richard Tucker, interview by Janet Bookspan [transcript], recorded 13 April, 5 June, 19 June, and 3 July 1973, William E. Wiener Oral History Library, American Jewish Committee, New York, 4.

85. Sargeant, "Pagliacci from Brooklyn," 127.

86. Drake, *Richard Tucker*, 60, 99.

87. Tucker's performance of "The Lord's Prayer" appears on *Joyous Christmas*, vol. 5 (Columbia C10396, 196?) and on *The Great Songs of Christmas*, album 5 (Columbia CSP 238 M [mono], CSP 238S [stereo], 196?), on which he also performs "O Little Town of Bethlehem."

88. Drake, *Richard Tucker*, 245, xv.

89. Ibid., 111, 137.

90. Leonard J. Leff, "A Question of Identity," *Opera News*, Dec. 2002, 37.

91. Drake, *Richard Tucker*, 171–172.

92. Ibid., xiv–xv.

93. Tucker, interview by Bookspan, 161.

94. Ibid., 148.

95. Leff, "A Question of Identity," 38.

96. Ibid., 38.

97. See Drake, *Richard Tucker*, 245.

98. See, e.g., David J. Baker, "Once in a Lifetime," *Opera News*, Dec. 2003, 27.

99. F. Paul Driscoll, "French Evolution," *Opera News*, Dec. 2003, 8.

100. Jacques Fromenthal Halévy, *La Juive* [DVD booklet] (Hamburg: Deutsche Grammophon, 2004), 8–9.

101. Quoted in Ira Siff, "Channeling *La Juive*," *Opera News*, Dec. 2003, 22.

102. "Rachel, quand du Seigneur" [short film], dir. Sidney Lumet, in Jacques Fromenthal Halévy, *La Juive* [DVD] (Hamburg: Deutsche Grammophon, 2004), disc 2.

103. This sketch appeared on the syndicated series *SCTV Television Network*, first aired 11 Oct. 1981.

104. The episode, "Like Father, Like Clown," first aired on Fox on 24 Oct. 1991.

105. Frank London, *Invocations* [sound recording] (Tzadik, 2000), liner notes.

106. David Vinik, dir., *Faith First: Second Career Clergy* [film] (Diva Communications for JTS, 2002), T2342, National Jewish Archive of Broadcasting, The Jewish Museum, New York. The documentary was telecast on WABC on 27 Jan. 2002.

107. Erik Greenberg Anjou, dir., *A Cantor's Tale* [film] (Teaneck, N.J.: Ergo Media, 2005).

108. Anthony Giddens, *Modernity and Self-Identity: Self and Society in the Late Modern Age* (Cambridge, U.K.: Polity, 1991).

109. Evan Eisenberg, *The Recording Angel: Music, Records and Culture from Aristotle to Zappa*, 2nd ed. (New Haven, Conn.: Yale University Press, 2005), 41–42.

110. See Mark Kligman, "The Media and the Message: The Recorded Music of Brooklyn's Orthodox Jews," *Jewish Folklore and Ethnology Review* 16, no. 1 (1994): 9–11.

NOTES TO CHAPTER 2

1. Jonathan Sarna, *American Judaism: A History* (New Haven, Conn.: Yale University Press, 2004), 274–275.

2. See Marshall Sklare, *Conservative Judaism: An American Religious Movement*, rev. ed. (New York: Schocken Books, 1972).

3. Max Arzt to members of the Rabbinical Assembly, 21 March 1944, as cited in Michael B. Greenbaum, "The Finkelstein Era," in *Tradition Renewed: A History*

of the Jewish Theological Seminary, ed. Jack Wertheimer (New York: Jewish Theological Seminary, 1997), 173.

4. Report to Board of Directors, 6 April 1941, as cited in Greenbaum, "The Finkelstein Era," 167.

5. On the Jewish Hall of Fame, see Greenbaum, "The Finkelstein Era," 187.

6. Marjorie G. Wyler, "The Eternal Light: Judaism on the Airwaves," *Conservative Judaism* 39, no. 2 (winter 1986–87): 18–19.

7. Marjorie Wyler, interview by Jeffrey Shandler (New York, 7 Dec. 1994).

8. Wyler, "The Eternal Light," 18.

9. Ibid., 19.

10. Wyler, interview.

11. See the minutes of the Board of Directors of the Jewish Theological Seminary of America, Executive Committee Meeting, 17 Aug. 1944, RG 2, JTS Archives.

12. "'The Eternal Light,' Program Series Drawn from Jewish Culture, Begins on NBC Oct. 8" [press release], 29 Aug. [1944], hectograph, RG 11C, box 26, folder 38, JTS Archives.

13. From a promotional poster published by JTS in the 1940s, reproduced in Nina Beth Cardin and David Wolf Silverman, eds., *The Seminary at 100: Reflections on the Jewish Theological Seminary and the Conservative Movement* ([New York]: Rabbinical Assembly and Jewish Theological Seminary of America, 1987), 186.

14. Everett C. Parker, Elinor Inman, and Ross Snyder, *Religious Radio: What to Do and How* (New York: Harper & Brothers, 1948), 7.

15. Telephone conversation between Milton Krents and Elihu Katz, 15 Nov. 1994, New York; see Jeffrey Shandler and Elihu Katz, "Broadcasting American Judaism: The Radio and Television Department of the Jewish Theological Seminary," in Wertheimer, *Tradition Renewed*, 394n. 7.

16. American Jewish Committee, "Radio Report," [Jan.] 1939, available online at www.ajcarchives.org/main.php?GroupingId=220 (accessed 6 Sept. 2006).

17. Stuart Svonkin, *Jews against Prejudice: American Jews and the Intergroup Relations Movement from World War to Cold War* (New York: Columbia University Press, 1997), 15, 17, 18, 20.

18. Ibid., 24, 37, 46.

19. Stewart M. Hoover and Douglas K. Wagner, "History and Policy in American Broadcast Treatment of Religion," *Media, Culture and Society* 19, no. 1 (Jan. 1997): 14.

20. Ralph Jennings, "Policies and Practices of Selected National Religious Bodies as Related to Broadcasting in the Public Interest" (Ph.D. diss., New York University, 1969), 4.

21. *Advisory Council of the National Broadcasting Company, Committee Reports, The President's Report, Second Meeting, March, 1928* (New York: National

Broadcasting Company, 1928), 14–15, as cited in Jennings, "Policies and Practices," 29.

22. David Sarnoff to Prof. Felix Frankfurter, 10 Feb. 1934, in David Sarnoff, *Looking Ahead: The Papers of David Sarnoff* (New York: McGraw-Hill, 1968), 67.

23. Address before the fifth annual Current Events Forum conducted by the *New York Herald Tribune*, New York City, 17 Oct. 1935, in Sarnoff, *Looking Ahead*, 70–71.

24. Memorandum to Cordell Hull, Secretary of State, Washington, D.C., 9 Jan. 1943, in Sarnoff, *Looking Ahead*, 76.

25. Address before the United States National Commission for UNESCO, Chicago, 12 Sept. 1947, in Sarnoff, *Looking Ahead*, 79.

26. Hoover and Wagner, "History and Policy," 10.

27. Erik Barnouw, *The Golden Web: A History of Broadcasting in the United States*, vol. 2, *1933–1953* (New York: Oxford University Press, 1968), 46.

28. *New York Times*, 27 Nov. 1938, 46, as cited in Hoover and Wagner, "History and Policy," 18.

29. Jennings, "Policies and Practices," 109.

30. See Stewart M. Hoover, *Mass Media Religion: The Social Sources of the Electronic Church* (Newbury Park, Calif.: Sage, 1988), 49–55; Peter G. Horsfield, *Religious Television: The American Experience* (New York: Longman, 1984), 3–7.

31. Radio listings, *New York Times*, 12 Nov. 1944, sec. 2, p. 6.

32. "The Eternal Light" [report, 1946?], hectograph, RG 11C, box 26, folder 40, JTS Archives.

33. Svonkin, *Jews against Prejudice*, 44.

34. Edward S. Shapiro, *A Time for Healing: American Jewry since World War II* (Baltimore: Johns Hopkins University Press, 1992), caption to illustration [no. 23] between 140 and 141.

35. Esther M. Klein, *Guidebook to Jewish Philadelphia: History, Landmarks, Donors . . .* (Philadelphia: Philadelphia Jewish Times Institute, 1965), 105–106.

36. Will Herberg, *Protestant—Catholic—Jew: An Essay in American Religious Sociology* (Garden City, N.Y.: Doubleday, 1955), 15, 40.

37. See Hoover and Wagner, "History and Policy"; Michele Rosenthal, *American Protestants and TV in the 1950s: Responses to a New Medium* (Basingstoke, U.K.: Palgrave, 2007).

38. Rosenthal, *American Protestants and TV in the 1950s*, 39, 40–41.

39. Ibid., 38, 42–43.

40. See Barnouw, *The Golden Web*, 66–70, 85–89, 116–121.

41. Morton Wishengrad, *The Eternal Light* (New York: Crown, 1947).

42. Wyler, "The Eternal Light," 19.

43. See "The Jewish Stage," in Gustav Karpeles, *Jewish Literature and Other Essays* (Philadelphia: Jewish Publication Society, 1895), 229–248; Martin Jacobs, "Theatres and Performances as Reflected in the Talmud Yerushalmi," in *The*

Talmud Yerushalmi and Graeco-Roman Culture, vol. 1, ed. Peter Schäfer (Tübingen: Mohr Siebeck, 1998), 327–347.

44. See, e.g., Milton Marks, Henry Hart, and Martin A. Meyer, *God Is One: An Historical Pageant of Israel's Loyalty* (New York: Bloch, 1914); Mignon L. Rubenovitz, *The Light of the Centuries and Other Historical Dramas* (Boston: Sisterhood of Temple Mishkan Tefila, 1938); *The Sabbath Angel: A Play in Two Acts* (Cincinnati: Department of Synagogue and School Extension of the Union of American Hebrew Congregations, 1929); Samuel Michael Segal, *Hitlerites and Chanukah Lights* (New York: Behrman's Jewish Book House, 1933).

45. Finkelstein, foreword to Wishengrad, *The Eternal Light*, viii.

46. "Art and Religion in Atmosphere of Creative Freedom Characterize 30 Years of 'Lamp Unto My Feet' Series," CBS News press release, 22 Feb. 1978, National Jewish Archive of Broadcasting, The Jewish Museum, New York.

47. Moshe Davis, transcript of interview by Pamela Jay, Jerusalem, 25 Dec. 1990, Ratner Center for the Study of Conservative Judaism, JTS, 6.

48. Wishengrad, *The Eternal Light*, 111; ellipses in original.

49. Ibid., 118, 119, 120.

50. See Julian Levinson, *Exiles on Main Street: Jewish American Writers and the Art of Return* (Bloomington: Indiana University Press, 2008), 23–25.

51. Hasia R. Diner, *The Jews of the United States* (Berkeley: University of California Press, 2004), 58.

52. Morton Wishengrad, *Akiba* (program no. 29, aired 29 April 1945); Irwin Gonshak, *The Days of a Poet* (Solomon Ibn Gabirol; no. 692, 12 Feb. 1961); Wishengrad, *Moses Mendelssohn* (no. 68, 24 Feb. 1946); Joseph Mindel, *A Lifetime Is Long Enough* (Vilna Gaon; no. 570, 8 Dec. 1957); Mindel, *A Heart of Wisdom* (Schick; no. 576, 19 Jan. 1958); Virginia Mazer, *The Man Who Knew Lincoln* (Rosewater; no. 489, 1 Jan. 1956); Judah Stampfer, *The Language of Hope* (Zamenhof; no. 653, 7 Feb. 1960).

53. Examples include Joseph Mindel, *An Unlikely Story* (Thanksgiving), based on Ida Uchill's *Pioneers, Peddlers and Tzadikim* (program no. 642, aired 22 Nov. 1959); William Wise, *The Man Who Rode like Revere*, the story of Francis Salvador, a revolutionary hero in South Carolina (no. 513, 17 June 1956); Marc Siegal, *Mr. Flanagan, the Chaplain and Mr. Lincoln*, on efforts to allow Jewish clergy to serve as chaplains during the Civil War (no. 723, 14 Jan. 1962); Joseph Bruck, *Enter to Learn, Depart to Serve* (Bethune; no. 616, 18 Jan. 1959); Harry Gersh, *David Dubinsky* (no. 597, 29 June 1958); Morton Wishengrad, *Emma Lazarus: A Modern Esther* (no. 21, 25 Feb. 1945); Virginia Mayer, *The Big Road* (Carver; no. 726, 4 Feb. 1962); Siegal, *An American Sampler* (tercentenary; no. 444, 21 Nov. 1954).

54. David Bernstein, "The American Jewish Tercentenary," *American Jewish Year Book* 67 (1956): 101–102. CBS, NBC, and Dumont all aired special television programs in conjunction with the tercentenary.

55. Morton Wishengrad, *Gandhi* (no. 252, 1 Jan. 1950); Marion Voigt, *Light against the Dark* (no. 473, 12 June 1955).

56. Stanley Silverman, *Isaiah and the Nations* (no. 102, 20 Oct. 1946); "The Eternal Light Celebrates Its First Birthday" [press release], October(?) 1945, hectograph, RG 11C, box 26, folder 50, JTS Archives, p. 6.

57. Val Adams, "'The Eternal Light': Religion Series Appeals to All Faiths and Stresses Dramatic Values," *New York Times*, 8 Jan. 1950, sec. 2, p. 15.

58. Examples include Meyer Levin, *Anne Frank: Diary of a Young Girl* (no. 366, 14 Dec. 1952); Morton Wishengrad, *My Father's Tallis* (no. 49, 14 Oct. 1945); Wishengrad, *A Sound of Music* (no. 59, 23 Dec. 1945); Wishengrad, *The Voice of Rachel* (no. 60, 30 Dec. 1945).

59. Geoffrey Wigoder, "Ecumenism," in *Contemporary Jewish Religious Thought: Original Essays on Critical Concepts, Movements and Beliefs*, ed. Arthur A. Cohen and Paul Mendes Flohr (New York: Scribner's Sons, 1987), 148.

60. S. Y. Agnon's *The Betrothed*, adapted by Joseph Mindel (no. 1260, 9 Jan. 1977); Isaac Babel's *The Phonograph*, adapted by James Yaffe (no. 1264, 6 Feb. 1977); a David Bergelson story was adapted by Morton Wishengrad as *The Tender Grass* (no. 75, 14 April 1946); Y. L. Peretz's *If Not Higher*, adapted by Norman Rosten (no. 47, 16 Sept. 1945); Henry Roth's *Call It Sleep*, adapted by Shimon Wincelberg (no. 1259, 2 Jan. 1977); Isaac Bashevis Singer's *Zlateh the Goat* (no. 1373, 9 Dec. 1979), Sholem Aleichem's *The Pocketknife*, adapted by Mindel (no. 1103, 27 Oct. 1946); *Joseph and the Indians*, adapted by Wishengrad (no. 3, 22 Oct. 1944); *Nathan the Wise*, adapted by Ben Kagan (no. 92, 11 Aug. 1946); *Athalie*, adapted by Harold Rosenberg (no. 91, 4 Aug. 1946); *The Wise Men of Chelm*, adapted by Milton Wayne (no. 87, 7 July 1946); Marc Siegel, *How Manny Got into the Seventh Grade* (no. 649, 10 Jan. 1960).

61. Davis, interview, 12–13.

62. Wishengrad to Davis, 8 Dec. 1949, box 1, folder 32, Morton Wishengrad Papers, JTS Archives.

63. Wishengrad to Michael [Gelber?], 28 June 1960, box 1, folder 40, Morton Wishengrad Papers, JTS Archives.

64. A press release marking the twenty-fifth anniversary of the series claims that listeners sent some 10,000 letters responding to Wishengrad's Warsaw Ghetto drama. "The Eternal Light" [press release], 26 Sept. 1969, hectograph, RG 11C, box 30, folder 42, JTS Archives, p. 2.

65. Wishengrad, *The Eternal Light*, 32. The last known airdate of *The Battle of the Warsaw Ghetto* is 2 Aug. 1985.

66. Ibid., 33; ellipses after "there was no release" in original.

67. Ibid., 41, 39.

68. "Political Affiliations" [an undated résumé documenting Wishengrad's anti-Communist activities], box 1, folder 47, Morton Wishengrad Papers, JTS Archives.

69. Wishengrad to Davis, n.d., box 1, folder 32, Morton Wishengrad Papers, JTS Archives.

70. Wishengrad to Ted Ashley, 2 March 1953, box 1, folder 19, Morton Wishengrad Papers, JTS Archives.

71. Wishengrad to Howard Singer, [1961], box 2, folder 8, Morton Wishengrad Papers, JTS Archives.

72. The first Hooper ratings were 3.3 (6 Oct. 1946), 3.6 (20 Oct.), and 4.4 (3 Nov.). By comparison, on 6 Oct. *The Catholic Hour* had a rating of 3.9; on 3 Nov. the *University of Chicago Round Table* had a 3.6 rating, and the Toscanini NBC Orchestra broadcast of that date had a 3.3 rating. See "The Eternal Light" [report, 1946?], hectograph, RG 11C, box 26, file 40, JTS Archives.

73. E.g., "6,000,000 Listen . . ." [brochure] ([New York]: JTS, ca. 1947), RG 11C, box 27, file 30, JTS Archives. The brochure notes that *The Eternal Light* is carried by "more than 75 [of NBC's] affiliated stations."

74. "The Eternal Light: Fact Sheet," 22 Oct. 1953, hectograph, RG 11C, box 26, folder 38, JTS Archives.

75. "Report to the Board of Overseers: The Eternal Light," Dec. 1948, hectograph, RG 11C, box 26, folder 38, JTS Archives, p. 2.

76. See, e.g., Jacob S. Golub, "Teacher's Guide for Scripts of 'The Eternal Light' Broadcasts," 15 Jan. 1945, hectograph, RG 11C, box 26, folder 39, JTS Archives.

77. [Untitled press release], 19 Jan. 1947, hectograph, RG 11C, box 26, folder 40, JTS Archives.

78. See "The Eternal Light Celebrates Its First Birthday," 1. Mrs. Roosevelt's syndicated column appeared on 10 Oct. 1944; see, e.g., "Hyde Park Visit; New Radio Series," *New York World-Telegram*, 17.

79. Rose., "The Eternal Light," *Variety*, 25 Oct. 1944, 38.

80. Parker, Inman, and Snyder, *Religious Radio*, 7.

81. Val Adams, "'The Eternal Light': Religion Series Appeals to All Faiths and Stresses Dramatic Values," *New York Times*, 8 Jan. 1950, sec. 2, p. 15.

82. *The Eternal Light: Tenth Anniversary Year* [brochure] [New York?, 1954?], RG 11C, box 30, folder 33, JTS Archives, p. 8; "The Eternal Light" [press release], 26 Sept. 1969, RG 11C, box 30, folder 42, JTS Archives, p. 2.

83. *The Eternal Light* received the Peabody Award for radio in 1962 and 1967. In addition, JTS received a Peabody Award in 1978 "for 'The Eternal Light,' a consistently noteworthy program broadcast for 35 Years on the NBC Radio Network." See Gita Siegman, ed., *World of Winners: A Current and Historical Perspective on Awards and Their Winners*, 2nd ed. (Detroit: Gale Research, 1992), 688, 686.

84. "Report to the Board of Overseers: The Eternal Light," Dec. 1948, hectograph, RG 11C, box 26, folder 38, JTS Archives, p. 2.

85. "Radio Listeners Say . . ." [brochure] (New York: Jewish Theological Seminary, [1945?]).

86. Ibid.

87. Ibid.

88. Ibid.

89. Philip Roth, *The Ghost Writer* (New York: Ballantine Books/Fawcett Crest, 1983 [1979]), 106–107.

90. Davis, interview, 7.

91. Arthur Hertzberg, *The Jews in America: Four Centuries of an Uneasy Encounter* (New York: Simon and Schuster, 1989), 322.

92. Albert I. Gordon, *Jews in Suburbia* (Boston: Beacon, 1959), 16.

93. Nathan Glazer, *American Judaism*, 2nd rev. ed. (Chicago: University of Chicago Press, 1989 [1957]), 116–117.

94. See Avram Kampf, *Contemporary Synagogue Art: Development in the United States, 1945–1965* (Philadelphia: Jewish Publication Society, 1966); Deborah Dash Moore, *To the Golden Cities: Pursuing the American Jewish Dream in Miami and L.A.* (New York: Free Press, 1994), chap. 5; Barbara Kirshenblatt-Gimblett, "Kitchen Judaism," in *Getting Comfortable in New York: The American Jewish Home, 1880–1950*, ed. Susan L. Braunstein and Jenna Weissman Joselit (New York: Jewish Museum, 1990), 78.

95. Zev Zahavy, *A History and Survey of Jewish Religious Broadcasting* (Ph.D. diss., Yeshiva University, 1959), 5, 19.

96. See, e.g., the records of speech teacher Arleigh Williamson, RG 3B, box 2, folders 21–27, JTS Archives.

97. See Sklare, *Conservative Judaism*, 191–195.

98. See, e.g., John Cogley, *Report on Blacklisting*, vol. 2, *Radio-Television* ([New York:] Fund for the Republic, 1956).

99. *The Eternal Light: Tenth Anniversary Year*, 7.

100. See Horace M. Newcomb and Paul Hirsch, "Television as a Cultural Forum: Implications for Research," *Quarterly Review of Film Studies* 8, no. 3 (summer 1983): 45–56; Paul C. Adams, "Television as Gathering Place," *Annals of the Association of American Geographers* 82, no. 1 (1992): 117–135.

101. See J. Hoberman, "The Goldbergs: A Chronology," in J. Hoberman and Jeffrey Shandler, *Entertaining America: Jews, Movies, and Broadcasting* (Princeton, N.J.: Princeton University Press, 2003), 124–129.

102. See, e.g., Lewis Herman and Marguerite Shalett Herman, *Foreign Dialects: A Manual for Actors, Directors, and Writers* (New York: Theatre Arts Books, 1943), 392–413.

103. Donald Weber, *Haunted in the New World: Jewish American Culture from Cahan to "The Goldbergs"* (Bloomington: Indiana University Press, 2005), 131, 135.

104. Gertrude Berg and Charney Berg, *Molly and Me* (New York: McGraw-Hill, 1961).

105. Morris Freedman, "The Real Molly Goldberg: Balebosteh of the Air Waves," *Commentary* 21, no. 4 (April 1956): 360.

106. See Weber, *Haunted in the New World*, 139.

107. Quoted in ibid., 133.

108. Ibid., 130.

109. For example, Wishengrad's play *The Remarkable Adventures of Deuteronomy Katz*, heard on the radio version of *The Eternal Light* on 9 June 1946 (program no. 83), was presented in an adaptation by the playwright for television on 8 Nov. 1953 (no. T-20).

110. *Schechter Revisited at Cambridge University* (no. 128, 15 Nov. 1965); *The World of Rembrandt* (no. 154, 10 Dec. 1967); *A Talent for Life: Jew of the Italian Renaissance* (no. 253, 2 Dec. 1979); *The Itinerary of Elie Wiesel: From Sighet to Jerusalem* (no. 200, 21 May 1972); *A Conversation with Ambassador Sol M. Linowitz* (no. 151, 19 Nov. 1967); *A Conversation with James Michener* (no. 160, 23 June 1968), *A Conversation with Itzhak Perlman* (no. 231, 7 Nov. 1976); *A Conversation with Karl Katz* (no. 172, 8 June 1969); *A Conversation with the Late Dr. Abraham Joshua Heschel* (no. 205, 4 Feb. 1973).

111. See Erik Barnouw, *Tube of Plenty: The Evolution of American Television*, 2nd rev. ed. (New York: Oxford University Press, 1990), 166.

112. Hoover and Wagner, "History and Policy," 23–24.

113. Hoover, *Mass Media Religion*, 56.

114. Form letter from Stanley J. Schaechter, Vice-Chancellor of JTS (addressed to "Dear Colleague"), 16 Feb. 1983, hectograph, RG 11C, box 27, folder 16, JTS Archives.

115. Rosenthal, *American Protestants and TV in the 1950s*, 37.

116. Svonkin, *Jews against Prejudice*, 178–179.

117. Michael Warner, "The Mass Public and the Mass Subject," in *Habermas and the Public Sphere*, ed. Craig Calhoun (Cambridge, Mass.: MIT Press, 1992), 377, 381, 380, 382, 383.

118. Hoover and Wagner, "History and Policy," 23.

119. Warner, "The Mass Public and the Mass Subject," 384.

120. Wishengrad, *The Eternal Light*, 2.

121. Warner, "The Mass Public and the Mass Subject," 382, 385.

122. "The Eternal Light" [press release], 26 Sept. 1969, 4.

123. See Hal Erickson, *Religious Radio and Television in the United States, 1921–1991: The Programs and Personalities* (Jefferson, N.C.: McFarland, 1992), 45, 82.

124. See Jeffrey Shandler, "At Home on the Small Screen: Television's New York Jews," in Hoberman and Shandler, *Entertaining America*, 258–263; see also Vincent Brook, *Something Ain't Kosher Here: The Rise of the "Jewish" Sitcom* (New Brunswick, N.J.: Rutgers University Press, 2003); Jonathan and Judith Pearl, *The Chosen Image: Television's Portrayal of Jewish Themes and Characters* (Jefferson, N.C.: McFarland, 1999); David Zurawik, *The Jews of Prime Time* (Hanover, N.H.: Brandeis University Press, 2003).

125. Jewish Heritage Video Collection, "About the JHVC," www.jhvc.org/about/index.php (accessed 1 Sept. 2006).

NOTES TO CHAPTER 3

1. For an overview of Holocaust theology, see Jack R. Fischel and Susan M. Ortmann, *The Holocaust and Its Religious Impact: A Critical Assessment and Annotated Bibliography* (Westport, Conn.: Praeger, 2004).

2. For Orthodox *kinot*, see, e.g., "Kinah [Elegy] in Memory of Our Six Million Martyrs Who Perished during 1939–1945," in *Tisha B'Av Compendium, Including Kinot for the Ninth of Av . . .*, trans. Rev. Abraham Rosenfeld (New York: Judaica Press, 1983), 173–175; for Reform Judaism, see *Gates of Prayer: The New Union Prayerbook* (New York: Central Conference of American Rabbis, 1975), 573–589.

3. See Jean-Jacques Rousseau, *Du Contrat Social ou Principes du Droit Politique* (1762), book 4, chapter 8.

4. See, e.g., Charles S. Liebman and Eliezer Don-Yehiya, *Civil Religion in Israel: Traditional Judaism and Political Culture in the Jewish State* (Berkeley: University of California Press, 1983).

5. Jeffrey Shandler, *While America Watches: Televising the Holocaust* (New York: Oxford University Press, 1999), xv.

6. On the challenges of Holocaust representation, see, e.g., Saul Friedlander, ed., *Probing the Limits of Representation: Nazism and the "Final Solution"* (Cambridge, Mass.: Harvard University Press, 1992); Brett Ashley Kaplan, *Unwanted Beauty: Aesthetic Pleasure in Holocaust Representation* (Urbana: University of Illinois Press, 2006); Berel Lang, *Holocaust Representation: Art within the Limits of History and Ethics* (Baltimore: Johns Hopkins University Press, 2000).

7. Annette Insdorf, *Indelible Shadows: Film and the Holocaust* (New York: Vintage, 1983), 3, 21; Ilan Avisar, *Screening the Holocaust: Cinema's Images of the Unimaginable* (Bloomington: Indiana University Press, 1988), 129.

8. Tim Cole, *Selling the Holocaust: From Auschwitz to Schindler: How History Is Bought, Packaged and Sold* (New York: Routledge, 1999), 76–77; Trudy Gold, "An Overview of Hollywood Cinema's Treatment of the Holocaust," in *Holocaust and the Moving Image: Representations in Film and Television since 1933*, ed. Toby Haggith and Joanna Newman (London: Wallflower, 2005), 197.

9. Lawrence L. Langer, *Using and Abusing the Holocaust* (Bloomington: Indiana University Press, 2006), xii.

10. For an inventory of *Eternal Light* broadcasts, see Eli Segal, *The Eternal Light: An Unauthorized Guide* (Newtown, Conn.: Yesteryear, 2005).

11. For a discussion of these dramas, see Shandler, *While America Watches*, chap. 3.

12. For a discussion of these telecasts, see ibid., 28–40.

13. See Hasia Diner, *Fitting Memorials: American Jews Confront the Holocaust, 1945–1962* (New York: New York University Press, 2008).

14. Michael Kammen, *Mystic Chords of Memory: The Transformation of Tradition in American Culture* (New York: Knopf, 1991), 13.

15. See, e.g., Beatrice S. Weinreich, "The Americanization of Passover," in *Studies in Biblical and Jewish Folklore,* ed. Raphael Patai, Francis Lee Utley, and Dov Noy (Bloomington: Indiana University Press, 1960), 354–355.

16. "Televizye un radyo" [Television and radio], *Jewish Daily Forward,* 19 April 1959, 10.

17. Jose., "The Final Ingredient," *Variety,* 22 April 1959, 50.

18. John C. Lyden, *Film as Religion: Myths, Morals, and Rituals* (New York: New York University Press, 2003), 12; Nathaniel Dorsky, *Devotional Cinema* (Berkeley: Tuumba, 2003), 16.

19. I discuss this dynamic with regard to the televised version of *Judgment at Nuremberg* in *While America Watches,* 69–79.

20. United Artists Pressbook, *Judgment at Nuremberg* [1961?], 2; Alan Mintz, *Popular Culture and the Shaping of Holocaust Memory in America* (Seattle: University of Washington Press, 2001), 92–93.

21. United Artists Pressbook, *Judgment at Nuremberg,* 5.

22. On the German premiere of *Schindler's List,* see Liliane Weissberg, "The Tale of a Good German: Reflection on the German Reception of *Schindler's List,*" in *Spielberg's Holocaust: Critical Perspectives on "Schindler's List,"* ed. Yosefa Loshitzky (Bloomington: Indiana University Press, 1997), 171–192.

23. This episode of *Seinfeld,* titled "The Raincoats," first aired 28 April 1994.

24. Mintz, *Popular Culture and the Shaping of Holocaust Memory in America,* 103.

25. "Watching Holocaust," *Moment,* April 1978, 34.

26. Martin Bernard, "NBC's Holocaust: The Trivialization of the Tragic," *Journal of Reform Judaism* 25, no. 3 (1978): 43–46.

27. James W. Carey, *Communication as Culture: Essays on Media and Society* (Boston: Unwin Hyman, 1988), 20–21.

28. See, e.g., Marcia Sachs Littell and Sharon Weissman Gutman, eds., *Liturgies on the Holocaust: An Interfaith Anthology,* rev. ed. (Valley Forge, Pa.: Trinity, 1996), which includes the text cited in the epigraph of this chapter.

29. On Holocaust memorial programs, see Lucia Meta Ruedenberg, "'Remember 6,000,000': Civic Commemoration of the Holocaust among Jewish Survivors in New York City" (Ph.D. diss., New York University, 1994).

30. *The Papal Concert to Commemorate the Holocaust* [videotape] (Los Angeles: Rhino Home Video, 1994) (R3 2180).

31. Daniel Dayan and Elihu Katz, *Media Events: The Live Broadcasting of History* (Cambridge, Mass.: Harvard University Press, 1995), 207–208.

32. Alan E. Steinweis, "Reflections on the Holocaust from Nebraska," in *The Americanization of the Holocaust,* ed. Hilene Flanzbaum (Baltimore: Johns Hopkins University Press, 1999), 172.

33. David Axelrod, *Requiem: The Holocaust* [sound recording booklet] (Liberty Records, 1993) (CDP-7-81258-2).

34. According to Rela Mintz Geffen, "The Shoah was a part of Tisha B'av as early as 1962 and 1963 in Camp Ramah in the Poconos. *Night and Fog* was already shown then." Email message to author, 13 March 2007.

35. Eric A. Goldman, "Film as Haggadah for the Holocaust," *Shoah* 4, nos. 1–2 (fall/winter 1983–84): 4.

36. Gunther Anders, "The Phantom World of TV," in *Mass Culture: The Popular Arts in America*, ed. Bernard Rosenberg and David Manning White (Glencoe, Ill.: Free Press, 1957), 360, 361.

37. Gerard Engel, "Campus Reactions to Eichmann," *Congress Bi-Weekly* 28, no. 11 (29 May 1961): 7.

38. Ibid., 7, 8.

39. Murray N. Rothbard, "Those Awards," in *Irrepressible Rothbard: The Rothbard-Rockwell Report Essays of Murray N. Rothbard* (Auburn, Ala.: Ludwig von Mises Institute, 1994), available online at www.lewrockwell.com/rothbard/rothbard112.html (accessed 4 March 2007).

40. Anita Meria, "Meet: Steven Spielberg—Calling the Shots," *NEA Today*, Nov. 1994, available online at www.findarticles.com/p/articles/mi_qa3617/is_199411/ai_n8723353/pg_1 (accessed 4 March 2007).

41. Quoted in Dotson Rader, "We Can't Just Sit Back and Hope," *Parade*, 27 March 1994, 7.

42. Institute for First Amendment Studies, "Religious Right Responds to 'Schindler's List,'" *Freedom Writer*, June 1994, available online at www.publiceye.org/ifas/fw/9406/schindler.html (accessed 4 March 2007).

43. Amy E. Schwartz, "Laughter in the Movie House," *Washington Post*, 16 March 1994, A19.

44. See Robert H. Abzug, *Inside the Vicious Heart: Americans and the Liberation of Nazi Concentration Camps* (New York: Oxford University Press, 1985); Telford Taylor, *The Anatomy of the Nuremberg Trials* (New York: Knopf, 1992).

45. Arthur A. Cohen, *The Tremendum: A Theological Interpretation of the Holocaust* (New York: Crossroad, 1981), 2–3.

46. New Jersey Commission on Holocaust Education, State of New Jersey Department of Education, "Mandate," www.state.nj.us/njded/holocaust/about_us/mandate.html (accessed 5 March 2007).

47. Facing History and Ourselves, "History and Mission," www.facinghistory.org/campus/reslib.nsf/sub/aboutus/historymission (accessed 25 Feb. 2007).

48. Peter Novick, *The Holocaust in American Life* (Boston: Houghton Mifflin, 1999), 261.

49. Yehuda Bauer, *Rethinking the Holocaust* (New Haven, Conn.: Yale Nota Bene, 2002), 188.

50. Novick, *The Holocaust in American Life*, 261.

51. Edward T. Linenthal, *Preserving Memory: The Struggle to Create America's Holocaust Museum* (New York: Viking, 1995), 52.

52. "Holocaust Museum Has Too Many Visitors," *New York Times*, 19 Nov. 1993, C3.

53. For further discussion of the MJH, see Jeffrey Shandler, "Heritage and Holocaust on Display: New York City's Museum of Jewish Heritage—A Living Memorial to the Holocaust," *Public Historian* 22, no. 1 (winter 1999): 73–86. See also Shandler, *While America Watches*, 229–239.

54. Barbara Kirshenblatt-Gimblett, *Destination Culture: Tourism, Museums, and Heritage* (Berkeley: University of California Press, 1998), 138.

55. Museum of Tolerance, "The Tolerancenter," www.museumoftolerance. com/site/c.juLVJ8MRKtH/b.1342591/k.A176/ToleranCenter.htm (accessed 20 April 2007).

56. Kirshenblatt-Gimblett, *Destination Culture*, 51.

57. United States Holocaust Memorial Museum, "Responding Today to Threats of Genocide: Analysis," www.ushmm.org/conscience/analysis/index. php?content=details.php%3Fcontent%3D2006-11-20%26menupage%3DSudan (accessed 16 Nov. 2006).

58. See Henry Greenspan, *On Listening to Holocaust Survivors: Recounting and Life History* (Westport, Conn.: Praeger, 1998); Oren Baruch Stier, "Framing the Witness: The Memorial Role of Holocaust Videotestimonies," in *Remembering for the Future: The Holocaust in an Age of Genocide*, vol. 3, ed. John K. Roth and Elisabeth Maxwell (Basingstoke, U.K.: Palgrave, 2001), 189–204.

59. Fortunoff Video Archive for Holocaust Testimonies, "About the Archive: Our Concept," www.library.yale.edu/testimonies/about/concepts.html (accessed 5 March 2007).

60. USC Shoah Foundation Institute, "Cataloguing and Indexing," http://college.usc.edu/vhi/cataloguingindexing/php (accessed 25 August 2008); "Indexing Guidelines" [report], USC Shoah Foundation Institute, 2006, 3.

61. See Toby Blum-Dobkin, "Videotaping Holocaust Interviews: Questions and Answers from an Interviewer," *Jewish Folklore and Ethnology Review* 16, no. 1 (1994): 46–50; Shandler, "Heritage and Holocaust on Display," 73–86.

62. "Survivors," *ABC News Nightline: Columbine High School*, 29 March 2000 (VHS no. N000329-01).

63. Shoah Foundation, *Giving Voice: Today's Kids Get Real about Bias* [DVDs and guidebook] (Princeton, N.J.: Films for the Humanities and Sciences, 2004).

64. Ibid.

65. "School's 'Holocaust' Experiment Upsets Parents; Dad: Son Cried over Becoming Jew for Day," WKMG TV 6 Central Florida, 29 March 2006, available online at www.local6.com/news/8345157/detail.html (accessed 27 April 2007).

66. Paula E. Hyman, "New Debate on the Holocaust," *New York Times Magazine*, 14 Sept. 1980, 67, 78.

67. Simone A. Schweber, "Simulating Survival," *Curriculum Inquiry* 33, no. 2 (2003): 140.

68. United States Holocaust Memorial Museum, "Identification Cards," www.ushmm.org/education/foreducators/resource/idcards.pdf (accessed 2 June 2008).

69. United States Holocaust Memorial Museum, "Activities and Resources for Use Following a Visit to the Permanent Exhibition," www.ushmm.org/visit/groups/information/following/ (accessed 2 June 2008).

70. Michael Taussig, *Mimesis and Alterity: A Particular History of the Senses* (New York: Routledge, 1993), 13.

71. Todd Strasser, *The Wave* (New York: Dell Laurel-Leaf, 1981).

72. Jack Kugelmass, "Why We Go to Poland: Holocaust Tourism as Secular Ritual," in *The Art of Memory: Holocaust Memorials*, ed. James E. Young (New York: Jewish Museum/Munich: Prestel, 1994), 175.

73. Ibid., 179.

74. Dean MacCannell, *The Tourist: A New Theory of the Leisure Class* (New York: Schocken Books, 1976), 7, 110.

75. March of the Living, "Mission," www.motl.org/mission.htm (accessed 21 March 2007).

76. March of the Living, "Programs: High School March," www.motl.org/programs/highSchool.htm (accessed 21 March 2007).

77. Ibid.

78. A. Hirchson, "Why Poland?" in *To Know and to Remember* (New York, n.d.), as cited in Rona Sheramy, "From Auschwitz to Jerusalem: Re-enacting Jewish History on the March of the Living," *Polin: Studies in Polish Jewry* 19 (2006): 308.

79. Gary Weintraub, "March of the Living: The Only Choice," March of the Living website, www.motl.org/alumni/alumni-mol-only-choice-weintraub.htm (accessed 4 April 2007).

80. Sheramy, "From Auschwitz to Jerusalem," 313.

81. Jonathan S. Woocher, *Sacred Survival: The Civil Religion of American Jews* (Bloomington: Indiana University Press, 1986), 51.

82. March of the Living, "Mission."

83. Commune di Arezzo, Assessorato alla Cultura, "*La Vita è Bella/Life Is Beautiful* di Roberto Benigni: Un itinerario guidato tra i luoghi cittadini, set del film/A guided tour through the places in town, where 'Life is beautiful' was filmed" [leaflet], acquired by author in 2004.

84. abc.KRAKÓW tour company, quoted on Modiya website, "Schindler's List Tours and Travel Diaries," http://modiya.nyu.edu/modiya/handle/1964/188 (accessed 27 April 2007).

85. Jagiellonian University, Summer Program's Schindler's List Tour, American Institute for Foreign Study, 2003, quoted on Modiya website, "Schindler's List Tours and Travel Diaries."

86. Franciszek Palowski, "Śladami 'Listy Schindlera'/Retracing 'Schindler's List'/Auf den Spuren von 'Schindlers Liste'" [brochure] (Cracow: Argona-Jordan Art, 1994), front cover.

87. See Ruth Ellen Gruber, *Virtually Jewish: Reinventing Jewish Culture in Europe* (Berkeley: University of California Press, 2002), 127–129.

88. Maurice Halbwachs, *On Collective Memory*, ed. Lewis A. Coser (Chicago: University of Chicago Press, 1992), 199.

89. On television coverage of the Bitburg controversy, see Shandler, *While America Watches*, 205–209.

90. "Remarks of Elie Wiesel at Ceremony for Jewish Heritage Week and Presentation of Congressional Gold Medal, White House, April 19, 1985," in *Bitburg in Moral and Political Perspective*, ed. Geoffrey H. Hartman (Bloomington: Indiana University Press, 1986), 241, 243.

91. Quoted in Edward Wyatt, "Next Book for Oprah Is 'Night' by Wiesel," *New York Times*, 17 Jan. 2006, E8.

92. Joshua Cohen, "Six Million Little Pieces?" *Forward*, 20 Jan. 2006, 1.

93. See Edward Wyatt, "The Translation of Wiesel's 'Night' Is New, but Old Questions Are Raised," *New York Times*, 19 Jan. 2006, E1, E7.

94. All citations from *The Oprah Winfrey Show*, 25 May 2006, Harpo Productions, transcription prepared by Burrelle's Information Services.

95. Elie Wiesel, *Night* (New York: Bantam, 1982 [1960]), 32.

96. Lee Siegel, "Thank You for Sharing," *New Republic*, 5 and 12 June 2006, 23.

97. James E. Young, *The Texture of Memory: Holocaust Memorials and Meaning* (New Haven, Conn.: Yale University Press, 1993), 4.

98. Fortunoff Video Archive for Holocaust Testimonials, "About the Archive: Our Concept."

99. Susan Stewart, *On Longing: Narratives of the Miniature, the Gigantic, the Souvenir, the Collection* (Durham, N.C.: Duke University Press, 1993), 70–71.

100. Marianne Hirsch, *Family Frames: Photography, Narrative, and Postmemory* (Cambridge, Mass.: Harvard University Press, 1997), 252, 254.

101. Stewart, *On Longing*, 89.

102. Quoted in Peter W. Schroeder and Dagmar Schroeder-Hildebrand, *Six Million Paper Clips: The Making of a Children's Holocaust Memorial* (Minneapolis, Minn.: Kar-Ben, 2004), 8–9.

103. Ibid., 12–14.

104. Ibid., 15–16.

105. Peter W. Schroeder and Dagmar Schroeder-Hildebrand, *Das Büroklammer-Projekt* (Munich: Elefanten Press Bei Bertelsmann, 2000).

106. Dita Smith, "A Measure of Hope," *Washington Post*, 7 April 2001, C1, C4.

107. Schroeder and Schroeder-Hildebrand, *Six Million Paper Clips*, 24.

108. Ibid., 26.

109. Ibid., 47.

110. Pavel Friedmann, "The Butterfly," in *I Never Saw Another Butterfly: Children's Drawings and Poems from Terezin Concentration Camp, 1942–1944* (New York: McGraw-Hill, 1964), 33.

111. Children's Holocaust Memorial and Paper Clip Project at Whitwell Middle School, www.whitwellmiddleschool.org/homepage_pc.cfm?id=78 (accessed 25 August 2008).

112. Schroeder and Schroeder-Hildebrand, *Six Million Paper Clips*, 7, 57.

113. Ibid., 51.

114. See, e.g., Novick, *The Holocaust in American Life*, 214–220.

115. Schroeder and Schroeder-Hildebrand, *Six Million Paper Clips*, 13.

116. Children's Holocaust Memorial, "The Beginning," www.whitwellmiddle-school.org/body_pc.cfm?id=85&0TopID=85 (accessed 25 August 2008).

117. Schroeder and Schroeder-Hildebrand, *Six Million Paper Clips*, 55.

118. Anti-Defamation League, "Paper Clips and ADL," www.adl.org/paper-clips/ (accessed 4 April 2007).

119. Robert Bellah, "Civil Religion in America," *Daedalus* 96 (winter 1967): 1–21.

120. Novick, *The Holocaust in American Life*, 15.

121. Hirsch, *Family Frames*, 22.

NOTES TO CHAPTER 4

1. Ivan G. Marcus, *The Jewish Life Cycle: Rites of Passage from Biblical to Modern Times* (Seattle: University of Washington Press, 2004), 10.

2. On Hollekreisch, see ibid., 64–65; Herman Pollack, *Jewish Folkways in Germanic Lands (1648–1806): Studies in Aspects of Daily Life* (Cambridge, Mass.: MIT Press, 1971), 27–28; Max Weinreich, *History of the Yiddish Language*, trans. Shlomo Noble (Chicago: University of Chicago Press, 1980), 197, 198.

3. Michael Renov, *The Subject of Documentary* (Minneapolis: University of Minnesota Press, 2004), 218.

4. Barbara Levine and Stephanie Snyder, *Snapshot Chronicles: Inventing the American Photo Album* (New York: Princeton Architectural Press/Portland, Ore.: Douglas F. Cooley Memorial Art Gallery, Reed College, 2006), 19.

5. Jonathan Z. Smith, *To Take Place: Toward Theory in Ritual* (Chicago: University of Chicago Press, 1987), 103; Ronald L. Grimes, *Rite Out of Place: Ritual, Media, and the Arts* (New York: Oxford University Press, 2006).

6. Barbara Myerhoff, "Rites of Passage: Process and Paradox," in *Celebration: Studies in Festivity and Ritual*, ed. Victor Turner (Washington, D.C.: Smithsonian Institution Press, 1982), 115; Clifford Geertz, *The Interpretation of Cultures: Selected Essays* (New York: Basic Books, 1973), 112.

7. Eric W. Rothenbuhler, *Ritual Communication: From Everyday Conversation to Mediated Ceremony* (Thousand Oaks, Calif.: Sage, 1998), 53.

8. Catherine Bell, *Ritual Theory, Ritual Practice* (New York: Oxford University Press, 1992).

9. Richard Chalfen, *Snapshot Versions of Life* (Bowling Green, Ohio: Bowling Green State University Popular Press, 1987), 10, 8.

10. James M. Moran, *There's No Place Like Home Video* (Minneapolis: University of Minnesota Press, 2003), 49–52; Chalfen, *Snapshot Versions of Life*, 99.

11. Peter Schweitzer, email message to author, 17 Jan. 2005.

12. Moran, *There's No Place Like Home Video*, xxi, 42.

13. Jean Rouch, *Ciné-Ethnography*, ed. and trans. Steven Feld (Minneapolis: University of Minnesota Press, 2003), 43–45.

14. Barbara Myerhoff, *Number Our Days* (New York: Touchstone, 1978), 144.

15. Daniel L. Schachter, *Searching for Memory: The Brain, the Mind, and the Past* (New York: Basic Books, 1996), 40–41.

16. Susan Sontag, *On Photography* (New York: Doubleday, 1989 [1977]), 15.

17. John Berger and Jean Mohr, *Another Way of Telling* (New York: Pantheon, 1982), 86–87.

18. Marianne Hirsch, *Family Frames: Photography, Narrative, and Postmemory* (Cambridge, Mass.: Harvard University Press, 1997), 22.

19. Chalfen, *Snapshot Versions of Life*, 138.

20. Ibid., 75–76.

21. Heather Norris Nicholson, "Seeing How It Was? Childhood Geographies and Memories in Home Movies," *Area* 33, no. 2 (2001): 129, 132, 137.

22. Marcus, *The Jewish Life Cycle*, 43; Hayyim Schauss, *The Lifetime of a Jew throughout the Ages of Jewish History* (New York: Union of American Hebrew Congregations, 1950), 14.

23. Daniel Boyarin and Jonathan Boyarin, "Self-Exposure as Theory: The Double-Mark of the Male Jew," in *Rhetorics of Self-Making*, ed. D. Battaglia (Berkeley: University of California Press, 1995), 16–42.

24. Moran, *There's No Place Like Home Video*, 41, 42.

25. I attended Eli Berliner's *bris*, which took place in New York City on 15 April 2004.

26. Efrén Cuevas and Carlos Muguiro, eds., *El Hombre sin la Cámara: El Cine de Alan Berliner/The Man without the Movie Camera: The Cinema of Alan Berliner* (Madrid: Ediciones Internacionales Universitarias, 2002), 128–129.

27. Renov, *The Subject of Documentary*, 219.

28. Alan Berliner, telephone conversation with author, 18 Sept. 2006.

29. Barbara Kirshenblatt-Gimblett, "The Cut That Binds: The Ashkenazic Torah Binder as Nexus between Circumcision and Torah," in *Celebration*, 136–146.

30. Vincent Crapanzano, "Rite of Return: Circumcision in Morocco," *Psychoanalytic Study of Society* 9 (1981): 33.

31. Jonathan Boyarin, email message to author, 1 Oct. 2003.

32. Nicholson, "Seeing How It Was?" 137.

33. On the history of bat mitzvah, see Paula E. Hyman, "The Introduction of

Bat Mitzvah in Conservative Judaism in Postwar America," *YIVO Annual of Jewish Social Science* 19 (1990): 133–146.

34. See, e.g., Jenna Weissman Joselit, *The Wonders of America: Reinventing Jewish Culture, 1880–1950* (New York: Hill and Wang, 1994), 95.

35. "CCAR Responsa: Contemporary American Reform Responsa 134: Taping in the Synagogue" (Nov. 1986), available online at http://data.ccarnet.org/cgi-bin/respdisp.pl?file=134&year=carr (accessed 22 Sept. 2006).

36. David H. Lincoln, "Videotaping on Shabbat," OH 340:3.1982a, 239, available online at www.rabbinicalassembly.org/teshuvot/docs/20012004/43.pdf (accessed 10 Sept. 2007).

37. Richard Hirsh, email message to author, 25 Sept. 2006.

38. Lincoln, "Videotaping on Shabbat," 241.

39. "CCAR Responsa: Contemporary American Reform Responsa 134."

40. Arnold Goodman, "May a Shabbat Service Be Taped?" OH 340:3.1989b, 302–303, available online at www.rabbinicalassembly.org/teshuvot/docs/19861990/goodman_taped.pdf (accessed 10 Sept. 2007).

41. Elliot Dorff and Gordon Tucker, "On Recording Shabbat and Yom Tov Services," OH 340:3.1989c, 308, available online at www.rabbinicalassembly.org/teshuvot/docs/19861990/dorfftucker_recording.pdf (accessed 10 Sept. 2007).

42. Mayer Rabinowitz and Dvora Weisberg, "Tape Recording and Photography on Shabbat," OH 340:3.1984, 249, available online at www.rabbinicalassembly.org/teshuvot/docs/20012004/45.pdf (accessed 10 Sept. 2007).

43. Jacob Agus, "Recording a Service on Shabbat," CJLS minority opinion, 1956, 1, as cited in Goodman, "May a Shabbat Service Be Taped?" 300.

44. Goodman, "May a Shabbat Service Be Taped?" 303.

45. Rabinowitz and Weisberg, "Tape Recording and Photography on Shabbat," 249.

46. Goodman, "May a Shabbat Service Be Taped?" 303.

47. Crapanzano, "Rite of Return," 32–34.

48. Mordechai Richler, *The Apprenticeship of Dudie Kravitz* (Boston: Little, Brown, 1959), 174–184.

49. Roger Bennett, Jules Shell, and Nick Kroll, *Bar Mitzvah Disco: The Music May Have Stopped, but the Party's Never Over* (New York: Crown, 2005), 59.

50. On rabbinic critique of lavish bar mitzvah celebrations, see, e.g., Jonathan Sarna, trans. and ed., *People Walk on Their Heads: Moses Weinberger's Jews and Judaism in New York* (New York: Holmes and Meier, 1982), 52, 76.

51. Bennett, Shell, and Kroll, *Bar Mitzvah Disco*, 9–10.

52. Bar Mitzvah Disco website, www.barmitzvahdisco.com (accessed 29 Jan. 2007).

53. Bar Mitzvah Disco, "Throw Your Own BMD Party!" www.barmitzvahdisco.com/party.php (accessed 29 Jan. 2007).

54. Rabinowitz and Weisberg, "Tape Recording and Photography on Shabbat," 243.

55. Marcus, *The Jewish Life Cycle*, 180.

56. Dushoff family footage, Archives of the YIVO Institute for Jewish Research, Film Collection, no. 111.

57. Gabriel Solomon Photography, "Weddings—Priceless Memories Captured Forever," www.gabrielsolomon.com/weddings.html (accessed 1 Nov. 2006).

58. Patricia R. Zimmerman, *Reel Families: A Social History of Amateur Film* (Bloomington: Indiana University Press, 1995).

59. Simchavision, "Services," www.simchavision.com/services.shtml (accessed 1 Nov. 2006).

60. Ibid.

61. Moran, *There's No Place Like Home Video*, 80.

62. Simchavision, "Services."

63. Jerry Meyer Studio, "Photojournalism," www.jerrymeyerstudio.com/photojournalism.html (accessed 1 Nov. 2006).

64. Notowitz Productions, "Our Unique Service and Style," www.notowitz.com/EventVideos/ServiceAndStyle.html (accessed 3 Nov. 2007).

65. Notowitz Productions, "Your Questions about Creating the Perfect Video Memory," www.notowitz.com/EventVideos/YourQuestions.html (accessed 3 Nov. 2007).

66. Melissa Shiff, *Promena Rituálu/Reframing Ritual* (Prague: Jewish Museum in Prague, 2006), 8, 24.

67. Emmanuelle Héran, *Le Dernier Portrait* (Paris: Musée d'Orsay, 2002); Geoffrey Batchen, *Forget Me Not: Photography and Remembrance* (Amsterdam: Van Gogh Museum/New York: Princeton Architectural Press, 2004); Clément Chéroux et al., *The Perfect Medium: Photography and the Occult* (New Haven, Conn.: Yale University Press, 2004).

68. Chalfen, *Snapshot Versions of Life*, 91.

69. Michelle Citron, *Home Movies and Other Necessary Fictions* (Minneapolis: University of Minnesota Press, 1999), 7.

70. Ellen Kellman, "Sholem Aleichem's Funeral (New York, 1916): The Making of a National Pageant," *YIVO Annual* 20 (1991): 277–304.

71. See, e.g., Jack Kugelmass and Jeffrey Shandler, "Going Home: How American Jews Invent the Old World" [exhibition brochure] (New York: YIVO Institute, 1989), 12.

72. Alden Films, "Jewish Death and Dying," www.aldenfilms.com/death.html (accessed 22 Oct. 2006).

73. Behrman House Publishers, book webpage, http://behrman.powerwebbook.com/productdetails.cfm?sku=704 (accessed 22 Oct. 2006).

74. Jewish Funeral Directors of America, "Publications," www.jfda.org/publications.html (accessed 22 Oct. 2006).

75. Carol Abadi, "Performing the Tahara," *Jewish Magazine* 105 (Aug. 2006), available online at www.jewishmag.com/105mag/tahara/tahara.htm (accessed 22 Oct. 2006).

76. "Ask Wendy: Video Greetings at Gravesite?" *Jewish World Review*, 9 Oct. 2003, available online at www.jewishworldreview.com/1003/wendy.html (accessed 25 August 2008).

77. Katy Stech, "Experts Say Webcasting of Services Will Keep Growing in Popularity," *Newsday*, 22 June 2006, available online at www.kitsapsun.com/bsun/bu_business/article/0,2403,BSUN_19060_4793172,00.html (accessed 22 Oct. 2006).

78. Marcelle S. Fischler, "Funeral Home Webcast Allows Out-of-Town Mourners to Pay Respects," *New York Times,* 8 Oct. 2006, sec. 14, p. 6.

79. Grimes, *Rite Out of Place*, 31.

80. Stech, "Experts Say Webcasting of Services Will Keep Growing in Popularity."

81. Fischler, "Funeral Home Webcast Allows Out-of-Town Mourners to Pay Respects."

82. Ibid.

83. Charles Lyons, "Dream Undertaken: Cemetery Sees Future in Vid Biopics," *Daily Variety*, 9 Nov. 1999, 64.

84. Forever Network, "About LifeStories," www.forevernetwork.com/lifestories/about.cfm (accessed 25 Oct. 2006).

85. Beth Olam of St. Louis, "Beth Olam St. Louis," www.betholam.com/St.%20Louis.htm (accessed 25 Oct. 2006).

86. Jill Kramer, "Green Burials," *Pacific Sun* (San Rafael, Calif.), 15 Dec. 2004, available online at www.pacificsun.com/story_archives/greenburial.html (accessed 25 Oct. 2006).

87. Ibid.

88. John Cloud, "Meeting Your (Film)Maker," *Time*, 10 July 2000, 66.

89. Beth Olam of St. Louis, "Beth Olam St. Louis."

90. Israel Abrahams, *Hebrew Ethical Wills* (Philadelphia: Jewish Publication Society, 1926), xxiii.

91. Kramer, "Green Burials." Elsewhere in this feature, Tyler Cassity characterizes Jewish burial practices as exemplary of "green" practices: using plain pine boxes, avoiding embalming or cosmetics on the corpse, and inviting the family to cover the grave with soil.

92. Moran, *There's No Place Like Home Video*, 93–95.

93. Roy Rappaport, "Ritual Sanctity and Cybernetics," *American Anthropologist* 73, no. 1 (1971): 72–73.

94. Daniel Dayan and Elihu Katz, *Media Events: The Live Broadcasting of History* (Cambridge, Mass.: Harvard University Press, 1995).

95. Myerhoff, *Number Our Days*, 32.

96. See, e.g., Chava Weissler, *Voices of the Matriarchs: Listening to the Prayers of Early Modern Jewish Women* (Boston: Beacon, 1998), which examines one example of popular religion that flourished following the advent of printed books among Ashkenazi Jews: Yiddish *tkhines*, or supplicatory prayers, composed largely for and sometimes by women.

97. Bruce Kapferer, "Introduction: Ritual Process and the Transformation of Context," *Social Analysis: Journal of Cultural and Social Practice* 1 (Feb. 1979): 6.

NOTES TO CHAPTER 5

1. "Oy Vay, Another Holiday!" [greeting card], design by Jim Lienhart, photography by David Jordano, copy and concept by Joe Murphy (Chicago: California Dreamers, 1984).

2. Joshua Eli Plaut, "Silent Night: Being Jewish at Christmas-time in America; Proclaiming Identity in the Face of Seasonal Marginality" (Ph.D. diss., New York University, 2004).

3. See Marc B. Shapiro, "Torah Study on Christmas Eve," *Journal of Jewish Thought and Philosophy* 8, no. 2 (1999): 319–353.

4. Jonathan Sarna, "Is Judaism Compatible with American Civil Religion? The Problem of Christmas and the 'National Faith,'" in *Religion and the Life of the Nation*, ed. Rowland A. Sherrill (Urbana: University of Illinois Press, 1990), 153.

5. Leigh Schmidt, *Consumer Rites: The Buying and Selling of American Holidays* (Princeton, N.J.: Princeton University Press, 1995), 32.

6. Stephen Nissenbaum, *The Battle for Christmas* (New York: Vintage, 1997), 195–196, 64.

7. "Spread of the Christian Religion," *Puck* 4, no. 94 (1878–79): 7.

8. C.P., "The Spirit of Christmas in New York," *Life*, 21 Dec. 1911, 1124; Walter G. Doty, "Keeping Up Old Customs," *Life*, 21 Dec. 1911, 1124.

9. Amos Alon, *The Pity of It All: A History of Jews in Germany, 1743–1933* (New York: Metropolitan, 2002), 231.

10. Jonathan Sarna, *American Judaism: A History* (New Haven, Conn.: Yale University Press, 2004), 136.

11. Barbara Kirshenblatt-Gimblett, "The Moral Sublime: Jewish Women and Philanthropy in Nineteenth-Century America," in *Writing a Modern Jewish History: Essays in Honor of Salo W. Baron*, ed. Barbara Kirshenblatt-Gimblett (New York: Jewish Museum/New Haven, Conn.: Yale University Press, 2006), 44.

12. For examples of accounts of East European Jews celebrating Christmas, see, e.g., Salcia Landmann, *Erinnerungen an Galizien*, 2nd ed. (Wiesbaden: Limes

Verlag, 1983 [1975]), 67–70; "G.S.," in *Awakening Lives: Autobiographies of Jewish Youth in Poland before the Holocaust*, ed. Jeffrey Shandler (New Haven, Conn.: Yale University Press, 2002), 265.

13. Marvin Herzog et al., eds., *Language and Culture Atlas of Ashkenazic Jewry, Volume III: The Eastern Yiddish-Western Yiddish Continuum* (Tübingen: Max Niemeyer, 2000), 294–297 (maps 118, 118S).

14. Ignats Bernshteyn, *Yidishe shprikhverter* [Yiddish proverbs] (Warsaw: Universal, 1912), 179; Nahum Stutchkoff, *Oytser fun der yidisher shprakh* [Thesaurus of the Yiddish language] (New York: YIVO, 1950), 729.

15. These were responses to a questionnaire published in *Literarishe bleter*, RG 223, part II, folder 165, YIVO Archives.

16. Ibid.

17. On *Toledoth Yeshu*, see Morris Goldstein, *Jesus in the Jewish Tradition* (New York: Macmillan, 1950), 147–166.

18. Mani-Leyb, "Nitl" [Christmas], in *Lider un baladn* [Songs and ballads], vol. 1 (New York: Congress for Jewish Culture, 1955), 327.

19. Tony Michels, *A Fire in Their Hearts: Yiddish Socialists in New York* (Cambridge, Mass.: Harvard University Press, 2005), 69, 93.

20. [A.] Lyesin, "Santa Klooz" [Santa Claus], *Jewish Daily Forward*, 25 Dec. 1897, 1.

21. "Santa Klauz, der malekh hamoves" [Santa Claus, the Angel of Death], *Jewish Daily Forward*, 26 Dec. 1901, 1; A.F., "Krismas gedanken" [Christmas thoughts], *Jewish Daily Forward*, 25 Dec. 1901, 7.

22. A. Ginzburg, "Kurtse bamerkungen" [Brief remarks], *Jewish Daily Forward*, 27 Dec. 1941, 4.

23. "Krismes—elter far Yesusen" [Christmas—older than Jesus], *Jewish Daily Forward*, 24 Dec. 1904, 4; "Vi kristmes iz geshmadt gevorn af a kristlikhn yontef" [How Christmas was converted into a Christian holiday], *Jewish Daily Forward*, 26 Dec. 1910, 4.

24. "Kristmes presents" [Christmas presents], *Jewish Daily Forward*, 24 Dec. 1910, 6. The article refers to a passage in Maimonides, *Guide to the Perplexed*, part 3, chapter 32.

25. "Frum zaynen zey, nor fun krismes halten zay oykh" [They're pious (Jews), but they also celebrate Christmas], *Jewish Daily Forward*, 25 Dec. 1904, 4.

26. "Der kristmes-yarid af di yidishe gasn fun Nyu-york" [The Christmas fair in New York's Jewish neighborhood], *Jewish Daily Forward*, 25 Dec. 1922, 5.

27. Morris Rosenfeld, "Erev kristmas" [Christmas Eve], *Jewish Daily Forward*, 14 Dec. 1910, 4.

28. Ab. Cahan, "Vi yidn filn zikh in der vokh fun krismes" [How Jews feel during Christmas week], *Jewish Daily Forward*, 27 Dec. 1941, 4.

29. Isaac Metzker, ed., *A Bintel Brief: Sixty Years of Letters from the Lower East Side to the Jewish Daily Forward*, vol. 1 (New York: Behrman House, 1971), 169.

30. A plot summary of *The Jew's Christmas* appears in *Moving Picture World*, December 1913, 1334; Anne Nichols, *Abie's Irish Rose: A Comedy in Three Acts* (New York: Samuel French, 1937 [1924]).

31. Emil G. Hirsch, "How the Jew Regards Christmas," *Ladies Home Journal*, Dec. 1906, 10.

32. Louis Witt, "The Jew Celebrates Christmas," *Christian Century*, 6 Dec. 1939, 1497–1499.

33. "Florida tandzsherins!" [Florida tangerines!] [advertisement], *Jewish Daily Forward*, 13 Dec. 1949, 6; "Resipis" [Recipes], *Jewish Daily Forward*, 24 Dec. 1949, 3.

34. Marie Badasch, "A Yiddish Christmas," *Jewish Daily Forward*, 28 Dec. 1924, English Section, 3.

35. Milt Gross, *De Night in de Front from Chreesmas* (New York: George H. Doran, 1927), 39.

36. Marie B. Jaffe, "Erev Krismes" [Christmas Eve], in *Gut Yuntif, Gut Yohr: A Collection in Yiddish of Original Holiday Verses and Popular English Classics in Translation* (New York: Citadel, 1991 [1965]), 12, 15.

37. "Twas the Night Before Chanukah," bangitout.com, www.bangitout.com/articles/viewarticle.php?a=1048 (accessed 8 Aug. 2007). See also Martin Gardner, ed., *The Annotated Night Before Christmas: A Collection of Sequels, Parodies, and Imitations of Clement Moore's Immortal Ballad about Santa Claus* (Amherst, N.Y.: Prometheus Books, 2005), 185–188.

38. Jeffrey Shandler, *Adventures in Yiddishland: Postvernacular Language and Culture* (Berkeley: University of California Press, 2005), 121.

39. Simon Dentith, *Parody* (London: Routledge, 2000), 9.

40. See, e.g., "Santa Kloz hot gekhalesht" [Santa Claus fainted], a children's story that is both antireligious and anticapitalist, in Betsalel Fridman, *Arbeter shul* [Workers' school] (New York: Internatsyonaler arbeter-ordn, 1934), 112.

41. S. J. Perelman, "Waiting for Santy: A Christmas Playlet," *Strictly from Hunger* (New York: Random House, 1937), 191–197.

42. Dentith, *Parody*, 33, 96.

43. Allan Sherman, *My Son, the Folksinger* [sound recording] (Warner Bros. WS1475, 1962), album cover.

44. "God Bless You, Jerry Mendelbaum" is sung in a medley called "Shticks and Stones" on *My Son, the Folksinger*; "The Twelve Gifts of Christmas" was first released as a single (Warner Bros. 5406, 1963), side A; it later appeared on Allan Sherman, *For Swingin' Livers Only!* [sound recording] (Warner Bros. WS 1569, 1964).

45. Jenna Weissman Joselit, *The Wonders of America: Reinventing Jewish Culture, 1880–1950* (New York: Hill and Wang, 1994), 229.

46. E.g., *The Eternal Light* telecasts in 1956 ("Cry a Warning"), 1957 ("The Liberators"), 1959 ("Oil but for One Day"), 1963 ("The Five Sons"), and 1964 ("The Legate").

47. Samuel Elkin, *A Time for Valor*, dir. Mende Brown (Jewish Chautauqua Society/Union of American Hebrew Congregations/Central Conference of American Rabbis, 1960), item no. T1639, National Jewish Archive of Broadcasting, The Jewish Museum, New York.

48. Grace Goldin, "Christmas—Chanukah: December Is the Cruelest Month," *Commentary* 10, no. 5 (Nov. 1950): 416–419.

49. James H. Barnett, *The American Christmas: A Study in National Culture* (New York: Macmillan, 1954), 68–69.

50. "Revised Statement as Suggested by Committee on Education, . . . Joint Conference on Religious Holiday Observances in the Public Schools, . . . Proposed Statement of Principles," [Sept.?] 1949, folder: "Church/State/AJC," vertical files, American Jewish Committee Archives, Blaustein Library, p. [1].

51. Thomas A. Clemente, "Double or Nothing," *Commonweal*, 22 Dec. 1950, 273–274.

52. Ruth S. Bernards, "Xmas in the Public Schools," *Hadassah*, Dec. 1961, 9.

53. Grace Paley, "The Loudest Voice," in *The Little Disturbances of Man* (New York: Penguin, 1985 [1959]), 53–63.

54. Charles E. Silberman, *A Certain People: American Jews and Their Lives Today* (New York: Summit Books, 1985), 230.

55. Stuart Svonkin, *Jews against Prejudice: American Jews and the Intergroup Relations Movement from World War to Cold War* (New York: Columbia University Press, 1997), 29.

56. Irving Canter, "Christmas and Jewish Teenagers," *Jewish Spectator*, Dec. 1961, 13.

57. Milton Matz, "The Meaning of the Christmas Tree to the American Jew," *Jewish Journal of Sociology* 3, no. 1 (June 1961): 129–137, passim. Matz's study was conducted in Chicago in 1958.

58. Marden D. Paru, "Tannenbaum and the Jewish Problem," *Jewish Social Studies* 35 (1973): 283–289.

59. Irving Canter, "Uncle Sam, the Hanukkah Man: Assimilation or Contra-Culturation?" *Reconstructionist* 27, no. 15 (1 Dec. 1961): 5, 7, 8.

60. Anne Roiphe, "Christmas Comes to a Jewish Home," *New York Times*, 21 Dec. 1978, C1.

61. Ibid., C6.

62. Anne Roiphe, "Taking Down the Christmas Tree," *Tikkun* 4, no. 6 (Nov./Dec. 1989): 58.

63. Cynthia Ozick, "The Holidays: Reply to Anne Roiphe," *New York Times*, 28 Dec. 1978, C6.

64. "Letters: Readers Respond on Jews Celebrating Christmas," *New York Times*, 28 Dec. 1978, C9.

65. Ibid.

66. Anne Roiphe, *Generation without Memory* (New York: Simon and Schuster, 1981), 206.

67. Silberman, *A Certain People*, 233. See also reviews of Roiphe's book by Christopher Lehmann-Haupt, "Books of the Times," *New York Times*, 22 May 1981, C29; and Eli N. Evans, "Looking for Roots," *New York Times Book Review*, 7 June 1981, 3.

68. See, e.g., David Greenberg, "Christmas for Jews: How Hanukkah Became a Major Holiday," *Slate*, 16 Dec. 1998, http://slate.com/id/10802 (accessed 20 Aug. 2007).

69. See, e.g., Alina Ever and Bonnie Wolf, "Being Jewish at Christmas," *Gay Community News*, 25 Dec. 1985–4 Jan. 1986, 5; "Interfaith Anxiety," *Psychology Today*, Dec. 1988, 6–7; Frank Reeves, "Dealing with a 'December Dilemma,'" *Philadelphia Inquirer*, 28 Dec. 1989, 4M, 5M, 21M; Ken Ringle, "Why Can't Jews Have Christmas Trees?" *Washington Post*, 23 Dec. 1992, C1, C4; Gerald L. Zelizer, "New Religion-Benders Blur Faith's Unifying Beam," *USA Today*, 24 Dec. 1997, 9A; Christian T. Iosso, "Christmas and Hanukkah: Feasts Share Great Meaning," *Gannett Newspapers*, 20 Dec. 1997, 10A; Jane Praeger, "When Is a Tree Not a Tree?" *Newsweek*, 21 Dec. 1998, 12.

70. The cards discussed in this section have been collected by Aviva Weintraub and me since the mid-1980s. Although they are usually published under copyright, most are undated and are frequently sold during the holiday season for several years. The earliest dated card in our collection is dated 1984. We termed these *December dilemma cards* in our article "'Santa, Shmanta': Greeting Cards for the December Dilemma," *Material Religion* 3, no. 3 (Nov. 2007): 380–403; it is not a term used by the cards' publishers and marketers. For an early survey of these cards, see Shulamith Z. Berger, "Merry Hanukkah: Santa Claus and Captain Hanukkah Team Up—Greeting Cards and Jewish-Gentile Relations in the 1980s," *Jewish Folklore and Ethnology Review* 13, no. 1 (1991): 13–16.

71. Selected from a list of holiday e-cards offered at www.bluemountain.com (accessed 14 Aug. 2006).

72. Schmidt, *Consumer Rites*.

73. Tomato Cards, Cornerstone Productions, "On the Eighth Day of Hanukkah . . ." [greeting card] (Chicago: Recycled Paper Greetings, n.d.).

74. Shelly Wasserman and Roger Wilder, Gerilyse Cards, "Happy Hanukkah from your Gentile friends" [greeting card] (Chicago: Recycled Paper Products, 1987).

75. "Happy Chanukah" [greeting card] (Berkeley, Calif.: Palm Press, 1990).

76. R. Long, "It's a Goy!" [greeting card] (Chicago: Recycled Paper Greetings, n.d.).

77. Henry Beard and Roy McKie, Well Defined Greeting Cards, "Cha-nu-kah (khä´noo kä´), n: . . ." [greeting card] (Bloomington, Ind.: Sunrise Publications, 1986).

78. Marilyn Wassy-Fried, "Bubbee . . . Why Can't We Have a Christmas Tree?" [greeting card] (Chicago: Recycled Paper Greetings, n.d.).

79. Jan Eliot, Laffs by Marcel, "Every year my entire family . . ." [greeting card] (Fairfield, Calif.: Schurman Fine Papers, n.d.).

80. American Jewish Committee, "News from the Committee" [press release], New York, 8 Dec. [1989].

81. Leslie Kaufman, "On Web, Season's Greetings Are Sent in One Size Fits All," *New York Times*, 7 Dec. 1999, C20.

82. Ibid., A1.

83. MixedBlessing, "About MixedBlessing and Its Creators," www.mixedblessing.com/aboutMB.php (accessed 9 Aug. 2007).

84. MixedBlessing, "Testimonials," www.mixedblessing.com/testimon.php (accessed 9 Aug. 2007).

85. Quoted in Lisa E. Bloom, *Jewish Identities in American Feminist Art: Ghosts of Ethnicity* (New York: Routledge, 2006), 98–99.

86. William B. Waits, *The Modern Christmas in America: A Cultural History of Gift Giving* (New York: New York University Press, 1993), 70–78.

87. For examples of Rosh Hashanah cards, see Gérard Silvain and Henri Minczeles, *Yiddishland* (Corte Madera, Calif.: Ginko, 1999), 371–390.

88. Joselit, *The Wonders of America*, 234.

89. See, e.g., Maury Sacks, "Computing Community at Purim," *Journal of American Folklore* 102, no. 405 (July-Sept. 1989): 275–291, which examines the transformation through computer technology of gift exchange among Orthodox Jews in New York on Purim.

90. *. . . And There Was Light: A Photographic Chronicle of the Public Chanukah Menorah Celebrations Sponsored by Chabad-Lubavitch around the World* (Brooklyn: Merkos L'inyonei Chinuch, 1987), 11, 13.

91. Nathaniel Popper, "Menorahs Light Path for Nativity Displays," *Forward*, 23 Dec. 2005.

92. U.S. Postal Service, "Special U.S. Postage Stamp Dedication at the Jewish Museum Honors First Night of Hanukkah" [press release], 27 Nov. 1996.

93. U.S. Postal Service, "U.S. Postal Service Joins Israel in Hanukkah Celebration" [press release], 8 Oct. 1996.

94. Hadley Robertson, "To My Love at Hanukkah . . ." [greeting card] (Chicago: Recycled Paper Greetings, n.d.).

95. Tomato Cards, Cornerstone Productions, "A True Story for the Holidays" [greeting card] (Chicago: Recycled Paper Greetings, n.d.).

96. Greeting Card Association, "History," www.greetingcard.org/thegreetingcard_history.html (accessed 8 Aug. 2007).

97. Dale Cards, "I Sincerely Wish . . ." [greeting card] (Chicago: RRP, n.d.).

98. Adam Sandler, "The Chanukah Song," *What the Hell Happened to Me?* [sound recording] (Warner Bros. Records, 1996), track 6.

99. December dilemma episodes are frequently discussed in works on the images of Jews on American television. See Elliot B. Gertel, *Over the Top Judaism: Precedents and Trends in the Depiction of Jewish Beliefs and Observances in Film and Television* (Lanham, Md.: University Press of America, 2003); Jonathan Pearl and Judith Pearl, *The Chosen Image: Television's Portrayal of Jewish Themes and Characters* (Jefferson, N.C.: McFarland, 1999); David Zurawik, *The Jews of Prime Time* (Hanover, N.H.: Brandeis University Press, University Press of New England, 2003).

100. Marshall Hershkovitz and Edward Zwick, *thirtysomething: Stories* (New York: Pocket Books, 1991), 101–102.

101. Ibid.

102. By having Michael fantasize that he is starring in *The Dick van Dyke Show* (CBS, 1960–1966), the creators of *thirtysomething* paid homage to a series that was itself an exercise in oblique self-portraiture on the part of its creator, Carl Reiner. In the earlier series, however, Jewishness was displaced from the series's protagonist; see David Marc, *Comic Visions: Television Comedy and American Culture* (Boston: Unwin Hyman, 1989), 84–118.

103. Virginia Heffernan, "Twice the Annoyance, but a Tradition Emerges," *New York Times*, 16 Dec. 2004, E1, E6.

104. Aviva Weintraub, "Pfeifen in Dunkeln: Juden und Weihnachten in Amerika von Portnoy bis 'South Park,'" in *Weihnukka: Geschichten von Weihnachten un Chanukka*, ed. Cilly Kugelmann (Berlin: Jüdisches Museum Berlin, 2005), 112.

105. Plaut, "Silent Night," 323–424.

106. Edward S. Shapiro, *A Time for Healing: American Jewry since World War II* (Baltimore: Johns Hopkins University Press, 1992), 233–234.

107. Egon Mayer, *Love and Tradition: Marriage between Jews and Christians* (New York: Plenum, 1985), 158–159. Mayer reports that 65 percent of conversionary families ("in which the non-Jewish partner has converted to Judaism") and 95 percent of mixed-marriage families he studied celebrated Christmas; 92 percent of conversionary families and 33 percent of mixed-marriage families celebrated Hanukkah.

108. Susan Weidman Schneider, *Intermarriage: The Challenge of Living with Differences between Christians and Jews* (New York: Free Press, 1989), 79, 192.

109. Ibid., 79.

110. Max Weinreich, "The Reality of Jewishness versus the Ghetto Myth: The Sociolinguistic Roots of Yiddish," in *To Honor Roman Jakobson: Essays on the Occasion of His Seventieth Birthday* (The Hague: Mouton, 1967), 2205.

111. WBtvshop, "The OC Chrismukkah," www.wbtvshop.com/cat/The-OC/Chrismukkah/ (accessed 18 Aug. 2007).

112. Ron Gompertz, *Chrismukkah: The Merry Mish-Mash Holiday Cookbook* (Bozeman, Mont.: Chrismukkah.com, 2005). See also Ron Gompertz,

Chrismukkah: Everything You Need to Know to Celebrate the Hybrid Holiday (New York: Stewart, Tabori and Chang, 2006).

113. Jennifer Traig and Victoria Traig, *Judaikitsch: Tchotchkes, Schmattes, and Nosherei* (San Francisco: Chronicle Books, 2002), 88.

114. These examples are drawn from programs offered on 25 December at the Jewish Museum, New York, 1995; Yeshiva University Museum, New York, 1997; and the Jewish Museum, San Francisco, 1998.

115. Tanqueray, "Mr. Jenkins wishes you . . ." [promotional card] (New York: Schieffelin & Somerset, 1997).

116. Virgin Mobile, "Virgin Mobile Holiday Campaign Tweaks Post-Election Obsession over 'Divided Nation' with Tongue-in-Cheek Celebration of Inclusiveness" [press release], Warren, N.J., 1 Dec. 2004.

117. The December dilemma itself, however, has been acknowledged and addressed in other modern diaspora Jewish communities living among Christian majorities. See, e.g., the discussion of assimilated Jewish families in interwar Poland in Anna Landau-Czajka, "Miedzy Chanuka a Gwiazdka: Swieta w asymilowanych rodzinach zydowskich okresu miedzywojennego," *Kwartalnik Historii Zydów* 210 (2004): 170–181.

118. Schmidt, *Consumer Rites*, 32–33.

119. Andrew R. Heinze, *Adapting to Abundance: Jewish Immigrants, Mass Consumption, and the Search for American Identity* (New York: Columbia University Press, 1990), 3–4.

NOTES TO CHAPTER 6

1. Estimates of the number of Lubavitcher hasidim vary considerably. See, e.g., Sue Fishkoff, *The Rebbe's Army: Inside the World of Chabad-Lubavitch* (New York: Schocken Books, 2003), 13, 25; Henry Goldschmidt, *Race and Religion among the Chosen Peoples of Crown Heights* (New Brunswick, N.J.: Rutgers University Press, 2006), 6; Samuel C. Heilman, *Sliding to the Right: The Contest for the Future of American Jewish Orthodoxy* (Berkeley: University of California Press, 2006), 73, 147, 233.

2. Union for Reform Judaism, "What Is Reform Judaism?" http://reformjudaism.org/ (accessed 25 August 2008); Hadassah, "About Membership," www.hadassah.org/pageframe.asp?section=about&page=membership/allaboutmem.html&header=membership&size=50 (accessed 28 May 2007).

3. Quoted in Fishkoff, *The Rebbe's Army*, 13.

4. Glenn Dynner, *Men of Silk: The Hasidic Conquest of Polish Jewish Society* (Oxford: Oxford University Press, 2006), 5–11.

5. S. M. Dubnow, *History of the Jews in Russia and Poland from the Earliest Times until the Present Day*, 3 vols. trans. I. Friedlaender (Philadelphia: Jewish Publication Society, 1916), 1:234, 381–382, 374.

6. Naftali Loewenthal, *Communicating the Infinite: The Emergence of the Habad School* (Chicago: University of Chicago Press, 1990), 212, 40.

7. Ibid., 44, 47.

8. Jerome R. Mintz, *Hasidic People: A Place in the New World* (Cambridge, Mass.: Harvard University Press, 1992), 6.

9. See Edward Portnoy, "Haredim and the Internet" (2004), Modiya, http://modiya.nyu.edu/handle/1964/265 (accessed 25 Dec. 2006).

10. Rabbi Joseph I. Schneerson, *Lubavitcher Rabbi's Memoirs*, vol. 1, 3rd ed. (Brooklyn: Otzar Hachassidim, 1956), x–xi.

11. Herbert Weiner, "The Lubovitcher Movement," part 1, *Commentary* 23, no. 3 (March 1957): 231.

12. Geoffrey Alderman, "Lubavitch Messianism" [review article], *Jewish Journal of Sociology* 45, nos. 1 and 2 (2003): 46.

13. The distinct nature of hasidic engagement with these portraits emerges in comparison to portraits of rabbis by nonhasidic Orthodox Jews; see Richard I. Cohen, *Jewish Icons: Art and Society in Modern Europe* (Berkeley: University of California Press, 1998), 114–153.

14. Maya Balakirsky Katz, "On the Master-Disciple Relationship in Hasidic Visual Culture: The Life and Afterlife of Rebbe Portraits in Habad, 1798–2007," *Images: A Journal for Jewish Art and Visual Culture* 1 (Sept. 2007): 68.

15. Ibid., 70–72.

16. Ibid., 68.

17. Shimon Schwab, "The Jewish Home Under Siege: Fighting Off the Forces of Cultural Assimilation," *Jewish Observer*, Feb. 1992, 6.

18. A. Fram et al., *Yidish leyenbukh far lererin: klas 1* (Brooklyn: Bais Rochel, 1977), 282–284.

19. *Handl erlikh* [board game] ([Brooklyn?], n.d.). For a discussion of the game, see Jeffrey Shandler, *Adventures in Yiddishland: Postvernacular Language and Culture* (Berkeley: University of California Press, 2005), 46–47.

20. Mintz, *Hasidic People*, 182.

21. See, e.g., the American feature films *The Chosen* (1981), *A Stranger among Us* (1992), *A Price above Rubies* (1998).

22. Samuel Heilman, *Defenders of the Faith: Inside Ultra-Orthodox Jewry* (New York: Schocken Books, 1992), 350; see also 95–97.

23. Menachem M. Schneerson, "The Advance of Scientific Discovery," *Likkutei Sichos* [Collected discourses], vol. 15, p. 42, trans. Uri Kaploun, available online at www.sichosinenglish.org/books/from-exile-to-redemption-1/13.htm (accessed 7 Aug. 2007).

24. Michel Foucault, *The Order of Things* (New York: Knopf, 1970), 319.

25. Jonathan Crary, *Techniques of the Observer: On Vision and Modernity in the Nineteenth Century* (Cambridge, Mass.: MIT Press, 1990), 79, 92.

26. Rabbi Shaul Shimon Deutsch, *Larger Than Life: The Life and Times of the*

Lubavitcher Rebbe Rabbi Menachem Mendel Schneerson, vol. 2 (New York: Chasidic Historical Productions, 1997), 167.

27. Menachem Mendel Schneerson, *Toward a Meaningful Life: The Wisdom of the Rebbe*, adapted by Simon Jacobson (New York: William Morrow, 1995), 189.

28. "Tanya on Radio," available online at www.sichosinenglish.org/essays/65.htm (accessed 25 May 2007).

29. Fishkoff, *The Rebbe's Army*, 281–282.

30. Donna Gaines, "Jewromancer: My Life with the Online Hasidim," *Village Voice*, 5 Sept. 1995, 31, 29.

31. Margaret Daly, "A Cable to Jewish Life: In Knowledge There Is Strength," *BCAT Program Guide*, 18–24 April 2004.

32. A Cable to Jewish Life, http://cablejew.com (accessed 25 May 2007).

33. Distributed by Tzivos Hashem on cassette, the program was also televised on the interdenominational Faith and Values cable channel. See "F & V Offers Chanukah Programs," *Jewish Advocate* (Boston), 15–21 Dec. 1995, 37.

34. For a discussion of the museum, see "Jewish Children's Museum: A Virtual Roundtable on Material Religion," *Material Religion* 3, no. 3 (Nov. 2007): 404–427.

35. Jewish Children's Museum, "Visit the Jewish Children's Museum: 3rd Floor," http://jewishchildren.museum/Levels3L.asp (accessed 25 May 2007).

36. See Yosef I. Abramowitz, "What Happens If the Rebbe Dies?" *Moment*, April 1993, 37.

37. Chabad, "About the Telethon," www.tolife.com/faf/home/ccp.asp?ievent=186922&lis=1&kntae186922=61B2E289A4CA4858A6C7BAE1F77AC4C0&ccp=61718 (accessed 31 May 2007).

38. Fishkoff, *The Rebbe's Army*, 179–181.

39. *Hakhel II: A Year in Lubavitch* [videocassette] ([Brooklyn]: Sholom B. Goldstein, 1994). On *hak'hel*, see Deuteronomy 31:10ff.

40. "The Year of Hakhel, Then and Now," available online at www.sichosinenglish.org/essays/36.htm (accessed 7 Aug. 2007).

41. *Farbrengen: An Evening with the Lubavitcher Rebbe—Yud Shevat 5732* [videocassette] (Brooklyn: Jewish Educational Media, 1997), back cover of packaging.

42. Comments by Naftali Loewenthal at Session 76: Modern European Cultural and Intellectual History, Twenty-seventh Annual Conference Association for Jewish Studies, Boston, 19 Dec. 1995.

43. Dubnow, *History of the Jews in Russia and Poland*, 1:227.

44. More recently, WLCC made audio recordings of the Rebbe available for listening online at www.wlcc.org (accessed 1 June 2007).

45. Yosef Yitshak Halbershtam, *Katalog Merkaz Shiduri Habad* [catalog] (Brooklyn: WLCC, 1993/4), 1. The texts originally appear in Menachem Mendel Schneerson, *Toras Menachem: Hisva'aduyos* [Teaching of Menachem: Public gatherings], vol. 1 (Brooklyn: Lahak Hanochos, 1992 [1950]), 51, 67.

46. Schneerson, *Toras Menachem*, 92. The text attributes this citation to Talmudic sources: Yerushalmi Shabbat 1:2, Shekalim 2:5, Kiddushin 1:7.

47. See Alter Eliyahu Friedman, *From Exile to Redemption: Chassidic Teachings of the Rebbe and the Preceding Rebbeim of Chabad*, vol. 1 (Brooklyn: Sichos in English, 1992).

48. Abramowitz, "What Happens If the Rebbe Dies?" 70.

49. "It's OK to Get Excited about Moshiach" [advertisement], [1992?].

50. David Berger, *The Rebbe, the Messiah, and the Scandal of Orthodox Indifference* (Oxford, U.K.: Littman, 2001), 23.

51. Ibid.

52. Quoted in Ari L. Goldman, "Debate Splits Lubavitcher Hasidim," *New York Times*, 29 Jan. 1993, B2.

53. Simon Dein, "What Really Happens When Prophecy Fails: The Case of Lubavitch," *Sociology of Religion* 62, no. 3 (fall 2001): 392.

54. Abramowitz, "What Happens If the Rebbe Dies?" 33. Quote from Schiffman originally appeared in *Long Island Jewish World*, 29 Jan. 1993.

55. Goldman, "Debate Splits Lubavitcher Hasidim," B1–B2.

56. Craig Horowitz, "Holy War," *New York*, 14 Feb. 1994, 28.

57. Berger, *The Rebbe, the Messiah, and the Scandal of Orthodox Indifference*, 10.

58. Laurie Goodstein, "Schneerson's Followers Cope with Void of Failed Expectations," *Washington Post*, 19 June 1994, A3.

59. "Lubavitch Leader Dies at 92," *New York Newsday*, 13 June 1994, 1, 4–6, 20–21 (encompassing several articles).

60. Dein, "What Really Happens When Prophecy Fails," 397.

61. Goodstein, "Schneerson's Followers Cope with Void of Failed Expectations," A3.

62. Craig Horowitz, "Beyond Belief," *New York*, 19 June 1995, 42. The custom of inviting the Rebbe to attend weddings in order to invoke his blessing was widely practiced while he was still alive.

63. David Berger, "Moshiach and The Rebbe" [letter to the editor], *Jewish Press*, 1 July 1994, 74.

64. William Shaffir, "When Prophecy Is Not Validated: Explaining the Unexpected in a Messianic Campaign," *Jewish Journal of Sociology* 37, no. 2 (Dec. 1995): 127–128.

65. Debra Nussbaum Cohen, "Campaign Expands to Airwaves to Declare Late Rebbe 'Moshiach,'" *JTA Daily News Bulletin* (Jewish Telegraphic Agency), 9 Feb. 1996, 2.

66. Ibid., 1–2.

67. Full-page advertisement, *New York Times*, 31 Jan. 1996, A11.

68. *International Demonstration of Unity to Greet Moshiach* [videocassette] (Brooklyn: International Campaign to Welcome Moshiach, 1996).

69. "Statement by Agudas Chassidei Chabad-Lubavitch" [advertisement], *New York Times*, 9 Feb. 1996, A23. The announcement is dated 30 Jan. 1996.

70. "The Time of Your Redemption Has Arrived" [advertisement], *New York Times*, 31 March 1996, sec. 1, p. 28.

71. Quoted in Frank Bruni, "To Some, Messiah Is the Message," *New York Times*, 25 Feb. 1996, sec. 1, p. 38.

72. Ibid.

73. Leon Festinger, Henry W. Riecken, and Stanley Schachter, *When Prophecy Fails: A Social and Psychological Study of a Modern Group That Predicted the Destruction of the World* (New York: Harper and Row, 1966 [1956]), 3, 209, 27, 28. The introductory chapter discusses past examples of false apocalyptic forecasts and pseudo-messiahs, including Shabbetai Zevi.

74. Dein, "What Really Happens When Prophecy Fails," 399, 383.

75. Ibid., 397.

76. Shaffir, "When Prophecy Is Not Validated," 129.

77. Chaim Potok, "Rabbi Schneerson: One of a Kind," *Philadelphia Inquirer*, 16 June 1994, as cited in M. Avrum Ehrlich, *The Messiah of Brooklyn: Understanding Lubavitch Hasidism Past and Present* (Jersey City, N.J.: Ktav, 2004), 173.

78. See, e.g., Rebecca Segall, "Holy Daze," *Village Voice*, 6 Oct. 1998, 52–55. On the larger phenomenon of disaffected hasidic youth, see Hella Winston, *Unchosen: The Hidden Lives of Hasidic Rebels* (Boston: Beacon, 2005).

79. See David Berger, "Messianism: Passing Phenomenon or Turning Point in the History of Judaism?" *Jewish Action* 56, no. 1 (fall 5756/1995), 44.

80. Shmaryahu Brownstein, "Open Up Your Door," and Avrumi Richter, "The Rebbe Lives," on *Oh Rebbe: The Rebbe Lives*, vol. 2 [sound recording] ([Brooklyn]: Y&M Music, 1997/1998), bands 1, 2.

81. Avrumi Richter and Daniel Green, "The Striking Sign," on *Oh Rebbe*, band 4.

82. *Hand in Hand: Children Learning from the Rebbe* [videocassette] (Brooklyn: Jewish Educational Media, 1996).

83. *Davening with the Rebbe: Audio Soundtrack* [sound recording] (Brooklyn: Jewish Educational Media, 2000).

84. Comments made by Samuel Heilman at "Looking Jewish: Photography, Memory and the Sacred," a colloquium convened by the Working Group on Jews, Media, and Religion, Center for Religion and Media, New York University, 29 April 2007. Transcribed from audio recording. See also Heilman's essay "Still Seeing the Rebbe," 5 Sept. 2001, available online at www.killingthebuddha.com/dogma/still_seeing_rebbe.htm (accessed 21 Aug. 2007).

85. Ibid.

86. According to a feasibility study, JEM's archive includes "98 Hours of Motion Film, 3,218 Hours of Video, 2,250 Hours of Audio, [and] 275,000 Photos." Jewish Educational Media Restoration and Preservation Study, Sept. 2006, 4.

87. Jewish Educational Media, "Update for Shluchim and Anash: An update regarding progress and future plans concerning the video, audio and photo archives of the Rebbe," 13 June 2007, http://home.jemedia.org/update.asp?aid=530159 (accessed 9 July 2007).

88. Jewish Educational Media, "The Archive—Unlocked," 5 June 2007, http://home.jemedia.org/update.asp?aid=535134 (accessed 9 July 2007).

89. Jewish Educational Media Restoration and Preservation Study, 4, 5, 7, 8, 17.

90. Jewish Educational Media Store, "Living Torah," www.jemstore.com/articles.asp?id=130 (accessed 12 July 2007).

91. Jewish Educational Media, "My Encounter with the Rebbe," www.jemedia.org/MyEncounter/ (accessed 12 July 2007).

92. Jewish Educational Media Store, "Holidays," www.jemstore.com/category_s/3.htm (accessed 12 July 2007).

93. Jewish Educational Media, "Announcement to Shluchim and Anash," http://home.jemedia.org/update.asp?aid=384224 (accessed 12 July 2007).

94. Chabad, "Ask the Rabbi," www.chabad.org/asktherabbi/default.asp; Chabad, "Dear Rachel," www.chabad.org/theJewishWoman/article.asp?AID=363801 (accessed 16 July 2007).

95. Chabad, "About Us," www.chabad.org/library/article.asp?AID=32812 (accessed 16 July 2006).

96. Jeff Zaleski, *The Soul of Cyberspace: How New Technology Is Changing Our Spiritual Lives* (San Francisco: HarperEdge, 1997), 14.

97. Ibid., 17.

98. Ibid., 18–19.

99. Ibid., 35.

100. Alderman, "Lubavitch Messianism," 50. See also, e.g., David Newman, "False Messiahs," *Jerusalem Post*, 17 June 1998, 10.

101. See, e.g., Sanford Pinsker, "The Rebbe Live," *First Things* 58 (Dec. 1995): 12–17.

102. Herbert Weiner, "The Lubovitcher Movement," part 2, *Commentary* 23, no. 4 (April 1957): 323.

103. Walter Burkert, *Creation of the Sacred: Tracks of Biology in Early Religions* (Cambridge, Mass.: Harvard University Press, 1996), 177–179.

NOTES TO THE AFTERWORD

1. DBS International Corporation, "Torah Treasures: The Computerized Torah Library" [promotional mailing] (Brooklyn, [2004]).

2. See H-JUDAIC Digest–19 Sep. 2007 to 20 Sep. 2007 (#2007-89), 22 Sep. 2007 to 23 Sep. 2007 (#2007-92), accessible at www.h-net.org/~judaic/.

3. See Marvin J. Heller, *Printing the Talmud: A History of the Earliest Printed Editions of the Talmud* (Brooklyn: Im Hasefer, 1992).

4. Jonathan Rosen, *The Talmud and the Internet: A Journey between Worlds* (New York: Picador, 2000), 8–14.

5. Susan M. Zakar and Dovid Y. B. Kaufmann, *Judaism Online: Confronting Spirituality on the Internet* (Northvale, N.J.: Jason Aronson, 1998), dust jacket, 176.

6. Open Source Haggadah Project, "About Us," www.opensourcehaggadah.com/aboutus.php (accessed 27 Sept. 2007).

7. Dafyomi.org, "Frequently Asked Questions," www.dafyomi.org/faq.php (accessed 27 Sept. 2007).

8. Shulshopper home page, www.shulshopper.com (accessed 27 Sept. 2007); JDate home page, www.jdate.com (accessed 27 Sept. 2007).

9. Second Life home page, www.secondlife.com (accessed 27 Sept. 2007).

10. Julian Voloj, "Virtual Sanctuary," *Forward*, 16 Feb. 2007; 2Life home page, www.2lifemagazine.com (accessed 27 Sept. 2007). The magazine's name puns on Second Life and the traditional Jewish toast, *l'hayyim* (literally, "to life").

11. Julian Voloj, "Subject: Virtual Judaism," email to jews-media-religion@lists.nyu.edu, 31 Aug. 2007.

12. 2Life home page.

13. "In the Grid: Your Guide to Jewish Sites in Second Life," *2Life* 1 (April 2007): 6, www.2lifemagazine.com/downloads/2Life_01.pdf (accessed 27 Sept. 2007). Matzohenge, created in Feb. 2007, is located on SoHo Island, SoHo (121, 21, 29).

14. "2Love" [advertisement], *2Life* 1 (April 2007): 9.

15. Daniel Treiman, "Virtual Journalism," *Forward*, 13 April 2007.

16. Ruth Ellen Gruber, *Virtually Jewish: Reinventing Jewish Culture in Europe* (Berkeley: University of California Press, 2002), 11, 8, 9, 27.

17. Voloj, "Subject: Virtual Judaism."

18. Voloj, "Virtual Sanctuary."

19. In fact, there are restrictions, including no gambling or pornography, according to Voloj, "Subject: Virtual Judaism."

20. Kafka Schnabel, "A Place to Meet and Discuss," *2Life* 1 (April 2007): 2.

21. "Five Questions for Second Life Resident Avram Leven," *2Life* 1 (April 2007): 7.

22. Tim Lenoir, foreword to Mark B. N. Hansen, *New Philosophy for New Media* (Cambridge, Mass.: MIT Press, 2004), xiv–xxii.

23. Jonathan Boyarin, "Jewish Geography Goes On-Line," *Jewish Folklore and Ethnology Review* 16, no. 1 (1994): 3–5.

Index

About the Author

JEFFREY SHANDLER is Professor of Jewish Studies at Rutgers University. His books include *Adventures in Yiddishland: Postvernacular Language and Culture*, *While America Watches: Televising the Holocaust*, and (with J. Hoberman) *Entertaining America: Jews, Movies and Broadcasting*, among other titles. He lives in New York City.